THE ICON CRITICAL DICTIONARY
OF POSTMODERN THOUGHT

THE ICON CRITICAL DICTIONARY OF POSTMODERN THOUGHT

EDITED BY

STUART SIM

ICON BOOKS

Published in 1998 by Icon Books Ltd.,
Grange Road, Duxford, Cambridge CB2 4QF
e-mail: icon@mistral.co.uk

Reprinted 1998

Distributed in the UK, Europe, Canada, South Africa and Asia by
the Penguin Group:
Penguin Books Ltd., 27 Wrights Lane, London W8 5TZ

Published in Australia in 1998 by Allen & Unwin Pty. Ltd.,
PO Box 8500, 9 Atchison Street, St. Leonards, NSW 2065

Cover illustration by Andrzej Klimowski
Design and layout by Christos Kondeatis
Text edited by Anne Rix and Sandra Stafford
Typesetting by Hands Fotoset, Leicester

ISBN 1 874166 65 X

Printed and bound in Great Britain by
Mackays plc., Chatham, Kent

CONTENTS

Editor's Introduction

From the Modern to the Postmodern

It is a cliché by now to say that we live in a postmodern world, and indeed 'postmodern' has become one of the most used, and abused, words in the language. Who has not heard the phrase 'that's postmodern' applied to some occurrence in everyday life? And doubtless replied with a knowing look, smile or laugh. Yet it is striking that few people can say with any sense of assurance what that term 'postmodern' actually means or involves. Some theorists have suggested that it is as much a mood or attitude of mind as anything else, but one nevertheless wants to know what constitutes that mood or attitude. That is what *The Icon Critical Dictionary of Postmodern Thought* is designed to answer.

In a general sense, postmodernism is to be regarded as a rejection of many, if not most, of the cultural certainties on which life in the West has been structured over the last couple of centuries. It has called into question our commitment to cultural 'progress' (that economies must continue to grow, the quality of life to keep improving indefinitely, etc.), as well as the political systems that have underpinned this belief. Postmodernists often refer to the 'Enlightenment project', meaning the liberal humanist ideology that has come to dominate Western culture since the eighteenth century; an ideology that has striven to bring about the emancipation of mankind from economic want and political oppression. In the view of postmodernists this project, laudable though it may have been at one time, has in its turn come to oppress humankind, and to force it into certain set ways of thought and action. It is therefore to be resisted, and postmodernists are invariably critical of universalizing theories ('grand narratives' or 'metanarratives' as they have been dubbed by the philosopher Jean-François Lyotard), as well as being anti-authoritarian in their outlook. To move from the modern to the postmodern is to embrace scepticism about what our culture stands for and strives for: *The Icon Critical Dictionary* will establish just what it is that motivates that scepticism.

STRUCTURE AND SCOPE OF THE VOLUME

Dictionaries aim to provide reference information, and *The Icon Critical Dictionary* certainly provides that, but is more ambitious in its scope than a standard reference dictionary – as the use of the term 'Critical' suggests. It is divided into two parts: (I) Essays, and (II) Names and Terms. Part I consists of 14 extended essays (3,000–5,000 words) tracing both the sources and the impact of postmodern thought, and includes such topics as 'Postmodernism and Philosophy', 'Postmodernism and Politics', 'Postmodernism and Feminism', and 'Postmodernism and Science and Technology', as well as a series of essays dealing with postmodernism and the arts (architecture, literature, film, music, etc.). The concluding essay, 'Postmodernism, Modernity, and the Tradition of Dissent', draws together the various strands of criticism of postmodernism, in order to demonstrate just how controversial the movement has turned out to be, and how much opposition it has managed to arouse even in such a relatively short time. Collectively these essays establish the breadth of postmodern thought that has transformed the cultural landscape of the late twentieth century. (A select bibliography for the essays as a whole can be found at the end of part I.)

In part II, the reader will find brief portraits of the leading theorists and creative artists who go to make up the postmodern world and its debates (well over one hundred figures listed), including influential voices from the past whose work either has been reappropriated by postmodernism, or has in some significant way informed its debates. It is difficult to engage with postmodernism without also engaging with, for example, the work of Marx, Kant or Nietzsche. Though brief, the portraits are pithy and informative, presenting the most relevant details of each figure's career and ideas, and placing him or her in the development of the postmodern movement. Alongside the portraits are short definitions of the key terms associated with postmodern thought. The object of the book is to provide accessible material on what can appear to be a forbiddingly complex and disparate area of discourse: a guide to 'who's who' and 'what's what' in postmodernism.

HOW TO USE THIS VOLUME

To facilitate cross reference, all the entries in part II (both names and terms) are picked out in bold when they appear elsewhere, and a comprehensive index is also provided to enable readers to follow up the various appearances of specific names and terms over the course of the volume as a whole, should they so wish. If, for example, you consult the entry on **postmodernism**, you will encounter the name of the philosopher Jean-François **Lyotard**, who features in an entry of his own. This entry makes it clear that Lyotard is one of the key figures in the development of postmodern philosophy, which leads you towards the opening essay 'Postmodernism and Philosophy'. Throughout that essay various other names will appear, picked out in bold type, such as Gilles **Deleuze**, Jacques **Derrida,** and Michel **Foucault**. Their entries in turn will deal with concepts and theories (again, in bold), such as **desiring-machines**, **deconstruction** and **genealogy**, which can then be followed up for more detail; as can other names mentioned in the course of these same entries (Félix **Guattari**, Roland **Barthes**, etc.). The index will provide yet more references to consult on any of the entries above.

The two sections of the *Dictionary* are designed to interact, allowing more- or less-detailed information to be accessed, depending on the reader's requirements. You may merely want to refresh your memory as to the definition of a term, or brush up on the work of a particular thinker, or go into more depth in, say, philosophy. Alternatively, you may simply wish to range around in the various networks of information the book offers, in order to build up your own particular picture of what postmodernism involves: dictionaries provide just that creative possibility for each individual reader, and the choice is yours.

POSTMODERNISM AND POSTSTRUCTURALISM

For our purposes here, postmodernism will be taken to encompass figures and debates within poststructuralism as well. Poststructuralism is a term that refers to a wide range of responses to the structuralist paradigm which dominated French thought during the middle decades of the twentieth century – responses such as the philosophically oriented 'deconstruction' of Jacques Derrida, the various 'archaeological' and 'genealogical' enquiries into cultural history of Michel Foucault, and the 'difference feminism' of such theorists as Luce Irigaray. It is always difficult to date movements such as this with any great precision, but poststructuralism has certainly been an influential part of the cultural scene since the 1960s. Nowadays it can be seen to be part of a more general reaction to authoritarian ideologies and political systems that we define as postmodernism. Postmodernism, we might say, subsumes poststructuralism, hence the inclusion of the latter in this present volume.

CONTRIBUTORS

The contributors to this volume are drawn from both academic and professional life, and are acknowledged experts in their particular fields. Their collective aim has been to map the postmodern such that its richness, diversity and cultural significance can be appreciated by the general reader. They are, in alphabetical order: Pamela Anderson, Adrian Baker, Peter Dempsey, Brian Dillon, Sara Dodd, Antony Easthope, Peter Every, Sarah Gamble, Iain Hamilton Grant, Sean Griffiths, Stan Hawkins, Valerie Hill, Stephanie Hodgson-Wright, Sam Jacob, Barry Lewis, Karin Littau, Anthony McGowan, Diane Morgan, Marc O'Day, Elisa Oliver, Danielle Ramsay, Derek Scott, Stuart Sim, Lloyd Spencer, John Storey, John Strachan, Sue Thornham, Colin Trodd, David Walker, Nigel Watson and Alison Younger.

I
POSTMODERNISM, ITS HISTORY AND CULTURAL CONTEXT

POSTMODERNISM
AND PHILOSOPHY

STUART SIM

Philosophy, particularly the recent French philosophical tradition, has been both a prime site for debate about **postmodernism** and a source of many of the theories of what constitutes postmodernism. Probably the leading figure in this regard is Jean-François **Lyotard**, whose book *The Postmodern Condition: A Report on Knowledge* (1979) is widely regarded as the most powerful theoretical expression of postmodernism. Lyotard's plea that we should reject the '**grand narratives**' (that is, universal theories) of Western culture because they have now lost all their credibility seems to sum up the ethos of postmodernism, with its disdain for authority in all its many guises. There is no longer any point engaging in debate with, for example, **Marxism**, the argument goes; rather we should ignore it as an irrelevance to our lives. Postmodern philosophy provides us with the arguments and techniques to make that gesture of dissent, as well as how to make value judgements in the absence of such overall authorities.

One of the best ways of describing postmodernism as a philosophical movement would be as a form of scepticism – scepticism about authority, received wisdom, cultural and political norms, etc. – and that puts it into a long-running tradition in Western thought that stretches back to classical Greek philosophy. Scepticism is an essentially negative form of philosophy, which sets out to undermine other philosophical theories claiming to be in possession of ultimate truth, or of criteria for determining what counts as ultimate truth. The technical term to describe such a style of philosophy is '**antifoundational**'. Antifoundationalists dispute the validity of the foundations of discourse, asking such questions as 'What guarantees the truth of your foundation (that is, starting point) in its turn?' Postmodernism has drawn heavily on the example set by antifoundationalist philosophers, perhaps most notably the iconoclastic nineteenth-century German philosopher Friedrich **Nietzsche**, whose call for a 'revaluation of all values' constitutes something of a battle-cry for the movement. Before considering postmodernism's sceptical credentials in greater detail, however, it would probably be helpful to say what, and who, can be regarded as falling under the heading of postmodern philosophy. It will

3

be taken here to mean not just the inclusion of such avowedly post-modernist thinkers as Lyotard, but also the various discourses, such as **deconstruction**, that go under the name of **poststructuralism**.

Poststructuralism's rejection of the **structuralist** tradition of thought constitutes yet another gesture of scepticism towards received authority, and can be considered as part of the postmodern intellectual landscape. Although postmodern philosophy is a somewhat disparate area overall, we can note certain common features, such as that gesture of scepticism, an antifoundational bias, and an almost reflex dislike of authority, that make it reasonable to discuss it as a recognizable style of philosophy in its own right.

Poststructuralism is a broad cultural movement spanning various intellectual disciplines that has involved a rejection not just of structuralism and its methods, but also the ideological assumptions that lie behind them. One can regard it as both a philosophical and a political movement therefore, as one can postmodernism in general. Poststructuralism called into question the cultural certainties that structuralism had been felt to come to embody; certainties such as the belief that the world was intrinsically knowable, and that structuralism gave us a methodological key to unlock the various systems that made up that world. Structuralism takes its cue from the linguistic theories of the Swiss linguist Ferdinand de Saussure, who revolutionized the study of linguistics in his posthumously published book, *Course in General Linguistics* (1916). Saussure's major point about language is that it was above all a system: a system with rules and regulations (or internal grammar) that governed how the various elements of language operated. Language was made up of **signs**, and signs consisted of two parts, a signifier (word) and a signified (concept), which combined, in an act of mental understanding, to form the sign. Although there was no necessary connection between a word and the object it named (they were 'arbitrary', as Saussure admitted), the force of convention ensured that they did not change at anyone's whim. There was at the very least a *relative* stability to language and the production of meaning, and language was to be viewed as a system of signs which induced a predictable response on the part of the linguistic community.

The linguistic model set up by Saussure formed the basis of structuralist analysis, which applied it to systems in general, making the assumption that every system had an internal grammar that governed its operations. The point of structuralist analysis was to uncover that grammar, whether the system in question was tribal myth, the advertising industry, or the world of literature or fashion. Ultimately, what poststructuralists object to is the overall tidiness of the structuralist enterprise, where there are no loose ends and everything falls neatly into place. Thus for a thinker like Claude **Lévi-Strauss**, or the early Roland **Barthes**, every detail of a narrative was significant in terms of the structure of the final product (there being no random elements), and narratives fell into specific genres, of which particular instances (say, a given tribal myth) were merely variations on a central theme. From such a perspective one system (or narrative) comes to seem much like any other, and the analysis of its grammar becomes a fairly predictable exercise, almost as if one knew beforehand what one was going to find; one could even argue, and poststructuralists did, that the analytical techniques being used by the structuralist *determined* the results. What structuralism seems to allow little scope for is chance, creativity or the unexpected. For a poststructuralist, these are much more important than all the similarities between systems, and there is what amounts to a commitment to finding, and dwelling on, dissimilarity, difference, and the unpredictability of analysis among poststructuralist thinkers.

Jacques **Derrida**'s deconstruction became one of the most powerful expressions of the poststructuralist ethos. Deconstruction was directed against the system-building side of structuralism, and took issue with the idea that all phenomena were reducible to the operations of systems, with its implication that we could come to have total control over our environment. What Derrida was concerned to demonstrate was the instability of language, and indeed systems in general. Signs were not such predictable entities in Derrida's view, and indeed there was never any perfect conjunction of signifier and signified to guarantee unproblematical communication. Some 'slippage' of meaning always occurred. For one thing, words always contained echoes and traces of other words, with their sound-quality, for example, invariably putting one in mind of a range of similar-sounding ones. Derrida provided evidence of this slippage in action by means of a concept called '**différance**', a neologism derived from the French word *différence* (meaning both difference and deferral). One could not detect which of the two words was intended in speech (they are pronounced the same), only in writing. To Derrida, what was revealed at this point was the inherent indeterminacy of meaning. Linguistic meaning was an unstable phenomenon: at all times, and all places, différance applied. (It is worth pointing out that Derrida denies that différance is a concept; for him, it is merely the identification of a process embedded within language itself.) The fondness for pun and word-play within deconstructive writing (a recurrent feature of all its major practitioners) has as its goal the illustration of language's instability, as well as its endlessly creative capacity to generate new and unexpected meanings.

Meaning is therefore a fleeting phenomenon, that evaporates almost as soon as it occurs in spoken or written language (or keeps transforming itself into new meanings), rather than something fixed that holds over time for a series of different audiences. Derrida contends that all Western philosophy is based on the premise that the full meaning of a word is 'present' in the speaker's mind, such that it can be communicated, without any significant slippage, to the listener. This belief is what Derrida calls the '**metaphysics of presence**', and for him it is an illusion: différance always intrudes into communication to prevent the establishment of 'presence', or completeness of meaning. The emphasis on difference, on what fails to conform to the norm or to system-building, that we find in deconstruction is very much characteristic of the postmodern philosophical ethos.

Michel **Foucault** is another thinker who turned against the system-building and difference-excluding tendencies of structuralist thought. Once again, it is the fact of difference that is emphasized. In Foucault's case, there is a particular interest in marginalized groups whose difference keeps them excluded from political power; groups such as the insane, prisoners and homosexuals. Post-Renaissance culture has been committed to the marginalization, even demonization, of difference, by its setting of norms of behaviour. Foucault has written a series of case studies describing how these norms were implemented in seventeenth- and eighteenth-century Western Europe, such that a whole new range of regimented institutions (insane asylums, prisons, hospitals) came into being in order to deal with the 'different'. For Foucault, these institutions are expressions of political power, of the way that a dominant group in society can impose its will on others.

In order to demonstrate how sexual difference had been demonized in modern society, Foucault turned back to classical times in his three-volume study *The History of Sexuality* (1976–84) to investigate how homosexuality functioned in Greek and Roman culture. Greek society was more tolerant of sexual difference than our own, although no less moral in its outlook. In Foucault's terms of reference, it had a different 'discourse' of sexuality, one in which no one norm of behaviour was imposed, but homosexuality and heterosexuality flourished side by side. Foucault contrasted this unfavourably to modern times, when heterosexuality was turned into a norm from which all other forms of sexual expression were regarded as deviations. This insistence on the norm at the expense of the different is all part of the authoritarianism that thinkers like Foucault associate with modern culture.

Gilles **Deleuze** and Félix **Guattari**'s *Anti-Oedipus* (1972) represented yet another poststructuralist attack on authoritarianism; in this case the authoritarianism embedded within psychoanalytic theory, which, through the mechanism of theories like the **Oedipus** complex, seeks to control the free expression of human desire. For Deleuze and Guattari, individuals are '**desiring machines**', who lack the sense of unity we generally associate with individual identity, but who find the opportunity to express their desire being curbed by the socio-political authorities (with fascism the most potent example of how the process works). Psychoanalysis becomes for Deleuze and Guattari a symbol of how desire is suppressed, and in opposition to it they posit '**schizo-analysis**', based on the experience of the schizophrenic – who in their scheme of things becomes some kind of ideal model of human behaviour. The political dimension to poststructuralist thought, often somewhat hidden under cloudy metaphysical discussions in deconstruction, is certainly foregrounded here.

Difference feminism can also be included under the heading of post-structuralism, in that it questions the supposed rigidity of gender categories. The argument is that gender identity, particularly female identity, is not something fixed, but instead a fluid process that cannot be reduced to any essence or norm of behaviour (in this case a patri-archally derived norm of behaviour). Theorists such as Luce **Irigaray** have used this form of argument to call into question the assumptions of patriarchy, in particular the assumption of specifically male and female gender traits that lead to the gender stereotypes that our society still largely adheres to, and uses as a basis for the suppression of women.

Lyotard remains the most influential voice of postmodern philo-sophy, and there is a consistent thread of anti-authoritarianism that runs through his philosophical career that we can now recognize as quintessentially postmodern. In his early career Lyotard can be described as a **Marxist**. He was a member of the group *Socialisme ou barbarie* (Socialism or Barbarism), who were dedicated to subjecting Marxist theory to a searching critique from the inside, and he acted as the spokesperson on Algeria for the group's newspaper. Lyotard's writings on the Algerian war of liberation in the 1950s and 60s reveal someone who is far from being an orthodox Marxist, and more than willing to call Marxist principles into question. The major objection he makes is that Algeria was being treated by the Communist Party hierarchy as a classic case of proletarian revolution, when in reality it was a peasant society where Marxism had little practical value.

After the break-up of *Socialisme ou barbarie* in the 1960s, Lyotard self-consciously distanced himself from his Marxist past. Like many French intellectuals of his generation he was disenchanted by the pro-establishment position adopted by the French Communist Party in the 1968 Paris *événements*, and in works such as *Libidinal Economy* (1974) he vented the frustration he felt by then towards official Marxism. *Libidinal Economy* claimed that Marxism was unable to encompass the various libidinal drives that all individuals experienced, since these unpredictable drives lay beyond any theory's control (the argument is similar to the one expressed in *Anti-Oedipus*). What was precisely wrong with Marxism was that it tried to suppress these energies, and in so doing revealed its latent authoritarianism. Behind the book's vicious attack on Marxism lay a belief on Lyotard's part that neither human nature nor historical process was as predictable, and therefore manipulable, as Marxist theory insisted. Lyotard asked us to accept that libidinal energy (something like the complex of sub-conscious drives identified by **Freud**) simply demolished any claim that Marxism may have had to be able to control events. The book can be seen as the beginning of the critique of 'grand narrative' that was to lie at the heart of Lyotard's most successful and influential work, *The Postmodern Condition*.

The Postmodern Condition argues that knowledge is now the world's most significant commodity, and that it may well become a source of conflict between nations in future. Whoever controls knowledge, Lyotard insists, now exerts political control, and he is keen to ensure that the dissemination of knowledge is kept as open as possible. His alternative to centralized political control of knowledge is to make all data banks accessible to the general public. Knowledge is seen to be communicated by means of narrative, and Lyotard is critical of what he calls grand narratives: theories that claim to be able to explain everything, and to resist any attempt to change their form (or 'narrative'). Marxism, for example, has its own particular narrative of world history which it feels is true and thus beyond any criticism or need of revision. It is not a narrative to be reinterpreted constantly in the light of changing cultural events, but an impregnable theory that holds over time and whose authority must never be questioned. To Lyotard, such an attitude is authoritarian, and he celebrates the cause of '**little narrative**' (*petit récit*) in its stead. Little narratives are put together on a tactical basis by small groups of individuals to achieve some particular

8

objective (such as the 'little narrative' combination of students and workers in the 1968 *événements*, calling for government reforms), and do not pretend to have the answers to all society's problems: ideally, they last only as long as is necessary to achieve their objectives. Lyotard considers that little narratives are the most inventive way of disseminating, and creating, knowledge, and that they help to break down the monopoly traditionally exercised by grand narratives. In science, for example, they are now to be regarded as the primary means of enquiry. Postmodern science, Lyotard informs us, is a search for paradoxes, instabilities and the unknown, rather than an attempt to construct yet another grand narrative that would apply over the entire scientific community.

Lyotard's objective is to demolish the authority wielded by grand narrative, which he takes to be repressive of individual creativity. 'We no longer have recourse to the grand narratives,' he declares; that is, we can no longer rely on them to guide our action, either at the public or private level. What we are enjoined to do is not to fight the grand narratives but simply to stop believing in them; in which case, they will be assumed to wither away. Although this is a somewhat idealistic view of the political process, something like this withering away did occur a few years after the writing of *The Postmodern Condition*, when Eastern European communism collapsed – largely without any violent clashes with the political authorities. In postmodern terms of reference, the populace simply stopped believing in the prevailing ideology, which then ceased to have any authority to enforce its will.

One of the problems we are left with when we dispense with grand narratives, or central authorities of any kind, is how to construct value judgements that others will accept as just and reasonable. Lyotard confronts this problem in *Just Gaming* (1979), where he argues that it is still possible to make value judgements, even if we have no grand narrative to back us up, on a 'case by case' basis (a form of pragmatism which he claims is operating in Aristotle's political and ethical writings). Operating on a case by case basis, where one is admitting the absence of any absolute criteria, is the condition Lyotard refers to as '**paganism**', and it becomes an ideal of how we ought to operate in a postmodern world. There never will be such absolute criteria, or foundations of belief, to guide us, but that need not, Lyotard insists, entail a collapse into social disorder, as critics from the grand narrative side are wont to suggest it will. What Lyotard is espousing here is antifoundationalism: a rejection of the idea that there are foundations to our system of thought, or belief, that lie beyond question, and that are necessary to the business of making value judgements. Postmodernist philosophy has proved to be resolutely antifoundational in outlook, and unwilling to accept that this renders it dysfunctional in any way as philosophy.

Lyotard's later philosophy is very much concerned with what he calls the '**event**', and also with the concept of '**differend**'. The event is for Lyotard an occurrence that dramatically alters the way we view the world, and calls all our ideological assumptions into question in the process. Auschwitz is one such event, the 1968 *événements* another. The former in particular is not something that can be explained away by the application of grand narrative theory; in fact, it represents the point at which grand narrative theorizing breaks down. The latter is some kind of explosion of libidinal energy which the system cannot deal with either. To acknowledge that there are events which cannot be predicted or encompassed within any neat universal theory, is to acknowledge not just the limitations of grand narrative but also the essential openness of the future. This openness becomes an article of faith to postmodernists: the future must not be considered to be determined in advance such that all human effort is rendered meaningless.

Differends are conflicts of interest between parties that cannot be resolved, but must be acknowledged and kept in view at all times (see particularly *The Differend* (1983)). Each party inhabits what Lyotard calls a different '**phrase** regime' whose objectives are incommensurable with the other, and neither of which has any ethical right to make the other conform to its wishes. What tends to happen in practice, particularly political practice, is that one party to the dispute enforces its view on the other, 'resolving' the dispute to its own advantage. In Lyotard's terms of reference, one phrase regime exerts dominance over another – a classic instance of authoritarianism in action. As an example of this in the everyday world, Lyotard cites the case of an exploited employee who cannot gain any redress for her exploitation if she brings an action against her employer, since the court that hears her plea is set up on the principle that such exploitation is legal. The employer's phrase regime is excluding the other from having a proper voice. It is the business of philosophers to help such suppressed phrase regimes find their voice, this being what Lyotard describes as a 'philosophical politics'. Philosophical politics, the search for new, counter-cultural, phrase regimes, can be considered the highest expression of postmodern philosophy.

Lyotard's most recent concern is the way that the forces of what he calls 'techno-science' (for which we can read the multinationals) are attempting to hijack the course of human history, by preparing for the end of life on Earth. Lyotard argues that techno-scientists are gradually eradicating humankind from the picture, by developing ever-more sophisticated computer technology with the ability to reproduce itself and to continue existing elsewhere in the universe when the Earth dies (an event some 4.5 billion years down the line). Techno-science's ultimate goal, Lyotard warns us in *The Inhuman* (1988), is to make thought possible without a body, and this represents a threat to humanity and its values that should be strongly resisted, being 'inhuman' in spirit. What techno-scientists want is to reduce humanity to its assumed essence, that is, thought, and to render this predictable in computer-program form. Given thought without a body there are no longer events or differends to worry about of course, nor the openness of the future that postmodernists so prize. It is another case of excluding the different and the unpredictable in order to exert control. What gets left out of the equation is the individual as well as the little narrative, neither of which has any place in the authoritarian scheme of things – and to wish to dehumanize mankind by reducing it to thought-process alone is an ultimate act of authoritarianism to Lyotard. Resistance at little narrative level becomes an ethical act on behalf of the cause of difference; and it is difference that must be protected at all costs in the postmodern world.

Jean **Baudrillard**'s work is yet another important expression of postmodern philosophy. He too came to be very critical of Marxism and structuralism, eventually rejecting the notion that there were hidden structures behind all phenomena which it was the analyst's task to identify and explain. For Baudrillard the postmodern world was a world of **simulacra**, where we could no longer differentiate between reality and **simulation**. Simulacra represented nothing but themselves: there was no other reality to which they referred. In consequence, Baudrillard could claim that Disneyland and television now constituted America's reality, and, even more intriguingly, that the Gulf War did not happen, but was merely a simulation (something along the lines of a video game, it would seem). Not surprisingly, this was a view that attracted a great deal of criticism for its apparent cynicism and lack of sensitivity to the human dimension involved.

Another argument of Baudrillard's that has inspired considerable controversy is that systems no longer need to be opposed, that they can instead be 'seduced' – by which he means beguiled into submission (see particularly *Seduction* (1979)). Feminists have been extremely critical of what they regard as the implicit sexism of the notion of **seduction**, and have accused Baudrillard of reinforcing sexual stereotypes by its use.

While acknowledging the force of the feminist argument, one might also regard seduction as yet another characteristically postmodern attempt to undermine systems by locating their weak spots. Postmodern philosophy in general sees no need for outright confrontation with systems of power, being more concerned to demonstrate how such systems (Marxism and communism being outstanding examples) can be made to implode.

The reaction against doctrinaire Marxism in the work of thinkers like Lyotard and Baudrillard can be regarded as part of yet another cultural trend that is now known as **post-Marxism**. Post-Marxism has become an important theoretical position, and includes not just figures who wish to reject their Marxist beliefs (Lyotard and Baudrillard, for example) but also those who want to revise Marxism in terms of new theoretical and cultural developments. Ernesto **Laclau** and Chantal **Mouffe** gave voice to the latter group when they published their controversial book *Hegemony and Socialist Strategy: Towards a Radical Democratic Politics* in 1985. In this study they argued that Marxism needed to align itself with the various new social movements that had been springing up (feminism, the **Greens**, ethnic and sexual minorities, for example); in other words, for Marxism to embrace political **pluralism** and drop its pretensions to be a body of received truth. Marxism also needed to take account of the various new theories that had been coming into prominence – theories such as deconstructionism or postmodernism. Once again, we can observe the characteristic postmodern distrust of grand narratives and their dogmatism coming to the fore. What is felt to be wrong with Marxism is that it has failed to move with the times, and to realize how various (or 'plural', to use the buzz-word) society has become. Marxism was instead stuck at the level of trying to impose its theories on others, on the grounds that it alone possessed the truth. Viewed from this perspective, Marxism is an authoritarian theory. Laclau and Mouffe, on the other hand, are putting the case for a more 'open' Marxism, able to adapt to changing cultural circumstances – and to attract new audiences in the process. Predictably enough, the Marxist establishment has been dismissive of Laclau and Mouffe's claims that Marxism is in need of drastic revision, or that it should strive to become pluralist, holding on instead to Marxism's supposed truth and universality of application.

It is this distrust of grand theory, and its authoritarian pretensions, that can be considered the distinguishing feature of postmodern philosophy, which maintains a libertarian attitude throughout its various expressions. In the Anglo-American philosophical world, we can find such views being espoused by the American pragmatist philosopher Richard **Rorty**, a well-known champion of the recent **continental philosophical** tradition. Rorty too has no time for grand theory and, in prototypically pragmatist fashion, is less interested in whether theories are true or false than whether they are useful and interesting. Philosophy, for Rorty, is no more than a form of conversation, and his own preference when it comes to finding a source of ideas to guide our behaviour is for other subjects such as literature. Rorty's turn to '**post-philosophy**', is, too, characteristically postmodern, in its rejection of the standard narrative associated with the Western philosophical tradition. Yet another authority is unceremoniously consigned to the historical dustbin.

Not surprisingly, not everyone has been happy with postmodernism's frequent recourse to the historical dustbin. The American critic Fredric **Jameson** has dubbed postmodern theory 'the cultural logic of late capitalism', regarding it as being, unwittingly or otherwise, in collusion with the powers-that-be in helping to maintain the political status quo. Postmodernists have consistently criticized the left's belief in the efficacy of ideological confrontation, and for a Marxist like Jameson that has the effect of serving the cause of the right, which has a vested interest in seeing apathy about the political process grow. Terry **Eagleton** has taken a similar view to Jameson, constantly drawing attention to the ideological implications of adopting the postmodern line, which he treats as inimical to the cause of socialism. Christopher **Norris** has been harshly critical of Baudrillard's work, in particular what he feels is his flippant attitude towards the Gulf War. For Norris, Baudrillard's denial of that war's reality is symbolic of postmodernism's emptiness as a cultural theory, and he cannot accept Baudrillard's apparent insensitivity to political turmoil and human suffering. Jürgen **Habermas**, too, finds postmodernism ideologically suspect, and has taken issue with Lyotard's philosophy on this ground. (For more on the topic of postmodernism's critics, see 'Postmodernism, Modernity, and the Tradition of Dissent' on page 158.)

Overall, postmodern philosophy is to be defined as an updated version of scepticism, more concerned with destabilizing other theories and their pretensions to truth than setting up a positive theory of its own; although of course to be sceptical of the theoretical claims of others is to have a definite programme of one's own, if only by default. Postmodern philosophy, therefore, can be seen as a deployment of philosophy to undermine the authoritarian imperatives in our culture, both at the theoretical and the political level. Whether such a trend will command interest for very much longer it is difficult to say. To some extent postmodernism has become its own grand narrative (there is a definite postmodernist 'line' to most philosophical issues), and therefore vulnerable to attack in its turn. It is also possible to argue that postmodern philosophers have overstated the decline of grand narratives, and one highly pertinent objection to Lyotard's dismissal of their continuing significance has been that religious fundamentalism (a grand narrative if ever there was one) has manifestly been on the increase in the closing decades of the twentieth century. The growth of Islamic fundamentalism in particular seems to call into question the validity of Lyotard's judgement on this score, given that it now controls the political life of an increasing number of countries in the Middle East and Asia, making it a significant influence on the global political scene.

Lyotard himself takes a cyclical view of cultural history, in which postmodernism and modernism continue to succeed each other over time in unending sequence. Thus there have been postmodernisms in the past (figures like Rabelais or Laurence Sterne qualifying as postmoderns for Lyotard), and there will be both modernisms and postmodernisms again in the future. It is just possible to argue that we are already into a post-postmodernist world, where different cultural preoccupations (such as the reconstruction of grand narratives) are making their presence felt. Certainly, scepticism has tended to go in and out of fashion over the course of philosophical history, and it may well be that the current round has served its usual purpose in drawing attention to the weaknesses of certain philosophical positions, and that a less negatively oriented philosophical programme can take its place for the immediate future.

POSTMODERNISM AND CRITICAL AND CULTURAL THEORY

ANTONY EASTHOPE

MODERNISM/POSTMODERNISM

Pablo Picasso: 'Les Demoiselles d'Avignon', circa 1907
© Succession Picasso / DACS 1998

Completed by Picasso around 1907, this picture, 'Les Demoiselles d'Avignon', is a foundational **text** in the **modernist** canon, shocking the viewer at every turn. The quattrocento tradition, the dominant form of Western art, carefully built up a convention in which objects were represented in linear perspective: in Picasso's work the face of the figure

15

bottom right, squatting on a bidet, is portrayed simultaneously from the front and from the side, an effect that shatters the tradition (as does the modelling of the bodies in general). This face and that of the one top right recall African masks, breaching any opposition between 'civilized' Europe and a 'barbaric' world outside. While the mainstream tradition had represented women as passive objects (generally naked, generally recumbent) who demurely return the viewer's gaze, these women (visibly shown as prostitutes) stare back with eyes that refuse to submit to any controlling look. Picasso's painting marks out a positive assertion that the past is dead, a false appearance, and that a new truth and different ways of painting must be found.

'The Old Man's Boat and the Old Man's Dog' (below), painted by the American artist Eric Fischl in 1982, invites questions. Does it show a pleasure cruise or the aftermath of a disaster? Should we attend to the sunny lower half or the dark background, in which a wave threatens to

Eric Fischl: 'The Old Man's Boat and the Old Man's Dog', 1982, oil on canvas.
Private collection, courtesy of the Mary Boone Gallery, New York.

engulf the craft? Are the figures naked for sexual pleasure or from destitution (is the woman at the centre sunbathing or dead?). While the figure in the bottom left corner fits the frame perfectly her pointing finger leads into a spiral which runs across the main figure, then round to the left through the two crawling men and beyond the picture altogether (one man's head is half out). With Fischl's painting no positive discrimination between the apparent and the real can be made – every line of enquiry is cancelled by another possibility.

These two paintings suggest a contrast between the confident, iconoclastic affirmations of **modernism** and a **postmodernism** founded on ambivalence. There must be a number of reasons for this kind of change. One would be that art obeys an imperative to move on, and so modernism is simply left behind because something new must be found. Modernism's intended impact has certainly diminished over time: in 1917 Marcel Duchamp horrified an art gallery by exhibiting a porcelain male urinal under the title 'Fountain', but when it was shown again at a Dada exhibition in the late 1950s, as Hans Richter remarked in *Dada: Art and Anti-Art* (1965), 'No trace of the initial shock remained.' And modernism became even further domesticated in the counter-culture of the 1960s.

Today we easily forget that in 1920 many people were terrified of an unknown future in which the working class would take over political power (the Soviet Revolution did little to allay these fears). Modernism was strongly linked to this anxiety. By the 1960s it had become clear the masses could be happily accommodated within existing institutions and a more benign and sceptical calm emerged in which postmodernism could recycle ideas and effects from modernism without causing any serious discomfort.

POSTMODERNISM: JENCKS

Three main uses of the term 'postmodernism' can be distinguished, one current in art history and architecture, a second in philosophy and a debate over whether truth needs and can have a foundation, and a third in a more general account of contemporary culture. The word appeared during the late 1960s to refer to the novels of John **Barth** and the dance of Merce Cunningham. Its first widespread currency came from Charles **Jencks** in his book, *The Language of Post-Modern Architecture* (1975).

Jencks gives a very specific and yet suggestive application to the notion of postmodernism. The modernist ideal in architecture was urban, universalizing and international; refusing decoration, it made a functionalist use of contemporary materials and is represented typically as a geometric glass and steel box, homogeneous in every direction, in which boundaries can be inferred between part and whole and from whole to part. Postmodernism for Jencks arises when modernism is joined to new technologies, producing a **pluralistic** admixture of styles and with it a different sense of space:

> Post-Modern space is historically specific, rooted in conventions, unlimited or ambiguous in zoning and 'irrational' or transformational in its relation of parts to whole. The boundaries are often left unclear, the space extended infinitely without apparent edge.

On this showing, while the modernist building is designed around a centre, its postmodern equivalent – through a use of diagonals, layering, demi-forms and shifted axes – is asymmetrical and decentred. This is not quite how Jencks expresses himself, for his concern is to give a detailed analysis of examples of contemporary architecture, but it is a way of summarizing his position that links it to the first, important advocate of postmodernism in philosophy and culture, Jean-François **Lyotard**.

LYOTARD AND BAUDRILLARD

Published in France in 1979, *The Postmodern Condition* enters from a somewhat unexpected direction: the status of science in the modern world. In the course of this discussion, however, Lyotard produces a radical and unsettling review of how knowledge has operated in the West since the Renaissance, starting from the viewpoint that for us today science has come to be deeply involved with language:

> Scientific knowledge is a kind of discourse. And it is fair to say that for the last forty years the 'leading' sciences and technologies have had to do with language: phonology and theories of linguistics, problems of communication and cybernetics, modern theories of algebra and informatics, computers and their languages, problems of translation and the search for areas of compatibility among computer languages, problems of information storage and data banks, telematics and the perfection of intelligent terminals, paradoxology.

With industrialization, iron and steel were commodities; today in a **post-industrial** world, knowledge itself has become a commodity, so that Lyotard refers to 'the mercantilisation of knowledge'. Not knowledge in the singular, however, but *knowledges*, since there is now a pluralist competition between knowledges. From this follows a problem of **legitimation**, for as Lyotard asks, 'Who decides what knowledge is?'

Traditionally, scientific knowledge has been defined in opposition to ideology or *doxa*. However, as Lyotard points out, this poses two problems, so putting into question the validity of science. First, if ideology is a kind of discourse, so also 'scientific knowledge is a kind of discourse', and this would entail the question 'How do we tell them apart?' Second, there is the problem of infinite regress: if scientific truth is obtained by evidence and proof, well, asks Lyotard, 'What proof is there that my proof is true?'

Lyotard argues that scientific knowledge never legitimated itself because it always relied on what he terms 'narrative knowledge' to support it. Narrative knowledge is customary, embedded in culture, enacted in forms of social competence as 'lived experience' which typically is represented as narration. Unlike scientific knowledge, narrative knowledge goes 'beyond the criterion of truth', and requires no further legitimation because it legitimates itself.

If this were all Lyotard had to say he would not have become a leading explicator of postmodernism. It is the next move and its consequence that give bite to his account, for Lyotard claims that the narrative knowledge called on by science has taken the form of one or other of two presiding, or grand, narratives. These have consisted of: (1) The narrative of emancipation, a story of 'freeing the people' for which science is believed to be a necessary means (Lyotard is thinking specifically of eighteenth-century rationalism in the service of the great revolutions, American and French, a rationalism which construes superstition as a bondage from which knowledge can release us), and (2) the narrative of the triumph of science as speculation or pure and authentic knowledge. (Arising with Renaissance culture, this narrative is continued by the **Enlightenment** and on into the work of **Hegel** and nineteenth-century positivism.) Noting the predominance of these two **grand narratives**, Lyotard adds dryly that **Marxism** 'wavered between the two models of narrative legitimation'.

All that has now gone. In the postmodern condition 'the grand narrative has lost its credibility . . . regardless of whether it is a speculative narrative or a narrative of emancipation'. Instead of totalizing and unifying narratives at the centre of culture – making a centre for culture – any former 'hierarchy of learning' has now given way 'to an immanent and, as it were, "flat" network of areas of inquiry . . .'.

At this point Lyotard slips over from description into advocacy. Knowledge now consists of a heterogeneity of competing local knowledges in which there are simply 'islands of determinism'. Knowledges have become performative, arbitrated no longer by the question 'Is it true?' but 'What use is it?', each discourse judged in terms of what Lyotard calls 'paralogy', the ability of parallel rather than hierarchically arranged knowledges to come up with a new move, an innovation. Lyotard welcomes what he envisages as the political outcome of this new condition, an end to the authoritarianism implicit in any claim to a totalizing understanding of the real – 'Let us,' he urges, 'wage a war on totality.'

In this account postmodernism is quite clearly defined: it character-izes a contemporary situation in which, as Lyotard phrases it, turning the knife, 'most people have lost the nostalgia for the lost narrative'. It would be a misunderstanding of Lyotard's analysis to respond that there are still grand narratives, his own history of how Enlightenment rationalism gave way to postmodern scepticism being one of them. At stake is not just an awareness but the active trust and belief supposed by the concept of narrative knowledge. More damaging would be a query as to whether narrative and scientific knowledge ever could be cut off from each other in the way Lyotard assumes. And some writers have simply disagreed with him, among them Jacques **Derrida** who, in an interview in *Radical Philosophy* (1994), says flatly: 'I have never gone along with these proclamations about the end of the great emancipatory and revolutionary discourses.'

Jean **Baudrillard** is an altogether less serious and committed thinker than Lyotard, and his discussion of postmodernism often deliberately challenges by being provocative and playful. If Lyotard stresses that in the postmodern condition you cannot found science in truth and so distinguish it from ideology (science itself being a discourse whose attempt to prove its own truth results in continual regress), Baudrillard conceives postmodernism as an endless circulation of **signs** from which any sense of reality has fallen away, a world in which there are **simulations** and only simulations.

Once upon a time (so Baudrillard might explain it), signs could be exchanged for reality in the sense that they were representations of it; in a second historical order, signs were related to other signs which referred to reality; now, in a 'third order', a postmodern order, signs have no connection to the real, signs indeed are more real than reality in what Baudrillard christens the '**hyperreal**'. Delighting in paradox, Baudrillard argues, for example, that Disneyland in the United States exists as it does to give the effect that the rest of America is real. Again, notoriously, he wrote two articles at the time of the Gulf War in 1990 proposing, first, that it couldn't happen, and then afterwards, that it hadn't. But there is a force in Baudrillard's exaggerations, for he makes us ask whether a war in which one side loses 200,000 combatants and the other about 70, almost all these killed by their own side in so-called 'friendly fire' incidents, is in any traditional respect a real war.

JAMESON

At this halfway point it may be helpful to list a cluster of effects which have been related to postmodernism.

1. Scepticism about the Enlightenment view that reason may rely on a firm founding for deciding between truth and falsehood, a tradition closely bound up with science.
2. Uncertainty about traditional humanism and ideas of progress.
3. An absolutely unprecedented development in the mass media, especially visual media (television, film, advertising, etc.), since 1950.
4. Widespread prosperity that seems to be here to stay, expressing itself in consumerism.
5. The weakening of any sense of central social authority in favour of a plurality of acceptable ethics and lifestyles.

If Lyotard and Baudrillard, with intellectual allegiances back to **Nietzsche** and Gilles **Deleuze**, come out for postmodernism, the American Hegelian–Marxist critic, Fredric **Jameson**, has made a resounding stand against it. Following the publication of Lyotard's book, at a time when the term 'postmodernism' was gaining currency but few people knew what to think of it, Jameson in 1984 published an article in the *New Left Review*, 'Postmodernism, or, The Cultural Logic of Late Capitalism' (later to become the title of a full book), which not only gave a clear explanation of what postmodernism was but also encouraged a decisive judgement on it.

Jameson confidently rests his own argument on a foundation of a single narrative as set out by Ernest Mandel in *Late Capitalism* (1975), a periodization in which the forces of production correspond to a stage of capitalist development and mode of cultural production:

after 1848: machinery and steam-driven power/market capitalism/ realism;
from the 1890s: electric and combustion motors/monopoly capital-ism/modernism;
from the 1940s: electronic and nuclear-powered apparatuses/ multi-national capitalism/postmodernism.

21

Eradicating older forms, this contemporary mode has extended itself into every aspect of life so that 'aesthetic production today has become integrated into commodity production generally' (*Postmodernism, or, the Cultural Logic of Late Capitalism* (1991)). Jameson's account of postmodernism annotates what are read as the cultural consequences of this logic.

Martin **Heidegger** had written compellingly about a Van Gogh painting of 1887, 'A Pair of Boots', and Jameson picks up his argument with enthusiasm: that the image discloses the truth about these peasant shoes, how they belong to a world of work and earth. Jameson contrasts this with Andy Warhol's image of five court shoes, 'Diamond Dust Shoes', produced by an artist who began as a commercial illustrator, that, Jameson argues, is passively complicit with the consumerism it depicts. The result, in the postmodern condition, is a loss of a sense of reality and so the emergence of 'a new kind of flatness, of depthlessness, a new kind of superficiality in the most literal sense'.

This effacement of the real through the 'commodification of objects', aesthetic and otherwise, has ramifications across the entire culture: not only in painting, architecture and the perceived organization of space but also in film, novels, poetry, and indeed in theory itself. Loss of historical reality in what has now become 'a field of stylistic and discursive heterogeneity without a norm' leads to the replacement of parody by pastiche. Whereas formerly parody imitated another style with the firm intention of mocking, satirizing or at least making a judgement on it, today pastiche reproduces formal features for the pleasure of citing them, in a practice of 'blank irony'. Increasingly, representation of the past ignores historical specificity and renders only a sense of the pastness of the past.

Loss of the real, in Jameson's view, leads to reduction of the traditional autonomy of the self, since with postmodernism the individual subject is no longer able to define itself reciprocally against a reliable, exterior object. Typically, Bob Perelman's poem, 'China', unfolds in the mode of radically incomplete syntax behind which Jameson detects 'schizophrenic fragmentation'. The Bonaventura Hotel in Los Angeles provides no space in which the subject might sustain its freedom and autonomy. It aspires to be 'a total space' without entrances, covered in a glass skin which repels and reflects the city outside, not even an area in which you can decide for yourself where to walk because 'a transportation machine' determines your passage. The 'alienation of the **subject**', enforced by modernism (Picasso's 'Demoiselles' – see pages 15 and 16), is displaced in postmodern culture by 'the fragmentation of the subject'; there is no affect, no depth, because there is 'no longer a self present to do the feeling'.

In sum, then, the totalization of consumerism and commodification corresponding to multinational diversification, eroding any awareness of reality in favour of pastiche and copies of copies, produced 'the disappearance of the individual subject'. What now appears to be lost is any critical distance on culture and the social formation which would allow collective action for change; the fear is that 'we are submerged' as it becomes ever more difficult to represent our present to ourselves.

Besides his many and brilliant examples, Jameson has essentially taken over the description from Baudrillard's (and to a lesser extent Lyotard's) account but given it a radically different interpretation. Although its range and vitality make it enormously suggestive overall as well as in detail, Jameson's theory of postmodernism is not difficult to interrogate. As a general theory surely it stands or falls with the 'productive force' Marxism avows as its own basis. It would seem hardly possible, after all these years of human culture, for a society to develop in which there are no longer any subjects, so Jameson's assertion is simply the outcome of a doubtful option: either the full subject or no subject at all. Do we need a sense of totality in order to enter a critical and resistance assessment or can we manage with something less than that? And how much of the analysis pertains more to the United States than anywhere else? (Could Jameson have written as he does about the Paris Disneyland?) Jameson nevertheless is foremost among the critics of postmodernism.

POSTMODERNISM AND THE REAL: NORRIS AND EAGLETON

As one might anticipate from a culture whose empiricism and obsession with the real is age-old and age-thick, British responses to postmodernism have been almost uniformly unsympathetic. Christopher **Norris** published two books criticizing it, *What's Wrong with Postmodernism?* (1990) and *The Truth about Postmodernism* (1993), Alex Callinicos and Terry **Eagleton** one each.

In an essay in *What's Wrong with Postmodernism* entitled 'Lost in the Funhouse', Norris chooses to take on Baudrillard because he has pushed his kind of writing as far as it will go, deliberately manipulating rhetoric as a weapon against opponents of the postmodern creed. Norris first of all attacks Baudrillard for retreating from rationality – for extrapolating 'far-reaching conclusions from limited evidence' and ignoring '**signs** that might complicate' his diagnosis as well as 'his habit of constantly jumping from one language-game to another'. But the main drive of Norris's antagonism is Baudrillard's insistence that in the postmodern condition, where signs are wall-to-wall, it is no longer possible 'to distinguish *truth* or its various surrogates – "science", "the real", "objectivity", "use-value", "need" or whatever – from the ideological representations which currently lay claim to that title'. Against this, Norris brings forward a number of arguments. One is to point out a passage by Baudrillard from *The Masses* in which he makes an opposition between truth and falsehood.

However, Norris rightly feels that such point-scoring is not enough and goes on to propose variously the following.

1. Baudrillard's own strategy of persuasion itself cannot escape the truth/falsehood opposition since no one will believe him, accepting his account of what the modern world is like, unless he can claim that it is accurate and informed (i.e. true). He thus becomes vulnerable to a knock-down argument used against relativism since the time of Plato, which Norris summarizes by saying: 'If he succeeds in undermining all appeals to truth . . . then there can be no grounds for counting him right . . . if he does not succeed . . . we are equally entitled to reject his case.'
2. Recent work in philosophy (Norris names Hilary Putnam and Donald Davidson) tends to show that rather than it being the case that a particular language or 'conceptual scheme' encodes its own sense of truth, the ascription to a language of a capacity to refer to reality is actually 'the *precondition* for our knowing any language'.
3. As Jürgen **Habermas** has argued, 'issues of truth and right reason are *inescapably* raised by any discourse that presents itself for serious appraisal in the mode of diagnostic commentary'; in other words, Baudrillard *has to* deploy rational argument and appropriate evidence if he is to be taken seriously (and clearly it is Norris's view that he is not and will not be since he begins his essay by urging us to 'forget Baudrillard').

Norris is keen to see off Baudrillard and postmodernism because, as he says, only the capacity to know truth and so work an effective opposition between knowledge and ideology makes possible a political critique aimed at transforming the very situation a writer such as Baudrillard describes so tellingly (and, adds Norris, with 'loathing').

In *The Illusions of Postmodernism* (1996) Terry Eagleton, writing from a 'broadly socialist perspective' takes an even stronger line than

Norris when he suggests that postmodernism, with its all-powerful consumerism, its relativism and celebration of plurality, is very much what one would expect to emerge at a time when mass political movements 'had temporarily gone out of business'. What his work adds to the arguments against postmodernism is a rejection of a tendency to dogmatize on the basis of some false oppositions:

> for all its talk of difference, plurality, heterogeneity, postmodern theory often operates with quite rigid binary oppositions, with 'difference', 'plurality' and allied terms lined up bravely on one side of the theoretical fence as unequivocally positive, and whatever their antitheses might be (unity, identity, totality, universality) ranged balefully on the other.

This is very well said, and Eagleton pursues the kind of criticism this opens up by arguing, for example, that culturalism is 'as much a form of reductionism as biologism', rejecting, therefore, an opposition between the view that since all bodily reality is interpreted through discourse, the body consists only of discourse on the one hand, and on the other, a simple belief that human behaviour is mainly determined by the body. With a similar **deconstructive** manoeuvre Eagleton refuses an opposition between social construction and free agency, and between **anti-essentialism** and essentialism; he goes on to assert that there can be no simple-minded choice between 'history as story-shaped and history as colourful chaos', or (putting a necessary question-mark against Lyotard) between the view that 'there is either a single **metanarrative** or a multiplicity of micronarratives'. Eagleton's intervention is sharp, pointed and often funny, though in this short, polemical book it is never clear exactly which proponent of postmodernism is under his cosh at any one time.

DERRIDA AS POSTMODERN

Since he affirms that no concept of knowledge founded in truth is still available, Lyotard faces a certain embarrassment in proving that his own version of reality (no grand narratives, only paralogy) is right. Jameson meets no such difficulty in his denunciation of postmodern culture since it is founded in the truth of historical materialism (or not). Norris and Eagleton also claim a reliable ground on which to criticize post-modernism.

In concluding, it may be instructive to refer to the writing of Jacques Derrida for a point of view on these issues. Since it is the work of Derridean deconstruction to breach and unsettle any **binary opposition** which seeks to preserve a sense of '**presence**', and since generally 'presence' has been felt as a necessary effect in the perception of truth, Derrida is widely regarded as *the* philosopher of postmodernism (for this he is severely criticized by Callinicos in *Against Post-Modernism* (1990)). Yet on three crucial questions – regarding reality, the nature of reason and the possibility of political critique – Derrida's position is surprisingly reassuring.

DERRIDA AND REALITY

Derrida, notoriously, has become associated with the claim (made in *Of Grammatology*), *'il n'y a pas de hors-texte'*, ('there is no outside-**text**'), a slogan Baudrillard would have been proud to have coined. Yet it is hard to know what a human world would be like in which there were only texts and the sign had no relation at all to anything beyond it. But we do not even have to speculate about this because if Derrida is read carefully, as Dominick LaCapra acutely remarks in *Soundings in Critical Theory* (1989), it is clearly his view that 'there is no inside-the-text either'.

Inside/outside the text: how could you ever decide fundamentally where text ends and reality begins? How could you ever occupy a position from which you could pronounce finally what is text and what reality? (Only God is really supposed to be able to do that.) The argument about knowledge does not necessarily have to go up the escalator Lyotard thinks is the only possible way to truth by asking 'What proof is there that my proof is true?' Text and reality, what is inside and outside the text, arrive together, a package deal.

DERRIDA AND REASON

The same Norris who condemns Baudrillard endorses Derrida's concern to put reason in question by trying (in Norris's words in his study *Derrida* (1987)) to 'demand a reason for reasonableness itself'. Or rather, again as Norris summarizes it, Derrida 'regards rationality in its current (technological and other) forms as a highly specific historical formation which cannot be appealed to some kind of ultimate ground'. This said, the whole of Norris's exposition demonstrates (perhaps even to excess) that Derrida *practises* rationality in his writing and that his arguments always invoke reason in being coherent, consistent and appropriately detailed. On this showing reason needs no 'ultimate ground' in reality to have its inherited effectiveness as rational discourse.

DERRIDA AND FUKUYAMA

In 1992 Francis **Fukuyama** published a book with the resoundingly postmodern title of *The End of History and the Last Man* and the resoundingly postmodern message that liberal democracy and consumer capitalism would soon have finally taken over the whole world, thus completing human history and bidding a last goodbye to the claims of any socialist or radical critique of the capitalist system. Derrida has little trouble (in *Specters of Marx* (1994)), first, in evidencing massive gaps and omissions in Fukuyama's version of the 'good news' – not all states are moving towards liberal democracy with the suave inevitability Fukuyama supposes, the free market does not necessarily produce political freedom (oh yes, and 'two world wars, the horrors of totalitarianism'). Second, Derrida asserts that Fukuyama's evangelistic tone invokes a narrowly 'Christian eschatology', that he constantly slides between actuality and an ideal, and that he assumes some universal definition of human nature ('man as man').

Throughout this devastating critique of Fukuyama, Derrida exhibits no reticence at all about adducing evidence from reality or sustaining a rational argument. Nor does he feel disqualified from affirming positive political alternatives to Fukuyama's free enterprise triumphalism. From the example of Derrida we might have to conclude either that he is not really a postmodernist or that postmodernism is not quite the irresistible contemporary force some of its exponents – and critics – have said it is.

POSTMODERNISM
AND POLITICS

IAIN HAMILTON GRANT

Ever since **postmodernism** hit the cultural news-stand, it has been incessantly interrogated as to its politics. With its 'anything goes' **pluralism** and its delirious celebration of **difference**; with reality, according to Jean **Baudrillard** – to many, the 'high priest of post-modernism' – 'no longer what it used to be', what grounds remain for a politics, necessary to counter the widespread and manifest injustices that remain in our postmodern world? Surely any prospect of tackling endemic racism, the horrors of the military-industrial-entertainment complex, the obviously economically motivated, console-cowboy overkill of the Gulf War, religious and political persecution or Chinese tanks crushing the bodies of protesting students, is given up in advance by any movement that, like postmodernism, renounces the modern ideals of universal freedom, equality and rights, without proposing any alternatives?

In many ways, 'postmodern politics' is a problem peculiar to the history of postmodernism in the English speaking world, where the term first arose in the world of art and architecture. Once postmodernism had reached a certain critical mass, it became irresistible to academic interests, and the path that it then took shifted from the arts to politics and philosophy, from which something known loosely as 'postmodern theory' began to emerge. The various elements from which theoretical postmodernism emerged were almost exclusively, however, fragments of French philosophy. It is to some extent a consequence of this speculation or free trade in theories divorced from their historical, political and philosophical contexts that the question of postmodern politics has appeared to be so open, and therefore, to host an apparently endless range of debates.

Two questions may therefore be asked. First, what impact has postmodernism had on politics in what Richard **Rorty** calls the North Atlantic bourgeois community, and second, what are the politics that inform the philosophy imported from France to this community in the guise of postmodern theory? The answers to both of these questions are linked through one of the very few **continental philosophers** to have directly addressed postmodernism. Jean-François **Lyotard**'s *The*

Postmodern Condition crops up in virtually every discussion of every aspect of these debates, so that his self-confessed extreme simplifications have assumed a definitive character with regard to postmodernism. With this text comes an entire history, and an entire politics, one that is generally replicated in all the European theorists who supply the resources for postmodern theory.

Before addressing this history directly, however, it is necessary, given the enormous credibility attaching to Lyotard's text, to consider some of its main points alongside critical reactions to them. While this may seem to over-restrict the full range of contributions to the theme of postmodern politics, it will get us to the core of many of the key debates in this area. Among the 'extreme simplifications' *The Postmodern Condition* announces, the one that has had perhaps the greatest impact concerns the status of what he calls '**meta-**' or '**grand narratives**'. While grand narratives such as the **Enlightenment** narrative of infinite progress in knowledge and liberty, or the **Marxist** narrative of progressive emancipation of labouring humanity from the shackles imposed upon it by industrial capitalism, have played a crucial role in anchoring knowledge and politics in **modernity**, **postmodernity** has entailed a crisis of confidence in them. One reason for this crisis is the rise of critical philosophy, begun, ironically, with the Enlightenment. While **Kant**, who initiated critical philosophy at the end of the eighteenth century, had intended it to supply human reason with the means for self-government, rather than relying on some divine arbiter or other unknowable phenomena, reason was to subject itself to criticism in order to know itself and its limits. By the end of the nineteenth century, however, criticism was being directed at the hard-won gains of the Enlightenment itself with **Nietzsche** proclaiming that God is dead, and that truth, morality and knowledge itself were mere illusions. Marx had also chipped away at the Enlightenment edifice, arguing that its politics had concentrated on ideals of progress at the expense of real progress in matters of human freedom, and that this idealism, rather than being a mistake, was a complex reflection of the ideals of the ruling classes. Meanwhile, in the late twentieth century, Marxism has not yet brought about the freedom it promised, but has instead produced a series of anomalies, such as the crushing of popular protest against Soviet rule in Budapest in 1956 and the bloody terrors of Stalin's gulags.

Progressive conflict between the narratives has therefore weakened them all, so that, at the end of the twentieth century, there seem to be no candidates to take over from them in tying all our knowledge and our actions to some coherent historical plan. All that is left is a field where the fragments left over from these grand narratives compete with one another and with new rivals. This field, however, is governed by a new alliance between technology and capitalism, constituting what some theorists have dubbed '**post-industrial** society'. But what big story does capitalism have to tell? Whereas it used to tell the Enlightenment tale of increasing liberty being best guaranteed by a free market capitalism that maximizes choice and minimizes state intervention in the lives and careers of individuals, under alliance with technology, the efficiency gains of, for example, computing fall into line with the drive to profit, so that 'minimum in, maximum out' becomes the only rule governing commercial, social and political concerns alike. Moreover, as a rule, it is its own justification: when profit is made and efficiency gained, the rule is justified, short-circuiting any appeal to larger-scale narratives to '**legitimate**' it. Indeed, the other side of this coin is that governments and other regulatory bodies are misled if they suppose they can control, by the imposition of political ends, the 'free' movements of capital across national boundaries. Governments and their economic policies no longer tell stories that affect the real movements of money: consider the inept wails of the UK government during 'Black Wednesday' and other recent bouts of international currency speculation.

While 'late capitalism', to use political theorist Ernest Mandel's phrase, popularized by Fredric **Jameson**, is a major player in post-modern or post-industrial societies, as noted by many critics and theorists, its presence in Lyotard's text is often overlooked. As we shall see later in this essay, it points to a very different evolutionary path for postmodernism than is often assumed by the celebrants of postmodern difference: the postmodern condition is a historical tale of the survival-of-the-fittest-narrative. To return then to the matter of narrative, with capitalism ultimately triumphant in the conflict of the narratives, no single story is left to hold things together; as many stories are told as there are groups to tell them. None, however, has any cultural, historical, philosophical or political priority over any other. It is in this field that, by common consent, postmodern politics finds itself: where there was unity, so the story goes, now there are only **differences**. Where the political will of a people, a nation or a culture used to be harnessed to long-term general goals, now fragmented groups engage in short-term struggles. The spread of identity politics over the last twenty years is testimony to this, with its emphasis on ethnicity, class, gender and sexuality replacing political credo.

Adherents of this state of affairs suggest that the celebration of the differences between such groups and identities allows for a politics to develop that no longer needs, as did ideals of the 'general will' of the people, or the political ideal of cultural revolution, to subjugate its members' interests to an orthodoxy. Instead, micropolitical alliances may unpredictably emerge that remain attentive to the differences between their constituent groups. Marxists, feminists, **Greens** and gays may thus find themselves in a loose coalition concerning one issue, but may equally find themselves at odds over another. Moreover, with the revolution off the agenda for the foreseeable future, direct action and issues-based politics assume a more urgent and realistic significance. Detractors, however, point to two main defects in such a view of the postmodern political condition. The first is, how can a culture organize itself around this liberal-pluralist, 'anything goes' ideology without the political muscle to back it up against those who, quite simply, are too different from ourselves, and who view Western liberalism in general, and the North Atlantic bourgeois community in particular, as pathologically weak and misguided? Consider, for example, the various fundamentalisms at work in the contemporary world. How does the North Atlantic bourgeois community respond when its basic rights are infringed, as happened when an ayatollah issued a *fatwah* against an author for blasphemy? If that community follows its liberal-democratic principles and continues to celebrate difference, how can it object to the death sentence? Such scenarios call for a basic commitment to enforcing certain laws and rights against those who are so different as to deny the value of difference. Second, by concentrating all its attention on 'micropolitical' issues, or on short-term, single-issue politics, the very real large-scale political structures that govern our everyday lives are disregarded and left uncontested to the enemy, which simply translates into covert support for, or actual complicity with, the status quo.

Meanwhile, of course, the champions of difference can point to a past riven with intolerance and the suppression of the majority of the world's population by a tiny minority of white, male, North Atlantic, well-educated and economically powerful individuals. Rather than celebrating difference, this regime has enacted a huge programme of colonization, political disenfranchisement and outright suppression. A postmodern world of differences opens up possibilities for the oppressed to find a voice with which to struggle against their oppression. Here, however, another aspect of postmodernism comes to the fore. Just as the Nation, the People or the Party are condemned for their totalizing aspirations, so too the ideal of a coherent and integrated self, such as promised by psychoanalysis, falls under suspicion. Once again, this is a problem that was initially opened up by Kant, who introduced an unbridgeable gulf between the knowable self and the knowing self, a gulf that was only provisionally held together by our ability to use the word 'I'. Nietzsche, seizing on the grammatical core of the Kantian **subject**, set about criticizing the belief in a coherent and integrated self as a product of a misplaced faith in grammar. **Freud** put paid to this idea by drawing attention to conflicts between aspects of the self, and located diverse parts of our 'psychical personalities', the unconscious bulk of which remains permanently inaccessible to us. Finally canonized in postmodernism as multiple or schizophrenic selves, postmodern difference seems to give with one hand what it takes with the other: for difference to offer any liberatory potential, the corrosion of the self must come to an end so that there is some identity that can serve as the basis of an identity politics. Such dilemmas are keenly felt and hotly debated in many fields, notably feminism. On the one hand, postmodern feminists like Judith **Butler** argue that there is no core identity, no essential self, nor any essentialist category 'woman' that would serve to unify the aims of a political mass movement. Instead, the self and its gender are realized only as performances. Others, however, argue for the maintenance of the essentialist category 'woman', since without it, what purpose could feminism conceivably serve? If we let go of the essential reality of women's oppression, we simultaneously take leave of our responsibilities to real women, making 'feminism' merely an academic ploy.

Apart from feminism's problematic alliance with postmodern theory, how do the main protagonists in the debates about postmodern politics line up? To develop this snapshot of the postmodern condition, I will continue to focus on positions that engage with Lyotard's version of postmodernism, since it has been one of the most influential and since a great deal more has, of course, been said about the themes of this essay than could be treated within it. As already noted, postmodernism came of intellectual age in the English speaking world in the early 1980s. Hal Foster's collection *Postmodern Culture* (1983) marks this transition well. Originally titled *The Anti-Aesthetic,* the retitling, in 1985, of this collection of essays by academic heavyweights such as Jürgen **Habermas**, Edward **Said**, Fredric **Jameson** and Jean Baudrillard, clearly signals postmodernism's shift away from the art world towards broader issues. Two contributors in particular made early forays into this new territory that have continued to focus debates ever since.

Jürgen Habermas's essay 'Modernity: an Unfinished Project' clearly signals his rejection of 'postmodernism'. If, according to Lyotard and other recent French philosophers, whom Habermas will later collectively call the 'young conservatives', none of modernity's narratives of emancipation and progress have borne fruit, this does not mean that they never will, but rather that they have *not yet* fully developed. Diagnosing the problem faced in late modernity as what he calls the 'fragmentation of the lifeworld' by the evolution, during modernity, of an increasing abstraction and specialization in the fields of knowledge (science), practical life (politics) and artistic practices, Habermas proposes to reinvigorate the **Enlightenment project** that directed all progress to the ideal benefit of the human race as a whole. Therefore, exponents of these rarefied practices ought to justify their abstractions to the lifeworld.

The means by which Habermas envisages this happening are found in the principles that govern **communicative action**: insofar as I speak to you, I give tacit assent to your speaking to me in return. Moreover, since speech replaces and modifies direct action (I do not just go ahead and change the world without asking), I also implicitly agree to be bound to seek agreement with you, rather than riding roughshod over your views. In other words, the aim of all rational communication is to reach agreement on what should be done. By not observing the rules implicit in all communicative action, I forfeit any right to engage in dialogue. Postmodernism, by insisting that this project is at an end, is simply not playing the game. That narratives are discredited and fragmented is no reason to assume that they need always be so. This merely poses us a problem that we must direct our efforts towards resolving.

Moreover, Lyotard, whose book *The Postmodern Condition* appeared in 1979 (Habermas's essay was first delivered in 1981), in relating a grand narrative about the end of grand narratives exposes a central contradiction in his account of postmodernism: if there is no longer any credulity in grand narratives, then what grounds could there be for accepting Lyotard's own account? If we do accept this account therefore, then paradoxically, it must be wrong about the status of grand narratives. Moreover, in offering it, Lyotard must himself believe that it must have some credibility, so that even Lyotard himself believes his account to be false.

Of course, in making these criticisms, Habermas effectively discredits Lyotard's extended analysis of *how it is* that this situation has indeed come about. We will return later to the roots of Lyotard's diagnosis of the condition of narrative under victorious capitalism. If Lyotard does not believe in the collapse of grand narratives, then, Habermas clearly does – certainly as regards Lyotard's narrative, at any rate! To the postmoderns, Habermas has too ideal a sense of what actually happens in communication: inevitably, interested parties set agendas, so that agreement must be won even by threat and coercion, that is, by the exercise of power.

Habermas's own suggestions for healing the splits in the everyday lifeworld in which we all live and act are riven with effects of power to which they remain blind: either agree or shut up. To the postmoderns, this merely emphasizes the illegitimacy of consensus as an ideal outcome, since it is won at the cost of suppressing dissent. The solution offered by Lyotard is therefore not to suppress, but rather to emphasize and even experimentally to aggravate dissensus. Rather than accept norms and rules imposed top-down by circumstance or project, open-ended experimentation will create new rules from the ground up. (As we shall see in 'Postmodernism and Science and Technology' (page 65), the scientific overtones in the language of experiment are crucial to understanding aspects of postmodernism that are often overlooked.)

While Habermas, following in the footsteps and the professorial chair of the **Frankfurt School** of Social Research, retains some of his forebears' commitment to the Marxist project along with his version of Kant's enlightened democracy, there are many other strands of the Marxist reaction to postmodernism. Ranging from Félix **Guattari**'s neo-communist outright dismissal of postmodernism as 'no philosophy at all . . . , just something in the air' like a fragrance or a 'flu virus, to Chantal **Mouffe** and Ernesto **Laclau**'s **post-Marxist** hybrid of Marxism and postmodernism, Marxist analyses have had, perhaps, the most to lose from the demise of the grand narrative of emancipated human labour and the postmodern disregard of large-scale political pheno-mena, such as the economy or the revolution. It is at least curious, then, that the renowned Marxist critic and theorist Fredric Jameson seems so positive about it. Even more paradoxically, his contribution to Foster's collection and his *Postmodernism, or, the Cultural Logic of Late Capitalism* (1991) – one of the largest books on postmodernism to have been written thus far and, along with Laclau and Mouffe's *Hegemony and Socialist Strategy* (1985), the most cited Marxist addresses to postmodernism – seem to buck the trend represented by Foster's collection to have moved postmodernism from aesthetics to philosophy and politics, insofar as they resolutely remain within the realm of the aesthetic. This paradox is only apparent, however.

The title of Jameson's book, which refers to postmodernism as the cultural logic of late capitalism, repeats the orthodox Marxist distinction between the economic base of society, and the cultural superstructure that reflects the conditions of this base. Art and philosophy are among the superstructural phenomena of a society, so that as Marx put it regarding philosophy, 'the ruling ideas in a society are simply the ideas of the ruling class'. By insisting that postmodernism has its roots in cultural phenomena, or, in other words, that it is located within this superstructural field, Jameson's book is a contribution to a long-running debate regarding the extent to which art and philosophy are to be regarded as simple expressions of fundamental economic shifts in society's base. A 'postmodern politics' would therefore be a misnomer, but the politics of postmodern culture can be revealed through the analysis of postmodern theoretical, philosophical and cultural artefacts. Rather than simply adopting the well-used strategy of criticizing it for its politics, Jameson is determined to gamble that by conducting such analyses, postmodernism may be susceptible to treatment by Marxist theory, and to find a place within the persistence of the Marxist dialectic. Against Lyotard, then, Jameson argues that incredulity in grand narratives is not a final position on postmodernism, but rather that this incredulity has its roots within economic phenomena. One of the themes to which Jameson constantly returns is therefore the prevailing nostalgia for the exuberant confidence and economic security of North American society in the 1950s evident in so much contemporary film and literature. It is the collapse of this economic utopia under the regimen of late capitalism, then, that lies at the root of the distrust of large-scale political narratives and provokes what Daniel **Bell** called, in 1960, 'the end of ideology', finding expression in so much contemporary philosophy and theory, so that postmoderns' vaunted theories of fragmentation turn out to be expressions of this, or analyses of these expressions.

Jameson does not, however, think that Marxism can survive these economic and cultural shifts without adapting its own theory to the new structures of the economic base effected by what sociologists such as Alain Tourraine have referred to as 'post-industrial society'. The analysis of postmodern culture will therefore have lessons for Marxism as well as postmodern political theorizing; for one thing, the strict separation of base and superstructure must be modified to take account of the dialectical effects on the base of cultural phenomena. After all, the idea that we can gain direct and unmediated access to economic reality by somehow sidestepping all theory and philosophy seems as untenable as the worst excesses of a 'just the facts, ma'am' scientism.

One of the holes in Jameson's book, which he explicitly and regretfully notes, is the absence of any discussion of recent **cyberpunk** fiction. As cyberpunk author Bruce Sterling notes, writing science-fiction in today's technologically sophisticated world faces a new challenge: the readers of such works have themselves, owing to an ever-increasing rate of technological change, grown up in a science-fictional world. Now, disregarding for the moment the problems this presents to science-fiction writers and readers, cyberpunk fiction none-the-less reveals a concern with the singular phenomenon of runaway technological development. This, nevertheless, is one of the concerns that animates Lyotard's report on the postmodern condition. While the ins and outs of this development will be further discussed in 'Postmodernism and Science and Technology' (page 65), it is important to note the extent to which Lyotard's account is an extension of the Marxist emphasis on the means of production to an analysis of changes in this sphere within post-industrial or computerized societies. That technology does not figure largely in Jameson's account demonstrates the possibility that the restriction of postmodernism to the field of culture and aesthetics is shaky, a shakiness compounded by his insistence that Lyotard's experimentalism is solely an advocation of the avant-garde practices enshrined in aesthetic modernism.

To develop this point, however, it is finally necessary to return to what this essay promised at the start: the political roots of Lyotard's postmodernism. Far from being particular to Lyotard, however, the French philosophies that have been imported into the English-speaking world to form that hybrid creature, postmodern theory, have all been shaped, to varying degrees, by these same political histories and events. To understand why this is, it is necessary to bear in mind the intellectual climate of post-war France. Between the two world wars, the names on everybody's contents pages were dominated by the 'three Hs': **Hegel**, **Husserl** and **Heidegger**. After the war, Sartre, whose existentialist philosophy was the culminating French expression of this holy trinity, began to attempt to move towards an accommodation with Marxism, finally declaring the latter to be the 'inescapable horizon of all thought in the twentieth century'. This reflected the rise to intellectual prominence of the so-called 'masters of suspicion': Marx, Nietzsche and Freud. One reason for this, apart from much cultural soul-searching following the ghastly spectacle of France's collaboration with the Nazis under the reviled Vichy regime, were the Paris lectures of Alexandre Kojève on Hegel's philosophy. Kojève's lectures, which brought a particularly Marxist slant to the reading of Hegel, had a defining influence on the entire generation of thinkers that were to rise to the dizzy heights of canonization as 'postmoderns'. Marxism, then, became that narrative against which the **legitimacy** of all others must be measured. In consequence, it is for the collapse of this narrative in particular that we must account in order to understand the passage from a Paris saturated with Marxism to its collapse in postmodernism.

The *événements* in Paris of May 1968 saw students and workers barricading the streets of a modern, first-world economic power to such an extent that the government was on the brink of being overthrown. When the unions, the parties, the intellectuals and the good men of the left condemned the popular insurrection in the streets of Paris in May 1968, Marxism's promise of a revolutionary future redeemed from capitalist exploitation, and hence its legitimacy among the intellectual left in general, evaporated. Lyotard, for instance, scandalized by the French Communist Party's condemnation of the occupation of the Nanterre campus of the University of Paris by the radical student group led by Daniel Cohn-Bendit, the 22nd March Movement (commemorating the arrest of the student leaders of an anti-Vietnam protest organization) supported them against the Party, the unions, the press, the university authorities, the government and ultimately, against the violent suppression of their occupation when Nanterre was stormed by the French riot police in early May. When the students reacted by taking to the streets in the company of the workers who, rejecting government pay policy, had staged a massively successful general strike, the failure of the Party and the unions to support the revolution, and their complicity with the state in helping to put it down in the name of a return to 'popular government', clearly demonstrated the left's betrayal of its revolutionary promise and its function as an organ of statist control. It is for this reason that Lyotard continued into the 1980s to regard May 1968 as a razor's edge severing the atrophied Marxist **metanarrative** from postmodernity. Hence, also, one of the slogans daubed on the walls of Paris during the *événements*: 'Comrades, humanity will never be happy until the last capitalist is hung on the guts of the last bureaucrat'.

Such a view had been vigorously championed by the **Situationist** International, whose pamphlet of 1966, 'On the poverty of student life', written in collaboration with Strasbourg student activists enraged against the university's role as a training ground for the managers of the '**spectacle**', forced the state to arrest, try and condemn the students – and to recognize the threat posed to the everyday banality of life under capitalism by the SI. The Situationists themselves made much of their role in the *événements,* commenting that their strategies had been implemented as if taken from a Situationist textbook; even taking to the streets was a strategy the situationists called 'drifting', a means of reappropriating the urban environment for the imagination: 'Beneath the paving stones, the beach!' Not only do elements of Situationist vocabularies and analyses find their way into Lyotard's texts from the late 1960s and early 1970s, it was also from this background that Jean Baudrillard's theses of a society of simulated desire emerged, taking its cue from Guy Debord's *The Society of the Spectacle,* with its theses concerning the management and production of desire through what remained, in de Gaulle's France, a state-run media. Whereas, however, the crux of Debord's analysis was that, under spectacular society, we either acquiesce as passive consumers of the spectacle of our own, alienated lives or, overthrowing the spectacle and its apparatus, we become active producers of revolution, for Baudrillard, a revolution against the spectacle can only take the form of a spectacle, since if it did not, it literally could not *take place,* would not register within spectacular society.

The immediacy of the revolution for which the Situationists agitated, while it found equally immediate expression in the streets of Paris, ran directly counter both to the Marxian ideal of revolution as an organic development from capital itself, and to its Trotskyite variant, for which the proletariat had to be helped to see how unfortunate and miserable they were by an intellectual and political vanguard. Neither war nor economic hardship had produced a revolution; but the stifling banality of the affluent society had. The failures of both these programmes to deliver the revolution, and the increasing bureaucratization of international Marxism, as evident at the Fourth International, had already prompted a large-scale re-evaluation of Marxism by groups such as *Socialisme ou barbarie* (Socialism or Barbarism), to which both Debord and Lyotard belonged. Between 1956 and 1964, Lyotard, a tutor in Algeria at the time, contributed analyses of the popular struggle for Algerian independence and the lessons for Marxism it contained. The group's basic thesis was that the bureaucratization of international communism revealed the extent to which it had become an organ of bureaucratic capitalism. After the group began itself to become rigid and doctrinaire, Lyotard left to join Workers' Power, where he remained until 1966, at which point, disillusioned, he became active in the emergent student politics and eventually joined the 22nd March Movement.

Although often enough at odds with each other, the Situationists, *Socialisme ou barbarie* and the enraged students all shared the conviction that Marxism no longer held the blueprints to the revolution. In other words, Marxism was already a thing of the past, for Lyotard, by the time of the *événements.* What then prompted him to claim so decisive a position, *vis-à-vis* Marxism, for these events? Surely Marxism was already at an end? Not so. While the immediate revolution of May 1968 demonstrated the unviability of Marxism as a political programme, the collapse of the Marxist grand narrative, that was to reach its culminating *synthesis* in the great, proletarian revolution arising out of capitalism itself, does not entail the rejection of Marxist *analysis,* merely a reorientation of its questions and a re-evaluation of its aims such as Lyotard had already been engaged in since 1956. Thus, if we look at the core questions asked in *The Postmodern Condition* – What form does capital take in postmodern society? How do the means of production in postmodernism differ from previous social formations? What form must a politics capable of responding to this situation take? – more rather than less continuity is revealed between the basic political orientation of Lyotard's thought on either side of the 'razor's edge' of May 1968.

What form, then, does postmodern capitalism take? As noted earlier, one crucial element of postmodern societies is the new alliance forged between capitalism and technology. It is this that provides the material basis for Lyotard's argument that capitalism emerges victorious from the conflict of the narratives: profit no longer need be legitimated by reference to a grand narrative of progressive realization of individual liberty through the market, since it is justified immediately by sharing its sole criterion of success with a technology that has become the means of production of knowledge, information and power. Thus, the means of production that secure power in postmodern societies are informational rather than industrial. Every time a computer maximizes the output of information from the minimum of input, every occasion when time or labour are saved by the implementation of a technology, capitalism immediately wins again. We cannot argue with capitalism, since within it there is no longer any role left for discursive reason. Nor does capitalism require propaganda: a self-confessed enemy of the state as much as of socialism, capital acts without loyalties, in accordance with its one rule of maximizing efficiency. The high ground of macropolitical reality is not therefore merely 'left to the enemy', as so many critics of postmodern politics have suggested; rather, the postmodern condition results directly from these new social structures. What form, then, should a postmodern politics take? Lyotard's advocacy of experimentation, mentioned earlier, must be applied to the context of the material organization of postmodern societies. Such a situation requires experimentation not only at the aesthetic level, as Jameson argues Lyotard's experimentalism reduces to, nor solely at the level of narrative: it requires that the media of techno-capital in which knowledge, power and information are stored, be the object themselves of radical experimentation.

This, then, is the history of the postmodern condition: on the one hand, a history of the evolution of capitalism into techno-capital, on the other, a history of the demise of the Marxist grand narrative and a response to the void left by this most accomplished of critical repertoires. The free trade in theory characteristic of postmodernism in the English-speaking world has, generally speaking, sacrificed the political history of the French philosophy of postmodernism to a kind of short-term expediency paradoxically derived, in large part, from theses propounded in such works. The rush for the new at the expense of its historical embeddedness remains, however, something of an experiment in forms of knowledge and political action, and the incursions made by postmodernism into fields such as law, political theory, and feminism clearly demonstrate the stakes of this experiment: if theory is regarded as a kit to be assembled not in accordance with some scholarly sense of its history, but variously according to the demands of the task at hand, then withdrawing it from the sterile catacombs of scholarly debate may yet have pragmatic benefit. Of course, ignorance of history, as is often remarked, condemns the ignorant to repeat it, but it is in the nature of an experiment to have an unknown outcome. Besides, if the tools of the past – Marxism, the Enlightenment project, market liberalism and so on – have been tried and found wanting, then experiment is demanded. As Lyotard says, the 'post' of 'postmodernism' does not signal that it comes at the end, but at the beginning of modernity. What new modernity might yet dawn from postmodern politics?

POSTMODERNISM AND FEMINISM

(or: REPAIRING OUR OWN CARS)

SUE THORNHAM

[Feminism] should persist in seeing itself as a component or offshoot of Enlightenment modernism, rather than as one more 'exciting' feature (or cluster of features) in a postmodern social landscape.

(Sabina Lovibond, in T. Docherty, ed., *Postmodernism: A Reader* (1993).)

[D]espite an understandable attraction to the (apparently) logical, orderly world of the Enlightenment, feminist theory more properly belongs in the terrain of postmodern philosophy.

(Jane Flax, in L. J. Nicholson, ed., *Feminism/Postmodernism* (1990).)

Any definition of feminism must see it above all as a social and political force, aimed at changing existing power relations between women and men. In Maggie Humm's words, 'The emergence of feminist ideas and feminist politics depends on the understanding that, in all societies which divide the sexes into different cultural, economic or political spheres, women are less valued than men' (*Feminisms: A Reader* (1992)). As a movement for social change, therefore, feminism's *theoretical* developments have been bound up with demands for political change. The beginnings of 'second wave' feminism, the term now usually used to describe the post-1968 women's movement, were thus marked both by new political groupings and campaigns, such as those organized around abortion legislation, demands for legal and financial equality, and equal opportunity at work, and by the publication of ambitious theoretical works such as Kate Millett's *Sexual Politics* and Shulamith Firestone's *The Dialectic of Sex* (both 1970). Both works offered themselves as texts of revolution, Firestone insisting that what she called the 'pioneer Western feminist movement' of the nineteenth and early twentieth centuries must be seen as only the first onslaught of 'the most important revolution in history', and Millett heralding the emergence of 'a second wave of the sexual revolution'. Both sought to re-claim a feminist history; both identified feminism as theoretical standpoint with the women's movement as political practice.

For feminism, then, politics and theory are interdependent. But feminist politics have operated in the spheres of knowledge and culture

41

as well as through campaigns for social and economic change. Feminist theorists from Mary Wollstonecraft (1759–97) onwards have identified as a primary source of women's oppression the cultural construction of femininity which renders women 'insignificant objects of desire' and opposes the category 'woman' to the category 'human'. As Annette Kuhn insists in *The Power of Image* (1985), 'From its beginnings, feminism has regarded ideas, language and image as crucial in shaping women's (and men's) lives.' Feminism has taken as an object of both analysis and intervention the construction of knowledge, meaning and representations. It has also been concerned with the struggle to find a voice through which such knowledges might be expressed. For the development of an autonomous female **subject**, capable of speaking in her own voice within a culture which has persistently reduced her to the status of object, is also part of feminism's project. As Rosalind Delmar describes it, feminism has sought to transform women's position from that of object of knowledge to knowing subject, from the state of subjection to subjecthood (in J. Mitchell and A. Oakley, eds., *What is Feminism* (1986)).

All of this would seem to place feminism as an offshoot of the 'emancipatory **metanarratives**' of **Enlightenment modernism**, and this is indeed where many feminist theorists would position themselves. If, as Lyotard suggests, two major forms of '**legitimation** narrative' have been used to justify the Enlightenment quest for knowledge and the importance of scientific research, both find their echo in feminist theory. The first, the 'narrative of emancipation', in which knowledge is sought as a means to liberation, finds a clear echo in the concept of 'women's liberation'. As Sabina Lovibond writes, 'it is difficult to see how one could count oneself a feminist and remain indifferent to the modernist promise of social reconstruction' (*Postmodernism: A Reader*). But **Lyotard**'s second legitimation narrative, that of the speculative mind, in which knowledge is sought for its own sake, also finds its feminist echo – in the practice of 'consciousness raising'. Through consciousness raising, greater insight into the operations of male power (a feminist 'enlightenment') is achieved through women's communal self-analysis and consequent rejection of internalized patriarchal assumptions and ways of understanding (what might be termed a patriarchal 'false consciousness'). Like **Marxism**, therefore, feminism's initial project ties theoretical analysis of oppression to a narrative of emancipation through social transformation.

Early feminism, then, had as its aim women's *equality,* through their admission to those spheres from which they had been excluded, and this included the spheres of rational thought and intellectual discourse. If women had been excluded from political theory, Marxism, philosophy, psychoanalysis and other dominant theoretical discourses, then women's inclusion would expand and perhaps transform those discourses, while at the same time their insights could be used to illuminate women's experience. Much feminist theory of the 1960s and early 1970s, therefore, set out to expand and transform existing theoretical models. But there are a number of problems with this approach. In the first place, it became clear that it was not possible simply to expand such theories to include women, for women's exclusion was not an accidental omission but a fundamental structuring principle of all patriarchal discourses. As Simone de Beauvoir pointed out in *The Second Sex* (1949), woman in Western thought has represented the **Other** that can confirm man's identity as Self, as rational thinking being. 'The category of the *Other*', writes de Beauvoir, 'is as primordial as consciousness itself', since the Self can only be defined in opposition to something which is not-self. Man, she writes, has assigned to himself the category of Self, and constructed woman as Other: 'she is the incidental, the inessential as opposed to the essential. He is the Subject, he is the Absolute – she is the Other.'

Moreover, even if women could be included within these discourses, it could be in terms only of *sameness* not difference, that is, within frameworks which could discuss women only in terms of a common, male-referenced humanity (what Luce **Irigaray** calls the 'hom(m)o-sexual economy' of men) not specifically as women. As *subjects* of these knowledges, therefore – that is, as thinkers and writers – women could occupy only a range of pre-given positions: they could write only as surrogate men. Indeed, it became increasingly clear that the 'universal subject' of Enlightenment modernism, far from being ungendered and 'transcendent', was not only gendered but very specific: a Western, bourgeois, white, heterosexual man.

Once this theoretical step is taken, a further step is inevitable: if feminists seek to construct a universal, 'essential' *woman* as subject and/ or object of their own thought, then that figure will be as partial, as historically contingent and as exclusionary as her male counterpart. Given her origins, she will simply be a Western, bourgeois, white, heterosexual *woman*. Feminist theory cannot claim both that knowledge and the self are constituted within history and culture and that feminist theory speaks on behalf of a universalized 'woman'. Rather, it must embrace **differences** between women and accept a position of partial knowledge(s). And once it occupies this position, feminist thought would seem to move away from its Enlightenment beginnings, and to have much in common with postmodernist theory. Barbara Creed, summarizing the arguments of Craig Owens in 'The Discourse of Others' (H. Foster, ed., *Postmodern Culture* (1983)), suggests a number of points of apparent convergence between the two. Both feminism and **post-modernism** argue that the '**grand**' or 'master' **narratives** of the Enlightenment have lost their legitimating power. Not only, they would both suggest, have claims put forward as universally applicable in fact proved to be valid only for men of a particular culture, class and race, the ideals that have underpinned these claims – of 'objectivity', 'reason', and the autonomous self – have been equally partial and contingent. Both also argue that Western **representations** – whether in art or in theory – are the product of access not to truth but to power. Women, as Owens points out, have been represented in countless images (and metaphors) throughout Western culture, often as a symbol of something else – Nature, truth, the **sublime**, sex – but have rarely seen their own representations accorded legitimacy. The representational systems of the West have, he argues, admitted only 'one vision – that of the constitutive male subject'. Both present a critique of **binarism**, that is, thinking by means of oppositions, in which one term of the opposition must always be devalued: we have seen in the discussion of de Beauvoir's work how fundamental this critique has been to feminist thought. Both, instead, insist on 'difference and **incommensurability**'. Finally, both seek to heal the breach between theory and practice, between the subject of theory/knowledge and its object. Women, of course, are both the subjects and the objects of feminist theory, and women's sense of self, it has been argued, is far more 'relational' than that of men.

Instead of an essential, universal man or woman, then, both feminism and postmodernism offer, in Jane Flax's words, 'a profound skepticism regarding universal (or universalizing) claims about the existence, nature and powers of reason, progress, science, language and the subject/self' ('Gender as a Social Problem', *American Studies* (1986)). But the alliance thus formed is an uneasy one, for feminism, as I have indicated, is itself a 'narrative of emancipation', and its political claims are made on behalf of a social group, women, who are seen to have an underlying community of interest, and of an embodied female subject whose identity and experiences (or 'truth-in-experience') are necessarily different from those of men. If, then, as Sarah Harding has suggested, we replace the concept of 'woman' by that of 'myriads of women living in elaborate historical complexes of class, race and culture' (H. Crowley and S. Himmelweit, eds., *Knowing Women* (1992)), as some theorists propose – if, in other words, we remove gender (or sexual difference) as a central organizing principle – how can a feminist political practice any longer be possible? If sexual difference becomes only one term of difference, and one that is not fundamentally constitutive of our identity, then how can it be privileged? Surely to privilege it becomes, in Christine Di Stefano's words, 'just another . . . totalizing fiction which should be **deconstructed** and opposed in the name of a difference that serves no theoretically unifying master' (*Feminism/Postmodernism*).

In throwing in its lot with postmodernism, then, might not feminism be colluding in its own eradication, accepting the demise of 'metanarratives of emancipation' at a point when women's own emancipation is far from complete? Feminists are understandably divided as to the answer to this question. Some, like Sabina Lovibond, insist that feminism must not be seduced by the attractions of postmodernism, for if feminism disowns 'the impulse to "enlighten"' it loses the possibility of all political and social action. Others take a very different line, arguing that the critiques of Enlightenment beliefs which feminist theory has mounted *must* place it as 'a type of postmodern philosophy'. Thus Jane Flax, for example, argues that feminist theories, 'like other forms of postmodernism, should encourage us to tolerate and interpret ambivalence, ambiguity, and multiplicity as well as to expose the roots of our needs for imposing order and structure no matter how arbitrary and oppressive these needs may be' (*Feminism/Postmodernism*). In this argument, postmodernism becomes a sort of therapeutic corrective to feminism's universalizing tendency. In similar vein, Nancy Fraser and Linda Nicholson, while rejecting the philosophical pessimism of Lyotard, wish to adopt his critique of metanarratives for a feminist social criticism. Such a feminist theory, they argue, would eschew the analysis of grand causes of women's oppression, focusing instead on its historically and culturally specific manifestations. It would also replace unitary conceptions of woman and female identity with '**plural** and complexly structured conceptions of social identity, treating gender as one relevant strand among others, attending also to class, race, ethnicity, age, and sexual orientation'. In a thoroughly feminizing metaphor, they conclude that such a theory 'would look more like a tapestry composed of threads of many different hues than one woven in a single color' (*Feminism/ Postmodernism*).

Another example of such an **anti-essentialist** critique can be found in the work of Judith **Butler** who, from a lesbian perspective, goes much further than Flax or Fraser and Nicholson, in arguing that the very category of gender is a 'regulatory fiction' which functions to enforce compulsory heterosexuality (everyone is either male or female; opposites complement/attract). For Butler, gender is 'a kind of impersonation and approximation . . . but . . . *a kind of imitation for which there is no original'*. The appearance of 'naturalness' that accompanies heterosexual gender identity is simply the effect of a repeated imitative performance. What is being imitated, however, is 'a phantasmatic ideal of heterosexual identity'. There is no essence of heterosexual masculinity or femininity which precedes our performance of these roles; we construct the ideal of that essence *through* our performances (D. Fuss, ed., *Inside/Out* (1991)). And we construct it in the service of a regulatory heterosexual binarism. Gender, like other categories of knowledge, then, is the product not of truth but of power expressed in discourse. Moreover, as a copy of a fantasized ideal, heterosexuality always fails to approximate its ideal. It is thus doomed to a kind of compulsive repetition, always threatened by failure and always liable to disruption from that which is excluded in the performance. Gender, in this view, is a performance which constructs that which it claims to explain. Rather than persisting in clinging to it as an explanatory category, therefore, feminists should celebrate its dissolution into 'convergences of gender identity and all manner of gender dissonance' (Butler, *Feminism/ Postmodernism*). Its abandonment promises the possibility of new and complex subject-positions and of 'coalitional politics which do not assume in advance what the content of "women" will be' (Butler, *Gender Trouble* (1990)).

Other feminists, however, while not wishing to return to a unitary concept of 'woman', are far more sceptical than Butler about the transformative possibilities of a feminism which embraces postmodernism. These theorists point to a number of major problems in this projected alliance. First, there is the tendency of male postmodernist theorists, when discussing feminism or attempting, as for example Craig Owens does, to 'introduce' feminism into the postmodern debate, to do so by presenting feminism as, in Owens's words, 'an *instance* of postmodern thought' (my emphasis). Postmodernism, that is, constitutes itself – where it considers feminism at all – as the *inclusive* category, of which feminism is merely one example. Second, to treat gender as only 'one relevant strand among others', as Fraser and Nicholson would wish, or as merely a 'regulative fiction', as Butler suggests, would render a politics based on a specific constituency or subject – women – impossible. The strategy proposed by Judith Butler, for example, is that of 'gender parody', in which gender is self-consciously and parodically performed, in a masquerade that subverts because it draws attention to the non-identity of gender and sexuality, to the multiple sexualities that can be written on our bodies. It is, as Tania Modleski points out in *Feminism Without Women* (1991), an 'extremely individualistic solution to the problem of women's oppression', and one which risks merely reinforcing the binary structure which it seeks to subvert. Parody, after all, depends on the stability of that which it imitates for its critical force. It is difficult, therefore, to envisage the 'coalitional politics' advocated by Butler as any more than a coalition in resistance, rather than a strategy for change.

A third problem inherent in the too-easy acceptance by feminism of postmodernism's embrace is, as Meaghan **Morris** points out, that while we may accept that there is a crisis in modernism's 'legitimation narratives', there is no reason to assume – simply because they have been termed '*master* narratives' – that this will benefit women – or blacks, gays, or other difference-based movements. It might just as well mean the disintegration of all motivating arguments for any kind of intervention or, as Donna **Haraway** puts it in *Simians, Cyborgs, and Women* (1991), 'one more reason to drop the old feminist self-help practices of repairing our own cars. They're just texts anyway, so let the boys have them back.' It might even, as Morris suggests, mean 'a state of permanent bellicosity in which Might . . . is Right' (*The Pirate's Fiancée* (1988)). With no arguments for change, power is ceded to the powerful. This last point takes us on to a further argument: that postmodernism may itself be a new 'master discourse', one which deals with the challenges posed by feminism by an attempted incorporation – as when feminism is offered inclusion in the postmodern debate as 'an instance' of postmodern thought.

That postmodernism has sought to deal with the feminist critique by offering itself as a 'framing discourse' for feminism is a point made by a number of feminist theorists. They have pointed to the fact that post-modernism's debate with – or deconstruction of – modernism has been conducted pretty well exclusively within and by the same constituency as before (white, privileged men of the industrialized West), a constit-uency which, having already had its Enlightenment, is now happy to subject that legacy to critical scrutiny. It is a debate in which the contribution of feminism, while acknowledged as a (perhaps even central) factor in the destabilizing of modernism's concept of a universal 'subject', must necessarily be (re-)marginalized: the central protago-nists are (as always) situated elsewhere. Feminist suspicions of this move are voiced by Nancy Hartsock. 'Why is it,' she asks, 'that just at the moment when so many of us who have been silenced begin to demand the right to name ourselves, to act as subjects rather than objects of history, that just then the concept of subjecthood becomes problematic?' (*Feminism/Postmodernism*). It is no accident, she argues, that just at the moment when those previously excluded begin both to theorize and to demand political change, there emerges uncertainty about whether the world *can* be theorized and about whether progress is possible or even, as a 'totalizing' ideal, desirable. For Hartsock, then, the intellectual moves of postmodernism constitute merely the latest accent of the voice of the 'master discourse', as it attempts to deal with the social changes and theoretical challenges of the late twentieth century.

Two further feminist suspicions are worth enumerating here. They concern the way in which postmodern 'gender-scepticism' permits an easy slide into what Susan Bordo calls the 'fantasy of *becoming* multiplicity – the dream of endless multiple embodiments, allowing one to dance from place to place and self to self' (*Feminism/Postmodernism*). This has two aspects. The first is that being everywhere is pretty much the same as being nowhere; in other words, postmodernism offers to its male theorists simply another version of the disembodied detachment which characterized the Enlightenment speaking position. The second is that 'becoming multiplicity' can also mean 'becoming woman' or occupying the feminine position. Thus, as Alice **Jardine**, Barbara Creed, and Tania Modleski all point out, male postmodern theorists have tended both to identify – in common with earlier thinkers – the position of 'otherness' with femininity, and to seek to occupy it. In this way, as Tania Modleski puts it, 'male power . . . works to efface female subjectivity by occupying the site of femininity' (*Feminism Without Women*), and the material struggles of embodied *women* are erased. Modleski goes on to argue further that for *women* to seek to occupy the postmodernist position, as postmodernist feminists do, is a cause for considerable feminist concern. The kind of disembodied, 'anti-essentialist' feminism which is produced is, she argues, a luxury open only to the most privileged of women. Only those who have a sense of identity can play with not having it.

How, then, can feminist theory both hold on to a belief in 'woman' *and* respect cultural diversity and difference? Or, as Rosi **Braidotti** puts it in *Nomadic Subjects* (1994), 'By what sort of interconnections, sidesteps, and lines of escape can one produce feminist knowledge without fixing it into a new normativity?' Attempts to answer this question – to, in Alice Jardine's words, 'dive into the wreck' of Western culture rather than simply pushing it aside – have produced some of the most exciting feminist thinking over the past decade. One possible answer is provided by what have been termed the feminist 'standpoint' theorists. These thinkers use for feminist ends the Marxist vision in which those who occupy subjugated or marginal positions in society not only produce different knowledges from those in positions of privilege; they also produce less distorted, less rationalizing, less falsely universalizing accounts. Nancy Hartsock presents the argument for this approach, arguing that 'we need to dissolve the false "we" I have been using into its real multiplicity and variety and out of this concrete multiplicity build an account of the world as seen from the margins, an account which can expose the falseness of the view from the top and can transform the margins as well as the center' (*Feminism/Postmodernism*). The task, she suggests, is to develop an account of the world which treats these alternative perspectives not – as they are seen from the centre – as subjugated or disruptive knowledges, but instead as primary and as capable of constituting a different world. This is an approach also embraced by black feminists like Patricia Hill Collins, who argues for what she terms a black women's or Afrocentric feminist epistemology. Like other subordinate groups, argues Collins, African-American women have not only developed distinctive interpretations of their own oppression, but have done so by constructing alternative forms of knowledge. The specific forms of black women's economic and political oppression and the nature of their collective resistance to this oppression mean, she argues, that African-American women, as a group, experience a different world from those who are not black and female. This distinctive experience in turn produces a distinctive black feminist consciousness about that experience, and a distinctive black feminist intellectual tradition. These 'engaged visions', in Hartsock's terms, can then produce the grounds for the recognition of commonalities, and 'the tools to begin to construct an account of the world sensitive to the realities of race and gender as well as class' (*Feminism/Postmodernism*).

There are problems, however, with this rather literal interpretation of what a 'politics of location' (Adrienne Rich, *Blood, Bread and Poetry* (1986)) might mean. It can become over-simplified and reductive (*this* set of experiences inevitably produces *that* mode of consciousness). It is difficult to know which set of experiences is constitutive of a particular group and mode of knowledge-production. It places an emphasis on experience which should perhaps more properly be placed on particular ways of *interpreting* that experience. Finally, the appeal to a commonality of experience can elide both differences between and differences within women. Collins's work, for example, persistently assumes that all black women are American, insisting, in 'The Social Construction of Black Feminist Thought', for example, that '[l]iving life as an African-American woman is a necessary prerequisite for producing black feminist thought' (B. Guy-Sheftall, ed., *Words of Fire* (1995)), and that all African-American women share a common position. On the other hand, once we allow for the multiplicity of positionings within every 'standpoint', the concept of a commonality of experience – and hence a distinctive standpoint – within oppressed groups can become lost.

The concept of 'situated knowledges' developed by theorists like Rosi Braidotti and Donna Haraway is a more complex answer to the question of how, in Braidotti's words in *Nomadic Subjects*, to 'figure out how to respect cultural diversity without falling into relativism or political despair'. The 'situatedness' envisaged here, however, is no simple affair. It is in the first place a position which insists on the embodied and therefore sexually differentiated nature of the female subject. But embodiment does not, in this context, mean 'essentialism', where essentialism is defined as implying a fixed and monolithic essence to female identity which is beyond historical and cultural change. The embodied female subject envisaged here is, on the contrary, a 'nomadic' subject, to use Braidotti's terminology. That is, she is 'the site of multiple, complex, and potentially contradictory sets of experiences, defined by overlapping variables such as class, race, age, lifestyle, sexual preference, and others'. Haraway goes further: in the contemporary high-tech world, feminist embodiment is about 'nodes in fields, inflections in orientations, and responsibility for difference in material-**semiotic** fields of meaning' (*Simians, Cyborgs, and Women*). What both thinkers are trying to do in these rather complex formulations is to insist both that the female subject is embodied – that women's knowledge and thought cannot be separated from their lived experience – and that this insistence does not mean that feminism cannot recognize the differences both between women and within each woman. Within all of us, argues Braidotti, there is an interplay of differing levels of experience, so that our identities, while situated, are not fixed but 'nomadic'. It is such situated knowledges – 'partial, locatable, critical knowledges', as Haraway describes them – which permit both a new definition of objectivity (objectivity as partial, situated knowledge) and the possibility of new political coalitions.

But this still leaves the difficulty of how, in Braidotti's words, to 'connect the "differences within" each woman to a political practice that requires mediation of the "differences among" women'. For it is difficult – to say the least – to see how women could unite around the formulations quoted earlier. In answer, Braidotti and Haraway offer 'political fictions' (Braidotti) or 'foundational myths' (Haraway) as a way of framing understanding. These 'politically informed images' (Braidotti), or 'figure[s] of hope and desire' (Patricia Clough, *Feminist Thought* (1994)), are offered as a means of empowering both a shared sense of identity and the struggle against oppression. Political fictions, argues Braidotti, may be more effective at this moment than theoretical systems. Braidotti's image is the figure of the nomad, who is neither exile (homeless and rootless) nor migrant (displaced and suspended between the old and the new); instead, 'situated' but mobile, the nomad employs a critical consciousness to cultivate 'the art of disloyalty to civilization', thus resisting incorporation by the host culture. Haraway's 'political fiction' is more challenging: the figure of the **cyborg**, a hybrid of body and machine, a 'kind of disassembled and reassembled, post-modern collective and personal self' (*Feminism/Postmodernism*). As hybrid figure, the cyborg blurs the categories of human and machine, and with it those other Western dualisms: self/other, mind/body, nature/culture, male/female, civilized/primitive, reality/appearance, whole/part, agent/resource, maker/made, active/passive, right/wrong, truth/illusion, total/partial, God/man. It is embodied but not unified, and being a figure of blurred boundaries and regeneration rather than (re)birth, it cannot be explained by reference to conventional narratives of identity. It is locally specific but globally connected: Haraway reminds us that 'networking' is a feminist practice as well as a multinational corporate strategy, a way of surviving 'in diaspora' (*Feminism/Post-modernism*).

It can be objected, however, that theorists like Braidotti and Haraway are trying to have it both ways: to be both situated and multiple, within and outside postmodernism. They can also be accused of substituting for a narrative of liberation directed at change in the real world, a utopian fantasy whose notions of 'embodiment' and 'situatedness' are slippery in the extreme. Susan Bordo, for example, criticizing Haraway's image of the cyborg, protests: 'What sort of body is it that is free to change its shape and location at will, that can become anyone and travel anywhere? If the body is a metaphor for our locatedness in space and time and thus for the finitude of human perception and knowledge, then the postmodern body is no body at all' (*Feminism/Postmodernism*). For Bordo, this kind of response to what Sandra Harding in *Knowing Women* calls the contemporary 'instabilities' of feminism's analytical categories will leave feminist thought 'cut . . . off from the source of feminism's transformative possibilities' (*Feminism/Postmodernism*). A similar charge is made by Tania Modleski (*Feminism Without Women*), who argues that it will leave us with a 'feminism without women'. Nevertheless, the dilemma that all these theorists articulate is the same: in Modleski's words, how to 'hold on to the category of woman while recognizing ourselves to be in the *process* (an unending one) of *defining* and *constructing the category*'. Since it is, as Donna Haraway comments, 'hard to climb when you are holding on to both sides of a pole, simultaneously or alternately' (*Simians, Cyborgs, and Women*), the various 'political fictions' offered by feminist theorists can be seen as a way of finding new terms in which to theorize a way forward. For the danger they recognize is also the same: that male postmodern theory will simply repeat the gesture of its modernist predecessors in appropriating 'femininity' as one of its multiple possible positions, at the same time as it erases and silences the work and lives of women. The task that is being addressed, then, is, in the words of Meaghan Morris in *The Pirate's Fiancée*, 'to use feminist work to frame discussions of postmodernism, and not the other way around'.

POSTMODERNISM AND LIFESTYLES
(or: YOU ARE WHAT YOU BUY)

NIGEL WATSON

In the early 1990s the *Independent on Sunday* asked the question: 'Why is Fergie like Batman, Ross Perot, Vimto, a Mazda and the new MI6 building?' The answer they gave was because all of these people and products had been labelled **postmodern**, they were all said to share a self-consciousness about the past and they all only fully made sense if an **ironic** sense of playfulness was acknowledged. The film *Batman*, for example, played upon references from comic books, while the Mazda MX5 was a contemporary recreation of the English sports car of the 1960s. This feature of postmodern styling and design has become best known as **retro** and a glance through catalogues of consumer goods will demonstrate the extent to which this trend has become part of everyday life, with telephones, radios, bathroom fittings and furniture all drawing upon our desire to recreate the mood of an imagined past.

The public images of Fergie and Ross Perot make sense by referring to the past rather than the future. Fergie because she draws upon a former age of royal decadence and Ross Perot because he appeals to the so-called lost values of a former America. John Major attempted a similar appeal in the UK by evoking an England of warm beer, cricket on village greens and spinsters cycling to church on balmy summer evenings. It has also been suggested that Ross Perot represents another feature of the postmodern in that he is a single-issue politician without roots in the traditions of party. The same could be said of Sir James Goldsmith's Referendum Party in the 1997 UK general election which had only one policy and which claimed that it would dissolve itself if its aim was achieved.

Postmodern politics are said to revolve more and more around particular campaigning issues in which previously disparate groups coalesce and then dissolve again. This is the so-called rainbow coalition of the 1980s and is best exemplified by the protests against live animal exports in which elderly Tory women, liberal academics and New Age travellers united against the injustice of sending animals to their deaths thousands of miles away and in the confined conditions of an animal transporter. At root this aspect of the postmodern condition is related to the dissolution of traditional class and status groupings. Values and allegiances are now more transitional and no longer centred in the old alliances of production-based relationships. Retro styling and the dissolution of tradition are only some of the features which characterize postmodernism and more of these will be explored in this essay.

Additionally the *Independent on Sunday* then went on to ask a number of celebrities if they could define the exact nature of the idea. Most were sceptical or dismissive, though some did attempt an answer. The Head of BBC Music and Arts said: 'Post modernism is a rather glib way of saying flexibility; of saying that hierarchies aren't what they used to be, that you can mix and match different hierarchies of culture.' He was a brave man because one of the most quoted writers on postmodernism and culture – Jean **Baudrillard** – refused the invitation and replied in this way: 'I cannot explain and I will not explain. Post modernism for me is nothing. I do not worry about this term. I am very exhausted with this post modernism. All that I will say is that the post modern is maybe postmodern.'

It is certainly true that as we approach the end of the 1990s there is still much confusion and controversy surrounding the concept and that for some philosophers, like Christopher **Norris**, the term is little more than a lazy way of collecting together some of the features of contemporary culture and combining these with partly digested aspects of **continental** thought. It is, they argue, only a transitory and relatively insignificant phase in our understanding of contemporary experience. However, it cannot be denied that postmodernism has had a major impact across a range of areas of thought ranging from geography to literary theory to cinema to architecture, and that for many writers it has provided a satisfactory way of explaining the significant changes in the nature of social experience over the last forty years or so.

This essay considers these changes in relation to consumer culture and in particular will reflect upon contemporary social identity. I try to answer the question whether the basis of everyday life can be said to have changed sufficiently to justify the claims of some writers that we are living in a new era or epoch – an era that can be called '**postmodernity**'.

POSTMODERNISM, IDENTITY AND LIFESTYLE

Although, for some, postmodernism remains a confused and vacuous term, it has been in use for long enough to have achieved at least a basic consistency of definition. Most commentators agree that there is a cluster of features which characterize contemporary culture and which when taken together can be called postmodern. Perhaps the most important of these for the purposes of this section is the suggestion that our experiences are now rooted in the processes of consumption rather than production. This can perhaps be illustrated by thinking of those regions of the UK which were once dominated by heavy industry. For most people in these largely working-class areas the future was one defined by a relationship with work and with, for example, the production of coal, or ships or cotton. The people were miners, shipbuilders or mill workers and the basis of social life was for these men and women their relationship with the process of production. Their personal, collective and cultural identities were rooted in the locality around the workplace and in the values of the industry for which they worked.

The last thirty years have seen a radical shift in the nature of this relationship. The land which used to house the factories and mines has now been developed for out-of-town shopping areas such as the Metro Centre in Gateshead or Meadow Hall in Sheffield, while the land by the rivers has been turned over to leisure marinas, theme parks and heritage museums. In fact the heritage museum, such as the one at Beamish in the north-east of England, epitomizes the postmodern process whereby a past is nostalgically recreated as a form of substitute reality. Ex-miners are employed to inform the rest of us about mining in a time in which they did not live, while the need for 'real' mining has all but disappeared. We pay our money and are entertained by consuming second-hand experiences which once formed the basis of social life. To a significant extent we have become tourists in our own cultures. Sunday no longer means a trip to church or chapel, but rather a visit to the cathedrals of consumerism. Shopping malls have become major sites of leisure activity, the pilgrimage is enough even without the act of buying.

We no longer conform to the traditions of the old occupational cultures and instead we choose a lifestyle. This term, not in itself a new one, was taken by the advertising and designer culture of the 1980s to stand for the individuality and self-expression that was the cornerstone of the free market revolution of that decade. The era of mass consumption, with its emphasis on conformity and similarity, has been replaced by an apparently endless choice and variety of consumer goods aimed at specific market segments. While it is important to remember that some people in developed societies and many throughout the world are excluded from this process, it is equally important to understand that the construction of identity through the acquisition of consumer goods is a voluntary one. Those of us who participate are not just fashion victims, we actively wish to join in and actively desire the opportunities for self-expression and display which are provided by the choices of the shopping malls. It is true that we may be targeted as dinkies (double income, no kids) or the infamous yuppies, but we like to identify with the style that best represents the way that we wish to be seen. Power has now come to be seen as the capacity to spend in order to find expression for an aspirational lifestyle.

Perhaps one of the most noticeable areas of growth in consumer markets has been in men's fashion and lifestyle accessories. The male body has been increasingly used in advertising not simply in a functional capacity as it would have been in the 1950s, but in a decorative one as well. Men are no longer just portrayed as the expert advisers to women on technical matters such as the choice of washing machine, they are as well at the aspirational heart of advertising style. Older, as well as young men, now articulate their identity through a conscious and selective process of consumption involving clothes, hairstyles and body decoration. From Levis' famous advertisement featuring Nick Kamen in a launderette through to magazines devoted to the latest electronic gadgets, men are the focus of a shifting process of consumerization in which image overrides utility. Even if the new man of the 1980s has become the bloke of the 1990s the construction of male identity is now inescapably a self-conscious, playful and sexualized process, unimaginable in the decades to which John Major so nostalgically referred.

The body is also a focus for identity construction in a more permanent and serious way. The opportunity for changing the shape and structure of our physical bodies through cosmetic surgery is widely advertised in fashion and style magazines. Noses can be reshaped, wrinkles removed, faces lifted, fat siphoned and breasts reduced or augmented. The body itself can be seen as a consumer commodity, and this is a process available and promoted to both men and women. In a competitive world it is not enough to be ordinary and we are all encouraged to approach more nearly the ideal of youthful bodily perfection in order to give ourselves added market value.

A massive, worldwide industry has developed devoted to assisting us in our responsibilities to maintain our bodies. The healthiness of the body has become associated with its appearance, and it is possible to buy into a bewildering array of products and services that trade upon the importance of the cultural values of youth and beauty. In this context youth and beauty are aligned with slenderness, muscularity and physical fitness, one extremity of which is represented by the increasing popularity of body-building for both men and women. The corollary of this is that the ageing body has become a source of anxiety, and the non-exercised and overweight body a source of shame and ridicule. Although we are surrounded by health-promoting messages which encourage us to exercise and to eat the 'right' foods, the drive for us to achieve fitness is related as much to the desire for surface attractiveness as it is to the protective dimensions of health promotion.

It is not a coincidence that management of our lifestyles is at the heart of the health-promotion process. We are encouraged to believe that our leisure time should be devoted to activities which will enhance our potential for healthy longevity. It is as important to be able to demonstrate and display an association with the correct attitude as it is actually to participate. Owning a mountain bike and Lycra shorts immediately confers the desired surface appearance, provided of course that unsightly bulges can be hidden. Similarly, eating low fat foods and the other acceptable commodities comprising a healthy diet gives an assurance of risk reduction and adequate body maintenance even if they are consumed in addition to, rather than instead of, proscribed food-stuffs. It is often the case that an emphasis on body maintenance is combined with the celebration of excess and indulgence. Postmodern fragmentation extends into dietary habits in which contradictory messages can be believed and simultaneously followed.

It can seem as if the efforts of the advertising industry are directed entirely towards the generation of false needs within us all, but one of the great strengths of the process of consumerism is that it is able to harness and direct our genuine needs, even if the goods and services on offer more often than not leave us frustrated and unfulfilled. Human-kind has almost certainly always desired better health, greater beauty, sexual fulfilment and longer life. The issue is, however, whether these are now sought at the expense of other more substantial aspects of life. It is also important to reflect what happens to the excluded in a world devoted to valuing the surface appearance. This will be returned to in the conclusion.

A FEW NECESSARY THEORETICAL POINTS

One of the features that emerges from the above discussion is that postmodernism emphasizes the importance of style and appearance over content. The construction of a personal lifestyle through the consumption of desirable consumer services has little to do with the usefulness of the goods and much to do with image and the way that they appear to others. This argument has also been applied to entertainment and to the arts. Many commentators have observed that the distinction between high art and popular culture has been lost because of the uncertainty which now surrounds establishing unequivocal criteria for judging the value of cultural forms. This is a difficult point, but essentially from a postmodern perspective it is not possible to assert that Shakespeare is better than *Coronation Street*. Certainly there are writers for whom this would be an absurd statement because they continue to believe in the traditional standards by which literary merit is judged, and who would counter any assault on these standards with bitter and hostile academic debate.

There is an important link here with one of the fundamental characteristics of most postmodern thought. The key thinkers have all identified a common theme in the scepticism of the twentieth century towards the once great certainties of history and society. We no longer unquestioningly accept the universal claims to knowledge and truth of the great stories which have organized our culture. These include religion, the progress of **modernism**, the progress of science, and absolute political theories like **Marxism**.

It is not always easy to grasp the significance of these abstract ideas for everyday life, but what is really in question is whether it is any longer possible to agree on absolute truth. We often hear on the television and radio about a breakdown in society because of the decline in shared values. Politicians of the main parties in the UK speak of the need to re-establish a common core of beliefs in order to bring society back together. From a postmodern perspective this does not make sense because the politicians are basing their claims on a mistaken belief in universal truths or **metanarratives**, as postmodern thinkers would say. The supremacy of Western thinking has been challenged throughout the twentieth century and especially with the decline of colonial empires. The explicit assumption that their cultures and ideas represented the progress of civilization is one that we no longer accept. It is now much more commonplace to assume that we cannot say that one society or culture is better than another one.

Postmodern thinkers also point to the fragmentation of experience and a compression of time and space as defining features of the late twentieth century. It is now accepted that changes in the structure of multinational companies have led to the globalization of production. Cars, for example, may now be assembled in the UK using parts which have been manufactured at factories throughout the world. Communication and transport systems have developed to allow links between countries to occur with great rapidity. European financial institutions are able to transmit their data electronically to be processed overnight on the Indian subcontinent, ready for return for business the next day.

The **Internet** allows us to view from home, and in real time, events on the other side of the world.

Whereas 40 years ago the family holiday might have been spent in Blackpool or Bournemouth, it is now unremarkable to travel to Florida, the Caribbean, or the Far East. It is quite possible for the more adventurous to explore the Himalayas or the Arctic. A visit to any supermarket provides the opportunity to purchase food from every culture on the globe and which was growing on the other side of the world perhaps only two days previously. The average high street in the UK contains restaurants and take-aways offering cuisine from every continent. All of these practical changes in our opportunities to experience the world mean that our conscious appreciation of time and of physical space is compressed when compared with even the middle of the twentieth century.

In the next section we will look at the implications of these ideas for our experience of leisure and entertainment, but before doing so we need briefly to consider the ideas of one particular theorist of the postmodern – Jean **Baudrillard**.

Baudrillard is associated, perhaps more than any other writer, with the cultural implications of postmodernism. His early writings provide a neo-Marxist critique of consumption in capitalist societies. However he later comes to criticize any theories, like psychoanalysis, Marxism, or structuralism, which depend upon looking beneath the surface appearance to an underlying truth or essence. Baudrillard is strongly influenced by a tradition in French philosophy called **semiology**. This leads him to look at the way that we understand **signs** and symbols in our culture, semiology being the science of sign systems which includes language as well as visual and social codes.

The basis of this tradition is that we make sense of the world around us by associating signs and symbols with objects or ideas which are called *referents*. Baudrillard has outlined four stages in the way that the signs relate to their referents and he has called this relationship **simulation**. It is possible to illustrate this in relation to the creation of images. While in medieval times the image was simply a direct reflection of reality, in the Renaissance period images were the individual and creative work of a single artist. The sign was *emancipated* and open to artistic interpretation; most importantly; it was unique and could not be reproduced in the same form. There is only one 'Mona Lisa'.

He then points to the Industrial Revolution and the emergence of processes of production which allow for the manufacture of endless copies of the same artefact. In terms of images the camera provides the best example of this. There is no original of a photographic image, although it refers to an external reality. Finally he suggests that with the start of postmodernism, we have entered the era of **hyperreality** in which the signs stand only for themselves. Signs are the reality and the imaginary and the real have become confused. This can be illustrated in relation to the imagery of the pop video in which time and place are hard to identify and in which a blend of styles and references mix together, teasing, but not depending upon our knowledge of previous artists. These brief and fast edited videos can then be watched in no particular order on music channels like MTV. Playful references to earlier musical styles like the Kinks or the Rolling Stones are at the core of successful bands like Blur and Ocean Colour Scene, while bands like Kula Shaker and Apache Indian blend an eclectic mix of cultural and musical styles including Asian, European and Afro-Caribbean. Similarly, in our pursuit of a healthy identity, the fitness bike or the home rowing machine has come to have a place of its own. Such aids depend upon our understanding of the real processes of rowing or cycling, but their usage has evolved into independent activities with a reality of their own. At the core of this series of observations is a central tenet of postmodern thinking. Images and cultural artefacts no longer refer to a single reality, but have instead become realities in their own right.

POSTMODERNISM, CITIES AND LEISURE

It was mentioned earlier that another of the features of postmodern analysis is the claim that there has been a breakdown in the distinction between élite art and popular culture. This is not a new observation and over sixty years ago the mass culture critics expressed concern that high culture would be undermined because of the commercial exploitation of mass taste. The major difference though between these early writers and the contemporary postmodern critics, is that the latter are celebrating these developments. One of the central claims made by writers who are optimistic about postmodern changes is that the process is demo-cratizing and potentially classless and this is an issue that will form the basis of the concluding section. However, we are now going to look at the impact of postmodern change upon leisure and the urban spaces in which we live and work.

The starting point for much of the debate about postmodern issues in the twentieth century has been architecture. It has even been suggested that the transition from the modern to the era of the post-modern can be specified as 3.32pm on 15 July 1972. This is the time when a prizewinning example of modern housing – the Pruitt-Igoe housing development in St. Louis – was blown up because it was considered unsuitable for human habitation even by those on low income. Modern architecture was characterized by the principles of architects such as Le Corbusier who was at his most influential in the 1920s, though his ideas are typified by the high rise flats which came to dominate our cities in the 1960s.

The modernist architects – like modernist writers and painters in their respective fields – rejected all previous forms and insisted that both traditional and classical forms of architecture should be replaced by buildings based upon rational and universal principles. In practice this meant an emphasis on plain functional design usually in concrete and glass. The building was decontextualized and universalized. The hearts of cities were flattened to be replaced all over the world by buildings which looked the same. This was the metanarrative of modernism.

In contrast postmodern buildings and cityscapes are characterized by a sensitivity to context and self-conscious playfulness in which different styles and references to different historical periods are mixed together in an ironic and eclectic way. There is a characteristic focus on appearance over substance and purpose. It contains a deliberate mixing of vernacular and classical features as part of the process whereby popular and élite culture are given equal value. In many of our cities the cobbled streets ripped up in the 1960s are being replaced and embellished with fibreglass reproduction gas lamps, in an attempt to evoke the past.

In a related sense the Metro Centre in Gateshead (north-east England) has shopping areas that are themed to provide us with a pastiche experience. In the Mediterranean village it is possible to eat pasta in an Italian trattoria or calamare in a tapas bar on opposite sides of the mall which shares the same twinkling lightbulbs designed to remind us of those longed-for sultry summer nights. If you are overcome by these feelings then travel agents are handily placed to complete the experience. Just around the corner we can enter a Dickensian world of cobbles, street-lamps and small-pane windowed shops where we can eat cream teas or buy humbugs. Many writers, including Baudrillard, have pointed to theme parks, and especially Disneyland, as examples of postmodern entertainment space. However, we have to travel to them. In the themed shopping mall we have the playful creation of alternative realities brought to us as part of an everyday experience of shopping.

A unique feature of the twentieth century has been the expansion and proliferation of electronic means of communication which fill our world with a confusion of images and sounds unimaginable a hundred years ago. The very existence of so much competing information means that our attention span is shortened and that the potential for a continuous narrative is undermined. Instead we mix and match styles and genres creating an eclectic mix of short-lived experience. This is exemplified by the increasing numbers of television channels across the world all of which can be surfed by using the remote handset. The television becomes like a magazine in which we flick from page to page, mostly just looking at the pictures, sometimes taking in sections but rarely completing a programme or article from end to end.

This dimension of discontinuity is even more marked in the development of the computer CD-ROM. While it is possible to disrupt the linear flow of television, the programmes are nevertheless made to be watched from beginning to end. Even the video recorder only provides a faster way of shifting the time experience, which nevertheless remains essentially linear. CD-ROM based reference materials like Encarta or Cinemania allow us to make a potentially infinite series of connections, creating our own sequences and patterns without the constraints of pre-given stories or argument. This is a truly postmodern experience in which time and content are separated and narrative is controlled by the viewer and is always in the present.

There have been a number of recent examples of television programmes which have been said to reflect postmodern culture. Perhaps the most often quoted is *Twin Peaks* which, like David **Lynch**'s films for the cinema, is characterized by disruptions of temporal and spatial relationships and elements of parody and pastiche. *Twin Peaks* is notable for the fact that the entire series centres on a murder which occurred before the action begins. It is spoken about and elements of it are glimpsed in flashback, but the murder itself is never depicted. Lynch chose instead to make a film for cinema which disclosed the events upon which the television series was based, but only after the series had finished its run. It is a matter of controversy as to whether this film had a life of its own, or whether it depended for its sense and coherence upon a knowledge of the television series. Certainly the sense of the television programmes was richest if the constant references to other television styles and series were appreciated. It has even been said that the programmes were as much about television as a medium as they were about the storyline, exemplifying the postmodern emphasis on surface and play.

It would be possible to give many other examples of the extent to which the characteristics of the postmodern can be seen in cinema, television and advertising. The films of Quentin Tarantino, especially *Pulp Fiction*, and television advertisements, such as the Guinness campaigns, all contain the elements which have been discussed so far in this chapter. It is clear that there has been a major shift in the field of representation and in the way that signs and symbols are presented to us. In essence it is no longer possible to be naive in our understanding of culture. It is characterized more often than not by a knowing irony which clearly marks out the difference between the modern and the post-modern.

Conclusion

In summary, this essay has examined two central and related themes. First, the extent to which our activities as consumers define our identities in the contemporary world, and second, the impact of the postmodern upon our day-to-day to lives. In particular the discussion has identified a shift from substance to style and has suggested that the certainties and metanarratives of the modern era are no longer sustainable.

If, as has been said, in the postmodern world the basic dictum is: *I shop therefore I am,* we need to reflect on the question of what happens to those who cannot shop and are therefore excluded from the basis of social identity. This is of particular importance as the old principles of the welfare state are challenged by new values of consumerism. In this new world, pensions, health care, and social support shift from the responsibility of the state to the responsibility of the individual. From a materialist perspective our capacity to consume these services constructs more than identity, it affects the physical basis of day-to-day life.

Critics of the postmodern perspective have pointed out that it can lead to an unprincipled emphasis upon personal and individual gratification at the expense of our responsibilities to others. For some writers this represents the capitalist market economy taken to its logical conclusion. For others, postmodern ideas are democratic, and it is argued that the dissolution of old class barriers and the strongholds of élite culture give all of us greater opportunities for full social participation.

I would like to finish this section with a quotation from the sociologist Zygmunt **Bauman**. In his recent writing he has explored the tension between acknowledging the reality of postmodern change and recognizing that it has led to the exclusion of many from a full and active part in society. This extract is taken from his book *Freedom* which was published in 1988.

> For most members of contemporary society, individual freedom, if it is available, comes in the form of consumer freedom, with all of its agreeable and less palatable attributes. Once consumer freedom has taken care of individual concerns, or social integration and systematic reproduction (and consumer freedom does take care of all three), the coercive pressure of political bureaucracy may be relieved, the past political explosiveness of ideas and cultural practices defused and a plurality of lifestyles, politics, moral or aesthetic views may develop undisturbed. The paradox is of course, that such freedom of expression in no way subjects the system or its political organisation to control by those whose lives it determines. Consumer and expressive freedoms are not interfered with politically, so long as they remain politically ineffective.

POSTMODERNISM AND SCIENCE AND TECHNOLOGY

Iain Hamilton Grant

Of all the worlds in which we might expect to discover signs of **postmodern** life, those of science and technology seem the least probable. Even those feedlines from science into culture that seem the most suited to **postmodernity**'s climate, such as the renowned uncertainties of **quantum** physics, stem not from narratives, but from nature. If postmodernism is simply, as Fredric **Jameson** has it, a cultural affair, then the sciences, reading only the book of nature, are surely unaffected by any postmodern 'loss of reality' – they never lost their way in the dead ends and labyrinths of the library of Babel. With postmodernism insisting, with **Heidegger**, that 'where word breaks off, no thing may be' – that beyond **signs** independent of speakers, beyond **text**, narrative, or discourse, there is nothing – it remains difficult to consider tectonic plate movements and earthquakes as self-contained texts or discourses. So, with postmodern narrative in ruins, still reeling under the gravity of its collapse, could science simply step in to show, with mathematical precision, why stories have never been a substitute for formulae and experiment in matters of reality? Nature, as Francis Bacon put it at the dawn of modern science, does not yield her secrets to the incantations of the poets or the bookish disputations of philosophers; the experimental sciences must *force* them from her. Moreover, with the postmodern 'empire of signs' leaving reality the victim of a crime so perfect, as Jean **Baudrillard** says, that even its corpse has disappeared, science and technology step onto the scene: what if this crime were a side-show, and the real is elsewhere?

With all these grounds for scepticism concerning the very idea of '**postmodern science**', it is surprising to find so much of science currently under the glare of postmodern scrutiny. Three aspects of science have in particular been singled out for postmodern interrogation: first, the study of science as a postmodern phenomenon; second, how postmodernism and science are negotiated within the scientific community; and finally, theories of postmodern science itself. Moreover, as will become increasingly apparent, technology, on which modern science becomes increasingly dependent, is also a crucial factor in this equation. Without compasses, printing presses, microscopes, computers and particle accelerators, whole chapters in the book of nature would remain illegible. Technology not only therefore emerges as what permits the study of nature, the 'racks' upon which Nature is laid to enable her secrets, in Francis Bacon's gruesome phrase, to be forced from her; the changing forms and functions of technology in the postmodern world have become inseparable from even the forms contemporary science takes, prompting some historians to consider technology itself as an evolutionary process, and some scientists to leave natural life behind for the 'sciences of the artificial' – **artificial intelligence** and **artificial life**. With these sciences, we are never far from science fiction, on the one hand, or from postmodern **simulation**, on the other. Given this unexpected convergence between the natural and the human sciences, technology, ironically, emerges as a vital component driving and shaping postmodern culture itself.

First, then, to the study of science as a postmodern phenomenon. Ever since Thomas **Kuhn**'s *The Structure of Scientific Revolutions* (1962), the world of natural science has been opened up to study by the social sciences. Arguing that the history of science shows a discontinuous series of breaks and radical departures (called '**paradigm shifts**' – a phrase that has enjoyed a certain celebrity in postmodern circles), rather than a progressive, linear accumulation of knowledge, Kuhn effectively demystified science as the 'disinterested search for facts', and showed how scientific agendas were set by faculty squabbles, funding pressures and peer groups as much as by theoretical problems and experimental results. Science may or may not be the study of nature, but it was necessarily also a culture to be studied like any other.

Of course, Kuhn's portrait of science-as-culture did not go unchallenged. Outraged scientists and philosophers queued up to knock holes in his theses. Some challenged the culturalist implications of Kuhn's ideas, insisting that since science was practised within a culture, it would be absurd to say that this was all there was to it. Apart from this cultural dimension, there was also the thorny problem of 'nature', to which science had so successfully devoted its productive career. While from the armchair or the questionnaire, science may look Kuhnian, laboratory work offered a very different, hands-on experience. Science could, therefore, be studied as a culture, but science itself studied nature. Out of these disputes in the Anglo-American world, there emerged what became known as science studies. In the UK, for instance, groups devoted to the sociological study of science formed in the universities of Edinburgh and Bath, while in the mid-1970s, the journal *Radical Science* began publication. These groups tended to examine the history and sociology of specific scientific and technological pro-grammes, such as the development of missile-guidance systems or the politics of IQ testing, asking questions concerning the funding, ideology, and politics of scientific knowledge. With scientific knowledge enjoying high status, and science studies being broadly **Marxist** in orientation, emphasis began to be placed on the role played by science in the social construction of broader questions. For example, while it is perhaps difficult to see 'life' as studied by biochemists as having any great social consequences, issues surrounding abortion make permanent appeal to scientific 'facts' about the age at which a foetus may be regarded as independently sentient, effectively defining the field in which these issues are contested and the roles of the contestants within it. Not only does the 'finished' science, science as a body of facts, therefore have enormous social implications, so too does science in action, leading sociologists of science to consider laboratory life as centred around both the practical (Which groups, in what circumstances and by what means, made what 'discovery'?) and ideological (How are class and gender positions implicated in scientific practice? What role does science play in constructing cultures?) construction of fact. If the first response to Kuhn had therefore been to 'naturalize' science, the second concen-trated on science as 'socialized' *power,* and set about exposing its class and gender biases.

Feminist science-studies, indeed, have yielded some of the most pertinent work from the perspective of postmodernism, science and technology. The medicalization of childbirth, for example, provides an early example of the way in which medical science (obstetrics) and hospital technology (bed, stirrups, forceps) position women in child-birth as passive bodies on which medicine acts. Childbirth is therefore no longer exclusively a female act; women require medical intervention to deliver a child, and so must submit to the medical regime as the dominant or active partner in the act of childbirth. Issues such as the gender composition (How many doctors are women?) and distribution (How many nurses are men?) of the medical workforce, begin to abut onto the complicity between medicine's representations of women and social **representations** of women: women are passive, while science and men are active, even in childbirth. The study of these situations is therefore crucial to understanding the relationship between science and the dominant social conceptions of femininity as well as the social roles of women.

Such concerns eventually led to the question 'Whose science, whose knowledge?' being asked. What if science was not simply statistically male (dependent upon the proportions of men to women working in the field), but also *epistemologically* male: does the way in which scientific knowledge is produced reflect, far from universal truths of nature, merely the results of a partial and therefore historically and culturally male experience of it? Francis Bacon's already-cited call to 'place Nature on the rack in order to force her to yield her secrets' clearly distributing gender roles to nature as a passive, scientific object and science as an active, knowing, male **subject**, seems to provide a vindication of this critical strand. Following many studies of science and its impact on the lives and social roles of real women alongside its role in the social construction of femininity, feminist science studies, in the work of Sandra Harding, Ludmilla Jordanova and Donna **Haraway**, began to move to what became recognizably postmodern science studies.

Suddenly, from being a practice and a body of unimpeachable fact inaccessible to study by the social sciences or by cultural criticism, science became first a socialized, ideological phenomenon susceptible to historical and sociological scrutiny, and second, a 'text', composed of representations that, regardless of their factual status, formed one set in a broader network of representations and discourses that themselves construct dominant images and concepts of women, animals and machines. It was insufficient to target local instances of the economic or lived reality of scientific intervention; rather, the discourses and representations produced by science, and even the discourses of science itself that perpetuate its immense power and prestige, must come under scrutiny. If this power was produced in a discourse of which the appeal to 'nature' or 'reality' was a component, critical science studies could not stop at demonstrating that nature is otherwise than science represents it.

The discourses that granted science its power and prestige had also to be challenged at the level of discourse itself. Not only therefore could scientific discourse be **deconstructed** to reveal its internal inconsistencies, other discourses could also be produced in which this challenge could be most powerfully mounted. Just as for early feminist studies in literary representations of women, the twin images of the goddess on a pedestal or the disease-ridden, whorish and inscrutable *femme fatale,* bent on the destruction of men, created the social reality according to which women were classified', so too, for postmodern, feminist science studies, the myth is indissociable from the reality of science. Thus Haraway, in a famous essay entitled 'A Manifesto for **Cyborgs**', concluded that, always the passive objects to active, scientific subjects, animals, machines and women formed an unstable network of unrealized alliances between both human and non-human actors.

Rather than stopping her critical labour at the point of exposing the ideological, fictional and mythic structures inhabiting scientific discourse (although this is precisely what she does in her epic study of the development of primatology in *Primate Visions* (1989)), Haraway accepted that science-as-mythology was a major component of its real situation and that science-fiction formed a core resource for its expansion. Memorably noting, therefore, that 'fact' is simply the past tense of 'fiction', both deriving from the verb 'to make' or 'to fabricate', Haraway puts a slice of **cyberpunk** politics into the cybernetic ideal of biology and technology unified under a single scientific paradigm. Accordingly, from the social and natural phenomena 'subjugated' by scientific mythology, she produces a 'hybrid', cybernetic mythology where 'nature' is a trickster, a wily coyote, and where women and machines fuse, feminizing the cybernetic ideal from within the discourses of science themselves, while simultaneously refusing representations of women that emphasize passivity and make technology a male thing. Thus Haraway concludes the cyborg manifesto with the dazzling line, 'I would rather be a cyborg than a goddess'.

Bizarre mixtures of images and cultural affinities aside, it may seem that the cyborg remains only an image, a cybernetic Minerva sprung fully formed from the head of a dreaming Zeus. Surely inventing such figures cannot of itself have any effects beyond the marginal realm of science-fiction fandom? As a 'non-human actor', however, a cyborg cannot merely be reduced to image; science and technology, indeed, are increasingly augmenting naturally occuring non-humans with artificial tones: nanomachines, robots, clones. While the postmodern reflex may be to ask in turn, 'Ah, but nothing, not even science, can escape this realm of signs. All cultural struggles are fought out there, in a world that is inescapably narrated rather than "natural", and science is a part of culture, after all', Haraway remains wary of claims to 'nature' being reducible to 'narrative', or science to signs. Rather, it is important to Haraway and other, postmodern science students, not to operate such a reduction, but rather to consider 'hybrids' as the points of connection between scientific, cultural and political issues without annexing reality to discourse. The hybrid and the network in which it is a node have become the crucial conceptual means of organizing science studies in postmodernity. Rather than *'either narrative or nature; either real or simulated'*, postmodern science studies such as Haraway, Michel Serres or Bruno Latour are engaged in emphasizing a 'hybrid' and inclusive approach to the network of events, problems, inventions, technologies, fictions, simulations and ideas that most adequately characterize the social role of science. Both the 'naturalizing' trend of early science studies and the 'narrativizing' bent of the more recent, deconstructive approaches present bad images of science. Haraway's cyborg therefore both combines the hybrid 'nature-culture' of the contemporary, scientifically, technologically, and critically sophisticated world, and the rise of 'non-human actors' in the contemporary world.

The concept of the hybrid and the network lend themselves to the postmodern imagination. Without core identities or essences sustaining 'the self', we postmoderns are hybrids of cultural influences, racial and sexual identities, histories, and memories both real (my memories) and artificial (my memories of that movie). Further, **Deleuze** and **Guattari**'s idea of two types of organizational structure, the one vertical, disconnected, top-down and 'arborescent' or 'tree-like', and the other horizontal, multiply connected, bottom-up and '**rhizomatic**', easily blends an apt image of postmodern conceptual relations where connections spread and multiply rather than being constrained by imposed and inflexible hierarchies, with methodologies being adopted in mathematics, physics and artificial intelligence research (in many ways, this coincidence of nature and culture is one of the most fascinating aspects of Deleuze and Guattari's work). Going further still, and prompting the question 'Science fiction or social fact?', networks, according to Jean-François **Lyotard**, have even become one of the most important, even definitive, non-human actors in the production of the postmodern world, even suggesting that the 'post' of 'postmodernism' refers not to coming after **modernism**, but to the 'posts' at which subjects and objects are connected in computerized societies.

While we can now see how easily science studies become susceptible to 'postmodernisation', it remains doubtful how far science itself could be regarded as postmodern. There are, perhaps, two ways of thinking about postmodern science. First, science that displays some of the features commonly associated with postmodernism; and secondly, science that *calls itself* postmodern. Much recent science invites description as 'postmodern' and, in *The Postmodern Condition,* Lyotard even canonizes René **Thom** and Benoit **Mandelbrot** as practitioners of postmodern science. Thom, in particular, seems to be postmodern in his 'hybrid' researches into mathematics, science, anthropology and **semiotics**. We know we are on postmodern tracks when we read that 'scientists are sorcerers'! Mandelbrot's **fractals**, meanwhile, have become an icon of the chaotic processes that seem so aptly to sum up the endless fragmentations of postmodernity, with mathematics now dumping the strategy of approximating the ideal and unchanging forms of a Euclidean world with a geometry of endless change and differ-entiation. If, under Mandelbrot, *geo*-metry goes back to the earth, then it is only to prove that the earth, once thought flat (premodern), then spherical (modern), is now fractal and infinite, and thus demonstrably postmodern. It is not, however, the possibility that this may be 'the truth' that makes it postmodern; rather it is the intensely paradoxical idea of a 'postmodern nature', and even the pursuit of paradox by **catastrophe theory** and fractal geometry that defines its aims as 'postmodern'.

Even among scientists, however, there are advocates of a postmodern turn. Although Lyotard had coined the term in 1979, 'postmodern science' in this more 'hardline' context first appeared in the subtitle of cosmologist Stephen Toulmin's *The Return to Cosmology* (1982). What Toulmin refers to is, however, less recognizably postmodern than the work of Mandelbrot and Thom mentioned above. As we have already seen in our discussion of Haraway, modern science, its practitioners and its philosophers, had drawn a picture of the world dominated by active subjects in pursuit of knowledge of essentially passive objects in that world. Moreover, nature was to be opened violently to the penetrating gaze of the scientist, as can be seen from all the narratives of scientific heroism filling the pages of popular accounts of great scientific 'discoveries'. Modern science, then, 'objectifies' nature, regarding it as something to be turned at will to the purposes of active subjects. With this bipolar split, science posed itself the insoluble problem of bridging the gulf between the subject's alleged knowledge and the actual consti-tution of the object in itself.

While such a characterization may seem excessively abstract and metaphysical, it comes into focus when we consider the debates about objectivity surrounding, for example, debates in primatology. Following Jane Goodall's well-publicized excursions into the field to study the great primates, a scandal broke out when it was revealed that she had solved the problem of making 'first contact' with a group of chimpanzees by laying out food for them. This, detractors argued, contaminated the evidence of her study since she had contaminated the habitat, inter-vened in an unacceptable manner to alter the conditions under which the chimps related to her, thus raising doubts as to the subsequent character of their behaviour.

Others have, of course, confronted this problem. The philosopher Willard van Orman Quine posited the following situation, which he called 'radical translation': suppose you were an anthropologist visiting a hitherto undiscovered culture. You want to understand their language, but since it has never been heard beyond that culture, you have nothing to go on. How do you set about assembling a dictionary? The anthropologist must, Quine responded, assume that the members of the other culture organized their linguistic world no differently, in all essential respects, than we do. As a result of this assumption, which Quine called 'the principle of interpretive charity', objectivity becomes meaningless. The culture under study is less an object than a group of subjects whose actions must be understood through the anthropologist's hands-on intervention. But what grounds do we have, other than sheer pragmatism, for making Quine's so-called 'charitable' assumptions? The anthropologist Claude **Lévi-Strauss**, for example, perpetually asked how, when studying other cultures, it was possible to avoid contaminating the specimen with imported prejudice specific to the culture of the scientist. Even the presence of the scientist significantly and irreversibly alters the situation, introducing **differences** where there were none, forcing the culture to confront, and thus to renegotiate its relations to, a new outsider. Lévi-Strauss's solution was not to try to minimize contact or disguise his presence, nor to assume that the differences were negligible, but to attempt to be absorbed into that other culture, to become, as he expressed it, 'the language spoken by its myths'.

If these scenarios problematize objectivity from an abstract point of view, primatologist Dian Fosse, following in Goodall's steps, brings the problem into a stark, moral focus. Fosse's objectivity was so shrouded in doubt that stories began to circulate about 'unnatural relationships' she may have been having with a gorilla. Things were exacerbated when hunters trapped and beheaded her favourite gorilla, prompting her to track the hunters in turn, only to become their next victim. In such circumstances, the question seems to be less one of how to maintain the proper scientific objectivity and detachment, but how pathological such detachment would be. Postmodern science, according to Toulmin, has learnt this lesson: nature is not an object, something that stands against us that we must subdue in order to know. Instead, postmodern science becomes part of 'man's new dialogue with nature', as complexity theorists Ilya Prigogine and Isabelle Stengers put it. After centuries of subjecting her to torture, the knowing subject decides nature is better conceived as a conversation partner. Like Richard **Rorty**'s ongoing 'North-Atlantic bourgeois conversation', postmodern science has discovered that, even without the purist, modern order of truth and objectivity, 'it's good to talk'.

The hermeneutic overtones in this version of postmodern science mark it out, however, as less postmodern than many a philosopher or **critical theorist** would recognize. Paradoxically, such postmodern science seems merely to have learnt the lessons of Martin **Heidegger**'s hermeneutic critique of the 'essence of modern science', over-polarized between maniacally mathematicizing subjects and indifferent, inactive objects, and insufficiently attentive to the being of nature, to how nature *is*. Modern science, Heidegger argued, has imposed an image upon nature that, rather than revealing or 'dis-covering' it, covered it over again, so that the 'age of the world picture' dominates all the procedures and dis-coveries of modern science. Heidegger, however, while no modernist, is perhaps better characterized as anti- rather than postmodern. And similarly, the 'discursive' turn to include nature as a partner in dialogue parallels Jürgen **Habermas**'s advocacy of the 'unfinished project of modernity' against a postmodernist renunciation of its ideals.

Once again, however, Heidegger's 'world-picture' brings us back to the issue of whether science studies nature or representations, substance or signs. Surprisingly, perhaps, it is along the lines of signs, representations and simulation that much of what is more recognizably postmodern in the sciences is currently leading. The sciences of the artificial have in effect mounted a two-pronged attack on modern science with its predilection for nature over representations, on the one hand, and analysis over synthesis, on the other. On the one hand, artificial intelligence research (AI) has always been less concerned with the programming of the functions of understanding as a key to intelligence than with *simulating* intelligence. Thus the 'Turing test' for machine intelligence, named after its inventor, Alan Turing, placed a person into a divided room and instructed them, by means of a typewriter, to engage the subject on the other side of the wall in conversation. The machine passed its intelligence test if the person was fooled into thinking that the machine was another person. Here the nature or essence of human intelligence is less important than its appearance: seeming or behaving intelligently is sufficient. As Lyotard says of postmodern knowledge in general, the goal is no longer truth but performance: we do not need to know what intelligence really is, just how to simulate it. Of course, AI therefore provokes questions concerning the nature of human intelligence, questions which, ironically, have resulted in machines modelling human intelligence, rather than humans providing the 'programme' for machines' intelligence. Moreover, the manner in which machines 'learn' in contemporary AI research is, in Deleuze and Guattari's terms, more 'rhizomatic' than 'arborescent': learning makes connections between things rather than mining a thing for as much information about it as possible. In AI, this approach is therefore called 'connectionism', and the hardware that learns through such means is called a 'neural net', eradicating the difference between real and artificial neurons. Rather than the image of arborescent 'supercomputers' such as HAL 9000 from the film *2001: A Space Odyssey,* that must be programmed with intelligence before carrying out intelligent functions, neural nets form rhizomatic networks of computers that interact with each other and, through this interaction, resolve random data into emergent patterns (see **Complexity theory** and **Fuzzy logic** in part II), thus actually learning. The 'cybernetic brains' of 1950s science-fiction have become the simulated reality of twentieth-century science.

Perhaps the most obviously postmodern of all the sciences, however, is that of artificial life (AL). Artificial life dispenses with nature altogether, studying instead the actions and simulated evolutions of pixel-creatures in a computer environment. Surely, at last, science is studying signs and representations rather than nature? Once again, however, the difference between the real and the artificial is what is eradicated. Thus, evolutionary biologist and AL researcher Thomas S. Ray twists this paradoxical science still further, stating, at this new discipline's fourth international conference in 1994, that the life processes studied in AL are not themselves artificial but natural; the resultant life-forms merely 'live' in an artificial environment. Thus AL naturalizes the artificial, making **simulacra** of life indistinguishable from their real-life counterparts. In a sense, Ray and other AL researchers are quite right: what current definition of life – self-moving, feeding and excreting, growing and reproducing – can rule these artificial aliens out of the natural world of evolutionary biology, even if the life in question is silicon- rather than carbon-based? And by the same token, who is to say that artificial intelligence will not result in the emergence of a new, synthetic species on the earth? The future historians of such a species may, as Manuel de Landa suggests, look back on the age when machines were assembled by humans as one in which the machines merely lacked their own reproductive organs and had to be aided by humans as pollinators at a certain stage of their evolution. Science fiction is certainly full of such emergent, machinic species – think of Skynet in *Terminator 2,* for instance, or the Terminator itself, 'evolving', through the intervention of scientist-pollinators, from a chip it left behind it in its own past – but bearing in mind Haraway's demonstration of the temporal continuity that turns fiction into fact, this does little to encourage the view that such a species is not just around the corner, or rather, waiting to descend upon us from the near future.

With the sciences of the artificial, we see a crucial link being established between science and technology in postmodernity: AL is unrealizable without the technological environment in which its creatures 'breed'. As in scientific simulation, so in its postmodern version. Jean Baudrillard, for instance, develops his theory of the simulacra on the basis of the functioning of the media; the 'society of the **spectacle**' is inseparable from the technology that underlies it. With simulation not simply a theory, but also a technological reality, things get a little complex, and it becomes impossible, as previously, to oppose the real to the artificial. Cyberpunk author Bruce Sterling points to the realist purchase science-fiction acquires in the science-fictional society in which we now live. When Fredric Jameson therefore omits any discussion of cyberpunk fiction from his mammoth *Postmodernism, or, the Cultural Logic of Late Capitalism* (1991), he not only misses a crucial component of postmodern culture, he also ring-fences that culture from the runaway technological development we have all witnessed in the rise of the computerized society. It is the omission of technology that allows Jameson to construct a portrait of post-modernism that remains exclusively a cultural phenomenon, merely reflecting rather than instigating economic and technological changes in social structures. It is precisely in this technological context, however, that Lyotard's *The Postmodern Condition* (1979) first coined the term 'postmodern science'. In order to see what postmodern science means in this context, we shall have to look at the technological background from which it emerges as a distinctly postmodern practice.

The postmodern condition is one where the credibility of **grand narratives** has collapsed. In their place, there are only distinct 'language games', the rules governing each of which are '**incommensurable**' from all others. Lifted from Thomas Kuhn's description of the 'lack of common measure' between different scientific 'paradigms', the incommensurability thesis means that there is no single set of rules according to which all language games must be played. For Lyotard as for Habermas, language, however, remains the way in which the 'social bond' is formed and perpetuated, so the consequences of incommensurability have enormous social and political consequences, affecting the way in which the various groups of which society is composed bond to form a single society. As Ludwig Wittgenstein has it, 'language games are not simply exchanges of verbal behaviour', they are indissolubly linked to 'forms of life'. Science, therefore, is one language game, one form of life, among others, such as shopping, politics, philosophy or work.

In the late twentieth century, however, science occupies a crucial post in the formation of the postmodern condition. This is less because of the content of scientific ideas than it is due to the increasingly powerful economic situation it enjoys under a capitalism that has become wedded to technological advance. Science can no longer afford to be the disinterested quest for the truth about nature, since its economic survival is bound up with the production of new technologies: science cannot simply desire to know, it must perform. Thus 'techno-science' is the principal vehicle for the evolution of capitalism in postmodern societies. Of course, insofar as capitalism has developed alongside technological change since the beginning of the industrial revolution, there is nothing new in this. The formation of factories and the rise of automation have always had an immediate impact on the working lives of individuals, and on the social structures arising from these changes. What is new in postmodern, capitalist techno-science is first that it is devoted to the maximization of efficiency, just as capital itself is devoted to the maximization of profit at any cost: minimum in (labour costs, machinery, maintenance, administration and regulation), maximum out (productivity, self-regulation, progressive automation and profit). Science therefore survives on the basis of its contribution to this regime: in the postmodern condition, owing to the collapse of grand narratives, science can no longer justify itself or legitimate its practices by appealing to the innate value of 'knowledge in itself', since knowledge in itself is not a saleable commodity. On the contrary, scientific knowledge must be translated into economic success, making techno-science commensurate with capitalism and aiding thereby the reduction of all language games to the single rule of profit.

Again, it might be objected that there is nothing new in this: science has always been subjugated to rule from outside, whether the state banning Galileo's hypotheses, thermodynamics co-opted by industrial capital or nuclear physics by the military. What is new in this situation is the extent to which capitalism has become reciprocally dependent upon techno-science in the form of the computerized society. Monies, capital itself, has become a stream of information, changing the stakes from the maximization of profit to the maximization of *information*. Techno-science is always capitalist owing to its subservience to capital's performativity rule; but capitalism has become techno-scientific in turn, so that capitalist techno-science now drives towards the maximization of private information. Where in modernity knowledge and capital vied for power, now postmodern capitalist techno-science has turned both into information as the measure of power. Hence Lyotard's otherwise bizarre comment, giving the 'solution' to the postmodern condition: 'Give the public free access to the databases' (can you imagine Marx simply advising capital to give the public free access to money?).

Of course, Lyotard's prescription of free access to information plays a language game that runs counter to the capitalist rule. It is for this reason that the game should be played experimentally, rather than in conformity with its rules. Nor should this call for experimentation be taken, as in Jameson, solely in aesthetic or cultural terms. Lyotard is not merely calling for an artistic renaissance along the lines of the early-century avant-gardes, he is also drawing attention to the situation of science under postmodern capitalism. Just as capitalist techno-science aims at maximizing the efficiency or 'performativity' of the game, so postmodern science aims to frustrate this rule, according to Lyotard, for purposes of seeking paradox. Instead of **legitimating** itself by reference to knowledge or progress, science now legitimates itself by vying with the capitalist game in quest not of 'winning', but of frustrating the rules and generating paradox. Thus Mandelbrot's thesis concerning the infinite fractal dimensions of the coastline of Britain, or Thom's thesis concerning the catastrophe that occurs when, at a certain morphological point, a frightened dog both flees from and attacks its assailant, offer to legitimate not the techno-scientific regime, but experiments in science as a language game, as an alternative form of life. Just as **Nietzsche** once claimed, the reign of the search for truth is over; long live the search for the false! It is in this sense that postmodern science is not simply about knowledge of the natural world, nor about the most efficient means to advance the computerization of a global society, but about inventing forms of social, technical, and political experimentation.

We can see then that there are several different approaches to the question of postmodern science, ranging from the mythic challenges of postmodern science studies, to the modernization of the scientific world-picture, to the quest for non-knowledge. Perhaps the single most defining feature of all in postmodern science, ranging across science as a cultural activity, to individual research methodologies in programmes such as the sciences of the artificial, to the new philosophies of postmodern epistemology, to the wild paradoxes associating late-twentieth-century science and 'primitive' magic or declaring the infinite duration of coastlines, is the phenomenon of the network, the rhizome, the neural net. Conjoining philosophy, science, nature, culture, technology, politics, the real, and the artificial in such a manner as to make their separation and purification impossible, perhaps the network, simultaneously conceptual, neural, defensive, capitalist dystopia, anarchist utopia, artificial and *really technological,* is not only characteristic of postmodern science, but of postmodern societies in general. While appearing fragmented, techno-science has ensured that postmodern societies are networked like never before, forming, as Lyotard claims, a 'second cortex' from which a postmodern, cybernetic, techno-scientific Leviathan now emerges, like an artificial owl of Minerva from Zeus's microchipped head.

POSTMODERNISM AND ARCHITECTURE

DIANE MORGAN

While motoring across the Californian desert, a young woman encounters a young male student engaged in the militant activities of May 1968. He is later shot by the police. Thanks to this encounter, her eyes are opened as to the capitalist materialism surrounding her; the prevalence of consumer culture; social inequality and the shady dealings of big business. She arrives at her destination in the middle of the desert, and enters her boss's house – a splendid **modernist** oasis, a cantilevered steel frame with strip windows, which perches on the edge of an arid rocky outcrop. She can now see through its refined design to its impure preconditions: its slick form, cleverly unobtrusive as it parasitically clings to the natural surrounding, sums up the exploitation rife in society at large. She exchanges knowing looks with the Native American servants in the house and appears to sense what natural values might be as she gives herself up to a waterfall in the grounds of the house. For her boss, by contrast, value is not something intrinsic in things or people but rather a product of commercial speculation. He reminds his business contact, hesitant about signing a deal with him for the development of a shoreside site, that 'the price of anything is neither high nor low except in relation to its potential use'. Value is only to be assessed in terms of what can be extracted financially. Water is not to be treasured for its natural properties but for the business opportunities it opens up, in this case, the construction of a marina, pier and airstrip, and perhaps hotel complexes, so as to turn the place into a marketable resort. Having understood the full significance of the house and its residents, the woman imagines it being blown up, being dramatically ripped apart by an explosive rejection. As the highly aesthetic modernist house bursts into flames, it is followed up by further iconoclastic demonstrations: fridges, clothes, all sorts of commodities are blasted into the air. These emblems of a materialistic culture epitomize a society gone astray, an instrumentalized world which 1960s' youth refuses in the name of fundamental rights and natural values.

The film I have just described is Antonioni's *Zabriskie Point* (1969) and it provides a good starting point for a discussion of **postmodern** architecture. In this film, modernist architecture is no longer associated

78

with the innovations of the avant-garde – as it was in the 1920s and 1930s – but with the establishment, the well-heeled, the older generation. Its pure, transparent style, the regime of living it offers to its residents, is equated with the arrogance of wealth and power. The sweeping away of its traces in the film marks the possibility of a radically new departure which is also a return to, or retrieval of, all too neglected values. This reinscription of the past conjoined with an enthusiasm for the variety of the actual world could serve as positive definition of postmodernism as understood by Charles **Jencks**, its most vocal of exponents on things architectural.

Jencks suggests that postmodern architecture at once continues the traditions of modernism and transcends them – his term for this process is '**double coding**'. Anxious to defend postmodernism against allegations that it is just an irresponsible free-for-all, whose lack of political commitment plays straight into the hands of those who want to maintain the status quo at any price, Jencks stakes out nobler aims. Postmodernism, he claims in *What is Post-modernism?* (1986), aims at a realization of 'the great promise of a **plural** culture with its many freedoms'. Whereas modernism was a 'univalent formal system' which suffocated dissenting voices in an attempt to impose general principles of taste, Jencks associates postmodern architecture with eclecticism and openness. For us to understand the stakes of this debate between postmodernist and modernist architecture, it is necessary to trace the latter's passage from the exciting and dynamic world of Bauhaus and Le Corbusier earlier on in the century through to the 1960s and 1970s where what used to be the avant-garde is now perceived as the enemy of change.

One of the most telling images of a modernist architect is given to us by Ayn Rand. In her bestselling novel, *The Fountainhead* (1947), the uncompromising architect, Howard Roark declares: 'I set my own standards. I inherit nothing. *I* stand at the end of no tradition. I may, perhaps, stand at the beginning of one.' Here, modernist architecture is represented by one who is unwilling to adapt his projects to the tastes of his public. Ahead of his time he will not pander to the retrograde mass demands for mock-classical buildings with their tacked-on pilasters, scrolls and leaves. His constructions are absolute in their demand for recognition: harsh, rigid glass skyscrapers and standardized mass housing which does away with individualized nooks and crannies, the idiosyncrasies of clutter, in the name of purity and clarity. Democracy, the negotiation of **differences**, is regarded by him as a levelling of genial creativity.

In *Decorative Art Today* Le Corbusier also announces a rejection of past standards. He kicks away the props and supports of conventional taste, castigating old-fashioned, artisanal values as redundant in the age of the machine aesthetic: 'Hand-made work. The cult of failures. The apologia for daubing. The relaxed hour of the inexact. The triumph of the limp ego. The jubilation of the free will, the respect for the as-for-me. The suppression of control.' Handed down assumptions must be put to the test, not just absorbed unquestioningly. The architect is a virile superman, an affirmative nihilist boldly overturning today's conventional values in an attempt to think and construct the future. In *Towards an Architecture* he explains that 'culture is the final outcome of an effort of selection. Selection means to put to one side, to prune, clean up, to bring out the naked and clear essential.'

This tough selection process, this jettisoning of all that is presumed to be superfluous, weak, and impure in the name of discipline and hygiene, coupled with Le Corbusier's personal admiration for technocrats and strong if not totalitarian states, brings together most of the worrying aspects of modernist architecture. A movement that started off with utopian visions of serving the masses, introducing standardization so as to set higher standards of living for all – not just the already privileged – seems to end up dictating to those same masses.

The same disquieting tendency can be detected with the Bauhaus. As *The Weimar Republic Sourcebook* (1994) makes clear, this school of thought saw in mass mechanical reproduction a solution to social injustice. Cheaply manufactured mass housing, rationalized into compact housing units, would not only reduce the difference between rich and poor by setting minimal standards for all, but would also, for example, emancipate the woman from household slavery by system-atizing the 'best and simplest way' to keep the house in running order. Such Taylorist efficiency would mean that household chores would become so self-evident and easy to accomplish that even husbands and children could contribute to 'making the beds, cleaning the washstand, etc. as necessary'! The final result would mean that the woman would save time and be freed up for other activities, intellectual or leisure pursuits as she wished.

This liberating aspect of Bauhaus' ethos has to be read alongside the other, more sinister, side of systematized rationalization. Consider this extract from Rudolf Arnheim's 'The Bauhaus in Dessau' (*Sourcebook*):

In a room hung with diagonal curtains, in which a sofa sits obliquely to the corner and ten different, fully loaded little tables are set up every which way, there is hardly any reason why a new floor lamp should be placed here rather than there. But the position of everything in a Bauhaus room can be decided with nearly lawlike precision. One will soon learn to understand theoretically that it is not a question here of subjective taste, but that such feelings are a very secure and generally valid psychological phenomenon that leads to very similar results from different people. That is why one can speak even in the case of such problems as those of 'objectively determined solutions'.

Here more manipulative overtones creep in. Instead of standardization promoting individuation, a general programmatization of taste is fantasized. In a Bauhaus flat there would only be one destination for your newly acquired lamp. Your flat would be designed in such a way that that particular item would belong to it *there* as if it were conforming to some ineluctable natural law. Emancipation tips over into dictatorial prescription; egalitarian standardization becomes totalitarian uniformity; the iconoclastic break with the past cashes out as a smashing of people's sense of place and rootedness; a disrespect for the all too human fondness for familiar localities.

For Jencks, the alienation felt by residents forced to fit into idealistic, overzealous modernist building schemes marks the failure of that movement (and the beginning of a more modest, *post*modernist reorientation). He describes how 'utopian' housing schemes gradually fell into disrepair, being progressively vandalized as the inhabitants tried to register their sense of despair at being abandoned to soulless, concrete jungles. In *The Language of Post-Modern Architecture* he writes:

Modern architecture died in St Louis, Missouri on July 15, 1972 at 3.32pm (or thereabouts) when the infamous Pruitt-Igoe scheme, or rather several of its slab blocks, were given the final *coup de grâce* by dynamite . . . Pruitt-Igoe was constructed according to the most progressive ideals of CIAM and it won an award from the American Institute of Architects when it was designed in 1951. It consisted of elegant slab blocks fourteen storeys high with rational 'streets in the air' (which were safe from cars but as it turned out, not safe from crime); 'sun, space and greenery', which Le Corbusier called the 'three essential joys of urbanism' (instead of conventional streets, gardens and semi-private space, which he banished). It had a separation of pedestrian and vehicular traffic, the provision of play space, and local amenities such as laundries, crèches and gossip centres – all rational substitutes for traditional patterns. Moreover, its Purist style, its clean, salubrious hospital metaphor, was meant to instil, by good example, corresponding virtues in the inhabitants.

Modernist architecture is regarded as having brutalized people in its attempt to rationalize, to impose a strict and systematic order on, their ways of living. Unfortunately for the idealist, humans are not entirely rational, ordered or disciplined. Their tastes are variable and mostly non-justifiable, and they are prone to fits of folly. For these reasons postmodern architecture, with its proclivity for crazy pastiche, its wacky blending of styles, its disrespect for monastic regularity and tolerance for historical referentiality is deemed more human than the rigours of modernist purism. As Jencks explains in *What is Post-modernism?* modernist architects were unsympathetic to human foibles: 'Ornament, polychromy, metaphor, humour, symbolism and convention were put on the Index and all forms of decoration and historical reference were declared taboo.'

Postmodern architecture is also more cautious about the uses technology can be put to and more sceptical about the merits of industrialization. Whereas mechanization was jubilantly celebrated by the modernists for its exactitude – see Le Corbusier's tirade against imperfect artisanal goods, cited above – its ability to dispel the stuffy **aura** of the past and to launch a fresh, disenchanted modern world, postmodernists are less optimistic. The world post-Auschwitz, post-Hiroshima, knows too much about the terrors of abstraction and instrumentalization. A dislocated, disembodied relation to the world results in people becoming figures to be 'processed' or materials to be 'recycled'. (Alain Resnais's documentary film, *Night and Fog* (1956), on the Nazi concentration camps, contains some of the most graphic evidence of the results of such abstraction. People are reduced to spare parts – divided up, sorted into piles: hair for stuffing cushions, skin for soap and lampshades.) Science should not be allowed to 'progress' according to its own self-generating laws, without due concern to its long-term impact on the world and its inhabitants. As a consequence, Jencks wants to suggest that postmodernist architecture draws on some of the ethical and ecological lessons the past has inadvertently taught us. As in *Zabriskie Point*, anyone who rejects the arrogant assumptions of the modernist élite, will rediscover the rights of the environment:

> Perhaps in the future with the environmental crises and the increasing globalization of the economy, communications and virtually every specialization, we will be encouraged – even forced – to emphasise the things which interact, the connections between a growing economy, an ideology of constant change and waste. They who don't realize the world is a whole are doomed to pollute it.

82

Reacting against the modernist disdain for personalized space and thereby reconsidering the artisanal respect for the local and the traditional, postmodern architecture reinscribes place while meeting the challenge of present-day globalization. It is this double articulation, the negotiation of place and that which threatens to erode it, the placelessness of global communication networks, which is a central concern for postmodern architects.

As architecture is the most down-to-earth art form, the most fixed in space, it has an intimate relation to questions of **presence**, origin, to rootedness and dwelling. All these concepts have taken a battering from postmodern thought. The virtual world of the **Internet** is one development which poses a serious challenge to architects used to concretizing projects in the here and now. If liberation is now to be equated with exhilarating surfing forays on the net, which seems to promise another, virtual world, not tied down to earthly restrictions or prejudices, how is the architect supposed to carry on constructing the future? As we have seen, in the past the architect felt it was incumbent on him, as heroic demiurge, to take upon his shoulders the burden of responsibility for building the right, improving context for society. In the postmodern world, the restrictions of a particular place appear to have been circumvented. One might not have, or know, any neighbours but instead be in regular, even intimate contact with people all over the globe whom one has never met *as such,* according to traditional notions of encounter.

Faced with such developments there can be no nostalgic return to an antiquated idea of place. Indeed any such hankering after precise geographical fixity and any such celebration of rooted, unproblematic identity is regarded as reactionary by this mobile global culture which espouses decontextualized hybridity, the intersplicing of cultural differences. Architectural theorists have reacted to such challenges to their profession in different ways.

Kenneth **Frampton**, who is no friend of Jencks and his version of postmodernism, nevertheless agrees that the modernist project is at an end and that what comes after is to be radically rethought. In his 'Towards a Critical Regionalism' (H. Foster, ed., *Postmodern Culture* (1982)), he accepts the fact that modernization can no longer be celebrated, as it was by his modernist predecessors, as the key to progress. Such a blind faith in the power of technology, as well as a nostalgic return to a pre-industrial past, cannot be sustained. Frampton at once, recognizes the dangers inherent in an avant-garde movement which has an overbearing sense of its own importance and truth, yet he is not prepared to lapse into apolitical quietism. He is still searching for a critical purchase on society and advocates that this stance is best achieved by an 'arrière-garde', not tempted by the **grand narratives** of modernism, which is still invested in resisting dominant forms of ideology.

Frampton's form of postmodernism focuses on architecture which can mediate between the 'ubiquitous placelessness of our modern environment' and a particular site. Frampton's stance can best be understood by juxtaposing him with what he is reacting against: consider this ecstatic celebration of the American city – that antithesis of the well-integrated environment, that enemy of the urban project – by the guru of postmodern euphoria, **Baudrillard**, in *America* (1988):

> No, architecture should not be humanized. Anti-architecture, the true sort (not the kind you find in Arcosanti, Arizona, which gathers together all the 'soft' technologies in the heart of the desert), the wild inhuman type that is beyond the measure of man was made here – made itself here – in New York, without considerations of setting, well-being, or ideal ecology. It opted for hard technologies, exaggerated all dimensions, gambled on heaven and hell . . . Eco-architecture, eco-society . . . this is the gentle hell of the Roman Empire in decline.

Baudrillard disdains a 'soft' consideration for human scale and local setting. Postmodernism, with its exciting new technologies, is not to be shackled by the dead weight of the human with his pedestrian concerns. Instead he extols the intricacies of the freeways and that antithesis of the European urban experience, Los Angeles:

> No elevator or subway in Los Angeles. No verticality or underground, no intimacy or collectivity, no streets or facades, no centre or monuments: a fantastic space, a spectral and discontinuous succession of all the various functions, of all signs with no hierarchical ordering – an extravaganza of indifference, extravaganza of undifferentiated surfaces – the power of pure, open space, the kind you find in the deserts.

Frampton exactly pitches himself against this uncritical acceptance of the decline of the urban project. He seeks to puncture this rhetoric of simulation and the **hyperreal** with buildings which, interacting with the singularity of their sites, resonate with a certain 'density' of experience. Subverting the otherwise unquestioned superiority of the eye over the remaining senses, Frampton calls on architecture to appeal to the tactile: 'The tactile resilience of the place-form and the capacity of the body to read the environment in terms other than those of sight alone suggest a potential strategy for resisting the domination of universal technology.' Touch, smell, the 'whole range of complementary sensory perceptions which are registered by the labile body' are evoked by Frampton as a way of reinscribing the human into an *experience* of place. Rejecting apocalyptic cries announcing the obsolescence of the body in this '**post-human**' age, Frampton sees his variety of postmodernism as permitting the resurgence of what Jean-François **Lyotard** might call '**little narratives**' or 'local **legitimacies**'.

Another theorist who, like Frampton, takes a stand against the prevailing placelessness of postmodernist architecture, is Fredric **Jameson**. In 'Postmodernism and Consumer Society' (A. Gray, ed., *Studying Culture* (1993)), he too recognizes the ossifying institutionalization of modernism against which postmodernism reacts. He also is trying to reinvent artistic experimentation – a sign of oppositional, critical art which rudely disrupts conventionalized ways of seeing – while not falling into the trap of modernism, which all too quickly became equated with élitism because of its uncompromising difficulty. For Jameson, the summation of postmodern despair, the total abandonment of any attempt to contribute positively to the urban environment, is encapsulated by the Bonaventura Hotel in Los Angeles. This building frustrates the experience of place. Whereas the nineteenth-century city, the home of the nomadic *flâneur,* provided a forum for enriching, if brief, encounters, this hotel preempts exploration. It discourages independent mobility, obliging the unsuspecting visitors passively to give themselves up to its 'transportation machines' which conduct them from one isolated point to another. Instead of the rich 'density of objecthood' sought by Frampton, this hotel thins out space by disallowing any appreciation of volume. No general impression of the building can be snatched, no transitory vantage point can be seized from which to gather some sense of place. However, this is not to say that, by contrast, modernist space provided the visitor with static, solid viewing platforms with nicely set up perspectival privileges from which to dominate the surroundings. Far from it. The modernists delighted in spaces which were dynamic, even vertiginous but which could be *experienced* as such. (Siegfried Giedion's book *Buildings in France: Building in Iron, Building in Ferro-Concrete* (1928) is packed full of exhilarating descriptions of buildings such as the Eiffel Tower and the Transporter Bridge in Marseilles, the precursors of modernist architecture, which orchestrate dizzy and destabilizing – yet enriching – experiences of space.) It is this paucity of experience which is lamented by Jameson. This building with its opaque reflecting surfaces, is seen to be repelling the fractured city outside, refusing any communication with it, and thereby to have self-destructively turned in on itself. It cannot generate any meaning from within itself and the result is a 'milling confusion'.

Jencks begs to differ. He reads postmodernism (in *What is Post-modernism?*) not as a destructive emptying out, or as a sceptical rejection of value, but rather as a paradoxical 'embracing of absolute relativism, or fragmental holism', a challenge to attempts to categorize postmodernism as any one thing. Robert **Venturi**, the other archi-tectural theorist most associated with the fate of postmodernism, also equates it with a medley of different styles and approaches:

> Architects can no longer afford to be intimidated by the puritanically moral language of orthodox Modern architecture. I like elements which are hybrid rather than 'pure', compromising rather than 'clean', distorted rather than 'straightforward', ambiguous rather than 'articulated', perverse as well as impersonal, boring as well as 'interesting'. . . I'm for messy vitality over obvious unity. I include the non sequitur and proclaim the duality (*Contradiction and Complexity in Architecture* (1988)).

Mocking the rigid and minimalist purity of modernist architects such as Mies van der Rohe, who had proclaimed earlier on in the century 'Less is more' – Venturi's response is 'less is a bore' – he celebrates the 'messy vitality' of places like Las Vegas. The casinos, diners, hotels and bars of Las Vegas are often mainly composed of enormous signs designed to catch the eye of touring motorists prowling the strip for somewhere to spend their money. As Venturi remarks in another of his books, *Learning from Las Vegas*, 'The sign is more important than the architecture . . . The sign at the front is a vulgar extravaganza, the building at the back, a modest necessity.' The signs are not just words but pictures, shapes and figures illustrating the enticing nature of the place. Venturi goes on to explain how Las Vegas would be blasphemous for modernist architects who strictly adhere to the biblical injunction against 'graven images' in the name of pure spatial expression:

> During the last 40 years, theorists of Modernist architecture . . . have focussed on space as the essential ingredient that separates architecture from painting, sculpture and literature. Their definitions glory in the uniqueness of the medium; although sculpture and painting may sometimes be allowed spatial characteristics, sculptural or pictorial architecture is unacceptable – because Space is sacred.

The example Venturi uses to illustrate his argument is a most convincing one: Mies van der Rohe's German Pavilion in Barcelona, described by Peter Behrens in *Le Style international* (Peter Joly, 1987) as 'the edifice which will be remembered as the most beautiful of all those constructed in the twentieth century'. Mies's 'universal grammar of steel I-beams' filled in with glass and brick is interrupted, but by no means disrupted, by the inclusion of a single statue, the Kolbe sculpture of a naked woman. As Venturi points out: 'Objects of art were used to reinforce architectural space at the expense of their own content. The Kolbe in the Barcelona Pavilion was a foil to the directed spaces: The Message was mainly architectural.'

Rather like the Bauhaus lamp mentioned above, the Kolbe statue is fitted into an overall design, not for its own sake but as the ornament that is required to adorn the building at that point, in that previously determined and circumscribed place. The statue, far from producing a dissonant note which upsets the harmony of the building actually effaces itself, symbolically communicating nothing boldly. In celebrating the language of **signs**, Venturi is praising the merits of 'an architecture of bold communication' over 'one of subtle expression'. However, the question can be raised: how boldly can one communicate if the vehicle one is using is one that consists of pastiche, play, incongruity, eclecticism and 'disjunctive variety'?

Returning to our initial point of departure: can we be so certain about the statement being made at the end of Antonioni's film, *Zabriskie Point* when the modernist house is blasted away? In the film there is a shift which can be registered between the dynamiting of the house and the ensuing images of exploding consumer items. The house itself is an example of the work of an architect such as Frank Lloyd Wright. He was hardly a purist, producing a textualized form of modernism, which made great use of building materials such as timber and stone. These blended gracefully into the natural surroundings in a eco-friendly sort of way. When the scene changes to the consumer items, the colours become artificially pastel and the music surges underscoring the release of tension as these symbols of materialist culture are jubilantly jettisoned. Whereas the woman appeared hesitant about doing away with the villa, the other objects are relinquished without delay. Is the woman actually rejecting modernism and embracing what comes after – that is, postmodernism? She is presumably putting into practice her newly found radical politics. Can this be equated with the postmodernist theories of Jencks and Venturi who have no scores to settle with capitalism and consumer culture? Indeed, the former goes so far as to declare that today's society showers us with a superabundance of choice; according to him we are overwhelmed with an *'embarras de richesses'* and bathed in an atmosphere of 'widespread pluralism'. He adds: 'With no recognised authority and centre of power many professional groups (and even whole countries) feel victimised by a world culture and market-place that jumps, sporadically, in different directions' (*What is Post-modernism?*).

These 'groups' and 'countries' who anxiously sit at the margins of an unpredictably expanding and contracting postmodern universe – suffering as they do from 'mild paranoia' – just cannot see the pleasures Jencks is trying to point out to them. They see mockery written into Ricardo Bofill's pastiche classical 'Versailles for the masses' and lament the fact that Venturi thinks they 'feel uncomfortable sitting in a square'. Maybe the postmodernist architectural theorists who would have most in common with the woman's reluctant destruction of the utopian modernist project turned élitist, and her unhesitating blasting of the symbols of consumer culture, would be Jameson and Frampton. At least they are still holding on to the notion of postmodern critique which is also a postmodern counter-culture. However, to cite Jameson's concluding words in 'Postmodernism and Consumer Society', this idea might have to remain elusive. It does not give us much solid to build on:

> We have seen that there is a way in which postmodernism replicates or reproduces – reinforces – the logic of consumer capitalism; the more significant question is whether there is also a way in which it resists that logic. But that is a question we must leave open.

POSTMODERNISM
AND ART

COLIN TRODD

Emerging as a critical tool describing certain characteristics of 'new' art in the 1970s and 1980s, **postmodernism** comes in at least six different versions: as that which resists the apparently all-pervasive power of the mass media through the defence of the inescapable uniqueness and critical authority of high art (the historico-mythological paintings of Anselm **Kiefer**); as that which, actively embracing popular culture, sets out to escape from the élitism of high culture by engaging with the techniques and technologies of the media (the collaged imagery of David Salle); as that which seeks to embody the desires and aspirations of those social and cultural groups that high culture has marginalized or ignored (the theoretical work of the feminist artist Mary Kelly); as that set of parodic or **ironic** practices which dig deep into the nature of contemporary experience in order to indicate that reality has been assimilated into the endless **simulatory** processes of the communication industries (the '**neo-geo**' paintings of Peter **Halley**); as that critical practice that wants to define consumption as the endlessly empty but structuring process in our social landscape (the photo-montage images of Barbara Kruger); and finally, as that form of 'demotic' representational art that is resolutely anti-**modernist** in its interests and values (the 'modern mainstream' photo-based figuration of **Gilbert and George**).

These multiple postmodernisms have enabled artists to attack the allegedly mandarin nature of **modernism**, reorient artistic practice, enlarge the productive range of art and develop an inclusive approach to the use of culture and its objects. Consequently, many artists and critics have seen in this diversification evidence of new cultural energies. But is it possible, one might ask, to see in these 'energies' some attempt to grapple with the social landscape of postmodernity? If so does artistic postmodernism comment upon the new economies of labour, leisure, and consumption? Does it have anything to say about a social realm characterized in terms of the deregulation of financial markets and the consequent mobility of capital, the inexorable growth of privatization, the internationalization of the division of labour, the introduction of 'flexible' manufacturing systems, the development of specialized product cultures and the ubiquity of 'customized' advertising campaigns? If it is possible to refer to different models of postmodernism, is it possible to make the distinction between a postmodernism which seeks to resist **postmodernity** and a postmodernism which embraces it? Is it possible, one might go on to ask, to distinguish between an oppositional postmodernism and an eclectic postmodernism? And, if we can make such a division, does it enable us to refer to 'good' and 'bad' forms of this art?

We begin to address such matters by returning to the way in which modernism was discussed in the late 1970s and 1980s. The criticisms of modernism, although taking many forms, centred on the belief that it was repressive, clinical and self-possessed. Thus, in opposition to the self-cancelling nature of a modernism condemned by its own conceits, postmodernism, through its redeployment of allegory, parody and narrative quotation, could be associated with the revivification of art itself. Including **installation art**, photography, painting and sculpture, postmodernism has been examined by such critics as Charles **Jencks**, Hal Foster, Rosalind Krauss, Douglas Crimp, Craig Owens, Benjamin Buchloh and Achille Bonito Oliva, all of whom were well versed in the writings of **Derrida**, **Foucault** and **Baudrillard**.

Is the division between a 'monolithic', 'universal', or 'closed' modernism and a 'diverse', 'pluralistic' and 'open' postmodernism, a division that is so apparent in Jencks's popular account of this new art, entirely accurate? This question is important because the critical power and value of postmodernism is entangled with its critique of modernism. We can get some purchase on this subject by examining in closer detail the nature of this reading of the development of modern art.

The dominant model for the explanation of modernist art has alleged that this is an art 'about' art. In the case of painting this meant the progressive uncovering of the formal essence of the medium. When the early modernist critic Clive Bell, writing in 1914, declared that all great painting registered significant form, he meant that such works possessed their own values and had to be judged by aesthetic criteria. This reading of modernism claims that, in the case of painting, the history of modern art is the history of self-purification by the eradication of all 'external' influences until we are confronted with absolute form in the pristine and spartan clarity of post-painterly abstraction.

This position, first articulated in explicitly philosophical terms by the American critic Clement Greenberg, became classic modernist dogma in the 1960s. For Greenberg, writing in *Modernist Painting* (1961), modernism, in establishing its autonomy of expression, generates the conditions for the emergence of a pure art that pursues its own unique agenda. In painting this meant that 'authentic' work would be made by drawing upon its own specific material nature. Thus Greenberg predicted that the modernist painter would devote more and more time to the nature of his medium: to the flatness of his canvas, to the physical reality of the picture-plane, to the luminosity or the opacity of his colour, to the shape of his support, to the presence of the frame. Organizing itself as an inward-looking practice, this form of modernism was to develop through the rigorous elimination of all decorative and ornamental elements. This celebration of the ineluctable uniqueness of modernism – its capacity to establish artistic value without making any critical engagement with social and political matters – became the dominant method of appreciating contemporary art practice; and in many ways Greenberg, who was the first critic to recognize the significance of Jackson Pollock's work, became the most important figure associated with this modernist model after the implosion of abstract expressionism in the late 1950s. It is notable that 'classic' American modernist artists of this period, such as Jules Olitski, Donald Judd, Robert Morris, Frank Stella and Dan Flavin, deployed versions of this Greenbergian rhetoric to justify the nature of their artistic experimentation.

Greenberg's success in offering a theory for the development of modern art as a process of internal development should not blind us from the realization that modernism has a far more complex history than this model allows. Indeed, it should come as no surprise that Greenberg's model of modernism found no place for Dada, surrealism and constructivism, all of which sought to connect art and politics in order to generate visions of social and cultural emancipation. In all three cases modernism involved disputing and contesting the shape and nature of modern society: criticizing the nihilism of capitalism; questioning the social management of ordinary experience; generating utopian visions in which art is integrated with the social fabric of modern life.

By assimilating all forms of modernist art into the Greenbergian model of modernism, postmodernist artists and critics contested the established cultural orthodoxy by developing three different strategies in the late 1970s and 1980s. Through these 'engagements' it became possible to claim that postmodernism was iconoclastic and radical. These attacks comprised: the presentation of a variety of text-based practices as radical examinations of the institutional machinery of the art world; the definition of the artist as the conduit for the dissemination of an impure but healing art; and the identification of **appropriation art** as a way of trumping the idea of the unity and uniqueness of the art object.

What were the motivations behind these three moves? First, the site-specific works of the Belgian artist Marcel Broodthaers and the German artist Hans Haacke are supposed to reveal the framing devices used by museums and art galleries. Second, the new figuration of the German painter Anselm Kiefer, in its identification of the picture-plane as a violent space where the **signs** of history are compressed and contorted, is taken to question modernism's residual commitment to the idea of beauty as truth. Third, in its most vivid form, that of the New York neo-geo or **simulationist** artist Peter Halley, the appropriation of modernist 'icons', such as Piet Mondrian and Barnett Newman, is seen as a way of tackling the relationship between modernism and the social, cultural and economic institutions of the modern capitalist state.

As these three moves are interrelated – the first deals with the idea of the governmental agencies of art, the second is concerned with the communicative and expressive qualities of painting, and the third addresses the flow of power within a 'globalized' economy – this essay will be organized around three different case-studies drawn from each of these practices.

The first of our case-studies involves the subject of installation art, which in the work of Broodthaers and Haacke questions the belief in the purity and self-defining nature of the modernist art object. Broodthaers' work, which developed a new intensity after the radical events of 1968, attempts to circumvent the intellectual division of labour that sustains and reinforces the authority of art galleries. Identifying himself with an imaginary museum – the Musée d'Art Moderne – he wrote accounts of his art from the position of the curatorial and cultural establishment. By conflating the realms of creativity and criticism he could make art 'speak' against the institutional languages that framed it. In this sense his denial of the division of labour established by the museum also challenged the articulation of cultural authority in cognate institutions.

In the work of Haacke it is not only the art object but the system that frames, manages and organizes the social networks of culture that is of importance. Thus he sets out to interrogate the institutions of modern art. By producing works that focus on the relationship between the art gallery and the corporations which sponsor them, he wants to examine the way in which business legitimizes itself through cultural patronage. He asks: what purpose does art serve in modern society and what interests are masked by corporate patronage? Two examples of this process are germane to this case-study. In 1971 the Guggenheim Museum cancelled Haacke's exhibition because the artist declined an offer to remove a couple of controversial pieces that dealt with the practices of some of its trustees. Entitled *Real Time Social Systems,* these works comprised diagrams, maps and photographs which constituted a visual 'plan' of the interplay between economic power and cultural identity. The 'plan' detailed the methods by which slum landlords transformed themselves into respectable figures by buying into the realm of culture. Examining the flow of capital from 'private' to 'public' spaces, the work addressed the relationship between the accumulation of different forms of authority and prestige.

Three years later Haacke was invited to exhibit at the Wallraf-Richartz Museum in Cologne. Once again, in drawing attention to the management of culture within capitalist society, his work met with suppression by the cultural managers of this institution. On this occasion Haacke's installation art involved the production of a detailed history of Manet's 'Bunch of Asparagus', which the museum had recently acquired from a local industrialist. This history took the form of inverting the relationship between the object and its elucidation: the 'art' comprised a series of wall panels, each one of which traced the history of the ownership of the Manet. These biographical vignettes concluded with an account of Hermann J. Abs, trustee of the museum and former owner of the Manet. Because his final wall panel drew attention to Abs's relationship with the industrial and economic policies of the Third Reich, the museum required Haacke to remove his installation.

Acting as the mediator between installation art and our second case-study, the so-called postmodernist **trans-avant-garde**, we find the anarcho-spiritual performance art of Joseph **Beuys**. For Beuys's art, as the embodiment of pure consciousness, is the dynamic force that will regenerate the social and material realm. This Beuysian pursuit of the mystic union of self and world is a noticeable feature of the work of his most celebrated student, Anselm Kiefer. Kiefer, echoing Beuys, is always in the process of declaring the redemptive quality of his art. Where Beuys's oracular rhetoric conflates the mystical version of Dada and the theatrical nature of performance art, Kiefer's art returns to German romanticism in order to confront its disturbing legacy. Like his teacher, Kiefer identifies the power of art as a form of magical fertility; the surfaces of his paintings are mobile forests of marks, wounds and growths. These skeins of paint – drifting, dripping and forming nomadic traces across the canvas – are forever entangled with new surfaces, new spaces and new morphologies. Evidently Kiefer identifies the authority of painting with its capacity to translate narrative into the transfiguring intensity of his materials. In such a scenario painting becomes a form of incantation and enchantment: it will raise the darkness of Teutonic mythology in order to face its primitivism and irrationality. This turning away from the 'universalism' of high-modernism is characteristic of the other main figures associated with this mode of postmodernism. The belief that the return to painting involves the return to the mythologies of national culture can be seen in the work of Kiefer's compatriots Markus Lupertz and Georg Baselitz, both of whom invoke Germanic culture in their work. Although less impressed by Beuys's sibylline utterances on the nature of art, they, like Kiefer, transform his 'post-modernism of immediacy' from the theatrical forms of 'body art' into a violent expressionistic style that hovers between 'myth' and biography.

The idea that the mystical totality of art forms a separate magical kingdom is also expressed by the Italian wing of this *trans-avant-garde* where Francesco Clemente and Sandro Chia led the return to the conventional media of oil painting and fresco. For the Italian critic Achille Bonito Oliva, the leading champion of this style, by rejecting the uniformity of modernism, these 'nomads' produce an art of 'desire' which battles against the repressive forces of 'the Law'. This re-introduction of 'painting into art', a reintroduction which includes descriptive and decorative elements, enables Oliva to claim that these artists are at once radical *and* traditional. According to Oliva, such work 'intentionally lacks character, does not hold heroic attitudes and does not recall exemplary situations'. Thus, it is the humbleness of this 'weak' work that establishes its 'healing' powers.

The idea that the artist acts as a spiritual or cultural healer, or that the resulting work is original because of its manipulation of mythological and classical sources, is firmly rejected by the figures associated with appropriation art, the third of our case-studies.

Instead of relying on practices that are supposed to merge the artist with the artwork, a marked characteristic of the romanticized mythology of the *trans-avant-garde,* Sherrie Levine, Cindy **Sherman**, Peter Halley, Haim Steinbach, and Jeff **Koons**, all of whom came to prominence in the late 1970s and early 1980s, produce work that resists the idea of individual **authority** and artistic creativity.

Levine and Sherman emerged in 1977 when their simulatory art was identified as a breakthrough in the formation of postmodernist aesthetics. Douglas Crimp, the recently appointed managing editor of *October,* the most important journal concerned with reframing art theory through the use of **poststructuralist** ideas, contrived a show entitled 'Pictures', which was held at the alternative gallery Artists Space in Lower Manhattan. This event was to be seminal because Crimp's catalogue essay, republished in expanded form in *October* in 1980, argued that the figures he had picked for this event subscribed to the notion that our experience of reality is organized and determined by the images we make of it. The importance of his exhibitors lay in their capacity to understand that the real is composed of the pictures we elaborate and assimilate in and through our dealings with the institutions of contemporary society. He asserted: 'to an ever greater extent our experience is governed by pictures, pictures in newspapers and magazines, on television and in the cinema. Next to these pictures, firsthand experience begins to retreat, to seem more and more trivial.' Thus the paradoxical power of work by Levine and Sherman was revealed in its capacity to assert that it *lacked* all authority: it registered that photography was always a *re*presentation. Furthermore, their self-conscious photography, which resisted the idea that **representation** could announce originality, was postmodernist because it confirmed the mythological status of 'authorship'.

Sherman's 'Untitled Film Still No. 21' is a classic example of her early technique. The female figure (it is Sherman herself), photographed in black and white, seems to have been taken from a film. The image, then, is made 'filmic' because Sherman seems to embody a moment in a sequence: she appears to be anxious; she is caught from an odd, almost elliptical, angle; there is something 'brooding' about this urban topography which bears down on the female subject. The image is neither portrait nor documentary narrative: it performs no 'ceremonial' function; it fails to delineate a story or depict a real situation. The image demonstrates something about how we perceive the social environments in which we move; and when we realize that it was part of an extensive sequence of images in which Sherman is shown in different scenarios, it becomes apparent that we are being asked to consider how female identity is established in our culture.

This denial of the referential nature of the photographic image is continued by Sherrie Levine. In her appropriation of canonical images by Edward Weston and Walker Evans, we see the same conflation of the idea of simulation and gender politics. It is certainly the case that these images declare that art is a representation of itself; that the burden of all art is its inescapable attachment to tradition; that it is somehow radical to criticize those conventions that claim to represent external reality. Here photography does not provide a window looking out into the world: it is a mirroring process that reflects its own conventionalized and normalized techniques for recording and framing the world. This interest in the 'fictive' quality of originality was continued in her 1984 show at the Nature Morte Gallery in New York, which comprised copies of drawings by Schiele and Malevich, the 'expressionistic' and 'classic' wings of early modernism.

Fascination with the nature of representation is also a marked feature of Peter Halley's work. Deploying cells and conduits within a grid-like geometric field, his art is informed by his reading of Foucault and Baudrillard. For Levine and Sherman, working through the photographic medium, representation never refers back to some pristine state of being in nature; compositions are imprisoned by the tradition which shapes, patterns and frames them; images are entangled within visual systems from which it is impossible to escape; photographic works are copies of copies. To this interest in representation-as-repetition, Halley, the main painter and theorist in this group, brings his concern with the relationship between representation and power. Looking at modernism is to see models, networks, movements, and flows of matter and energy. Thus Stella's aluminium 'grid' paintings of the late 1950s, generally regarded as the zenith of late modernism, are made to reveal the massive interstate highways which traverse America.

Halley concentrates on the idea of geometry in order to ask why modern society associates it with freedom, light, reason and truth. In 'Notes on Painting' (*Collected Essays* (1987)) abstraction is identified as a form of confinement: non-representational art, hollowed out of its utopian rhetoric, is assimilated into the visual languages of multinational corporations. The modernist artefact has become part of the logic of late monopoly capitalism: in its geometrical and grid-like forms Halley discovers social, governmental and financial networks. Modernism's search for absolute visual purity is no longer 'innocent': instead of its association with idealist aesthetics, Halley locates it in the imprisoning spaces of consumer capitalism. Thus he claims that his paintings 'are a critique of idealist modernism. In the "colour field" is placed the jail. The misty space of Rothko is walled up.'

Far from being a process of social enlightenment, geometry is, in fact, an instrument of social control. Therefore he links the geometric sign to what he sees as the dominant image of surveillance: the grid. He writes: 'On the grid, there are no monuments. Only the grid itself is a monument to its own endless circulatory nature . . . On the grid there is only the presentness of unending movement, the abstract flow of goods, capital and information.' Public space has been hollowed out and private space has collapsed into a zone of endless, empty consumption. It is in this context that we should approach a painting such as 'Day Glow Prison' (1982). Deliberately disorienting, it seems to combine elements of kitsch and abstraction, that is junk-culture and high modernism. On the one hand there is the garish, electric light colour, on the other the rigour of geometric modernism.

This is a weird mutation: it is as if the colour scheme of suburbia has entered the 'pure' space of modern art. By appropriating the day-glow colour scheme of Stella's work from the early 1960s, he affirms that such apparently pure art is an echo of the social furniture of modern life. By including Roll-a-tex, a mock-stucco, to 'adorn' the square figure that commands the image, colour becomes coloration: it is that which is produced and reproduced by instruments and that which registers the nature of its own reproduction. Colour does not 'refer' to nature but to Roll-a-tex. If the structure of the image, collapsing form and content, deals with the imprisonment of experience in the techniques of 'advertising', it eschews the hedonistic qualities of pop, which, in many ways, embraced the consumer culture that Halley criticizes. In opposition to say, Warhol, who endlessly repeats the look of consumer images, Halley engages with the multiple styles of modernism in order to criticize it. If, like Warhol, he replaces the cult of originality with the practice of repetition, he does so in order to confront the reproductive technologies which inform the social and political systems of **post-industrial** society.

The presentation of postmodern art as something which emerges from the networks of leisure and consumption in contemporary society is continued in the work of Haim Steinbach and Jeff Koons. If Halley sees the geometric sign as the essence of modernity, both these artists are fascinated with the world of shopping; and it is the objects of consumption that they replicate. In the case of Steinbach, shopping becomes a form of urban tourism in which commodities act as souvenirs: by buying something an attempt is made to hang on to the experience which compelled the purchase in the first place.

This simulated art takes as its reference point that most contemporary of environments: the shopping mall. A parade of parody and pastiche, in which historical and cultural styles are knitted together in 'unique' configurations, the shopping mall is the fabricated space of pure fantasy. Reproducing shopping as a leisure 'experience' through the articulation of 'themed' spaces, the shopping mall blends the 'ordinary' and the 'exotic', transforming consumption into something 'exciting'. Here shopping becomes the fantasy of escape, the fantasy of holiday. Shopping, we might say, contains and recreates the world: shopping is tourism.

Steinbach, who in a 1986 panel discussion which included Halley and Koons, opined 'in a sense the media have been turning us into tourists and voyeurs outside our own experience . . . in my case I spend a lot of time shopping', creates objects and microenvironments. Or more accurately, he manages products. Placed on Formica shelves resembling plinths, these products are the very commodities we purchase in shopping malls.

The products produced by Steinbach play games with the way in which we use, collect and value ordinary commodities. His achievement is to connect two realities – the shopping mall and the home – and to express the way in which the experience of both is built around a comforting, homely, tranquillizing banality. If in such a world the objects of consumption, the commodities we buy, have become the modern equivalent of primitive totems, this may be because in our world shopping has become a kind a religion, a dream of purity. At the same time there is an inescapable emptiness here, a great void which cannot be redemptive precisely because consumerism is based on the idea of endless consumption. **Desire** is aroused but never satisfied and the commodity generates a sense of loneliness which must be overcome by yet more consumption.

In Britain a self-consciously whimsical or quirky attitude to appropriation is found in the work of Tony Cragg, Bill Woodrow and Edward Allington, all of whom make reference to forms of mass-production, although the allusions to the world of commerce and kitsch tend to be 'poetical' rather than 'political'. Elsewhere the camp, sentimental militarism of Gilbert and George assimilates the iconic powers of medieval art and Soviet socialist realism, generating tableaux which are obsessed with masculinity, fecundity and death. Does this appropriated iconography, which reduces the world to a series of pictograms or iso-types, confirm that we dealing with banal art or art about banality? Appropriation of a different kind is found in the work of the young 'Brit-pack' artist, Damien **Hirst**. From his dead cows and sheep, which allude to such sources as Rembrandt's 'The Flayed Ox', to his recent 'dot' paintings, which allude to Peter Taaffe's simulation of Op Art during the 'golden-age' of New York simulationism in the 1980s, Hirst's work has acknowledged the endless entangling of 'high' and 'low' subjects in the iconography of European art.

At the beginning of this essay it was asked whether there is anything of value to be gained by coupling artistic postmodernism with social postmodernity. Well, if there are no simple alignments between the processes of cultural heterogeneity and social fragmentation – alignments that enable us to distinguish between 'good' and 'bad' art – we can at least conclude our investigation by confirming that some forms of contemporary practice establish more interesting and more critical dialogues with modernism and the social landscape of late monopoly capitalism than others. In the case of the American sculptor Richard Serra we find works that confront those public spaces that 'shopping mall' postmodernism declares to have vanished into the simulated spaces of replication and miniaturization. The sheer physicality of Serra's sculptures, which tend to inhabit the open-air urban environment, encourage spectators to reflect upon the nature of the lived experience of built space. That the nature of this art could be something other than an emphatic embrace of postmodernist consumer culture can be seen in the controversy surrounding his 'Tilted Arc', a work that was destroyed after its removal from New York's Federal Plaza in 1989.

In its combination of brute matter and indomitable form the 'Tilted Arc' resisted the idea that public art should decorate, adorn or aestheticize public space. There was nothing about the 'Tilted Arc' to suggest it supported the rhetoric of 'urban renewal'; nothing that resembled the bovine pastoralism of much contemporary public art. The object was in no sense charming or pleasing. Indeed, its capacity to block any real sense of spatial orientation was an insistence that people should be obliged to address its bulky ugliness. To be sure, the work denied people the opportunity to scan or survey the immediate environment. To this should be added the ghostly nature of the thing: here the matter of industrial engineering returns to a deindustrialized governmental, financial and consumer sector of the city, bringing with it the buried history of industry. This registration of the uncanny was compounded by the dimensions of a work that suggested both vertigo and claustrophobia: this was an object whose presence was both ubiquitous and elusive; at once inviting the individual to 'merge' with its form and resisting the idea of absorption.

It was the unhomely nature of the object – its ability to resist urban assimilation by its insistence on the inescapable strangeness of urban space – that brought this postmodernist work back to one of the central themes of literary and philosophical modernity: that consciousness is marked by its sense of transcendental homelessness. In the writings of Schlegel, Baudelaire, Kierkegaard, **Benjamin**, Kafka, **Adorno** and **Heidegger** we find the idea that being is a form of alienation; that life is a form of exile or the registration of an inescapable and catastrophic loss. It is, then, the simultaneous strength and weakness of art that it is generated from this experience of estrangement from the world; and it is through this paradoxical nature, combining both utopian hope for a better world at the same time that it confirms its melancholy separation from this immediate world, that, no matter what appellation is used to describe them, there is always a positive dimension to the most intractable or commanding works of art. In an age where museums and art galleries begin to resemble shopping malls by processing and marketing consumption and leisure as 'experiences', perhaps it is those forms of art that reach for the utopian through the melancholic that deserve our greatest attention. Is it possible, therefore, to draw some form of ironic comfort from the fact that the new 'deindustrialized' postmodern classes, with their bases in the media, advertising, financial services, marketing, merchandising, leisure and retailing were the very groups whose campaign resulted in the destruction of the 'Tilted Arc'? If so, we are obliged to resist the apocalyptic or iconoclastic rhetoric of those forms of postmodernism that tell us we are condemned to a simulated world, and insist that the most controversial forms of contemporary art continue to engage with the most compelling themes of modernism itself.

POSTMODERNISM AND
THE CINEMA

VAL HILL AND PETER EVERY

Postmodern cinema ironically has a history now. In 1984, Fredric Jameson observed that contemporary culture seemed to be expressing a new form of 'depthlessness' – a concentration on style and 'surface'. For Jameson these features represented a retreat from the need to supply a univocal narrative closure to the postmodern text, predicated on the fragmentation of mass culture, the end of a rigidly fixed signifying system, a loosening of **binary differences** and the emergence of the individual consumer in relation to the reconfiguration of multinational capital.

In the wake of this change, postmodern film criticism has celebrated the vivid intensity of the surface and the multivocal readings 'against the grain' that it allows. Recently, however, some critics (such as Steven Connor and Linda Nicholson) have begun to question if this surface, and its intertextual pleasures, is all there is to the postmodern cinematic text. They are asking again what (under)pins the text and if the position of the reader is as 'free' as has been claimed by the theorists of relativism. Implicit in these questions is an examination of the contradictions brought about by absolute **pluralism** – an exploration of the limits imposed by an absence of values.

In this essay, we wish to emphasize that the *thematic* concerns produced within postmodern cinema reveal a very particular set of values. We argue that the scenarios found in many postmodern films express a number of repetitions, particularly around the issues of gender, sexuality and ethnicity, that make the notion of free-floating signification problematic. We wish to question why, in the light of a reflexive critical sophistication towards the strictures of the **text**, do audience, director, and critic continue to collude, most often pleasurably, in the maintenance of narrative structures which repetitively replay the gains and losses of 'difference', albeit in new and mutated forms.

MODERNISM, POSTMODERNISM AND FILM CRITICISM

Film theory within the discursive space of critical **modernism** strove to reveal the work of the text – especially its attempt to position the spectator, to keep the world firmly within the parameters of capitalism and patriarchy and heterosexuality. For directors such as Godard, and critics such as Comoli and Narboni, the fantasy was to make a film that clearly spoke to and for the proletariat, the colonized and women in a way that did not partake of the bourgeois realist narrative structures characteristic of Hollywood. This desire to contest the text, to make the right film, to suggest that we are positioned in a way that is both collusive and exclusive, yielded up a rich vein of theoretical work. Laura Mulvey, for example, concentrates her earlier work on the cinematic narratives of Hollywood movies of the 1940s and 1950s – a period when American culture was very visibly engaged in negotiating and controlling the 'monsters' produced by the Second World War. The most obvious 'monster', within popular cinema, was the femme fatale of *film noir* who, for the transgression of stepping 'out of her place', became a woman punished and domesticated by death or marriage, mutating from Joan Crawford to Marilyn Monroe in a relatively short period as the female form was pulled back into the service of reproductive patriarchal relations. Mulvey rightly sees the 1940s and 1950s as paradigmatic of what Hollywood movies are and do.

At the same time, the political and cultural events of May 1968 produced in their wake the disillusion of the organized left, the defeat of the trade union movement and the inexorable marginalization of the working class in terms of a mass politics. These events, however, also allowed for the emergence of single-issue politics and a sensitivity, at least in theory, towards the particular circumstances of individual identity.

In the 1970s, the Vietnam War became a sort of stand-in signifier for discussions of all colonial struggles. In the fallout ensuing from America's defeat, mainstream cinema audiences began to experience 'difficult' films such as *Taxi Driver* and *Apocalypse Now*. The conspiracy films which proliferated in the early 1970s such as *All the President's Men, The Conversation* and *The Parallax View* attempted to negotiate the contradictions and paranoias produced by a radical loss of political and national certainty: 'You mean there's a CIA inside the CIA?' Each attempt, however, to uncover 'the truth' or to recover some form of normality by exorcizing the demons of a compromised state took the cinema, audience and all, further from 'safe ground' – until the phrase 'there's no place like home', spoken once with such reassuring naivety in *The Wizard of Oz*, began to signify the uncanny rather than apple pie.

The critique of dominant modes of **representation**, combined with the normalization of 'the shock of the new', became a sort of Trojan horse that opened the door of the city to the theoretical and practical work that has had the 'p' word applied to it. The work of modern theory requires a critical distance – a position from which it can 'speak' in order to judge and value the text. In its critical reflexivity – a mode already latent in critically modernist theory – postmodernism weakens the authority of theory in that it is revealed as *a* position rather than *the* position. The loosening of this critical distance has generated a large volume of work around 'reading the text differently'.

However, in the sleep of reason marked by the eschewal of textual authority, postmodernism still produces monsters. How does this happen? In the following section, we will argue that postmodernism 'knows' the histories outlined above, knows the codes of representation that have become our pleasure, even if it is a pleasure that knows how compromised it is. Hollywood cinema has never been without contradiction, but postmodern cinema plays this contradiction within a frame that works to allow its pleasures, to make visible the contradiction, but still, somehow, manages to 'tidy it up' and put the world back in place.

THE NATURE OF POSTMODERN CINEMA

The endlessly circulating commodity of postmodern cinema contains signifying systems that carry with them both the values of capitalism and the contradictory **signs** of the struggle produced within it. This means that the stories of postmodern cinema are particular stories that work through very particular themes. Now obviously this can be said of any period of history or culture, which is precisely why it must be said about postmodern cinema. The postmodern cinematic market-place is dominated by American products. This domination has consequences both for the form of the American film, and for other national, local and independent cinemas which tend to be absorbed, ignored or marginalized. At the same time, the American film is required to reduce its own cultural specificity in order to satisfy the demand to be 'global'. So, while the forms, codes, conventions and narrative structure of postmodern cinema possess a strong resemblance to that of the mass-produced cinema of **modernity**, the need for globalization produces both an intensification of its formal specificities and an allowed and necessary address to difference. We are doubly stressing 'difference' here, to refer both to the organization of sexual and ethnic difference within the structure of the text and to the visibility of those representations of difference within the play of the text. Difference is allowed, celebrated and commodified. The cultural politics of difference becomes the cultural commodity of difference. Postmodern cinema celebrates, at surface level, its own exchange and use value. We are told how it was made, how much it cost and what it is about. This is especially true for what, in a sense, is a paradigmatic instance of postmodern cinema, the action film.

In the action film the history and conventions of many Hollywood genres (the western, the thriller, the horror film, the war film, the romance and the family drama) are distilled and intensified to produce a commodity that contains all of the pleasure, all of the pain, and works in as many markets as possible – while never quite eschewing American values. We would argue that these 'intensifications' produce the sort of observations made by Jameson and **Baudrillard** in terms of the intensity of the surface of the postmodern film. They also produce the critical emphasis on the reflexive nature of the postmodern text. The film and its audience, one could say, 'know their own histories'. The pleasure of the texts consciously spills over into an audience's knowledge of other films, other performances, other musics. One only has to think of the success of *Reservoir Dogs* and *Pulp Fiction* to see the power of these commodities to reference not only social life but, more importantly, all other forms of popular culture. The referent becomes part of the treasure house of signifiers that constitute popular culture. Some theorists, like Baudrillard, extend this line of argument to conclude that the social world 'outside' of popular cultural terms has 'gone away', cinema can now *only* refer to other signifiers of popular culture.

Postmodern theory speaks of the end of history, the loss of the referent, the impossibility of critical distance and the celebration of 'new-found' difference. However, if you add the first three of these to the last one, then you are forced to ask: 'What is difference?' Without history, without reference to the social, without some sense of distance (what one might call an ethics or politics) the notion of difference, itself, is placed under question. It is this tension between the desire to celebrate difference within the commodity form and, at the same time, the need to construct a commodity world without history or social referent, that lets loose the kinds of difference that emerge in postmodern cinema.

THE INTENSIFICATION OF DIFFERENCE

The weakening of the **grand narratives (Lyotard)** releases difference from the tidy shackles of modernism – this does not, however, just mean that previously subjugated others are released into a different, more intense visibility (and one thinks, here, of the continued marginalization of 'third' cinema from Latin America) but also that the 'old' binaries themselves mutate towards a more exaggerated, almost parodic, existence or are displaced through the production of new forms of **otherness**. Gender attributes wander across the old binary divide; Linda Hamilton, in *Terminator 2,* can have muscles and we can all derive voyeuristic pleasure from Brad Pitt's butt in *Thelma and Louise.* Difference itself becomes a crucial organizer and signifier within the texts of postmodern cinema. In a sense, the transmutation and seeming erosion of 'modern' difference allows the *absolute* of difference to emerge, uncannily, in the gap – a gap within which, if we are 'allowed' the pleasure of Linda Hamilton's muscles or Brad Pitt's butt, we can also begin to sense the enormous cost of these signifiers.

The strong version of masculinity, as played out by Schwarzenegger and Stallone in the action movie, embodies a desire for a fixed relation to the symbolic, the world where the law still operates, made less possible by the weakening of the grand narratives that also kept difference in place. Indeed. *First Blood* (1982) could be argued as a film in which the weight of historical trauma is borne by the body of Stallone, a new and shocking male body soon to be commodified and multiplied in the forms of Schwarzenegger, Van Damme and others. The desire to win a war that had already been lost signified in so many of the Vietnam films can itself be seen as a form of nostalgia for a present that never was. What is important for this essay is the observation that, although these bodies are on one level superhuman, too much, hysterical, they are also suffering, immolated bodies – almost to the point of death. We have become used to suffering male bodies in film genres dependent on male–male relationships, but in the post-Rambo action movies, the 'buddy' is absent and it is not homosexuality that is defended against, but *psychosis.*

This brings us back to Fredric Jameson. In 'Postmodernism, or, the Cultural Logic of Late Capitalism' Jameson uses Lacan's definition of schizophrenia – a form of psychosis – as a metaphor to carry his description of the fragmentation of **subjectivity** and the emergence of an 'eternal present' at 'the end of history', which he sees at work in the postmodern condition. It is significant, for this essay, that Jameson does two other things. He dismisses the paternal signifier (the guarantee of the law) from his use of the metaphor of schizophrenia, as does postmodernism when it gives up on the **Enlightenment project**. He also, in two places in his essay, invokes the image of Marilyn Monroe, once as 'Marilyn Herself', almost as something, someone, that stays in place when all else is fragmented and lost. For Jameson the slide of the signifier is halted by the image of a woman and the difference she represents. In a sense, Jameson performs the same sleight of hand as postmodern cinema, denying a fixing point that should not be there but is.

THE PRODUCTION OF OTHER OTHERS

The contradictions within postmodern cinema's celebration of difference can be seen in the way that a transmuted otherness emerges within particular narratives. In *Predator 2* (1990) Danny Glover moves from the place of 'black sidekick who usually dies first' to that of black hero who survives. At the same time as Glover's textual liberation from stereotype, however, the predator is constructed as an other that carries signifiers of blackness – its 'hair' resembling dreadlocks, its figure that of a hunter or warrior. Similarly, Sigourney Weaver in *Aliens* (1986) plays the good mother to the alien bad mother – both protecting their children. The latter, however, the hyperbolic feminine, is represented as dripping and oozing and carrying signifiers representing the *vagina indentata*. The film almost gives itself away when the child 'mothered' by Ripley is given the name 'Newt' – a touch of the alien.

Blade Runner (1982) presents the transmutation of difference and otherness in a more complex way, setting humans against **cyborgs**. One can read the film as one in which the cyborg other reproduces humanity at the point at which the human race has 'lost it'. However, the emergence of the cyborg, the unhuman, can be read differently. Cinema and other popular cultural forms of the 1980s and 1990s contain either the fantasy of 'leaving the meat' (body) or the possibility of a transformation of the body into something more, something different (*Lawnmower Man*, *Nightbreed*, *Cocoon*). The disappearance of the human race is on the agenda in the 1990s – and maybe we should argue that this is nothing more than a coding of the imagined disappearance of white dominance. The union of Rachel and Deckard at the end of *Blade Runner*, however, speaks of an escape from the misery of the human condition, into a fantasy rural idyll. The twist in the tale – the possibility that the new Adam and Eve are both cyborg, and the certainty that at least one is (something not seen before as anything other than a threat), reveals, perhaps, the depths of contemporary anxiety about the future.

DEATH AND THE MAIDEN: THE BODY IN THE TEXT

The female corpse is a very insistent signifier in postmodern cinema. In the failure of the text satisfactorily to 'put things back together' in the face of the commodification of difference she/it becomes the currency through which to repay an impossible debt. For example, in *Basic Instinct* (1992) we are 'allowed' to see a strong beautiful woman, Sharon Stone, maybe get away with murder. She is bisexual; getting both the men and the women that she wants. However, in order for her to achieve her end, Michael Douglas and the ice-pick under the bed, the text produces corpses – most notably those of her girlfriend Roxy, a strongly, if conventionally represented, lipstick lesbian with a taste for voyeurism and a female psychiatrist previously 'contaminated' by Stone's seduction. (This also shows that the 'free-play' of difference is not that free!)

Silence of the Lambs (1991) reproduces the same pattern. The wonderful Jodie Foster, lesbian icon, wins out, but at the same time the text produces a trail of flayed female corpses. Other films and cultural texts may be called into evidence at this point: *River's Edge* (1987) – the female corpse as a *thing* to be poked with a stick; *Manhunter* (1986) – 'something about the woman'; *Blue Velvet (1986)* – the abjected, less than perfect body of Isabella Rossellini; *Rising Sun* (1993) – the digitally encoded and replayed sexual murder of an unnamed woman; *Twin Peaks* and *Murder One* – the twin female corpses wrapped in plastic.

The intensity of the gaze at the female corpse could be seen as another aspect of the intensification, and loss of distance, in the postmodern text. It is almost like pornography – what is it we are looking at and why? In the films outlined above, a woman's corpse sutures the narrative producing a double emptying of the female body, a double death; the weight of sexual difference is removed from the body, it becomes a thing, both a blockage and a suture – it makes sense of the narrative, compensates for a femininity 'out of place', while making no sense itself. It emerges in the real outside of signification.

AND DEATH SHALL HAVE NO DOMINION

At this point, it might also be useful to replay another postmodern characteristic differently. The notion of the 'eternal present' has been seen as concomitant with the end of history. However, what one observes when one confronts, particularly, 'early' postmodern films is that the present, the contemporary, has become a difficult category, a category in crisis. Some of the most popular films of the early 1980s – *Terminator, Blade Runner, Alien* – involve dystopic representation of a near future, while others attempt a flight into the past of cinema itself (*Purple Rose of Cairo, Barton Fink*).

By the mid to late 1980s another, more utopian, tendency could be observed within mainstream cinema represented initially through the Oedipal revisionism of *Back to the Future* (1985) and *Peggy Sue got Married* (1986) in which the world and the American dream are put firmly back into place. The tenderness of the incestuous 'time-loop paradox' represented by the love scene in *Terminator* (1984) is replaced by the horror on the face of Michael J. Fox when his mother makes a pass at him. It is as if the narrative resolution becomes dependent on the abolition of the limit of time. This abolition also involves a negotiation with death.

Two of the most popular movies of the early 1990s, *Field of Dreams* (1989) and *Ghost* (1990) are examples of a whole cluster of films in which death itself is overcome. *Ghost*, which operates around a dead man, is interesting in that it combines another favourite concern of the 1980s – Wall Street – with the idea of life after death. Justice is only achieved through divine intervention and the spectral colonization of the body of a black woman by a dead white man.

Field of Dreams is a Reaganite fantasy where the *unheimlich* becomes *heimlich* (literally German for unhomely and homely – two words used by **Freud** in his essay 'The Uncanny', to give a sense of something we thought was safe, homely, turning into something terrifying that we do not recognize, something uncanny). In a devastating series of loops predicated on the near death of a small girl, the film allows a man to 'have it all': the house, the wife, the child, the dead father and the entrance fee of twenty dollars. Costner's dream is resecured in the present, but only by bypassing the limit term of death. It is also important that the central character is a man, a father, a son and a husband – patriarchy is secured and the dead father placated.

However, in postmodernist cinema, death is not an equalizer and its limit-line becomes an organizer of gender. *Thelma and Louise* (1991) suffer a very different fate to that of Kevin Costner's character in *Field of Dreams*. What Thelma and Louise try to avoid is 'Texas', a place in this film where women get raped; rape here being constructed as the high point of heterosexual difference. In attempting to 'go around' Texas they are caught by the law – in the end, to borrow a phrase from the first series of *Star Trek*, 'they attempt to boldly go where no man has gone before', beyond patriarchy, signification and difference, but they can't. The image freezes, time goes into reverse. We celebrate their past, not their broken bodies, in a frozen, almost **sublime** moment at the edge of the collapse of difference.

CONCLUSION

We would like to suggest that there has been a shift in the formal and aesthetic structuring within the films that may be called postmodern. This shift may be marked historically, but as with modernism and postmodernism, there is no pure break. Films such as *Blade Runner*, *Terminator*, *Alien* and *Brazil* show an anxiety concerning both the present and the future constructed out of the visual detritus of the past and the signifiers of historical trauma. For example, the scenes of the future catastrophe in *Terminator* could be argued to be drawing their signification from the Holocaust, Hiroshima or Cambodia after Pol Pot's Year Zero.

However, in more recent films the real relations of capital become occluded, fetishized, from the total space of the film – only to return in/on the body of an appropriate other, be it woman, alien or black. *Reservoir Dogs* (1992) and *Forrest Gump* (1994) are films that strongly represent this tendency. *Reservoir Dogs* is a film in which all others (almost) are held at the level of speech. The 'Dogs' worry around the signifiers of woman, black people, Jews and homosexuals. However, we would like to suggest that there is a resonance here between the hystericized bodies of men already commented on and the hystericized speech of men in this film. This speech is predicated on anxiety. So although we are presented with what is almost a cloning of a certain kind of white heterosexual masculinity as a defence against the postmodern condition, and the fetishistic pleasures of the visual and aural surfaces of the film as it attempts to defend against any suggestion of crisis, the particularities of the speech of the 'Dogs' says something else: 'What do women want? Are they virgins or whores? Do they earn to much of too little? In the case of black women, are they strong or subservient to their men?' The sexuality of black men and women carries with it the intensity we have spoken of earlier in this essay; but it is the sexuality of black men that is the real problem for the 'Dogs', especially when combined with the 'threat' of homosexuality. The difficulty of a film full of men – a subject already well documented in modernist film theory – is displaced and projected into the discourses of homophobia and racism. What it finally produces is their deaths; the real conditions of existence return revealing a white heterosexual masculinity in crisis.

Forrest Gump, on the other hand, rather than holding anxiety at the level of speech gives two accounts of the period of US history from Vietnam until the present day, accounts which are gendered, and where the benefits and costs are placed on opposite sides of the gender divide.

Once again, the trauma is absorbed by the body of the woman from her abused childhood to her death from AIDS. Gump goes from success to success, never stopping, never understanding. In the film *Forrest Gump*, as Slavoj Zizek has said, 'ideology lays its cards on the table, reveals the secret of its functioning, and still continues to function'. Gump, like the 'Dogs', is a perfect representation of 'subjectless subjectivity', 'the absolute proletarian' (Zizek after **Marx**). He understands nothing, does everything he is told and becomes a hero and a billionaire. (In fact, the 'stupid' man as hero has become a new Hollywood sub-genre: *Dumb and Dumber*, *Beavis and Butthead*, the characters played by Jim Carrey, *The Hudsucker Proxy*, *King Ralph* and Homer Simpson.) This is very different from the work of sexual difference in Ridley Scott's *Alien* (1979) – a film we would see as representative of early postmodern cinema. In *Alien*, we can witness the beginnings of the trauma concerning the emergence of strong women – but we also see capital, in the form of the Company, represented very negatively. The alien itself could be read as the embodiment of the desire of the Company, not a representation of the 'absolute proletarian', but rather of the absolute of capital itself. Conversely, in *Reservoir Dogs* and *Forrest Gump* there is an attempt to protect masculinity from the demands of the new postmodern market-place where the play of difference is permitted so long as it is commodifiable.

So, we are suggesting that later postmodern cinema attempts to deal with the conditions of late capitalism but gets caught in the meshes of the logic of difference. It might be useful here to look at *Barton Fink* (1991), a Coen Brothers film which, like *Gump* and *Dogs,* demonstrates the formal and aesthetic signifiers of a thoroughly postmodern text (it is one of Jameson's nostalgia movies). However, unlike the former films, it can be read *thematically* and *politically* as an allegory of the postmodern condition. Set in 'the golden age of Hollywood' (on the verge of the USA's entry into the Second World War), the film shows the pathetic impossibility of Barton Fink's position as a left-wing Jewish writer 'bought' by, appropriately, Capital Pictures, and set to work producing hack scripts about 'big men in tights'. He finds that he can no longer write. All he can do is look at the pin-up someone has left on the sweating wall of his hotel bedroom. His neighbour, Charlie Meadows, who sweats as much as the hotel walls, is a travelling insurance salesman who 'eases the pain' of his clients/victims by shooting and decapitating them. Fink sleeps with the abused partner of his former idol, a drunken writer reminiscent of William Faulkner. Not only is she the true creator of the writer's scripts (again a woman structures the narrative!), but she is also the serial killer's next victim while she and Fink sleep after sex (a woman's corpse sutures the narrative). After her death Fink is able to reproduce his own stories about working-class fishmongers. In this, he neither satisfies the demands of Hollywood nor hears the other tales of the human condition continually offered to him by the one representative of the working class in the film – the killer. The final sequence tells the story in terms of a destroyed masculinity, a destroyed left politics and a femininity split into its extreme corporeal components. Fink sits on a beach, his ideal woman, the pin-up from his hotel bedroom, appears 'in the flesh' (indeed the whole *mise-en-scène* is that of the pin-up photograph). Next to him is a box that we all know contains the head of the woman murdered in his bed. His destruction produces a thoroughly imaginary fetish, and a little piece of the real, at the point of the greatest military conflict the world has ever seen. The dream and the horror are brought together on this beach, with Fink unable to grasp either of them fully.

The discourse of the Enlightenment can be accused of hiding its history of slavery and oppression – part of the very conditions that made it possible. Postmodernism raises those conditions to the level of the signifier, making them part of the pleasure of the text, whether we are talking about the space of drugs, crime and deprivation inhabited, at the level of signification, by most of black Hollywood at the moment, or the female corpses that litter the postmodern movie scene. As audiences we view, and yet do not see, that the blood, torture, death and horror that visually enframes the postmodern narrative, that provides the very meat of its drama, are psychic compensations for the vivid yet blank perfection of its commodity form.

POSTMODERNISM AND
TELEVISION

MARC O'DAY

Television is arguably the **postmodern** medium *par excellence*. Whether we are discussing postmodernism, postmodernization, **postmodernity** or just the postmodern in general, television offers us compelling examples of the ideas and trends invoked by these terms. Many of the buzz-words of postmodern debate – **simulation, hyper-reality**, fragmentation, heterogeneity, decentring, **intertextuality**, pastiche and so on – are ready-made for application to TV. Indeed, several of them were stimulated by facets of TV in the first place. The rapid evolution of television into a diverse, multinational, well-nigh global industry exemplifies the socio-economic processes of postmodern-ization, while the fractured, conflicting ideologies of programmes on burgeoning numbers of TV channels fluidly incarnate the experience of postmodernity. Particular channels or programmes, from MTV, *Miami Vice* and *Moonlighting* to *Twin Peaks*, *Ren and Stimpy* and *Fantasy Football League*, provide us with some of the best formal examples of postmodernism in any medium. At the same time, not all television is postmodern and postmodern perspectives provide only one set of approaches, albeit compelling ones, to TV.

The following sections aim to sketch in some of the key features of TV considered as a postmodern phenomenon.

HYPERREALITY AND CONSUMERISM

The postmodern theorist Jean **Baudrillard**, in his book *Simulations* (trans. 1983), uses the terms 'simulation' and 'hyperreality' to describe the 'mediatization' of reality in contemporary society. Given his tendency towards abstract and totalizing theory, he rarely mentions television by name but his speculations make most sense in the context of watching TV. He argues that with the massive increase in **signs** and images circulating in postwar media society, the distinction between objects and their **representations** has disappeared. We are, he alleges, now living in a world of 'simulation', where media-generated images function independently of any reality external to them. Signs and meanings float in a self-referential 'hyperreality' – an excessive reality and also one which is literally 'hyped' by advertisers and others.

Baudrillard overstates his case, yet there are indeed numerous examples where the reality of television problematizes or even replaces everyday reality. For instance, while many studies have shown that people are perfectly capable of distinguishing between soap-opera reality and real life, this doesn't stop a few of them from abusing the real-life actor or actress who plays the role of a currently unpopular character (at the time of writing, Helen Grace, who plays the incestuous Georgia Simpson in *Brookside*, has been having a bad time of it). Much of the promotion of soaps, of course, actively encourages such a (largely enjoyable) confusion. Another example: how do we know that the events ritually narrated on the news actually happened? Baudrillard once provocatively argued that the Gulf War did not take place except as a simulation. More generally, television may have contributed to a mutation in everyday perception, insofar as our view of the world is increasingly mediated by the vast mental image-bank we each store in our minds. Thus, when I go to Paris or New York, I have already visited them in representation – probably in *Holiday* or *Wish You Were Here?* – and may be disappointed if they don't live up to those idealized TV images. (No, I'm kidding. Of course I know the difference . . .) As John Fiske argues in his essay 'Postmodernism and Television' (1991):

> In one hour's television viewing, one of us is likely to experience more images than a member of a non-industrial society would in a lifetime. The quantitative difference is so great as to become categorical [...] We live in a postmodern period when there is no difference between the image and other orders of experience.

Closely allied to the postmodern claim that 'TV is the world' is another, advanced by Fredric **Jameson**, that postmodernism is nothing less than 'the cultural logic of late capitalism'. For Jameson television functions as the social glue in an increasingly subcultural and privatized postmodern consumer culture. The post-war growth of consumer society, first in the United States and then in Europe and elsewhere, was fuelled by the simultaneous expansion of the media, especially television, which promoted the desirability of commodities and reproduced a consumerist ideology. Writing from a neo-**Marxist** position Jameson, in his book *Postmodernism* (1991), sees the aesthetic forms and techniques of the avant-garde and **modernism** being placed at the service of consumerism in postmodern aesthetics. Thus the emphasis on style, novelty and innovation which motivated the avant-garde is co-opted into the packaging and marketing of everyday commodities, while the history of art becomes a vast cultural repertoire to be raided by advertisers looking for a new 'take' on a product. The promotion of 'lifestyle' options in advertising where the imaginary, symbolic and associational qualities of homes, furniture, fixtures and fittings, cars, clothes, cosmetics or food and drink is more important than their physical uses has become, for Jameson, the real business of television and other media.

Again the case is overgeneralized – and again there is an unwillingness to discuss television overtly in any detail – but there is no doubt that from this rather reductive perspective commercial TV is, and always has been, ruled by the economic necessity to sell audiences to advertisers. We are all, in a sense, working for capital when we watch television. Some people joke that advertisements are the 'real' programmes – and often the best. For this line of thought, Levis 501 ads are the sexiest and most entertaining TV around. And maybe they ought to be, since more money is spent on advertising than on any other kind of programming except rare prestige drama. Programme segment lengths (and hence, up to a point, formats) and the overall schedule are, within regulatory limits, largely determined by advertisers' needs. Remember those plans to divide football matches into four quarters for the 1994 World Cup Finals, held in the United States? Mercifully they were refused. Increasingly, programmes are brand-named by sponsorship. Recent British examples include Beamish/*Inspector Morse* and Cadbury/*Coronation Street*. Product placement in drama and the blurring of the distinction between advertising and other forms of programming illustrate the commercial imperative which underpins television in a postmodern consumer culture. As competition hardens, TV channels also spend much more time promoting themselves at programme junction points. There's nothing absolutely new in these trends, though they continue to intensify. What is new, however, is the way that they operate within the heterogeneous environment of the postmodernized TV industry, whose audiences understand and enjoy the intertextuality, recycling and self-conscious play which permeates postmodern TV.

POSTMODERNIZATION, INDUSTRY AND AUDIENCE

In the 1960s, Marshall **McLuhan** characterized post-war media society as an 'electronic global village'. Changes in the structure of the television industry over the last 20 years or so, along with the arrival of other information technologies, have confirmed the relevance of this ever-so-slightly-glib label (village?). Ien Ang, in the introduction to her book, *Living Room Wars: Rethinking Media Audiences for a Postmodern World* (1996), remarks on these changes: 'Television itself has undergone massive postmodernization – manifested in a complex range of developments such as **pluralization**, diversification, commercialization, commodification, internationalization, decentralization – throwing established paradigms of how it operates in culture and society into disarray.' It may not be strictly necessary to describe these changes as 'postmodernization'; nevertheless, they are arguably homologous with changes in other spheres of the postmodern.

Since the early 1980s, there has been a diversification and a fragmentation in the technologies by which television is transmitted. Broadcast television has been supplemented and challenged by the arrival of satellite, cable and (more recently) digital and interactive TV. The diffusion of these technologies has been encouraged by 'deregulation', which has seen market forces become increasingly prevalent. In the United States, for instance, the network TV system dominated by the giants ABC, CBS and NBC has been transformed by large numbers of more specialized and local channels. In Europe, the traditional public-service broadcasting systems have, to an extent, been undermined by competition from commercial subscription satellite and cable channels. At the same time, the extended reach of these technologies has opened up large areas of the world to penetration by international and multinational media conglomerates. Postmodernization aspires to a genuinely global reach (and, alongside this, somewhat paradoxically, an increased local reach). Together, these changes have led to a volatile, competitive market which typifies the postmodern processes of so-called 'disorganized capitalism'. In fact, it is anything but disorganized; it is, however, relatively fluid, flexible and fast-changing.

What are the implications of this for the television audience? In the postmodern era producers, while they remain obsessed with success and delivering the desired audience to sponsors and advertisers, recognize the need to build 'coalition audiences' from diverse constituencies, which may differ by gender, class, race, region or lifestyle and may be mobilized to watch a programme for a variety of reasons. Niche marketing is increasingly the name of the game as audiences become more fragmented and heterogeneous. In the case of pay-per-view TV, for instance, used in particular for boxing and other sporting events, an audience will be built on a one-off basis. Researchers, for their part, have tended to move away from the traditional audience models employed within the sociology of mass communications. The effects model conceptualized the audience as passive, and has come to be seen as an offshoot of earlier, modernist ambitions to deploy television as an instrument of social management. The uses and gratifications model, although it posited an active individual viewer, was also instrumental in its understanding of the TV–viewer relation, and lacked any real social context which could account for ways in which TV is embedded in the culture of everyday life. In place of these models, the trend since the 1970s has been towards ethnographic and other studies of variable audiences engaged in watching television in various contradictory ways, making active choices concerning what they watch and when, in particular viewing contexts. Here the emphasis is on the diversity and situatedness of viewing practices, very much in line with the postmodern turn towards **difference** and micropolitics of all kinds.

The shorthand term for this trend, 'the active audience', may seem to empower the audience too much. The best research in this area, however, by David Morley, Ien Ang, Henry Jenkins and Maria Gillespie among others, is well aware of the dangers inherent in constructing a transgressive, pleasure-seeking viewer completely free to 'graze' the galaxy of sumptuous signifiers which is postmodern television. Choices, providing we can pay, may appear to be unlimited but they are still the choices that the fashion system of postmodern consumer culture makes available to us. In this sense, it might be argued that not watching TV, not consuming the media, is the more genuinely transgressive act.

Since hardly anyone, however, doesn't watch at least *some* television, we can ask what the postmodern viewer is up to today. It is easy, of course, to produce an identikit postmodern hedonist: the archetypal decentred subject with a maximum attention span of three minutes. Living in a world of schizophrenically fragmented instants, she cruises the surfeit of channels available to her, **zapping** her remote control and hopping between channels and programmes unconnected by time, space or genre. She is unconcerned with narrative, coherence or rational understanding; rather, she constructs a largely random bricolage out of bits and pieces of television, which she connects with only in a bored and distracted fashion. She is the viewer, figured in a cryptic and almost science-fictional way, by Baudrillard in his essay 'The Ecstasy of Communication' (trans. 1983), who is merely an extension of small-screen technology: 'With the television image – the television being the ultimate and perfect object for this new era – our own body and the whole surrounding universe become a control screen.'

Over against this in many ways nonsensical model, we can posit an alternative postmodern viewer (though no less an identikit, if truth be told). He is aware of the choices that the new TV technologies offer, and how much they cost. He knows what kind of programmes he likes, and why. He is happy watching television in different environments (home, bar, shopping mall) with various social groups (alone, partner, children, whole family, best friend, group of friends, strangers) and with varying degrees of attention (from 'literary mode' – serious, attentive, diligent, analytic, watching from beginning to end in the right order – through to 'video mode' – playful or distracted, hopping, pausing, replaying, sampling, indulging, ignoring). He integrates television into his everyday life, taking full advantage of the postmodernization of TV while being able to switch deftly between postmodern and other modes of viewing.

One more point about both these viewers. Though still in front of iconic small screens, a lot of the time they aren't watching broadcast or narrowcast TV at all. Still using the TV set, in conjunction with the VCR they may be time-shifting, watching material recorded off-air or prerecorded material not available on television; or they may be playing video games. Equally, they may be using their personal computers to surf the **Internet** and 'talk' to their friends (who they may never have met).

POSTMODERN PROGRAMMES

This essay may seem to have delayed an approach to actual pro- grammes. I hope the reason why is clear: we cannot think about the formal features of postmodern programmes apart from the contexts in which they are produced and viewed or the wider relationship between postmodern television and society. TV, as a cultural technology and as an apparatus, involves complex interrelationships between producers, advertisers, **texts** and audiences. Its postmodern dimensions emerge most fully within these interrelationships and in thinking more broadly about TV as a social and cultural phenomenon.

It is also the case that, within the specificities of TV as a medium combining image and sound and transmitted 24 hours a day, many of the postmodern formal features of particular channels or programmes closely resemble those in other arts and media: thus postmodern TV is characterized by a high degree of excess, fragmentation, heterogeneity, hybridization, aestheticization, stylization, **intertextuality**, recycling, bricolage, self-referentiality, and parody and pastiche. Postmodern programmes are often ontologically unstable, playfully foregrounding production contexts and environments (never doing this in the sober and revelatory fashion of the modernist text), shifting between realistic and fantasy worlds without comment, blurring the boundaries between fact and fiction or past, present and future, and casually using computer graphics and special effects to warp or wipe out televisual worlds. It is television which in many respects assumes a sophisticated and playful audience with a highly developed TV literacy; an audience, in short, who have been watching lots of television all their lives, and for whom TV is culture which is (second-)nature.

The initial 1980s accounts of postmodern TV were dominated by 'M' channels and programmes: MTV, *Miami Vice*, *Moonlighting* and *Max Headroom*. E. Ann Kaplan, in her book *Rocking Around the Clock: Music Television, Postmodernism, and Consumer Culture* (1987), argues that MTV, the generic Music Television channel, is paradigmatically postmodern in its function, structure and (partly) content. Functionally, MTV's inception in 1981 was emblematic of the emergence of specialist, genre-based cable (and later satellite) television in phase with the prerogatives of postmodern consumer culture. It was, and remains, devoted to selling popular music. Pop videos were shot initially as promotional visual material for the songs they accompanied; very quickly, however, they became commodities in their own right, an alternative or complementary format in which to consume one's favourite performers. Structurally, MTV also typified the increasing fragmentation and specialization of postmodern TV: in its purest form (it has since diversified somewhat) it showed pop videos non-stop. Theoretically, viewers could spend their whole lives watching it. In terms of content, Kaplan argued that while the overall form of MTV was postmodern, there were five principal types of video featured: romantic, socially conscious, nihilist, classical and postmodernist. The actual categories, which were much disputed even at the time, matter less than the recognition that the majority of individual videos were not, for Kaplan, postmodern in form.

Various postmodern features were also noted in other programmes of the mid 1980s. Lawrence Grossberg, in his gloomily titled 'The Indifference of Television' (1987), berated the American cop show *Miami Vice* for its stylization and empty intertextuality: '*Miami Vice* ... is all on the surface. And the surface is nothing but a collection of quotations from our own collective historical debris, a mobile game of Trivia ... The narrative is less important than the images.' The pop video aspects of *Miami Vice*, which always featured rock music soundtracks, have since passed into the mainstream, not least in the pneumatic erotics of the massively popular *Baywatch*. The playful, pastich-ey ambience of the comedy crime series *Moonlighting*, which paired Cybill Shepherd and Bruce Willis as private detectives engaging in war-of-the-sexes screwball banter as they lightheartedly pursued capering criminals, was also much discussed by TV critics. More generally, in programmes which are not formally postmodern, hybridization between 'masculine' and 'feminine' genres has been a feature of TV series from *Cagney and Lacey* through to *The Bill*. Lastly from this period, the British *Max Headroom*, a computer-generated DJ and talking head based on the actor Max Frewer, exemplified both the foregrounding of electronic production processes and the blurring of the gap between the human and the technological in postmodern subjectivity. He *was* Baudrillardian (and extremely irritating with it).

In the 1990s, the intertextuality, recycling and self-referentiality of postmodern form have also passed into the TV mainstream. At a fundamental level, the expanding number of TV channels has created an ever-increasing demand for programming of all kinds. One effect of this is that much more of television's past is on TV *now*, albeit often watched by relatively small audiences. This in turn has partly underpinned the self-referentiality of much television made today. It is only exaggerating slightly to claim that the entire popular cultural archive of the last forty years and beyond is now available to raid and recycle. Many comedy, drama, music, chat, news and current affairs shows, for instance, literally or parodically reuse past television within their formats. In terms of comedy, for instance, think of Victoria Wood, *The Comic Strip Presents*, *French and Saunders*, *The Day Today*, *Knowing Me, Knowing You with Alan Partridge*, and *The Mrs Merton Show* to name but a few.

Three more brief examples are worth mentioning. First, no discussion of postmodern television can ignore *Twin Peaks* (UK broadcast 1991–92). Within its finite serial format, *Twin Peaks* typified postmodern genre-mixing, moving between the classic detective investigation, melodrama and science-fiction/horror with wild changes of tone and register, serious at one moment, comic or bathetic the next, then bizarre and hallucinatory, and so on. It was hard to know how to take it (except, ultimately, **ironically**?). However, much of the marketing for the programme, it seems to me, employed modernist and romantic strategies by focusing on David **Lynch** as auteur and *Twin Peaks* as quality television. Second, two of my own personal postmodern favourites. One is the incomparable American comedy animation series, *Ren and Stimpy* which, within the traditional animal duo format (Ren is a chihuahua and Stimpy a fat cat), manages more intertextual nuances and changes of tone per minute than any programme to date while occasionally being, dare I say it, profound. It can certainly be watched as just a knockabout cartoon but at the same time it encodes the viewer with an extraordinarily wide cultural competence. The other is the recent British comedy football show, *Fantasy Football League*. An outcropping of the 'bourgeoisification' of football, it was fronted by comedians Frank Skinner and David Baddiel, with the able assistance of Angus 'Statto' Loughran. Combining elements of the magazine, quiz-show, chat and comedy-sketch genres, it fully acknowledged yet remorselessly parodied the authentic, anorak, blokey culture of football. (It was salutary and moving to see the format collapse when something *really* serious happened; the presenters were so genuinely upset by Germany's defeat of England in the 1996 European Championship semi-finals that they found it hard to be funny.)

However, as I mentioned at the outset, we shouldn't assume that all TV is postmodern. Much programming and viewing is reassuringly traditional. I for one regularly sit and watch the conventional realist narratives of *Coronation Street* and *EastEnders* pretty much from beginning to end, with little or no zapping or hopping (though I do some timeshifting now and again).

POSTMODERNISM AND LITERATURE

(or: WORD SALAD DAYS, 1960–90)

BARRY LEWIS

The dominant mode of literature between 1960 and 1990 was **postmodernist** writing. A few inaugural and closing events can be aligned with these dates (give or take a year or so either way).

> The assassination of John F. Kennedy and the *fatwa* decree against Salman **Rushdie**.

> The erection and demolition of the Berlin Wall.

> Philip Roth's essay 'Writing American Fiction' (1961) and Tom Wolfe's 'Stalking the Billion-Footed Beast: A Literary Manifesto for the New Social Novel' (1989).

The killing of Kennedy, and the death threat against Rushdie for writing *The Satanic Verses* (1989) provided two sinister book-ends for a period of history that was rife with terrorism and doubt. The Berlin Wall was the most potent symbol of the Cold War and its accompanying suspicion. This was a world uneasy with rapid technological change and ideological uncertainties.

The essays by Roth and Wolfe indicate how literature responded to this climate. Roth's piece declared that the daily news was more absurd than anything fiction could render. This gave hundreds of novelists the go-ahead to experiment with fantasy and self-consciousness. Wolfe's manifesto, on the other hand, was a rallying-cry for a return to realism. He claimed that postmodernist novelists had neglected the task of representing the complex life of the city. His own work *Bonfire of the Vanities* (1988) was an attempt to redress the balance by applying the journalistic methods of Balzac and Thackeray to the urban New York jungle.

Another plausible set of benchmarks for this postmodern period involves *Naked Lunch* (1962) by William Burroughs, a novel that challenged every norm of narrative unity and decorum upon its original French publication in 1959. The Boston Superior Court created a sensation when it concluded that the book's portrayal of the hallucinations of a drug addict was nasty and brutish (and not particularly short). Few eyelids were batted, however, in 1992 at the release of the feature film *Naked Lunch* (directed by David Cronenberg). Despite its lurid depiction of talking anuses and virulent cockroaches, the movie met with apathy and not apoplexy, disdain and not disgust. This suggests not only a rise in schlock-tolerance levels, but also a change in attitudes towards transgressive fictional forms.

Indeed, the **aura** formerly attached to the avant-garde is now fading. When an offbeat television series such as David Lynch's *Twin Peaks* is as popular as *Peyton Place* was in its day, it is certain that the demarcation between mainstream and fringe art has eroded. The printed word can no longer compete with the visual media as far as surrealism is concerned.

Is, then, the literature of exhaustion (John **Barth**'s phrase for the last-gasp attempt of the novel to achieve pre-eminence in the electronic global village) now itself exhausted? De Villo Sloan, in his essay 'The Decline of American Postmodernism' (1987) thinks it is: 'Postmodern-ism as a literary movement . . . is now in its final phase of decadence'. Malcolm Bradbury and Richard Ruland, in their sweeping survey *From Puritanism to Postmodernism* (1991) think so too: 'Postmodernism now looks like a stylistic phase that ran from the 1960s to the 1980s.' Therefore a large proportion of writing published after 1990 which is dubbed 'postmodernist' is really 'post-postmodernist', or 'post-pomo' for short.

Bradbury has done much to chart the territory and promulgate the perception of post-1960s writing as a self-contained period. He admits that the problems of mapping contemporary literature are considerable, and that its diversity presents problems for the would-be cartographer. Postmodernism is, of course, only part of the total landscape, but like a mountain-range it looms over everything else, and plodding over its peaks and valleys is no easy task. Luckily there have been other intrepid explorers whose treks can assist our tours of its contours and reliefs. The most useful guides are Patricia Waugh's *Metafiction* (1984), Larry McCaffery's *Postmodern Fiction* (1986) and Brian McHale's *Post-modernist Fiction* (1987). Also aiding orientation are dozens of more local sketches of individual writers and their works.

Postmodernist fiction is an international phenomenon, with major representatives from all over the world: Günter Grass and Peter Handke (Germany); Georges Perec and Monique Wittig (France); Umberto **Eco** and Italo **Calvino** (Italy); Angela **Carter** and Salman Rushdie (Britain); Stanislaw Lem (Poland); Milan Kundera (former Czechoslovakia); Mario Vargos Llosa (Peru); Gabriel Garcia Márquez

(Colombia); J. M. Coetzee (South Africa); and Peter Carey (Australia). Yet, despite this cosmopolitanism, Malcolm Bradbury has quipped that 'When something called postmodernism came along everyone thought it was American – even though its writers had names like Borges, Nabokov, Calvino and Eco.' This is because the number of Stateside writers who can be placed under the postmodernist rubric is large. Here are twenty names usually included in such lists:

Walter Abish	Raymond Federman
Kathy Acker	William Gass
Paul Auster	Steve Katz
John Barth	Jerzy Kosinski
Donald Barthelme	Joseph McElroy
Richard Brautigan	Thomas Pynchon
William Burroughs	Ishmael Reed
Robert Coover	Gilbert Sorrentino
Don DeLillo	Ronald Sukenick
E. L. Doctorow	Kurt Vonnegut

Raymond **Federman** states in 'Self-Reflexive Fiction' (1988), that 'it cannot be said that these writers . . . formed a unified movement for which a coherent theory could be formulated'. It is difficult to disagree with this, as the novels and short stories of these authors vary a great deal. However, they do have certain things in common. Some of the dominant features of their postmodernist fiction include: temporal disorder; the erosion of the sense of time; a pervasive and pointless use of pastiche; a foregrounding of words as fragmenting material **signs**; the loose association of ideas; paranoia; and vicious circles, or a loss of distinction between logically separate levels of discourse. Traits such as these are encountered time and time again in the bare, bewildering landscapes of contemporary fiction. John W. Aldridge puts it like this in *The American Novel and the Way We Live Now* (1983):

> In the fiction of [postmodernist writers] . . . virtually everything and everyone exists in such a radical state of distortion and aberration that there is no way of determining from which conditions in the real world they have been derived or from what standard of sanity they may be said to depart. The conventions of verisimilitude and sanity have been nullified. Characters inhabit a dimension of structureless being in which their behaviour becomes inexplicably arbitrary and unjudgeable because the fiction itself stands as a metaphor of a derangement that is seemingly without provocation and beyond measurement.

The following brief survey will concentrate on the characteristic derangements of contemporary novels and short stories. Postmodernism has influenced all the literary forms. Yet, as Chris Baldick observes in *The Concise Oxford Dictionary of Literary Terms*, '[it] seems to have no relevance to modern poetry, and little to drama, but is used widely in reference to fiction'. For this reason, this introduction will focus on postmodernist fiction, although it is possible to find many of the features it discerns in other types of contemporary writing.

TEMPORAL DISORDER

Postmodernism, according to Linda Hutcheon in *A Poetics of Postmodernism: History, Theory, Fiction* (1988), is a 'contradictory enterprise: its art forms . . . use and abuse, install and then destabilize convention . . . [in] their critical or **ironic** re-reading of the art of the past'. She argues further that postmodernist writing is best represented by those works of 'historiographic metafiction' which self-consciously distort history. This can be accomplished by several means, as Brian McHale notes in the study mentioned earlier: apocryphal history, anachronism, or the blending of history and fantasy.

Apocryphal history involves bogus accounts of famous events. Take Kazuo Ishiguro's *The Remains of the Day* (1989). This novel implies that a butler in a stately home played a small but significant role in the appeasement policy adopted by Britain towards Germany before the Second World War. Anachronism disrupts temporal order by flaunting glaring inconsistencies of detail or setting. In *Flight to Canada* (1976) by Ishmael **Reed**, Abraham Lincoln uses a telephone, and his assassination is reported on television. Tom Crick, a schoolteacher in Graham Swift's *Waterland* (1983), blurs history and fantasy by combining his account of the French Revolution with personal reminiscences and unsubstantiated anecdotes about his own family history.

Postmodernist fiction does not just disrupt the past, but corrupts the present too. It disorders the linear coherence of narrative by warping the sense of significant time, *kairos,* or the dull passing of ordinary time, *chronos*. *Kairos* is strongly associated with those modernist novels which are disposed around moments of epiphany and disclosure, such as James Joyce's *A Portrait of the Artist as a Young Man* (1916). Postmodernist novels such as *Gerald's Party* (1986) by Robert **Coover** chuckle at such solemnities. The sheer abundance of incidents that occur over one night (several murders and beatings, the torture of Gerald's wife by the police, and the arrival of an entire theatre group) distends time beyond recognition. Realist writing specialises in *chronos,* or common-or-garden clock time, and this too is ridiculed in some postmodernist texts. Nicholson **Baker**'s *The Mezzanine* (1990), for instance, comprises a series of extended meditations on why the central character's shoelace snapped during one particular lunchtime.

Postmodernist writing is full of these kinds of temporal disorder. As Coover writes in *The Public Burning* (1977), 'history does not repeat. . . there are no precognitions – and out in that flow all such assertions may be true, false, inconsequential, or all at the same time'. Or, as Inspector Pardew, a character from *Gerald's Party*, remarks about time: 'It's the *key* to it all, it *always* is, the key to *everything*!'

PASTICHE

The Italian word *pasticcio* means 'A medley of various ingredients: a hotchpotch, a farrago, jumble' (*OED*), and is the etymological root of the word 'pastiche'. Pastiching an individual writer is rather like creating an anagram, not of letters, but of the components of a style. Pastiche is therefore a kind of permutation, a shuffling of generic and grammatical tics.

The mere presence of pastiche in postmodernist writing is not in itself unique. The infancy of the novel form itself was marked by a succession of parodies, from Samuel Richardson to Laurence Sterne. Yet as John Barth points out in his essay 'The Literature of Exhaustion' (1967) and its sequel 'The Literature of Replenishment' (1980), there is certainly something peculiar and distinctive about the contemporary mania for impersonation.

Barth's earlier essay epitomizes a mood in the late 1960s, when critics such as Susan Sontag were busy greatly exaggerating rumours about the death of the novel. The traditional devices of fiction seemed clapped-out, unable to capture the complexities of the electronic age. At first it was thought that Barth, by stressing the exhaustion of both realism and **modernism**, had not only joined the novel's funeral procession, but was volunteering to be chief pall-bearer. However, the critics overlooked his claim (reasserted in the later essay) that the corpse could be revivified by stitching together the amputated limbs and digits in new permutations: by pastiche, in other words.

Pastiche, then, arises from the frustration that everything has been done before. As Fredric **Jameson** notes in 'Postmodernism and Consumer Society' (1983), 'the writers and artists of the present day will no longer be able to invent new styles and worlds . . . only a limited number of combinations are possible; the most unique ones have been thought of already'. So instead of honing an unmistakable signature like D. H. Lawrence or Gertrude Stein, postmodernist writers tend to pluck existing styles higgledy-piggledy from the reservoir of literary history, and match them with little tact.

This explains why many contemporary novels borrow the clothes of different forms (for example: the western, the sci-fi yarn and the detective tale). The impulse behind this cross-dressing is more spasmodic than parodic. These genres provide ready-made forms, ideal for postmodernist miscegenation. The western, as Philip French observes, is 'a hungry cuckoo of a genre . . . ready to seize anything that's in the air from juvenile delinquency to ecology'. In other words, it is already a bastardized form. Examples of the postmodern western include *The Hawkline Monster* (1974) by Richard Brautigan, *Yellow Back Radio Broke-Down* (1969) by Ishmael Reed, and *The Place of Dead Roads* (1984) by William Burroughs. Science-fiction is another popular source for postmodernist pastiche. Some critics assert that it is the natural companion to postmodernist writing, because of their shared ontological occupations. (See especially *Solaris* (1961) by Stanislaw Lem, *Cosmicomics* (1965) by Italo Calvino, and *Slaughterhouse-Five* (1969) by Kurt **Vonnegut**.) Lastly, the detective genre is another candidate for the post of true companion of postmodernism. The pursuit of clues appeals to the postmodernist writer because it so closely parallels the hunt for **textual** meaning by the reader. The most popular postmodernist detective fictions are *The Name of the Rose* (1984) by Umberto Eco, *The New York Trilogy* (1987) by Paul **Auster** and *Hawksmoor* (1985) by Peter **Ackroyd**.

FRAGMENTATION

John Hawkes once divulged that when he began to write he assumed that 'the true enemies of the novel were plot, character, setting and theme'. Certainly many subsequent authors have done their best to sledgehammer these four literary cornerstones into oblivion. Either plot is pounded into small slabs of event and circumstance, characters disintegrate into a bundle of twitching desires, settings are little more than transitory backdrops, or themes become so attenuated that it is often comically inaccurate to say that certain novels are 'about' such-and-such.

'Too many times,' as Jonathan Baumbach observes in a short story in *The Return of Service* (1979), 'you read a story nowadays and it's not a story at all, not in the traditional sense.'

The postmodernist writer distrusts the wholeness and completion associated with traditional stories, and prefers to deal with other ways of structuring narrative. One alternative is the multiple ending, which resists closure by offering numerous possible outcomes for a plot. *The French Lieutenant's Woman* (1969) by John Fowles is the classic instance of this. The novel concerns the love of respectable amateur naturalist Charles Smithson (engaged to the daughter of a wealthy trader) for Sarah Woodruff, an outcast rumoured to have been scandalously involved with a French lieutenant. Although the book is set in Lyme Regis in 1867, and follows several love story conventions, it is far from being a regular historical romance.

Fowles disrupts the narrative by parading his familiarity with **Marx**, Darwin and others. He directly addresses the reader, and even at one stage steps into the story himself as a character. The multiple endings are a part of these guerrilla tactics. Fowles refuses to choose between two competing dénouements: one in which Charles and Sarah are reunited after a stormy affair, and the other in which they are kept irrevocably apart. He therefore introduces an uncertainty principle into the book. He even dallies with a third possibility of leaving Charles on the train, searching for Sarah in the capital: 'But the conventions of Victorian fiction allow, allowed no place for the open, the inconclusive . . .'

Another means of allowing place for the open and inconclusive is by breaking up the text into short fragments or sections, separated by space, titles, numbers or symbols. The novels and short stories of Richard Brautigan and Donald **Barthelme** are full of such fragments. Some authors go even further and fragment the very fabric of the text with illustrations, typography, or mixed media. As Raymond Federman puts it in the introduction to *Surfiction: Fiction Now . . . and Tomorrow* (1975): 'In those spaces where there is nothing to write, the fiction writer can, at any time, introduce material (quotations, pictures, diagrams, charts, designs, pieces of other discourses, etc.) totally unrelated to the story.'

Willie Masters' Lonesome Wife (1967) by William Gass does just about all these things in its sixty-odd pages, and is a postmodernist text *par excellence.* The pages themselves come in four different colours: jotter blue, khaki green, strawberry red and glossy white. The nude woman lounging full-frontal on the title-page is Babs. She is a frustrated spouse who figuratively embodies the language/lovemaking equation examined by Gass. The layout is so eccentric it might have been designed by Marshall **McLuhan** on mescaline. Multiple typefaces (bold, italic), fonts (Gothic, script), characters (musical symbols, accents), and miscellaneous arrangements (columns, footnotes) jostle for air alongside some visual jokes (coffee-cup stains, huge asterisk). In a review, Ronald **Sukenick** called it 'a cloudburst of fragmented events'. 'Monsoon' is nearer the mark.

With works such as these by Fowles, Brautigan, Barthelme and Gass it is difficult not to be reminded of the famous epigraph to E. M. Forster's *Howards End*: 'Live in fragments no longer. Only connect...' We can counterpoint this with an utterance by a character in Barthelme's 'See the Moon?' from *Unspeakable Practices. Unnatural Acts* (1968): 'Fragments are the only forms I trust.' These two statements evince a crucial difference between modernism and postmodernism. The Forster phrase could almost be modernism's motto, as it points to the need to find new forms of continuity in the absence of the old linear plots. Conversely, Barthelme's gem hints at postmodernist fiction's wariness of wholeness.

LOOSENESS OF ASSOCIATION

Another means by which many postmodernist writers disrupt the smooth production and reception of texts is by welcoming chance into the compositional process. The infamous *The Unfortunates* (1969) by B. S. Johnson, for instance, is a novel-in-a-box which instructs the reader to riffle several loose-leaf chapters into any order. Only the first and last chapter are denominated, otherwise the sections can be freely mixed. The point of this contrived format is not just to perform a cold, technical experiment. Rather, Johnson wishes to recreate the unique disposition of his thoughts on a particular Saturday afternoon, when reporting a football match in Nottingham for the *Observer*. It was the first time he had returned to the city since the death of his friend, Tony. The peculiar form of the novel mirrors his churning feelings. So, ironically, the loose-leaves of *The Unfortunates* are not intended to be random at all, but strive to render the workings of the mind more naturally.

William Burroughs also forays frequently into serendipity. The arrangement of the twenty-two individual sections of *Naked Lunch* (1962) was regulated solely by the adventitious order in which they happened to be sent to the publishers. Indeed, the untidiness of the room in which the manuscript was assembled sometimes disturbed the sequence of pages. Small wonder that Burroughs confessed that 'You can cut into *Naked Lunch* at any intersection point'. Burroughs wields chance less randomly in three novels from the 1960s which are often grouped together as a trilogy: *Nova Express* (1966), *The Soft Machine* (1967) and *The Ticket That Exploded* (1967). These books make methodical use of the cut-up. The cut-up is the brainchild of the artist Tristan Tzara, who envisaged it as a verbal equivalent to the cubist and Dadaist collages in the visual arts.

Further extensions of the idea can be traced through the poetry of T. S. Eliot and Ezra Pound, and the newspaper pastiches of John Dos Passos. The cut-up was taught to Burroughs by Brion Gysin. It involves placing excised sentences from a range of texts into a hat or other container, shaking them, then matching together the scraps of paper which are picked out at random. This rigmarole has prompted sceptical critics to make unflattering comparisons between Burroughs and monkeys with typewriters.

Another chance technique favoured by Burroughs is the fold-in, in which a page of text is folded vertically, and then aligned with another page until the two halves match. Just as the cut-up allows writing to mimic cinematic montage, the fold-in gives Burroughs the option of repeating passages in a specifically musical way. For example, if page 1 is folded-in with page 100 to form a composite page 10, phrases can flash forward and back like the anticipation and recapitulation of motifs in a symphony.

The fold-in, like the cut-up, strains to evade the manacles of ordinary fiction. Few texts directly borrow these techniques, but Burroughs' spirit of chance-taking is decidedly congenial to the postmodernist writer. In this respect he is rather like the musician John Cage, who opened up tremendous ground for exploration by later composers, although his experiments with dice and the *I-Ching* proved to be unrepeatable. Nevertheless, as Julian Cowley noted in an essay on Ronald Sukenick (1987), in both music and writing 'Readiness to ride with the random may be regarded as a characteristically postmodern attitude . . .'

PARANOIA

Paranoia, or the threat of total engulfment by somebody else's system, is keenly felt by many of the dramatis personae of postmodernist fiction. It is tempting to speculate that this is an indirect mimetic representation of the climate of fear and suspicion that prevailed throughout the Cold War. The protagonists of postmodernist fiction often suffer from what Tony Tanner calls in *City of Words* (1971) a 'dread that someone else is patterning your life, that there are all sorts of invisible plots afoot to rob you of your autonomy of thought and action, that conditioning is ubiquitous'.

Postmodernist writing reflects paranoid anxieties in many ways, including: the distrust of fixity, of being circumscribed to any one particular place or identity, the conviction that society is conspiring against the individual, and the multiplication of self-made plots to counter the scheming of others. These different responses are immanent in three distinct areas of reference associated with the word 'plot'. The first meaning is that of a piece of ground of small or moderate size sequestered for some special purpose, such as a plot for growing vegetables or building a house. A stationary space, in other words, intimidating to the postmodern hero. Randle McMurphy in Ken Kesey's *One Flew Over the Cuckoo's Nest* (1962), Yossarian in Joseph Heller's *Catch-22* (1962) and Billy Pilgrim in Kurt Vonnegut's *Slaughterhouse-Five* (1969) are each confined to their own 'plots' in this sense by the authorities. McMurphy is committed to a mental hospital, Yossarian is conscripted to the air force, and Billy Pilgrim is interned in a German prisoner-of-war camp. A vindictive bureaucracy controls these mavericks by medication, red tape or the force of arms.

In each instance the imprisoning of the individual by outside powers propagates a panic of identity. So McMurphy's protests that he is sane prove his insanity. Pilgrim's belief that he is the subject of an experiment is belied by the offhand way his German captors treat him. To compensate for the hopelessness of their predicaments, these paranoids long for a state of complete fluidity and openness. However, their impulse towards freedom is tainted both by their terror of the actual open road and their cynicism about possible escape. McMurphy, Yossarian and Pilgrim are simultaneously safe and insecure in their 'plots' of the Oregon Asylum, the Pianosa air-force base, and the Dresden slaughterhouse.

A second meaning of 'plot' is that of a secret plan or conspiracy to accomplish a criminal or illegal purpose. The protagonist of the postmodernist novel sometimes suspects that he or she is trapped at the centre of an intrigue, often with some justification. McMurphy is right to be afraid of Nurse Ratched and the Combine, who eventually force him to undergo shock treatment and an unwarranted lobotomy. Yossarian's parachute is stolen by Milo Minderbinder and replaced by a useless M&M Enterprises voucher. General Peckham sends Yossarian's squadron out on dangerous bombing missions simply to obtain decent aerial photographs for the magazines back home. Nately's whore stabs Yossarian, in the belief that he killed her lover. In *Slaughterhouse-Five*,

Billy Pilgrim also correctly perceives that others wish to control his welfare. His daughter commits him to a mental institution and Paul Lazarro later kills him as a revenge for allegedly allowing Roland Weary to die.

There's but a small step from these private apprehensions to a more distressing speculation. Perhaps the whole of the society is a plot against the citizen. What if all the major events of history are really side-shows orchestrated by unseen ringmasters for hidden motives? This is known as paranoid history. Thomas **Pynchon** is enthralled by the topic. Stencil in *V.* (1963), Oedipa Maas in *The Crying of Lot 49* (1966), Slothrop in *Gravity's Rainbow* (1973), and Prairie in *Vineland* (1990) each stumble upon subterranean schemes and cabals which threaten the rights of the individual. As Pynchon remarks in *Gravity's Rainbow*, their multiplying anxieties are triggered by 'nothing less than the onset, the leading edge, of the discovery that everything is connected, everything in the Creation'.

The third, more mundane, meaning of plot is, of course, that of a plan of a literary work. In an interview, John Barth called this 'the incremental perturbation of an unstable homeostatic system and its catastrophic restoration to a complexified equilibrium'. This humorous definition suggests that a plot has a particular shape: somebody is challenged, certain obstacles are overcome, a new state of affairs is reached. Plot is shape, and shape is control. Several postmodernist writers proliferate plot, as if to prove through zealous mastery that they are free of the straitjackets of control by outside forces. The best of these maximalist works are *Foucault's Pendulum* (1988) by Umberto Eco, *Life: A User's Manual* (1978) by Georges Perec and *Letters* (1979) by Barth himself.

VICIOUS CIRCLES

Vicious circles arise in postmodernist fiction when both text and world are permeable, to the extent that we cannot separate one from the other. The literal and the metaphorical merge when the following occur: short circuits (when the author steps into the text) and double binds (when real-life historical figures appear in fictions).

The short circuits which plague postmodernist fiction rarely occur in other forms of fiction. In realist literature, for example, there is an unbroken flow of narrative 'electricity' between text and world. The author never appears directly in his or her fictions, other than as a voice that indirectly guides the reader towards a 'correct' interpretation of the novel's themes. Conversely, much modernist fiction is motivated by the desire to expunge the author from the text altogether. Think of James Joyce's image of the artist standing behind the work, paring his fingernails. This again ensures that there is little chance of confusing the world inside the text with the world outside the text. In the post-modernist novel and short story, however, such confusion is rampant. Text and world fuse when the author appears in his or her own fiction. The best examples of this occur in Ronald Sukenick's *The Death of the Novel and Other Stories* (1969) and *Out* (1973), and Raymond Feder-man's *Double or Nothing* (1971) and *Take It or Leave It* (1976).

The double bind is a concept elaborated by Gregory Bateson and others to explain an inability to distinguish between different levels of discourse. When a parent chastises a child, for instance, they may undermine the punishment by smiling as they smack. If these kinds of contradictory messages are repeated obsessively, it may lead to the child's breakdown. The boundaries separating the literal and the meta-phorical will never fully form, and any moves to resolve matters result only in further entanglement. It is well known that schizophrenics often confuse fact and fantasy in their delusions. The patient who thinks he is Jesus Christ manifests a typical symptom of the illness.

The equivalent of the double bind occurs in postmodernist fiction when historical characters appear in a patent fiction. We are used to the idea of the historical novel, which shows famous people from the past acting in ways consistent with the verifiable public record. A common alternative is to sketch in the 'dark areas' of somebody's life, and again care is usually taken not substantially to contradict what we already know about them. In postmodernist writing, however, such contradictions are actively sought. So in Max Apple's *The Propheteers* (1987), the motel mogul Howard Johnson plots against Walt Disney. In Guy Davenport's 'Christ Preaching at the Henley Regatta' (1981), Bertie Wooster and Mallarmé stand on the banks watching the boat race. In E. L. Doctorow's *Ragtime* (1975), **Freud** and Jung go through the Tunnel of Love together at Coney Island. These are just some of the many derangements of postmodernist fiction.

POSTMODERNIST WRITING AND LANGUAGE DISORDER

The comparisons between the derangement of postmodernist writing and insanity are appropriate. Some major **poststructuralist** thinkers enlist ideas connected with schizophrenia in their diagnoses of post-modern society. Jean-François **Lyotard**, for instance, employs the metaphors of fragmentation in *The Postmodern Condition* (1979) to convey the splintering of knowledge into a plethora of incommensurate discourses. He states in 'The Ecstasy of Communication' (1983) that 'we are now in a new form of schizophrenia'. Gilles **Deleuze** and Félix **Guattari** speak of '**schizoanalysis**' in *Anti-Oedipus* (1977). For all the recondite terminology, their rhetoric makes a surprisingly everyday equation between mental breakdown and the contemporary moment. Lastly, Fredric Jameson's full-length study *Postmodernism, or, The Cultural Logic of Late Capitalism* (1991) employs schizophrenia as an analogy for the collapse of traditional socio-economic structures.

This recurrent linking of mental illness, the fractures of late capitalist society and the linguistic experiments of contemporary writing is not accidental. Temporal disorder, involuntary impersonation of other voices (or pastiche), fragmentation, looseness of association, paranoia and the creation of vicious circles are symptoms of the language disorders of schizophrenia as well as features of postmodernist fiction. It is in this alignment that we can find the primary contrast between the modernists and postmodernists.

A possible objection to a postmodernist poetics that emphasizes elements of style is that these characteristics are not unique. Modernist writers such as James Joyce, Virginia Woolf and Marcel Proust also experimented with distortions of narrative time, pastiche, fragmentation and so on. This cannot be denied, but perhaps we can argue that the derangements of works such as *Ulysses* (1922), *To the Lighthouse* (1927) and *Remembrance of Things Past* (1913–27) have different motivations. These were homeopathic attempts to protect culture against the chaos of technological change and ideological uncertainty in the wake of the First World War. Following the Second World War, writers faced a situation which R. D. Laing would no doubt call 'radical ontological insecurity'. Postmodernist authors between 1960 and 1990 no longer believed that the old cultural values were recoverable after the Holocaust. They simply gave up the struggle and delighted in delirium. The alienation effects of *their* fictions express the effects of alienation upon themselves.

POSTMODERNISM AND
MUSIC

DEREK SCOTT

Postmodernism began to have an impact upon music and musicology in the 1980s when it became evident that a **paradigmatic shift** in thought was needed in order to find answers to the theoretical impasse that had been reached in several areas.

First, the idea that a mass audience did no more than passively consume the products of a culture industry had become discredited. Yet tacit acceptance of this idea explains why, for instance, the legendary jazz saxophonist Charlie Parker does not appear in the *New Oxford History of Music* and the rock guitarist Jimi Hendrix is absent from *The New Grove Dictionary of Music and Musicians*. Anyone caring to peruse the index of the *Oxford History* will indeed find a Parker listed, but this is the American organist and composer Horatio Parker (1863–1919). Giving priority to the latter makes a clear statement of value: Horatio is of greater musical importance than Charlie. Today, it is evident that classical music is as involved in the market-place as pop and jazz (conductors and singers can become superstars, and even a 'serious' composer like Górecki has appeared in record charts). Moreover, the serious versus light opposition that kept mass culture theory going is also found repeated in jazz and rock – for example, 'real' jazz versus commercial dance band; 'authentic' rock versus superficial pop.

Second, the musical genealogical tree had needed surgery too often: lines connecting composers, charting musical developments and influences, had been redrawn too many times. One has only to consider the major reassessment of Monteverdi and Berlioz in the 1960s. The linear paradigm works to include and to exclude: those who do not obviously connect are out (for example, Kurt Weill and Benjamin Britten). The related issue of the evolution of musical style was now questioned: if atonality was presented as an inevitable stylistic evolution, then clearly Duke Ellington was a musical dinosaur.

Third, the neglect of the social significance of music had become more apparent, especially the way cultural context often determines the legitimacy of styles of playing and singing, and changing social factors alter our response to existing works. For example, would we any more wish to hear John Lee Hooker attempting Puccini's 'Nessun Dorma' than Luciano Pavarotti singing 'Chicago Bar Blues'?

Fourth, the impact of technology had to be considered, especially the effects that sampling and remixing had on the concept of the composer as originating mind.

Furthermore, students who had grown up during the 'rock revolution' were inclined to see the **modernist** inclinations of university departments of music as the new orthodoxy. Perhaps more disturbing still was that it became common for a composition tutor to find students earnestly composing a type of music that they would never dream of actually going to a concert hall to hear. Other factors bearing upon the present situation were the rise of period instrument performances making old music seem new (and arguably a replacement for the new), and crossovers between 'classical' and 'popular' idioms by increasing numbers of performers and composers.

Consequently, the time was ripe for postmodernism to offer a new theoretical perspective. Its impact is discussed below under a number of headings; these are not to be taken, however, as representing a particular hierarchical order.

'ART FOR ART'S SAKE' CHALLENGED

Postmodernism ousted notions of universalism, internationalism and 'art for art's sake', and replaced them with concerns for the values of specific cultures and their differences. 'Art for art's sake', a nineteenth-century doctrine born of distaste for industrialization, had proved to be an insuperable obstacle to the production of music that satisfied widespread social needs. Indeed, by the time Debussy was composing, the élitist attitude that 'art' is of no use to 'the masses' was common. However, by the 1980s there was a growing interest in uncovering the complicity between art and entertainment rather than drawing a contrast between these two terms. Among the middle classes and the 'educated' – and among 'serious' musicians – attention drifted away from high culture to popular culture. It was no longer pressing to debate whether Boulez, Cage or Tippett represented the 'way ahead' for high culture since, to echo a well-known song, those taking the high road had been overtaken by those taking the low road. Moreover, since the 1960s there had been a remarkable similarity in marketing techniques used for the classical repertoire and for pop music.

The opposition 'art versus entertainment' is an assumption of mass culture theory and may be regarded as an ethical rather than aesthetic opposition. To choose examples from the careers of major figures in the classical canon, one can show that Mozart abandoned a flute concerto in mid-composition because a commissioner failed to pay up; the same composer was persuaded by a concert promoter to change a movement of his Paris Symphony; and it was a publisher who persuaded Beethoven to replace the finale of his late String Quartet in B flat with something more conventional. Today, Michael **Nyman** does not feel associations with businesses compromise his artistic integrity: 'MGV' was commissioned to mark the opening of the Paris to Lille high-speed rail link, and car manufacturer Mazda UK Ltd commissioned a concerto in 1997.

THE COLLAPSE OF HIGH AND LOW: CROSSOVERS AND NEW GENRES

The amount of 'crossover' between 'serious' and 'popular' culture has been increasing since the late 1950s. An example of the widening influence of pop is heard in the soundtracks of films: in the 1940s Flash Gordon conquered the universe to the strains of Liszt, whereas in the 1980s his crusading was accompanied by the rock band Queen. In the 1980s, performance artist Laurie **Anderson** had a remarkable crossover hit with 'O Superman'. In recent years, the violinist Nigel Kennedy has tried his hand at rock, while blues guitarist Eric Clapton has performed an electric guitar concerto. The Kronos String Quartet has an arrangement of Jimi Hendrix's 'Purple Haze' in its repertoire. Opera singers of the calibre of Kiri Te Kanawa and Placido Domingo have ventured into the popular arena.

Some works now cannot easily be categorized, for example: Philip **Glass**'s 'Low' and 'Heroes' symphonies (both based on albums produced in the 1970s by David Bowie and Brian **Eno**); *The Juliet Letters* by Elvis Costello and the Brodsky Quartet; and the peculiar mixture of medievalism and jazz in the albums *Officium* by Jan Garbarek and the Hilliard Ensemble, and *Terror and Magnificence* by John Harle. Along with this, there is a tendency for contemporary composers to label their ensembles 'bands' (John Harle Band, Steve Martland Band, Paul Robinson's Harmonie Band).

THE END OF GRAND NARRATIVES

Modernists have continually seen works as 'pointing forwards' to others, thus reinforcing a sense of self-determining progress in the arts. But can *Tristan und Isolde* really be said to point forward to the sudden and rapid developments of 1908–1909, such as Strauss's *Elektra* and Schoenberg's *Erwartung*? If a 50-year gap is possible, why not concede a 300-year gap and allow the idea that Gesualdo pointed forward to Debussy? A major problem for 'linear modernism' is that, while Beethoven and Wagner appear to follow an evolutionary 'progress' in their music, many otherwise impeccable modernists, like Debussy and Schoenberg, do not. What is more, modernist composers are not even reliable in their tastes: Debussy admired Gounod and Richard Strauss but not Schoenberg; Stravinsky admired Weber and Tchaikovsky but loathed Wagner.

The dominant **grand narrative** for musical modernism was that of the evolution and dissolution of tonality. Schoenberg claimed that serialism grew out of necessity, yet this necessity was itself born of a set of particular cultural assumptions. Empirical data can be used to demonstrate that the change from extended tonality to atonality was an evolution, but it can equally well show that this was a qualitative leap. A belief in the historical necessity of atonality led to the neglect of many areas of twentieth-century music history, such as the importance of Vienna to Hollywood (Korngold) or of Puccini to 'The Generation of the 1880s' in Italy. Worst of all, perhaps, was the almost complete disregard of jazz.

The BBC's thinking is still informed by modernist **metanarratives**: admiration for 'forward-looking' composers, and of 'progressive' music is part of the left luggage from the years when Sir William Glock controlled the Third Programme's output but, all the same, it is dispiriting for anyone who completely rejects that theoretical paradigm. It is as if the arguments from **poststructuralism**, **deconstruction** and postmodernism have fallen on deaf ears. Nyman feels that the musical establishment has given him the cold shoulder, as evidenced by the neglect of his music by BBC Radio 3 and his lack of Proms commissions.

It is erroneous to believe that an 'adventurous' style requires greater compositional skill than a 'simple and direct' style; such a position serves only to offer a facile proof, for example, that Birtwistle must be better than Pärt. As a criterion of musical value, the important thing is the relationship of style and idea.

SOCIOCULTURAL CONTEXT REPLACES AUTONOMY

The romantic and modernist interpretations of music history emphasized formal and technical values, novelty and compositional 'coups'. The stress was on the composition in itself and its place in an autonomous musical process. A well-known example of how Mozart's life and music may be interpreted through this reading of history is offered by Peter Shaffer's *Amadeus*, in which art is seen as a reflection of life (a corruption of the distinction between romantic self-expression and the baroque 'Doctrine of Affections'); art is perfection, the artist is a visionary (Salieri cannot understand Mozart's unique vision in the 'confutatis' of his *Requiem)*, and social and political issues are cast aside (Mozart, a member, it seems, of the republican Illuminati, says he is 'not interested in politics', and *The Magic Flute* with its Masonic messages is described as a vaudeville). It is all too easy when constructing the history of a cultural practice to assume one is dealing with facts and not interpretation.

Raymond Williams has pointed out how lines are drawn to link ancestors within a cultural tradition. However, with the passage of time some lines become weaker, some are erased and new ones drawn. At the beginning of the twentieth century, the reputations of Gounod, Spohr and Borodin were high, but are no longer so. Since the 1960s, lines from Josquin and from Monteverdi have been strengthened, and in the 1970s eclectic modernists like Ives and Varèse were brought in from the margins following the failure of attempts to establish a common practice in total serialism (an attempt to impose order on length and loudness of notes as well as their pitches). This enabled the USA to take its place in the history of modernism, since a line drawn from Varèse to Cowell to Cage could be used to illustrate progressively radical exploration of sound colours.

The linear paradigm works to create canonic figures and marginalize others. Canons imply an autonomous cultural development, and those who fail to participate in that particular development, or who seek alternatives, are marginalized, as were Korngold and Eisler for rejecting modernism. The linear paradigm is a means of defending a single authentic culture, but that requires a common practice and modernism failed to establish one.

Aesthetics cannot always be easily divorced from social significance. Can anyone listen to those old recordings of Castrati who survived into the twentieth century with an aesthetic sensibility unmoved by the knowledge that these singers were mutilated as children? Social factors affect our response to music in a variety of ways. For example, French concern at the lack of an operatic tradition, which led to the unearthing of Rameau's *Hippolyte at Aricie* early in the twentieth century, developed in the context of nationalism arising from political defeat. Changing social factors affect our response to works which may have previously provoked quite different reactions: *Così fan tutte* is not the same after the cultural impact of the Women's Movement of the 1970s, and *Peter Grimes* has become problematic owing to the greater awareness of child abuse that developed in the 1980s (we are no longer so ready to accept Grimes as a tortured idealist).

THE END OF THE 'INTERNATIONAL STYLE'

The belief in a universal aesthetics, that 'art music' transcends social and cultural context, lay behind the internationalist aspirations of modernism. Having developed his atonal style, Schoenberg gave voice to his conviction in 1910 that by 1920 every talented composer would be writing that way. Modernism was never internationalist in a **pluralist** sense, but in the sense of a *single* culture with *universal* values. Composers of different nationalities and different musical traditions were shown to be moving towards the same end, usually that of embracing 12-note music.

The ambitions of modernist music towards internationalism have been overtaken by pop, which has already become a more widely accepted international style. The social history of our times is inseparable from pop music so that, measured in terms of social significance, the 12-bar blues may be said to have been of greater importance to twentieth-century music than the 12-note row.

Today, after all the efforts expended by ethnomusicologists, it would appear impossible to avoid the conclusion that music is no more international than other forms of cultural expression. The acceptance of modernism's international ambitions led to distortions and contradictions in the way music history was interpreted. For example, the supposed poor state of English music during the first half of the twentieth century was blamed on insularity, yet the English musical 'rebirth' at the end of the nineteenth century was usually credited to composers' acceptance of 'Englishness' instead of 'Germanness'.

RELATIVISM REPLACES UNIVERSALISM

Modernism, an attempt to defend one universalist culture, was often forced to attack regionalism as parochialism, nationalism as chauvinism, popular music as entertainment not art, and ethnic music as primitivism or 'ghetto culture'. The postmodern alternative is to accept that we are living in an age of **cultural relativism**. Cultural relativism, a perspective taken from anthropology, was the key to socio-musicological interpretation in the 1980s. The argument that cultural values could be historically located was already familiar and was expanded by the recognition that significance could also be socially located. The last idea fuelled the main argument against mass culture theory: that meaning could be made in the act of consumption – consumption was not simply passive.

STYLES AS DISCURSIVE CODES

Contrary to Stravinsky's opinion that expressive devices are established by convention within an autonomous musical practice, they are established as conventions through social practice and can be related to social changes. Musical meanings are not labels arbitrarily thrust upon abstract sounds; these sounds and their meanings originate in a social process and achieve their significance within a particular social context. Musical signifiers develop in tandem with society. The opening of Vivian Ellis's *Coronation Scot* uses no musical technique or dissonant vocabulary which would have surprised Beethoven, yet it is meaningless unless one is familiar with the sound of a steam train pulling away. The piece could not have been written before the advent of the steam locomotive. Indeed, what would boogie-woogie piano or much of the characteristic style of blues harmonica have been without trains?

Schoenberg's free atonal period can be related to the new science of psychoanalysis and **Freudian** investigations into the inner reaches of the human psyche. Expressionist artists envied the supposed power of music to express the composer's internal life. Just as Kandinsky spoke of 'inner necessity', Schoenberg placed his trust in 'unconscious logic'; yet, if atonality was historically inevitable, this trust was as much a corollary as a catalyst to his adopting a new musical language. Even so, it would appear odd that the development of an extreme chromatic language should coincide merely by chance with an expressionist interest in extreme emotional states.

At the same time, it is important to recognize that style codes have developed from the solidification of conventions and that these involve technical features as well as socially constituted meanings. Although style codes may be subject to further development and change, that cannot be achieved by rupturing, negating or contradicting their most important and defining attributes. The music-historical problem for jazz has been its resistance to assimilation into the Western 'art music' tradition because of fundamental aesthetic conflicts. The criteria for determining what is a beautiful or 'legitimate' style of singing and playing in jazz, for example, are frequently at odds with the criteria that prevail in 'art music'. The classical operatic voice can be related to instrumental techniques and standards of beauty of tone production within that style. Jazz has its own range of associated vocal techniques, many of which are not found in classical music – scatting, growling and smearing or bending notes – and can also be related to instrumental techniques within that style (for example, the use of a plunger mute to create a growling sound on trumpet or trombone). The existence of distinct musical style codes in the nineteenth century is made evident in the incompatibility of Beethoven's Viennese style to the Scottish airs he arranged.

An even more distinct style code, *piobaireachd* – a unique kind of bagpipe music that originated among the Gaelic communities of the Scottish Highlands and Islands – may be used to illustrate the way meaning depends on socio-cultural context rather than on universally valid musical devices. The interval of the tritone (that between fah and te in tonic sol-fa) conveyed emotional anguish to seventeenth-century Venetians, as we know from their madrigals and operas; yet, it evidently did not carry this meaning to seventeenth-century Scottish Highlanders. There is an old *piobaireachd* of uncertain date bearing the title 'Praise of Marion' ('Guileagag Moraig') which, in one variation alone, contains 29 tritones within 32 bars.

A final example of how style codes have their own conventions and construct their own meanings is revealed by comparing Richard Strauss's 'Dance of the Seven Veils' (from his opera *Salome*) with David Rose's 'The Stripper'. In the latter, one notes the quasi-vocal slides on trombone and the wailing *tremolando* on a 'blue' seventh followed by 'jungle' drums: these were among the devices developed originally by Ellington at the Cotton Club to signify the wild and the primitive for his white patrons, and which soon became associated with wild, predatory female sexuality. The eroticism of the Strauss, on the other hand, is encoded in the sensual richness (timbral and textural) of a huge orchestra, the quasi-oriental (that is, exotic) embellishment of melody, and the devices of crescendo and quickening pace. However, it is surely no coincidence that, despite the anachronism, the Viennese waltz with its connotations of *fin de siècle* decadence lies just below the surface of the Strauss piece, as the foxtrot lies below that of Rose. There is no sense, of course, in which one of these pieces of music is really sexier than the other; each encodes eroticism in a different way and for a different function. It would be just as ludicrous to imagine 'Dance of the Seven Veils' being played in a seedy strip club as to imagine 'The Stripper' being incorporated into *Salome*.

MEANING AS AN EFFECT OF DISCOURSE

Seeing seven colours in a rainbow is an effect of Newtonian discourse (Newton having added the colour indigo in his determination that a rainbow should have seven colours), just as hearing an octave divided into twelve semitones is an effect of a particular Western musical discourse (that of equal temperament tuning). An empiricist would argue that a transcendental subject acquires knowledge by observing or listening, but other cultures see five or six colours in a rainbow and divide an octave into intervals that differ from the Western classical norm. If a discourse divides the spectrum into certain named coloured segments, then those are the ones that are seen. If a musical discourse – that is, a domain of musical practice or a musical style – divides an octave into quarter tones, these may be perceived in another cultural context as out-of-tune notes or 'corrected' by the ear to the nearest semitone.

EMPHASIS ON RECEPTION AND SUBJECT POSITION

It has become important to ask who the implied audience might be for a piece of music. Whom do Nanci Griffith, Shirley Bassey or Kiri Te Kanawa think they are singing to? The way the music sounds may indicate that it is intended, for example, for a salon, a concert hall or outdoors. If so, has this affected the composition in terms of form and instrumentation, or has the composer been guided only by imagination in choice of timbre? Why did Beethoven not make folk-song arrangements for guitar and voice? Certain ensembles carry greater status than others: for example, a string quartet would be regarded in some circles as more refined and 'elevated' than a saxophone quartet, no matter what music had been written for each. Music has more status in a concert hall than in a pub; because of this, the status of jazz was negatively affected for many years. Some of the Edinburgh bourgeoisie may well have found Beethoven's Scottish folk-song arrangements convincing, since they sought a 'refined' or 'improved' version of their musical heritage. The subject position one occupies can radically affect reception: until the 1980s, few critics in the West recognized the extent of Shostakovitch's use of **irony** in his music.

THE DISAPPEARING 'REAL', THE SIMULACRUM AND PROBLEMS OF AUTHENTICITY

With poststructuralism, notions of an 'inner essence' and a 'real' have disappeared. 'Authenticity' can be seen to be constructed as one more style: values of truth and authenticity will be set up in the dress-codes and styles of singing of performers (folk singers do not wear pin-stripe suits), perhaps in the instruments they play (for example, acoustic instruments tend to signify such values better than electronic instruments). A performer who can be pinned down to a particular image, such as Bruce Springsteen, will communicate a deeper impression of authenticity than a performer who plays multiple roles, such as David Bowie.

In some areas of music there are examples of **Baudrillard**'s **simulacra**, where there is not even an attempt to be real, or where reality has been appropriated by a fiction. The 'jungle music' created by Ellington's band, or Hollywood 'cowboy songs', are ready examples. A more complex matter is **orientalist** music. In spite of the differences that developed over the years in Western **representations** of the East in music, the successive orientalist styles tended to relate to previous orientalist styles more closely than they did to Eastern ethnic practices. It is not surprising, because orientalist music is not poor imitation of another cultural practice: its purpose is not to imitate but to represent. Representations, however, rely upon culturally learned recognition, and this may have much to do with a person's existing knowledge of Western signifiers of the East and little to do with the objective conditions of non-Western musical practices. Indeed, a composer may bring something new into being which displaces and stands in for the Orient.

Musicology has also had to take on board the lessons of **Derrida**'s deconstruction, which is concerned with demonstrating the privileging of one term over another in metaphysical oppositions. There is no longer a case to be made for supposedly 'pure' music. Even the music of a composer like Bruckner can be deconstructed to expose ideological assumptions behind what, on the surface, may seem to be abstract musicological choices. In his music, meaning is created by differing and deferring (Derrida's *différance*): minor is governed by major and therefore the minor opening of the Third Symphony is not mistaken for the dominant term; we know major will triumph. Minor is *always* the antithesis – but not a true antithesis, because Bruckner privileges major over minor. In Bruckner's music, major is the commanding term for ideological and not structural reasons: major connotes light and minor connotes darkness; or, we might say, minor is major with a lack, as darkness is light with a lack. There is no structural reason why minor should not command major: for example, in Mahler's Sixth all light is extinguished (adumbrated early on by the major triad's turn to minor).

DEATH OF THE COMPOSER AS ORIGINATING GENIUS

Music technology, especially sampling, which allows existing sounds to be recorded and reused or manipulated at will, has had a major impact on ideas of originality, creativity and ownership. So has the wide availability of pre-programmed features on sound modules, synthesizers, drum machines and keyboards. The producers and DJs in hip-hop, house, techno and underground dance, who select parts of records, add sounds, blend features, combine tracks, restructure or remix, eat away at notions of **authorship**. We must also recognize that postmodernist theory, poststructuralism and deconstruction have strongly challenged notions of organic unity and the composer's expressive presence within his or her music.

POSTMODERN MUSICOLOGY

The rise in recent years of 'feminist musicology', 'critical musicology', and 'gay and lesbian musicology' prompts the question, 'Are we living in an age of alternative musicologies, or are we witnessing the disintegration of musicology as a discipline?' Some critical musicologists consider that the unitary concept of a discipline is part of a now discredited paradigm for musicological thought. The alternative is to view musicology no longer as an autonomous field of academic inquiry but, in the French psychoanalyst and **semiotician** Julia **Kristeva**'s terms, a field of transpositions of various signifying systems. Critical musicology has revealed what it means to regard musicology as an *intertextual field*, and why this, rather than the notion of a *discipline*, offers a more productive epistemological framework for their research.

A Critical Musicology Group was founded in the UK in 1993 to discuss the character and purpose of critical musicology and whether it extends or challenges other forms of musicological inquiry. The term was chosen to indicate a concern with critique, including a critique of musicology itself. The growth in numbers attending meetings over the next two years led to a major conference in Salford in 1995, which attracted some seventy delegates, representing thirty different universities. The group consists not only of those working in more recent fields, such as film music, music semiotics, and constructions of gender and sexuality in music, but also of researchers in ethnomusicology and the psychology of music who have long felt themselves to be out of the musicological mainstream. A *Critical Musicology Journal* was launched on the **Internet** in 1997.

Critical musicologists in the UK are generally agreed that the biggest problem facing current musicology is the collapse of the binary divide between pop and classical; it is the fundamental importance accorded to this perception that sets them apart from the 'new musicologists' of the USA, who tend (with few exceptions) to concentrate on canonic works. The disintegration of high and low as aesthetic values has, of course, been felt already in other subject areas: consider how far cultural studies has encroached upon English as an academic discipline. Critical music-ologists maintain that a new theoretical model capable of embracing all music is urgently needed. Such a model might encompass the following (the intention here is not to put forward a manifesto, but to mark out a terrain and an identity for postmodern musicology).

A concern with social and cultural processes, informed by arguments that musical practices, values and meanings relate to particular historical, political and cultural contexts.

A concern with critical theory and with developing a musical hermeneutics for the analysis of the values and meanings of musical practices and musical texts.

A concern to avoid teleological assumptions of historical narrative (e.g. the 'inevitability' of atonality). Causal narration in musical historiography has been found problematic: genealogical lines connecting one composer (or musical style) with another are forever being redrawn or erased, and music is occasionally conjured up from nowhere (for example, New Orleans jazz).

A readiness to engage with, rather than marginalize, issues of class, generation, gender, sexuality and ethnicity in music, and to address matters such as production, reception and subject position, while questioning notions of genius, canons, universality, aesthetic auto-nomy and **textual** immanence.

A readiness to contest the binary divide between 'classical' and 'popular', since both may be perceived as intimately related to the same social formation.

A readiness to study different cultures with regard to their own specific cultural values, so that a cultural arbitrary is not mis-recognized as an objective truth, but also to recognize the necessity of extending the terms of such study beyond explicit cultural self-evaluation.

A readiness to consider that meanings are intertextual, and that it may be necessary to examine a broad range of discourses in order to explain music, its contexts and the way it functions within them. For example, questions of music and sexuality cannot be considered in isolation from political, biological, psychological, psychoanalytical and aesthetic discourses. There may be no intention, however, to document each area comprehensively.

A readiness to respond to the multiplicity of music's contemporary functions and meanings (for example, the fusions of practices variously described as 'time-based arts' and 'multimedia arts'). This may be achieved by adopting the epistemological position and methodology outlined above (one requiring intertextual study and the blurring of discipline boundaries); it contrasts with a narrow discipline-based study of music as performance art or as composition (typically represented by the printed score).

POSTMODERNISM AND POPULAR CULTURE

JOHN STOREY

Most contributions to the debate on **postmodernism** agree that whatever else it is or might be, postmodernism has something to do with the development of popular culture in the late twentieth century in the advanced capitalist democracies of the West. That is, whether postmodernism is seen as a new historical moment, a new sensibility or a new cultural style, popular culture is cited as a terrain on which these changes can be most readily found.

POPULAR CULTURE AND THE ORIGINS OF POSTMODERNISM

It is in the late 1950s and early 1960s that we see the beginnings of what is now understood as postmodernism. In the work of the American cultural critic, Susan Sontag (*Against Interpretation* (1966)), we encounter the celebration of what she calls a 'new sensibility'. As she explains: 'One important consequence of the new sensibility [is] that the distinction between "high" and "low" culture seems less and less meaningful.'

The postmodern 'new sensibility' rejected the cultural élitism of **modernism**. Although it often 'quoted' popular culture, modernism was marked by a deep suspicion of all things popular. Its entry into the museum and the academy as official culture was undoubtedly made easier (despite its declared antagonism to 'bourgeois philistinism') by its appeal to, and homologous relationship with, the élitism of class society. The response of the postmodern 'new sensibility' to modernism's canonization was a re-evaluation of popular culture. The postmodernism of the 1960s was therefore in part a populist attack on the élitism of modernism. It signalled a refusal of what Andreas Huyssen in *After the Great Divide* (1986) calls 'the great divide . . . [a] discourse which insists on the categorical distinction between high art and mass culture'. Moreover, according to Huyssen, 'To a large extent, it is by the distance we have travelled from this "great divide" between mass culture and modernism that we can measure our own cultural **postmodernity**.' The American and British pop art movement of the 1950s and the 1960s,

147

with its rejection of the distinction between popular and high culture, is postmodernism's first cultural flowering. As pop art's first theorist Lawrence Alloway explains:

> The area of contact was mass produced urban culture: movies, advertising, science fiction, pop music. We felt none of the dislike of commercial culture standard among most intellectuals, but accepted it as a fact, discussed it in detail, and consumed it enthusiastically. One result of our discussions was to take Pop culture out of the realm of 'escapism', 'sheer entertainment', 'relaxation', and to treat it with the seriousness of art (quoted in John Storey, *An Introduction to Cultural Theory and Popular Culture* (1997)).

Seen from this perspective, postmodernism first emerges out of a generational refusal of the categorical certainties of high modernism. The insistence on an absolute distinction between high and popular culture came to be regarded as the 'unhip' assumption of an older generation. One sign of this collapse can be seen in the merging of art and pop music. For example, Peter Blake designed the cover of the Beatles' *Sergeant Pepper's Lonely Hearts Club Band*; Richard Hamilton designed the cover of their 'white album'; Andy Warhol designed the cover of the Rolling Stones' album, *Sticky Fingers*.

POPULAR CULTURE IN THE DEBATE ON POSTMODERNISM

By the mid-1980s, the postmodern 'new sensibility' had become a condition and for many a reason to despair. According to Jean-François **Lyotard** the postmodern condition is marked by a crisis in the status of knowledge in Western societies. This is expressed as incredulity towards '**metanarratives**', such as God, **Marxism**, scientific progress. Steven Connor (*Postmodernist Culture* (1989)) suggests that Lyotard's analysis may be read 'as a disguised allegory of the condition of academic knowledge and institutions in the contemporary world'. Lyotard's 'diagnosis of the postmodern condition is, in one sense, the diagnosis of the final futility of the intellectual'. Lyotard is himself aware of what he calls the contemporary intellectual's 'negative heroism'. Intellectuals have, he argues, been losing their authority since 'the violence and critique mounted against the academy during the sixties'. Iain Chambers (*Popular Culture* (1988)) makes much the same point but from a different perspective. He argues that the debate over postmodernism can in part be understood as 'the symptom of the disruptive ingression of popular culture, its aesthetics and intimate possibilities, into a previously privileged domain. Theory and academic discourses are confronted by the wider, unsystemized, popular networks of cultural production and knowledge. The intellectual's privilege to explain and distribute knowledge is threatened.'

Like Chambers, Angela McRobbie (*Postmodernism and Popular Culture* (1994)) welcomes postmodernism, seeing it as 'the coming into being of those whose voices were historically drowned out by the (modernist) metanarratives of mastery, which were in turn both patriarchal and imperialist'. Postmodernism, she argues, has enfranchised a new body of intellectuals; voices from the margins speaking from positions of **difference**: ethnic, gender, class, sexual preference; those whom she refers to as 'the new generation of intellectuals (often black, female, or working class)'. Kobena Mercer (*Welcome to the Jungle* (1994)) makes a similar point, seeing postmodernism as in part an unacknowledged response to 'the emerging voices, practices and identities of dispersed African, Caribbean and Asian peoples [who have] crept in from the margins of postimperial Britain to dislocate commonplace certainties and consensual "truths" and thus open up new ways of seeing, and understanding'.

For Jean **Baudrillard** (*Simulations* (1983)), hyperrealism is the characteristic mode of postmodernity. In the realm of the **hyperreal**, the 'real' and the imaginary continually implode into each other. The result is that reality and what Baudrillard calls '**simulations**' are experienced as without difference – operating along a roller-coaster continuum. Simulations can often be experienced as more real than the real itself – 'even better than the real thing', in the words of the U2 song.

The evidence for hyperrealism is said to be everywhere. For example, we in the West live in a world in which people write letters addressed to characters in soap operas, making them offers of marriage, sympathizing with their current difficulties, offering them new accommodation, or just writing to ask how they are coping with life. Television villains are regularly confronted in the street and warned about the possible future consequences of not altering their behaviour. Television doctors, television lawyers and television detectives regularly receive requests for advice and help. Baudrillard calls this 'the dissolution of TV into life, the dissolution of life into TV'.

John Fiske claims in *Media Matters* (1994) that postmodern media no longer provide 'secondary representations of reality; they affect and produce the reality that they mediate'. Moreover, in our postmodern world, all events that 'matter' are media events. He cites the example of the arrest of O. J. Simpson: 'Local people watching the chase on TV went to O. J.'s house to be there at the showdown, but took their portable TVs with them in the knowledge that the live event was not a substitute for the mediated one but a complement to it. On seeing themselves on their own TVs, they waved to themselves, for postmodern people have no problem in being simultaneously and indistinguishably livepeople and mediapeople.' These people knew implicitly that the media do not simply report or circulate the news, they produce it. Therefore, in order to be part of the news of O. J. Simpson's arrest, it was not enough to be there, one had to be there on television. In the hyperreal world of the postmodern, there is no longer a clear distinction between a 'real' event and its media **representation**. In the same way, O. J. Simpson's trial cannot be neatly separated into a 'real' event that television then represented as media event. Anyone who watched the proceedings unfold on TV knows that the trial was conducted at least as much for the television audience as it was for those present in the court. Without the presence of the cameras this would have been a very different event indeed.

Fredric **Jameson** is an American Marxist cultural critic who has written a number of very influential essays on postmodernism. According to his account postmodernism is a culture of pastiche, disfigured by the 'complacent play of historical allusion'. Postmodern culture is 'a world in which stylistic innovation is no longer possible, all that is left is to imitate dead styles, to speak through the masks and with the voices of the styles in the imaginary museum'. Rather than a culture of pristine creativity, postmodern culture is a culture of quotations. Instead of 'original' cultural production, we have cultural production born out of other cultural production. It is a culture 'of flatness or depthlessness, a new kind of superficiality in the most literal sense'. A culture of images and surfaces, without 'latent' possibilities, it derives its hermeneutic force from other images, other surfaces. Jameson acknowledges that modernism itself often 'quoted' from other cultures and other historical moments, but he insists that there is a fundamental difference – postmodern cultural **texts** do not just quote other cultures, other historical moments, they randomly cannibalize them to the point where any sense of critical or historical distance ceases to exist – there is only pastiche.

Perhaps his best-known example of the postmodern culture of pastiche is what he calls the 'nostalgia film'. The category could include a number of films from the 1980s and 1990s: *Back to the Future I* and *II*, *Peggy Sue Got Married*, *Rumble Fish*, *Angel Heart*, *Blue Velvet*. He argues that the nostalgia film sets out to recapture the atmosphere and stylistic peculiarities of America in the 1950s. But the nostalgia film is not just another name for the historical film. This is clearly demonstrated by the fact that Jameson's own list includes *Star Wars*. Now it might seem strange to suggest that a film about the future can be nostalgic for the past, but as Jameson explains in 'Postmodernism and Consumer Society' (H. Foster, ed., *Postmodern Culture* (1985)), *Star Wars* 'does not reinvent a picture of the past in its lived totality; rather, [it reinvents] the feel and shape of characteristic art objects of an older period'.

Films such as *Raiders of the Lost Ark*, *Independence Day* and *Robin Hood, Prince of Thieves* operate in a similar way to evoke a sense of the narrative certainties of the past. In this way, according to Jameson, the nostalgia film either recaptures and represents the atmosphere and stylistic features of the past and/or recaptures and represents certain styles of viewing of the past. What is of absolute significance for Jameson ('Postmodernism, or the Cultural Logic of Late Capitalism', *New Left Review* (1984)) is that such films do not attempt to recapture or represent the 'real' past, but always make do with certain cultural myths and stereotypes about the past. They offer what he calls 'false realism', films about other films, representations of other representations (what Baudrillard calls simulations). In this way, history is effaced by 'historicism . . . the random cannibalisation of all the styles of the past, the play of random stylistic allusion'. Here we might cite films like *True Romance* or *Pulp Fiction*. More than this, Jameson insists that our awareness of the play of stylistic allusion 'is now a constitutive and essential part' of our experience of the postmodern film. Again, it is an example of a culture 'in which the history of aesthetic styles displaces "real" history'. This relates to a second stylistic feature Jameson identifies, what he calls schizophrenia. The schizophrenic, he claims, experiences time not as a continuum (past–present–future), but as a perpetual present, which is only occasionally marked by the intrusion of the past or the possibility of a future. The 'reward' for the loss of conventional selfhood (the sense of self as always located within a temporal continuum) is an intensified sense of the present – what Dick Hebdige, in *Hiding the Light* (1988), calls 'acid perspectivism' (suggesting the experience is similar to that of 'tripping' on LSD).

To call postmodern culture schizophrenic is to claim that it has lost its sense of history (and its sense of a future different from the present). It is a culture suffering from 'historical amnesia', locked into the discontinuous flow of perpetual presents. The temporal culture of modernism has given way to the spatial culture of postmodernism.

Two examples of postmodern popular culture

A discussion of postmodernism and popular culture might highlight any number of different cultural forms and cultural practices: television, music video, film, pop music, advertising. I will consider here two prime examples: pop music and television.

Postmodern pop music

As Frith and Horne point out in *Art into Pop* (1987), 'Pop songs are the soundtrack of postmodern daily life, inescapable in lifts and airports, pubs and restaurants, streets and shopping centres and sports grounds'. Connor argues that pop music is perhaps 'the most representative of postmodern cultural forms'.

Jameson distinguishes between modernist and postmodern pop music, making the argument that the Beatles and the Rolling Stones represent a modernist moment, against which punk rock and new wave can be seen as postmodern. In 'Popular Music and Postmodern Theory' (*Cultural Studies* (1991)), Andrew Goodwin quite correctly argues that for various reasons this is a very difficult position to sustain. The Beatles and the Rolling Stones are as different from each other as together they are different from, say, the Clash and Talking Heads. In fact, 'it would be much easier to make an argument in which the distinction is made between the "artifice" of the Beatles and Talking Heads and the "authenticity" of the Rolling Stones and the Clash'.

Goodwin considers a number of ways of seeing pop music and pop music culture as postmodern. Perhaps the most cited aspect is the technological developments that have facilitated the emergence of sampling. He acknowledges the parallel with some postmodern theorizing, but suggests that what is often missed in such claims is the way in which sampling is used. For example, he claims that sampling has a 'historicizing function'; it is often deployed 'to invoke history and authenticity'. To call this process pastiche is to miss the way 'contemporary pop opposes, celebrates and promotes the texts it steals from'.

Rap is perhaps the best example of sampling being used in this way. When asked in an interview to name *the* black means of cultural expression, the African-American cultural theorist Cornel West answered, 'music and preaching'. He went on to say:

> [R]ap is unique because it combines the black preacher and the black music tradition, replacing the liturgical ecclesiastical setting with the African polyrhythms of the street. A tremendous *articulateness* is

syncopated with the African drumbeat, the African funk, into an American postmodernist product: there is no **subject** expressing originary anguish here but a fragmented subject, pulling from past and present, innovatively producing a heterogeneous product (John Storey, ed., *Cultural Theory and Popular Culture* (1997)).

One can make similar claims for British rap as postmodern. Angela McRobbie, as we noted earlier, claims that postmodernism appeals 'to what might be called the new generation of intellectuals (often black, female, or working class)'. The Ruthless Rap Assassins, for example, are black and working class: three street intellectuals articulating their politics with 'a funky North Hulme beat'. They engage in postmodern pla(y)giarism, not as an end in itself, but to construct compelling critiques of the everyday racism of British society. They would certainly reject Jameson's claim that their work is an example of postmodern pastiche. Their **intertextual** play of quotations is not the result of aesthetic exhaustion, but the telling combination of found fragments from a cultural repertoire which by and large denies their existence. These are not the fragments of modernism shored against aesthetic ruin, but fragments combined to condemn those who have sought to deny them a voice within British culture.

Perhaps the best way to think of the relationship between pop music and postmodernism is historically. In most accounts, the moment of postmodernism begins in the late 1950s – the same period as the emergence of pop music. Therefore, in terms of periodization, pop music and postmodernism are more or less simultaneous. This does not necessarily mean that all pop music is postmodern. Using Raymond Williams's model of social formations always consisting of a hierarchy of cultures – 'dominant', 'emergent' and 'residual' – postmodern pop music can be seen as 'emergent' in the 1960s with the late Beatles, and the rock music of the counter-culture, as principal examples, and in the 1970s with 'art school' punk, to become in the late 1980s the 'cultural dominant' of pop music. To see the relationship in this way avoids the either/orism of 'it is all postmodern' or 'none of it is postmodern'. This would allow for the claim that all pop music is in some sense postmodern (potentially so), but that all pop music is not necessarily postmodern.

It is also possible to see the consumption of pop music and the surrounding pop music culture as in itself postmodern. Instead of an approach concerned with identifying and analysing the postmodern text or practice, we might look instead for postmodernism in the emergence of particular patterns of consumption; people who actively seek out and celebrate pastiche. The notion of a particular group of consumers, people who consume with **irony** and take pleasure in the weird, is very suggestive. Fred Pfeil, for example, claims, in 'Postmodernism as a "Structure of Feeling"' (C. Nelson and L. Grossberg, eds., *Marxism and the Interpretation of Culture* (1988)), that in America at least, postmodernism is a particular style of consumption; the way of consuming of a specific social grouping, the professional managerial class. Umberto **Eco** (quoted in R. Boyne and A. Rattansi, eds., *Postmodernism and Society* (1990)), using Charles **Jencks**'s notion of '**double coding**', identifies a similar postmodern sensibility exhibited in an awareness of what he calls the 'already said'. He gives the example of a lover who cannot tell his lover 'I love you madly', and says instead: 'As Barbara Cartland would put it, I love you madly.' We might think also of the hedonistic irony of those for whom flying ducks and garden gnomes are always displayed in knowing inverted commas. Seeing the world in inverted commas can be a way of attacking the normative standards of dominant patterns of taste, but it can also be a means of patronizing those supposedly without taste – those who display their ornaments without the inverted commas.

While academics and other cultural critics argue about whether postmodernism is best understood as text and practice, or as reading formation, the music industry has not been slow to bring text and consumption into combination. There is now a generic/sales category of pop music called postmodern: perhaps the most notable example of this (1988–93) was MTV's programme *Post Modern MTV*. The presenter described the music played on the programme as 'a slightly alternative mix'. This description and the general content of the programme suggested that postmodernism was being used as perhaps little more than another way to market so-called 'indie pop'. This usage has also been taken up by record companies who now market certain performers as postmodern.

POSTMODERN TELEVISION

Television, like pop music, does not have a period of modernism to which it can be 'post'. But, as Jim Collins points out in 'Postmodernism and Television' (R. C. Allen, ed., *Channels of Dicourse, Reassembled* (1992)), television is often seen as the 'quintessence' of postmodern culture. This claim can be made on the basis of a number of television's textual and contextual features. If we take a negative view of postmodernism, as the domain of Baudrillardian simulations, then television seems an obvious example of the process – with its supposed reduction of the complexities of the world to an ever-changing flow of depthless and banal visual imagery. If, on the other hand, we take a positive view of postmodernism, then the visual and verbal practices of television can be put forward, say, as the knowing play of intertextuality (the way one text is inscribed with other texts) and 'radical eclecticism', encouraging and helping to produce the postmodern 'sophisticated bricoleur' (someone who takes pleasure in the intertextuality of a text). For example, a television series like *Twin Peaks*, both constitutes an audience as bricoleurs and in turn is watched by an audience who celebrate its bricolage.

Collins uses *Twin Peaks* as a means of bringing together the different strands of the relationship between postmodernism and television. *Twin Peaks* is chosen because it 'epitomises the multiple dimensions of tele-visual postmodernism'. He argues that the postmodernism of the series is the result of a number of interrelated factors: David **Lynch**'s reputation as a film maker, the stylistic features of the series, and, finally, its commercial intertextuality (the marketing of related prod-ucts: for example, *The Secret Diary of Laura Palmer*). At the economic level, *Twin Peaks* represents an attempt by American network television to win back affluent sections of the television audience lost to cable and video. In this sense, *Twin Peaks* marks a new era in network television's view of the audience. Instead of seeing the audience as an homogeneous mass, the series was part of a strategy in which the audience is seen as fragmented, consisting of different segments – stratified by age, class, gender, geography and race – of interest to different advertisers. Mass appeal now involves attempts to intertwine the different segments to enable them to be sold to different sections of the advertising market. The significance of *Twin Peaks*, at least from this perspective, is that it was marketed to appeal to those most likely to have been tempted away from network television by VCR, cable and cinema. In short, the so-called 'yuppie' generation.

Collins demonstrates this by addressing the way the series was pro-moted. First, there was the intellectual appeal – Lynch as auteur, *Twin Peaks* as avant-garde television. This was followed by *Twin Peaks* as soap opera. Together the two appeals soon coalesced into a postmodern reading formation in which the series was 'valorised as would-be cinema and would-be soap opera'. This was supported and sustained by the **polysemic** play (capacity to generate multiple meanings) of *Twin Peaks* itself. The series is, as Collins suggests, 'aggressively eclectic', not only in its use of conventions from Gothic horror, police procedural, science fiction and soap opera, but also in the different ways – from straight to parody – these conventions are mobilized in particular scenes. Collins also notes the play of 'tonal variations . . . within and across scenes' – moving the audience from moments of parodic distance to moments of emphatic intimacy, continually playing with our expectations. Although this is a known aspect of Lynch's filmic technique, it is also a characteristic 'reflective of changes in television entertainment and of viewer involvement in that entertainment'. In other words, this fluctuation in generic conventions 'describes not just *Twin Peaks* but the very act of moving up and down the televisual scale of the cable box. Viewing perspectives are no longer mutually exclusive, but set in perpetual alternation.' What makes *Twin Peaks* different from other soap operas is not that it produces shifting viewing positions, but that it 'explicitly acknowledges this oscillation and the suspended nature of television viewing . . . [It] doesn't just acknowledge the multiple subject positions that television generates; it recognises that one of the great pleasures of the televisual text is that very suspension and exploits it for its own sake.' In this way, *Twin Peaks* is not a reflection of postmodernism, nor is it an allegory of postmodernism, it is a specific address to the postmodern condition – a postmodern text – and as such it helps to define the possibilities of entertainment in the contemporary capitalist world.

Postmodernism, popular culture and questions of value

Postmodernism has disturbed many of the old certainties surrounding questions of cultural value. It has become somewhat of a commonplace to demonstrate how canons of value form and re-form in response to the social and political concerns of those with cultural power. To the less watchful eye, the changes often seem insignificant – changes at the perimeters, relative stability at the core – but even when the canonical texts remain the same, how and why they are valued certainly changes. So much so that they are hardly the same texts from one historical moment to the next. As the Four Tops put it, in a slightly different context: 'It's the same old song / But with a different meaning since you've been gone.' Or to put it in a less danceable discourse, the cultural text under the sign of the postmodern is not the source of value, but a site where the construction of value – variable values – can take place.

Perhaps the most significant thing about postmodernism for the student of popular culture is the recognition that there is no absolute categorical difference between high and popular culture. This is not to say that one text or practice might not be 'better' (for what/for whom, etc., must always be decided and made clear) than another text or practice. But it is to say that there are no longer any easy reference points that will automatically preselect for us the good from the bad. Some might regard such a situation (or even the description of such a situation) with horror – the end of standards. On the contrary, without easy recourse to fixed categories of value, it calls for rigorous, if always contingent, standards, if our task is to separate the good from the bad, the usable from the obsolete, the progressive from the reactionary. As John Fekete points out in *Life after Postmodernism* (1987): 'The prospect of learning to be at ease with limited warranties, and with the responsibility for issuing them, without the false security of inherited guarantees, is promising for a livelier, more colourful, more alert, and, one hopes, more tolerant culture that draws enjoyment from the dappled relations between meaning and value.'

Fekete's point is not significantly different from the argument made by Susan Sontag in *Against Interpretation* at the birth of the postmodern 'new sensibility'. As she explains: 'From the vantage point of this new sensibility, the beauty of a machine or of the solution to a mathematical problem, of a painting by Jasper Johns, of a film by Jean-Luc Godard, and of the personalities and music of the Beatles is equally accessible.'

Postmodernism has certainly changed the theoretical and the cultural basis on which to think about popular culture. In fact, the collapse of the distinction (if this is the case) between high and popular culture may signify that at last it may be possible to use the term popular culture and mean nothing more than *culture* liked by many people.

POSTMODERNISM, MODERNITY, AND THE TRADITION OF DISSENT

LLOYD SPENCER

It is perhaps characteristic of our age – the age of designer labels, when almost every aspect of culture and identity seems amenable to 'packaging' – that there should be such a fearsome fuss over the label '**postmodern**'. As the novelist and critic Gilbert Adair notes in *The Postmodernist Always Rings Twice* (1992), few 'isms' have provoked as much perplexity and suspicion as postmodernism.

The very term 'postmodern' is a paradox and a provocation. **Modernity**, in the sense of the 'now' which surrounds us, is not something we can be 'post'. But the modernity referred to is not the 'now' of the thoroughly modern. Modernity is a long epoch of historical change, fuelled by scientific and technological development and dominated by the spread – *extensively* across the world and *intensively* into every nook and cranny of the soul – of the capitalist market economy. Throughout the modern era, cultural, philosophical and political debates have marked out an intellectual space between the declining authority of the Church on the one hand and, on the other, the economic and technical imperatives forcing the pace of change.

Modernity even in this sense, of a centuries-old tradition of change and debate about change, can hardly be said to have come to an end. The declining role of religion and the pace of economic and technological change are factors that will shape the future as decisively as they have shaped our past. But in the latter part of the twentieth century something has changed in the very nature of tradition and in the way that we relate to the past. Every aspect of the past is made accessible, available. But it is *made* available: mediated, packaged, presented and re-presented. Postmodernism could be described as that variant of **modernism** which has given up hope of freeing itself from the ravages of modernity or of mastering the forces unleashed by modernity.

I

'Modernity' – however it is conceived – had a history several centuries old before it came to be formulated under that label. Modernism in art was echoed in the debates that arose in philosophy and social theory. But it should not be forgotten that there were reactionary modernisms as well as progressive, and that most forms of modernism were a compound of quite disparate, ill-assorted ideas. If modernism implies enthusiasm about some aspects of modernity, it was usually accomplished – in the same writers, in the same works – by despair at other aspects of modernity. Modernism is as much an antidote to modernity as it is to its party-programme.

If we choose to call these times we live in 'postmodern' then we have to recognize as 'postmodern' intellectuals of a wide variety of cultural and political orientations. That at least should be clear from the variety of positions and postures, beliefs and commitments evidenced in this dictionary. If 'postmodernity' is a way of describing the times in which we live, then we may justly characterize as 'postmodernism' a diverse range of responses to those times. We use labels such as 'modernity', 'modernism' to refer to historical epochs and trends which we feel constrained to grasp *in their complexity*. The 'postmodernism' of our own time demands similarly to be viewed in its complexity.

Our own postmodern age is extraordinarily self-conscious. It subjects itself to the most glaring scrutiny and to endless commentary. Writers, theologians and artists have their part in this process as do academics and other intellectuals. So far the cast-list of these scrutinizers and commentators is a familiar one. What has changed is the role of these agents in the age of the mass media. The postmodern age is one in which cultural activity is dominated by media industries capable of appealing directly to a public (itself the beneficiary of 'mass education') over the heads of any cultural élite.

Mass media and the culture industries, informatics and cybernetics, virtual reality and an obsession with 'image' – postmodernists and their detractors map the changes in the increasingly synthetic fabric of social life in very similar ways. Postmodernists present postmodernism as the set of critical tools needed to grasp and criticize new and changing circumstances. For critics of postmodernism the very 'appropriateness' of postmodernist ideas is grounds for suspicion. Some postmodernists (**Baudrillard** is the obvious example) write in a style that is ostentatiously 'postmodern' when they write about postmodernism. The close fit between the tools of criticism and the circumstances criticized opens postmodernists to the accusation – which has been oft-repeated – that their thinking is itself symptomatic of the ills that need to be diagnosed.

II

Postmodernism, like modernism before it, has produced a profusion of definitions and redefinitions. So it is only appropriate that it should call forth this dictionary. Readers who come to this volume in search of clear and stable definitions may begin to feel a sense of vertigo as they explore the entries. Not only does what counts as 'postmodern' change from writer to writer, but what is 'meant' by most other terms depends on who is doing the 'meaning', and what they mean by 'meaning'.

One of the symptoms of the 'postmodern condition' is a hyper-sensitivity to the ways in which words are strategically defined and polemically deployed. In the early years of this century, the poets of the age of high modernism seemed each to produce their own virtual thesaurus of the language. Now towards the end of the century sociologists and other theorists have been made aware of the constraints imposed by language and engage in related processes of linguistic gymnastics (or linguistic mud-wrestling).

Not only are 'postmodernism', 'postmodernity' and 'the postmodern' difficult to define, but like their ('-modern-') counterparts, they refer to processes of definition and redefinition. At the heart of debates concerning modernism/postmodernism lies the question of 'meaning' itself (or of *the meaning of 'meaning'*) and a host of heated arguments over the meanings of particular key terms (including the various cognates of 'the modern' and 'the postmodern'). The result is that in many contemporary debates these labels (and their cognates) obscure more than they clarify. Inherently vague, ambiguous and slippery, these terms are continually used in conflicting and even contradictory ways. Even when this confusion is acknowledged, there seems to be no obvious way out of the maze – and no route back to a simpler clear view of the intellectual landscape.

III

Dissenting from postmodernity is difficult for at least three interrelated reasons. First, postmodernity is still so amorphous. Although it is all-but ubiquitous it remains ill-defined. Second, the 'postmodern' emerges into fierce debates about the role of language and almost all commentators self-consciously deploy their terms and definitions with strategic, often combative intention. On all sides, agreeing the terms of the debate is less important than acting politically on and in the domain of language itself. The result is a multiplicity of competing definitions of post-modernity. Third, dissent from postmodernism is especially difficult because postmodernism – the awkward label announces this at the very least – is itself so thoroughly imbued with the spirit of dissent. By constantly striking an attitude of dissent, postmodernism both declares its difference from a previous tradition of dissent – modernism – and at the same time accentuates the attitude which it shares with its predecessor. Postmodernism is always having it both ways: it is both the definitive end and overcoming of modernism and, at the same time, modernism under new management.

Although it has become established in cultural and intellectual discussion over recent decades the term 'postmodernity' has never gained any precise or clear definition; it has gained currency instead as a vague and all-embracing notion referring to a wide variety of ways in which we have succeeded to the ambiguous legacy of modernity and of its late apologists, the modernists. Postmodernism is much less a programme or intellectual framework than it is a mood or *Stimmung* – the *Zeitgeist*, a 'feeling in the air'.

If postmodernism can be most accurately described as a certain mood or *Stimmung*, then it is one characterized by ambivalence and uncertainty. Postmodernism did not announce itself bravely and proudly but seems to have slunk over the horizon. Postmodernism has been characterized by dissent and disillusionment in equal measure. Although some of the products or manifestations which are grouped under the heading of postmodernism are playful or joyous, 'postmodernism' often seems to revert to an attitude of an awkward and petulant teenager, wavering between anger and revolt on the one hand and sullen reproach and refusal on the other. Postmodernism presents itself as a 'historical complex' – complete with its neuroses and obsessions. And legions of therapists and counsellors are constantly at work on the personality disorders of the *Zeitgeist*.

IV

Throughout its long history, modernity, in all its guises, has been characterized by the tension between impulses which were critical or sceptical – destructive or negative impulses – and other impulses which were more positive, affirmative – impulses of hope and longing. Constructive and **deconstructive** tendencies have been closely intertwined.

Postmodernism can be seen as an extension of the critical, sceptical, dissenting – even nihilistic – impulse of modernity. It is treated in this way by many of its critics. And for many critics of postmodernity, this is exactly their difficulty. Under the 'postmodern condition' dissent becomes generalized: it can seem to involve 'dissent in principle' or even 'dissent from everything possible'.

At the same time, postmodernism is sometimes claimed to be a new form of realism. Postmodernism includes also the call for a return to common sense, for pragmatism in the face of the wilder utopian visions indulged in by modernism. As such it is reproached by its critics, especially **Marxist** ones, as leading to easy assimilation or accommodation with the status quo. Consider this attack on Baudrillard by Douglas Kellner:

> Baudrillard is still read and received as a political radical, and those who are becoming increasingly attracted to his thought generally perceive themselves as 'radicals' of some sort ... Baudrillard is the latest example of critical criticism which criticizes everything, but rarely affirms anything of much danger to the status quo ... A court jester of the society he mocks, he safely simulates criticism, advertises his wares and proceeds to enjoy the follies of the consumer and media society (*Jean Baudrillard: From Marxism to Postmodernism and Beyond* (1989)).

It is a recurrent gesture of the 'postmodern' moment to be 'critical' – of Western rationality, **logocentricism**, humanism, the legacy of the **Enlightenment**, the centred **subject**, etc. The most frequent refrain among dissenters from postmodernism is 'Critique in the name of what?' Richard J. Bernstein offers one of the most eloquent explorations of this quandary: '[T]he very "grammar" of critique requires some standard, some measure, some basis for critique. Otherwise there is – as **Habermas** claims – the danger of the critical impulse consuming itself.' And he goes on to cite Jacques **Derrida**, so often claimed by friends and foes as a prototypical postmodernist: 'I cannot conceive of a radical critique which would not be ultimately motivated by some sort of affirmation, acknowledged or not' (Richard Kearney, ed., *Dialogues with Contemporary Continental Thinkers* (1984)).

V

Nihilistic, subjectivist, amoral, fragmentary, arbitrary, defeatist, wilful; the terms sound familiar. They constitute some of the core vocabulary used in criticism of postmodernism. It is worth pausing to reflect that these terms are not only in wide circulation today – they have much justification – but that they have a surprisingly long and respectable pedigree.

In the first half of this century disapproving critics, such as Georg Lukács, deplored the tendencies (nihilism, irony, fragmentation) of *modernist* literature (Dostoyevsky, Kafka, Musil) in just these terms. In doing so they – intentionally – echoed the warnings issued a hundred years earlier by **Hegel** against the subjectivism of his romantic contemporaries (Novalis, the brothers Schlegel, Schleiermacher and Fries).

The fact that postmodernism – or, at least, the nihilistic tendency it contains – has such a long tradition is fully recognized by leading postmodernists. Jonathan Arac long ago put forward the hypothesis that postmodernism always has been in search of tradition while pretending to innovation. In diagnosing what he called *The Postmodern Condition*, Lyotard presented this condition as one that occurs again and again throughout history: 'What, then is the postmodern? . . . It is undoubtedly a part of the modern . . . A work can become modern only if it is first postmodern. Postmodernism thus understood is not modernism at its end but in the nascent state, and this state is constant.'

Lyotard has unearthed many worthy precursors of the postmodern. In considering the criticisms levelled at postmodernism it might be worthwhile to follow his example and to examine an important precedent.

Denis Diderot (1713–84) gave twenty years of his life to editing the great French *Encyclopédie*. Diderot was at the centre of French Enlightenment circles. In 1761, in *Rameau's Nephew*, Diderot drew a portrait of the new man. Rameau's nephew is a *philosophe* like himself and like his former friend, Jean-Jacques Rousseau. He is an assertive, self-conscious and self-**ironizing** citizen of the republic of letters. Rameau's nephew has absorbed all of the ('**antifoundational**') arguments against traditional forms of moral authority, the Church, the state. The result is that Rameau's nephew declares himself to be utterly amoral, absolutely self-seeking and nihilistic.

Rameau's nephew is the classical prototype of the nihilist tendencies which have drawn fire from the critics of postmodernism. But Diderot's tale gives the devil the best tunes and offers no effective antidote to the dangerous amoralism and subjectivism so successfully evoked. So the tale itself could be claimed for the very postmodernism it attacks.

Diderot himself felt the tale so dangerous that he left it unpublished. Diderot's most personal reflections show how very much he wanted to be a good man, a moral person. But they show, too, Diderot's awareness that if moral codes were not handed down from above then moral awareness will inevitably involve uncertainty, ambiguity and doubt.

That a moral impulse can and must survive in the postmodernist landscape is a message repeated in book after book by Zygmunt

Bauman. Bauman's postmodern ethics – which include the notion that we must not attempt to eradicate ambiguity but instead must learn to face it, and to live with it – would be well-understood by his Enlightenment precursor, Diderot.

VI

When postmodernism is advanced in a thoughtful, non-polemical form – such as in the various recent writings of Bauman – it demands a new ascetism and modesty. It demands that we be scrupulously responsible not only about our actions but even about our hopes and dreams.

To dissent from the prevailing postmodern disenchantment with all previous theoretical frameworks, programmes, social movements appears to make one guilty of wanting to resuscitate worn-out illusions, to re-enchant one's world, or at least one's outlook on it.

One way of drawing the line between postmodernism and its critics is to focus on postmodernism's refusal of the utopian, dream-like elements which have accompanied the constant change of modernity. Modernisms, including Marxism, dreamt of a better world. Legislating for this world on the basis of this dream of a better one is seen as the cardinal sin of that modernism which postmodernism seeks to go beyond.

The antagonism between many postmodernists and many neo-Marxists revolves around this fraught issue. Postmodernists treat the authoritarianism of communist regimes as a result of having tried to realize an unrealizable dream, or having tried to lay hands on utopia and to engineer it in real societies.

Marx himself criticized what he ridiculed as the 'utopian' socialists. He always respected the Jewish prohibition on investigating the future. But for Marx, his refusal to speculate on a future communist society was an aspect of the 'scientific' nature of his socialist social science.

It could not be clearer that, for Marx, capitalism – the unique object of Marx's historical materialism – is a *moral* issue. Throughout his life, Marx's thinking expressed his fierce political commitment. And the question of the relation of theory to practice has always been a crucial one within the Marxist tradition. For seventy years after Lenin's victory in Russia this question became increasingly entangled and intransigent for Western Marxist intellectuals. Although many Western communist parties and trade union organizations developed authoritarian forms of organization, the totalitarian form of communism established in Soviet Russia attracted relatively few supporters among leading Western

Marxist intellectuals. On the other hand, Chinese communism and especially the 'Cultural Revolution' initiated in China by Mao was viewed with some enthusiasm by many during the student protests of the late 1960s.

Many of the leading figures associated with French postmodernism, including Lyotard and Baudrillard, emerged from Marxist and 'post-Marxist' groupings within France. Reaction against totalitarianism within the Soviet Union had its parallels in reaction against the closed minds and authoritarian practices within the politicized French left. By the late twentieth century both Marxism and modernism had become easy targets for the dissenting impulse within postmodernism. Both had been institutionalized, both had become associated with an 'establishment' – even where this was the 'establishment' of oppositional groups, trade unions, party organizations, academic faculties.

Today the very notion of Marxist political practice has a paradoxical ring to it. On the other hand, Marx's theoretical insights and achievements are now so widely accepted that they have long since ceased to be the property of any particular political orientation or grouping. Whoever seeks to understand society today in sociological and historical terms will find themselves borrowing, correcting and extending Marx's ideas. Or, as the Marxist historian Eric Hobsbawm puts it, 'we are all Marxists now'.

Not surprisingly much of the fiercest criticism of postmodernist trends has come from writers who feel that they continue to work within the Marxist tradition in one way or another: Alex Callinicos, for example, is a Marxist who stresses that the nature of exploitation remains fundamentally unchanged. In order to understand the changes taking place in society it is essential to begin by analysing the mechanisms whereby surplus-value is extracted. Fredric **Jameson** has developed a Lukácsian or Hegelian–Marxist perspective on historical development and treats postmodernism as expressing the 'logic of late-capitalism'. In other words, postmodernism is treated as symptomatic of the capitalist system at a particular phase in its development. In order to develop a critical perspective appropriate to our consumerist cyber-society Douglas Kellner, in *Jean Baudrillard*, has argued that the **Critical Theory** tradition of the **Frankfurt School** has more to offer than currently fashionable French theory:

> I am not sure that we have now transcended and left behind modernity, class politics, labour and production, imperialism, fascism and the phenomena described by classical and neo-Marxism, as well as by other political and social theories which Baudrillard rejects out of hand.

Kellner, like Jameson, has conducted a very serious engagement with postmodern thought and shows in his own analyses of contemporary society that he has drawn a great deal from the postmodernists. Nevertheless, he insists, French postmodernists have been over-hasty in their dismissal of the neo-Marxist tradition of cultural analysis:

> New French Theorists like Baudrillard, Lyotard and Foucault have made a serious theoretical and political mistake in severing their work from the Marxian critique of capitalism precisely at a point when the logic of capital has been playing an increasingly important role in structuring the new stage of society which I conceptualize as a new stage of capitalism – capitalism as techno-capital.

For the postmodernists, Lyotard represents the view that in all the advanced societies '(socialist) struggles and their instruments have been transformed into regulators of the system'. Against the postmodernists, neo-Marxist critics allege that postmodernist criticism is always already complicit in the system that it criticizes.

VII

Postmodernism is a label one can attach to cultural manifestations across the entire globe. Postmodernism in philosophy and cultural theory, however, has had a distinct French accent. Leading cultural theorists such as Baudrillard and Lyotard developed away from variants of Marxism with which they were familiar in Paris. Unfortunately there has been no sustained attempt on the part of French intellectuals to engage seriously with the way in which the Marxian tradition was developed in the German-speaking realm. It has largely been left to English-speaking writers, such as Jameson and Kellner, to bring the two traditions into critical engagement with one another.

The one notable exception to this generalization would seem to be the way in which Lyotard's French theory has defined itself in opposition to the thinking of the German social theorist, Jürgen Habermas. In *The Postmodern Condition* Lyotard develops his most-quoted definitions of postmodernism (as a suspicion of **metanarratives**) as an explicit critique of Habermas's ambitious intellectual project. Habermas is singled out for this unique distinction because his aims remain unashamedly synthetic and constructive (rather than analytical and deconstructive). Habermas acknowledges ideals (albeit highly abstract ones) which he claims as universal and his social theory is continually related to accounts of human evolution (including the phases of history). Particular difficulty has surrounded Habermas's notion of an 'interest in consensus', which occupies a crucial role at the heart of his extensive theorization of communication and discourse. Habermas, for whom the concept of modernity is central, is frequently taken to be the boldest defender of the unfinished project of modernity, a forceful champion of the Enlightenment legacy.

Habermas presented an early response to postmodernism in social theory in an essay entitled 'Modernity versus Postmodernity' (*New German Critique*, 22 (1981)) in which he drew comparisons between postmodern theory and the neo-conservatism. A more sustained and substantial treatment of what Habermas sees as the flaws and dangers of postmodernism was presented in his twelve lectures on *The Philosophical Discourse of Modernity* (1985). But here, too, the engagement is anything else but direct. Habermas treats of **Foucault** and Derrida as well as the antecedents of postmodern thinking in **Nietzsche**, **Heidegger** and the surrealist Georges Bataille. But he is more concerned to trace what he sees as a more promising basis for understanding modernity (and post-modernity) through the insights of Hegel and the theorization of late capitalism (and late modernism) by **Horkheimer** and **Adorno**. In a collection of essays devoted to *Habermas and Modernity* (Richard J. Bernstein, ed. (1985)) Richard **Rorty** gives a succinct summary of the way in which Habermas and Lyotard talk past one another:

> Anything that Habermas will count as retaining a 'theoretical approach' will be counted by an incredulous Lyotard as a 'meta-narrative.' Anything that abandons such an approach will be counted by Habermas as 'neo-conservative,' because it drops the notions which have been used to justify the various reforms which have marked the history of the Western democracies since the Enlightenment, and which are still being used to criticize the socio-economic institutions of both the Free and the Communist worlds. Abandoning a standpoint which is, if not transcendental, at least 'universalistic,' seems to Habermas to betray the social hopes which have been central to liberal politics. So we find French critics of Habermas ready to abandon liberal politics in order to avoid universalistic philosophy, and Habermas trying to hang on to univer-salistic philosophy, with all its problems in order to support liberal politics.

VIII

As Richard J. Bernstein has reminded us in *The New Constellation* (1990), the 'most fundamental, powerful – and perhaps seductive – theme in Hegel's philosophy is the promise and fulfilment of reconcili-ation (*Versöhnung*)'. Habermas's treatment of communication and discourse partakes of this spirit and on this basis seeks to transcend 'systematically distorted communication': 'The "postmodern" celebration of contingency, fragmentation, fissures, **singularity**, **plurality**, and ruptures (that defy reconciliation) are profoundly anti-Hegelian gestures.' From Hegel to Habermas (and beyond in many other traditions still active) there persists the hope not only of reconciliation among the living but also reconciliation with the dead. The postmodernist attitude of citing, parodying, pastiching, using and reusing the past is surely a significant symptom of our times. The postmodernist intellectual metropolis is one without a cemetery – there is no 'dead centre' to its town.

At the start of the eighteenth century a great debate raged between the 'ancients' and 'moderns'. The 'ancients' held that the classical civilizations of Greece and Rome were the source of all standards and all literary ideals. The 'moderns' contended that new times required new standards and new forms of expression. What we should remember in this context is that this was a debate between men raised on Greek and Latin. Even those who belonged to the 'modern' camp, from whom emerged the leading figures of the Enlightenment, were steeped in the classics. All the participants to the debate were on familiar terms with Aristotle and Aristophanes, with Tacitus and Cicero.

To be 'modern' in the sense of feeling superior to, and hence cut off from, all one's ancestors would be an extraordinarily disorienting and alienating experience. We need to acknowledge the authority of at least some of the ancients. Throughout modernity the canon of 'classics' is continually recreated. But until fairly recently, the search always led back to the huge variety off prototypes and precedents played out in the ancient world. From this stems both the universalism and the 'élitism' which characterizes various forms of modernism, from the reforming zeal of the Enlightenment *philosophes* to the aesthetic experiments of the twentieth-century avant-garde.

The evolution of mass education is one of the key factors in shaping the social history of the twentieth century. Education is the one 'great hope' which, at the end of the century, we have not entirely given up. One precondition (and effect) of universal education was a dramatically reduced role for Latin, Greek and classics. For the first half of this century, modernism operated in an intellectual landscape in which the classics, in this sense, still represented an active if ambivalent legacy. Classics came more and more to be the cornerstone of a privileged education, allowing privileged access to the heritage of the past. At the same time among disaffected, yet almost always 'well-educated', intellectuals, the perennial subversiveness of classical authors and classical themes (myths and mythemes) fuelled the radical universalism of modernism.

Meanwhile the demands of the market turn yesterday's fashions into something already ancient, utterly out of date – into something ripe for revival as 'classic'. The cycles of history are driven by the mandarins of a commercial culture, in order that they, and others, might turn a profit. Among all the culture industries, it is the heritage industry which experiences the most sustained boom.

IX

The radical avant-garde wish was to overcome the gulf between art and society or between art and everyday life. The aestheticized world prophesied by a modernist avant-garde in the earlier half of this century has, in our own time, become all too real: it has become the **hyperreal**. And this state of hyperreality has been achieved not by the artistic avant-garde but by commodities and the countless creative workers who sustain our consumer culture. After surrealism, no new aesthetic movement of collective importance operative across more than one art form emerged. As Douglas Kellner has pointed out in *Jean Baudrillard*, postmodernism is continually parodying the revolutionary gestures of the avant-garde earlier in the twentieth-century. This is true of at least one brand of postmodernism which, when it came on the market, announced itself with shrill insistence as something utterly new:

> [A]lmost every discussion of Baudrillard in English seems to presuppose that he is right, that we are in something like a postmodern condition, that we have left modernity behind and are in a qualitatively new society where the old categories and old distinctions no longer hold. Such a vision rests, I believe, partly on wishful thinking . . .

We have lately learnt to be more modest in our modernity, more cautious in our hopes, more sceptical of the promise of the future. We cannot any longer take the project of modernity simply on trust. Even this postmodern tentativeness is no longer new. Postmodernity is ready to enter dictionaries and encyclopedias as it has already entered into countless textbooks. Debates over the traditions of modernity, late-modernity, and postmodernity will continue, and will continue to generate sober reflection on where we have come from and where we are going.

SELECT BIBLIOGRAPHY

The following is a select bibliography of works on postmodernism and related issues discussed over the course of the essays. Where the original date of publication differs from a translation (or from a later revised edition), the former is given in square brackets after the title.

Adair, Gilbert, *The Postmodernist Always Rings Twice: Reflections on Culture in the 90s* (London: Fourth Estate, 1992).

Allen, R. C., ed., *Channels of Discourse, Reassembled* (London: Routledge, 1992).

Ang, Ien, *Living Room Wars: Rethinking Media Audiences for a Postmodern World* (London: Routledge, 1996).

Baudrillard, Jean, *America* [1986], trans. Chris Turner (London and New York: Verso, 1988).

Seduction [1979], trans. Brian Singer (Basingstoke and London: Macmillan, 1990).

Simulations, trans. Paul Foss, Paul Patton and Philip Beitchman (New York: Semiotext(e), 1983).

Bauman, Zygmunt, *Freedom* (Milton Keynes: Open University Press, 1988).

Bernstein, Richard J., ed., *Habermas and Modernity* (Oxford: Polity Press, 1985).

Boyne, R. and Rattansi, A., eds., *Postmodernism and Society* (London: Macmillan, 1990).

Bradbury, Malcolm and Ruland, Richard, *From Puritanism to Postmodernism: A History of American Literature* (London: Routledge, 1991).

Braidotti, Rosi, *Nomadic Subjects: Embodiment and Sexual Difference in Contemporary Feminist Theory* (New York: Columbia University Press, 1994).

Butler, Judith, *Gender Trouble: Feminism and the Subversion of Identity* (New York and London: Routledge, 1990).

Callinicos, Alex, *Against Post-Modernism: A Marxist Perspective* (Cambridge: Polity Press, 1990).

Connor, Steven, *Postmodernist Culture: An Introduction to Theories of the Contemporary* (Oxford and New York: Basil Blackwell, 1989).

Debord, Guy, *The Society of the Spectacle* (Detroit: Black and Red, 1970).

Deleuze, Gilles and Guattari, Félix, *Anti-Oedipus* [1972], trans. Robert Hurley, Mark Seem and Helen Lane (London: The Athlone Press, 1984).

Derrida, Jacques, *Of Grammatology* [1967], trans. Gayatri Chakravorty Spivak (Baltimore and London: The Johns Hopkins University Press, 1976).

Specters of Marx: The State of the Debt, the Work of Mourning, and the New International, [1993], trans. Peggy Kamuf (New York and London: Routledge, 1994).

Docherty, Thomas, ed., *Postmodernism: A Reader* (Hemel Hempstead: Harvester Wheatsheaf, 1993).

Eagleton, Terry, *The Illusions of Postmodernism* (Oxford: Basil Blackwell, 1996).

Fekete, John, ed., *Life after Postmodernism: Essays on Value and Culture* (Basingstoke and London: Macmillan, 1987).

Fiske, John, *Media Matters* (Minneapolis: University of Minnesota Press, 1994).

Frith, S. and Horne, H., *Art into Pop* (New York and London: Methuen, 1987).

Foster, Hal, ed., *The Anti-Aesthetic: Essays on Postmodern Culture* (Port Townsend, WA: Bay Press, 1983). Reprinted as *Postmodern Culture* (London and Concord, MA: Pluto Press, 1985).

Foucault, Michel, *The History of Sexuality*, I–III. I, *The History of Sexuality: An Introduction* [1976], trans. Robert Hurley (Harmondsworth: Penguin, 1981); II, *The Use of Pleasure* [1984], trans. Robert Hurley (Harmondsworth: Penguin, 1987); III, *The Care of the Self* [1984], trans. Robert Hurley (Harmondsworth: Penguin, 1988).

Fukuyama, Francis, *The End of History and the Last Man* (New York: The Free Press, 1992).

Fuss, D., ed., *Inside/Out: Lesbian Theories, Gay Theories* (London: Routledge, 1991).

Goodwin, Andrew, 'Popular Music and Postmodern Theory' (*Cultural Studies*, 5, 1991, pp. 174–203).

Gray, Ann and McGuigan, Jim, eds., *Studying Culture: An Introductory Reader* (London: Edward Arnold, 1993).

Habermas, Jürgen, *The Philosophical Discourse of Modernity* [1985], trans. Frederick Lawrence (Cambridge and Oxford: Polity Press and Basil Blackwell, 1987).

Halley, Peter, *Collected Essays 1981–1987* (New York: Sounabend Gallery, 1987).

Haraway, Donna, *Simians, Cyborgs, and Women* (London: Free Association Books, 1991).

Humm, Maggie, ed., *Feminisms: A Reader* (Hemel Hempstead: Harvester, 1992).

Hutcheon, Linda, *A Poetics of Postmodernism: History, Theory, Fiction* (New York and London: Routledge, 1988).

Huyssen, Andreas, *After the Great Divide: Modernism, Mass Culture, Postmodernism* (Bloomington: Indiana University Press, 1986).

Jameson, Fredric, *Postmodernism, or, The Cultural Logic of Late Capitalism* (Durham, NC: Duke University Press, 1991).

Jencks, Charles, *The Language of Post-Modern Architecture* [1975], 4th revd. edn. (London: Academy Editions, 1984).
  What is Post-modernism? (London: Art and Design, 1986).
Kaplan, E. Ann, *Rocking Around the Clock: Music, Television, Postmodernism, and Consumer Culture* (New York and London: Routledge 1987).
Kellner, Douglas, *Jean Baudrillard: From Marxism to Postmodernism and Beyond* (Cambridge: Polity Press, 1989).
Laclau, Ernesto and Mouffe, Chantal, *Hegemony and Socialist Strategy: Towards a Radical Democratic Politics* (London: Verso, 1985).
Lyotard, Jean-François, *The Differend: Phrases in Dispute* [1983], trans. George Van Den Abbeele (Manchester: Manchester University Press, 1988).
  The Inhuman: Reflections on Time [1988], trans. Geoffrey Bennington and Rachel Bowlby (Oxford: Blackwell, 1991).
  (with Jean-Loup Thebaud), *Just Gaming* [1979], trans. Wlad Godzich (Manchester: Manchester University Press, 1985).
  Libidinal Economy [1974], trans. Iain Hamilton Grant (London: The Athlone Press, 1993).
  The Postmodern Condition: A Report on Knowledge [1979], trans. Geoffrey Bennington and Brian Massumi (Manchester: Manchester University Press, 1984).
McCaffery, Larry, *Postmodern Fiction: A Bio-Biographical Guide* (Westport, CT: Greenwood, 1986).
McHale, Brian, *Postmodernist Fiction* (New York and London: Methuen, 1987).
McRobbie, Angela, *Postmodernism and Popular Culture* (London and New York: Routledge, 1994).
Mercer, Kobena, *Welcome to the Jungle* (London: Routledge, 1994).
Modleski, Tania, *Feminism Without Women: Culture and Criticism in a 'Postfeminist' Age* (New York and London: Routledge, 1991).
Morris, Meaghan, *The Pirate's Fiancée: Feminism, Reading, Postmodernism* (London: Verso, 1988).
Nicholson, L. J., ed., *Feminism/Postmodernism* (London: Routledge, 1990).
Norris, Christopher, *The Truth about Postmodernism* (Oxford: Basil Blackwell, 1993).
  What's Wrong with Postmodernism: Critical Theory and the Ends of Philosophy (Hemel Hempstead: Harvester Wheatsheaf, 1990).
Storey, John, ed., *Cultural Theory and Popular Culture* (Hemel Hempstead: Harvester Wheatsheaf, 1997).
  An Introduction to Cultural Theory and Popular Culture (Hemel Hempstead: Harvester Wheatsheaf, 1997).
Toulmin, Stephen, *The Return to Cosmology: Postmodern Science and the Theology of Nature* (Berkeley, CA: University of California Press, 1982).
Venturi, Robert, *Contradiction and Complexity in Architecture* (New York: The Museum of Modern Architecture, 1968).

Learning from Las Vegas: The Forgotten Symbolism of Architectural Form [1972] (Cambridge, MA and London: MIT Press, 1977).

Waugh, Patricia, *Metafiction: The Theory and Practice of Self-Conscious Fiction* (London and New York: Methuen, 1984).

II
NAMES AND
TERMS

A

ABJECTION A term coined by the French psychoanalytical theorist and **semiotician** Julia **Kristeva**. In 1982 she published *Powers of Horror: An Essay on Abjection*, in which she argued that the 'abject' constitutes anything that is excluded from the symbolic order, the site of the social and unambiguous subjectivity. In order to take up a position within such an order, the **subject** must repress that which reminds it of its own material nature by categorizing it as unclean or disgusting. This attempt at exclusion can only ever be partially successful, and thus the abject preserves an ability to render the subject's inclusion in the symbolic order problematic. At moments when the subject is forced to recognize this, the resultant reaction is one of extreme repulsion – what Kristeva terms an 'act of abjection'.

ACKER, KATHY: NOVELIST (1948–97) Acker began publishing a string of texts in the mid-1970s with small underground presses. Her move to London in the mid-1980s coincided with her reaching a larger audience when a major publisher brought out *Blood and Guts in High School* (1984). She now lives in New York. Her work draws upon Sade, Bataille, post-war French fiction and, most clearly, the 'cut-up' and collage techniques of William Burroughs. Often depicting the global adventures of a young girl beginning with a sado-masochistic sexual relationship with a patriarchal figure (usually her father) in various confined spaces (harems, family homes) her work is marked by a complete absence of the usual features (and pleasures) of fiction – consistent characterization, plot and psychological motivation. It is notorious for its extremely graphic descriptions of sex and violence, though the reader has some difficulty deciding which is the more unpleasant. Examples in this manner are *Blood and Guts in High School, Empire of the Senseless* (1988) and *Don Quixote* (1986). 'I wanted to stick a knife, a little one, up the ass of the novel', she has said.

In many ways her books are textbook examples of what **postmodern** fiction can be in its most avant-garde form; here we find sexual transgression, passages of lyricism, occupations of the space of '**otherness**', the use of different genres (romance, science-fiction, pornography, adventure), the plagiarizing of high and popular cultural works (Dickens, Cervantes, William **Gibson**), the representation of fluid subjectivities and the questioning of notions of originality and realism. The hilarious *Hello, I'm Erica Jong* (1984) is a send-up of the consciousness-raising, sexually liberated feminist fiction of the 1970s, of which Jong's *Fear of Flying*

(1973) is a prime example. It plays with Jong's realist aesthetics and links sex and death in ways the relentlessly upbeat Jong would never do. It is also a skit on the '**death of the author**' and concludes with a drawing of a tombstone which bears the legend 'RIP E. J.'. *I Dreamt I Was a Nymphomaniac* (1975) is, Acker says, 'an experiment with the word "I"', while *Kathy Goes to Haiti* (1978) alternates chapters of seeming autobiography with material lifted from pornographic sources. Using *Treasure Island* as her starting point, Acker's latest novel, *Pussy, King of the Pirates* (1996) relates once more the adventures of a young girl through a landscape that doubles for the female body. These 'belated', highly mediated texts reflect Acker's belief that 'our reality now, which occurs so much through the media, *is* other texts'. Needless to say her work has been controversial; to some it is merely 'pornobabble'. For others it represents in fiction the possibility of a kind of **Deleuzian** 'flow'. At its best it gives the reader a glimpse of the possibilities of contemporary fiction. It offers us the disturbing suggestion, as Jonathan **Dollimore** has put it, that power and pleasure are not mutually exclusive but reinforce one another and this, finally, may prove to be the most unpalatable aspect of her work.

ACKROYD, PETER: NOVELIST, BIOGRAPHER, CRITIC (1949–) Born in London, Ackroyd has worked as an editor and critic. A prolific writer, he has produced many critically acclaimed novels. *Chatterton* (1987), *First Light* (1989), *English Music* (1991), *The House of Doctor Dee*

(1993) and *Dan Leno and the Limehouse Golem* (1995) are all, in one way or another, historical fictions which involve the attempt to solve some kind of mystery. Ackroyd has also written successful biographies of T. S. Eliot, Dickens and William Blake. He is at work on a biography of Sir Thomas More, author of *Utopia* (1516). These biographies, as well as the majority of his novels, are, in a sense, about London – where Ackroyd was born and lives. His third novel was the gruesome (and gruesomely funny) *Hawksmoor* (1985), which made his name and which exemplified what were to be his recurring themes; the presence of the past, occult knowledge and the irrational. The novel tells the tale, in alternating chapters, of a series of parallel murders – one group in the eighteenth century, the other in the twentieth – and the ways in which they might be linked. While Ackroyd's self-conscious historical pastiches can be seen as **postmodern** in style, they are profoundly anti-**modern** in sentiment; *Hawksmoor* uses the figure of the architect-scientist Sir Christopher Wren to send up the **Enlightenment**'s belief in human progress and human perfectibility. In doing so, his stylistically exhilarating, philosophically conservative and deeply pessimistic fiction questions the intellectual and ethical foundations of modernity.

ACTIVE INTERPRETATION Jacques **Derrida**'s term for what **deconstruction** involves as a form of critical writing. Active interpretation is not so much a reading of a **text** (in the standard sense of a critical interpretation, or *explication de texte*, designed to reveal the text's underlying meaning) as an exercise in creative writing, where the language of the text forms a pretext for imaginative play and the production of new meanings. Punning, wordplay and association of ideas, those staples of the deconstructive writing manner, come into their own in such a context, and the critic can indulge his or her linguistic ingenuity to the full. Active interpretation is therefore a tactic to challenge the claims of **logocentricity**, in that it reveals the text to be a source of multiple meanings that go on almost indefinitely. There is no one central meaning to any text, but a **plurality** of possible meanings. From such a perspective conventional criticism is a pointless act, since it is based on the notion that each text has an essential meaning which it is the critic's duty to present to the reader. Active interpretation represents an explosion of this assumption, since by its manipulation of the text's language it continually discovers new meanings.

ADAMS, JOHN: COMPOSER AND CONDUCTOR (1947–) Adams has played a crucial role in the development of the **minimalist** tradition, building upon the foundations laid down by composers ten years his senior, such as Steve **Reich** and Philip **Glass**. Adams was thoroughly schooled in the **modernist** approach to composition (i.e. the European post-war avant-garde – Boulez, Stockhausen, etc.) which he felt was not only going against his instincts but against the natural forces of music. It was only after graduating (from Harvard in

1971) and moving to San Francisco that Adams was exposed to the minimalist music of Reich, **Riley**, and Glass. This music, with its rich polyrhythmic textures and defiantly static harmony, was to be hugely inspirational to Adams, offering an alternative to the modernist musical language.

Minimalism, at least in its early days, rejected self-expression and any form of sentimentality in favour of processes, gradual change and a kind of objective detachment from the music. Adams, along with other composers, was to adopt many of the minimalist techniques but to adapt them to his own more expressive, more climactic and often more dissonant musical language. The tag, 'post-minimalism' has often been employed to describe this music. One of Adams's early pieces 'Shaker Loops' (1978) employs the familiar minimalist techniques of steady pulse, repetitive structures, tonal stability and polyrhythm, yet develops an emotional and dramatic narrative.

Adams has composed two operas. The first, *Nixon in China* (1987), takes as its subject-matter the historic meeting in 1972 between Richard Nixon and the Chinese leader Mao Zedong. This full-length three-act work, being described by some as 'realist' and by others as 'surrealist', makes no overt political statements and resists political satire. His second opera *The Death of Klinghoffer* (1990) is inspired by the 1985 Palestinian hijacking of the cruise ship *Achille Lauro* and offers a reflective look at the continuing conflict between the Arab and Jewish people. Leaving the world of opera for five years, Adams concentrated on orchestral works, 'El Dorado' (1991), the Chamber Symphony (1992) and the Violin Concerto (1993), which allowed him to develop a more complex, contrapuntal and dissonant musical style. Returning to the world of music theatre in 1995 he composed the piece 'I was Looking at the Ceiling then I saw the Sky'. This collaboration with the director Peter Sellars and poet June Jordon was not only scaled down and more compact than his operas but also allowed him to return to a simpler, more accessible compositional style. It is clear that not only has Adams developed and expanded the genre of minimalism but also that he has gained for it a sense of respectability with the 'classical' music establishment.

ADORNO, THEODOR WIESENGRUND: PHILOSOPHER (1903–69) Along with Max **Horkheimer** and Herbert **Marcuse**, Adorno is the major representative of the 'critical thought' developed by the members of the Institute of Social Research, or **Frankfurt School**. At university in Frankfurt Adorno studied philosophy, sociology, psychology and music. Then, in 1925, he studied musical composition with Alban Berg in Vienna and gained a deep appreciation of the atonality of the 'new music' being developed by Arnold Schoenberg. As well as writing numerous musical compositions, Adorno wrote copiously on music. In this and in other areas of aesthetics Adorno remained a commited advocate of the radical, critical impulses within modernism. In philosophy, however, Adorno's work can be read as equally close to **modernism** (if one concentrates on certain ideas or pronouncements) or postmodernism (if one allows for the performative element, the reflexive dramatization of movement of critical thinking – 'thinking against thought' – itself).

Adorno's most important philosophical debt is to **Hegel**. Like Hegel, Adorno's own thinking constantly circles around the dialectical tension between individual and society, between the particular and the universal. On the other hand, Adorno – like **Marx** – regards Hegel's fundamental claim (to have effected the reconciliation of these dialectical poles) as condemning Hegel to illusory forms of idealism. Adorno regards all fantasies of 'organic wholeness', including the Hegelian, as in some ways regressive. The '**negative dialectics**' proposed by Adorno aim at constantly undermining and defeating any final synthesis.

When the Institute for Social Research was forced into exile from Nazi Germany, Adorno went through a profound engagement with mass culture in its American, commercial forms. The result was an analysis of the culture and social organization of late capitalism which stressed its propensity to become an integrated, closed, or 'total', system. Adorno contributed many studies of the manipulation of consciousness by what he called the 'culture industries'. These became the cornerstone of a damning portrait of what Adorno saw as an increasingly 'administered world'.

Against an increasingly irrational and intractable world Adorno seeks to mobilize all the powers of philosophical reason. ('We are wholly convinced . . . that social freedom is inseparable from enlightened thought.') Yet, for Adorno, reason, in the form of scientific rationality and means–end calculations, is itself part of the problem. In *Dialectic of Enlightenment* (1947), Adorno collaborated with Max Horkheimer to diagnose the dark side of the development of reason. According to the allegory of the voyage of Odysseus, which Adorno constructs within the book, the repressive potential of reason does not arise with the eighteenth-century **Enlightenment** conception of reason (which Adorno labels 'identity logic' or 'the philosophy of identity') but has its origins in the very beginnings of Western culture. The rationality bound to identity has always felt compelled to deny, repress and violate singularity, **difference** and **otherness**. Its extraordinary success in offering mankind domination over nature leads inexorably to domination of men over men (and over women).

In the face of the darkness of this vision, Adorno self-consciously affirms the wildest utopian dream of the Enlightenment of all: an end to *human suffering*. 'The only philosophy which can be responsibly practiced in the face of despair is the attempt to contemplate all things as they would present themselves from the standpoint of redemption . . . Perspectives must be fashioned that displace and estrange the world, reveal it to be, with its rifts and crevices, as indigent and distorted as it will appear one day in the messianic light.'

ALTERITY 'Alterity' is often used interchangeably in **poststructuralist** discourse with '**Other**'. The 'Other' in the work of Michel **Foucault**, for instance, consists of those who are excluded from positions of power, and are often victimized within a predominantly liberal humanist view of the **subject**. Much of Foucault's work is therefore dedicated to retrieving for history and philosophy those who have been excluded from intellectual consideration, and have consequently had their political rights either ignored or erased. The 'Other' in this context are homosexuals, women, the clinically insane, non-whites and prisoners. These figures, collectively and individually, are seen by post-structural and **postmodern** thinkers to exist on the margins of Western society, and are often the negative opposition in **deconstructive** discourse.

AMERICAN DECONSTRUCTION **Deconstruction** made such a huge impact on American academic circles from the 1970s onwards, that some commentators have seen it as the dominant form of academic discourse in the American humanities through into the 1990s. Jacques **Derrida**, the leading proponent of deconstruction, was a visiting professor at Yale and Johns Hopkins at frequent points during that period, and clearly had a galvanizing effect on those with whom he came into contact. Although it is primarily a form of philosophical discourse, deconstruction in America had its greatest success in the field of literary studies (with the **Yale School** being an outstanding example), where it has evolved into a particularly free-wheeling and linguistically exuberant form of critical writing, with a strong emphasis on the pun. Derrida himself has been less than happy with what has taken place under the name of deconstruction in America, and has even gone on record as saying that he regards it as something of a travesty of his original intentions – somewhat ironic though this is for a movement of thought which has taken it for its special brief to challenge notions of truth and intention.

AMIS, MARTIN: NOVELIST (1949–) Amis has written eight blackly satirical novels, all showing a technical virtuosity and verbal brilliance unmatched by his contemporaries. He has displayed all of the formal trickery expected of the **postmodern** novelist: unreliable narrators (two of them in *Success),* bizarre authorial interventions (he plays chess with the main character, John Self, in *Money)* and temporal manipulation (most spectacularly in *Time's Arrow,* which plays the life of a concentration camp doctor backwards).

Amis's first two novels, *The Rachel Papers* (1973) and *Dead Babies* (1975), portray the selfish pursuit of pleasure by the young in a world without traditional moral values. His following two novels, *Success* (1978) and *Other People: A Mystery Story* (1981), show an increasingly adventurous experimentation with form: in the latter the world is seen through the defamiliarizing, innocent gaze of an amnesiac. *Money: A Suicide Note* (1984) and *London Fields* (1989) show Amis at his best, integrating complex formal structures with devastating moral satire. In the former the greed and decadence of the Reagan–Thatcher years and in the latter the seedy moral depravity of

the criminal underclass are caught by Amis's brilliant phrasemaking. Amis's latest novel, *The Information* (1995) exposes the fear and loathing running through London's literary élites.

The postmodernist aesthetic that shows in Amis's familiar technical flourishes is matched by a carefully considered postmodernist ethic. Amis is well aware of the critique of **Enlightenment** values, of the crumbling concept of the self and of the coupling together of power and knowledge.

ANDERSON, LAURIE: PERFORMANCE ARTIST, COMPOSER (1947–) Laurie Anderson is **postmodern** in her defiance of categorization. Throughout her work, Anderson has destabilized barriers such as those between art, music and performance, craft and technology, avant-garde and commercial. In her performances she challenges traditional limits of gender and technology while making use of assumptions about them. The 45-minute piece *For Instants* (1976). incorporated explanations of the technical difficulties in making the work plus postmodern distinctions between 'what happened' and 'what I said and wrote about what happened'. She performed on her viophonograph – a turntable on a violin with a needle mounted onto a bow – playing a recording of her own voice and accompanying it with live singing.

In a later piece she replaced the bow's horsehair with recording tape, playing pre-recorded words on an audio head mounted onto the violin. Effects were designed so that incompleteness could make new meanings, as in Lenin's 'Ethics is the aesthetics of the future', which became *Ethics is the Aesthetics of the Few(ture)* (her title). In *Songs for Lines/Songs for Waves* (1977) she reversed recorded words, exposing the arbitrariness of signifiers.

The 1980s multimedia *United States* used her famous vocoder, tape loops and synthesizers to create a robotic chant which unsettled gender expectations. 'O Superman' condemned the excesses of technological and media control while making use of them. *Language is a Virus* (from William Burroughs's 'Language is a virus from outer space') subverts 'natural' expression, combining media images and computer graphics with Anderson's voice, staccato phrasing and mechanical gestures. The ironic distancing produced by decoding her voice and incorporating other sounds stresses the mediation involved in communication.

ANTI-ESSENTIALISM **Postmodernist** thinkers invariably describe themselves as anti-essentialist, meaning that they reject the notion of there being any essence to phenomena such as truth, meaning, self or identity. Traditional philosophy is taken to be essentialist in believing that there is such a thing as absolute truth underpinned by logical formulae such as the law of identity ($A = A$, or a thing equals itself). This law has been challenged by postmodernists, who claim that it does not always hold (a thing might not equal itself if it is in a continuous process of change over time, for example). Traditional philosophy also tends to posit an essential self (as in the case of Descartes, where

the mind is the essence of selfhood, 'I think therefore I am'), which postmodernism has similarly called into question. Self is in fact seen to be a very fluid entity in postmodernist thought, particularly in feminist circles, where the notion of an essentialist self is regarded as part of patriarchal oppression.

ANTIFOUNDATIONALISM To challenge the grounds of someone's system of belief, or thought, is to be antifoundationalist. **Poststructuralist** and **postmodernist** thinkers tend to be self-consciously antifoundational in outlook. **Derrida**, as a case in point, has challenged the validity of the law of identity (that a thing equals itself, $A = A$), arguably *the* foundation to thought and argument in the West. The basic problem is that any system of thought, indeed any system aspiring to make value judgements of any kind (true or false, good or evil, etc.), requires a starting point, or initial assumption (say, that $A = A$), that is self-evidently true and beyond all possible doubt. Antifoundationalists point out that the starting point itself requires a prior assumption. Poststructuralism and postmodernism are merely more extreme versions of positions that have been outlined earlier in the history of Western philosophy. Sceptics in general, such as the eighteenth-century philosopher David Hume, are antifoundationally inclined in that they are less concerned with what their opponents say than their ground of authority for making any kind of value judgement at all. Antifoundationalism in recent times has argued that foundationalism is authoritarian in intent, and it has become a rallying cry for an attack on the status quo and the Establishment.

APORIA From the Greek, meaning, literally, 'the absence of a passage', and hence a perplexing difficulty or state of being at a loss, aporia denotes in rhetoric a figure in which the speaker or writer expresses doubt about how or where to begin a discourse, or how to overcome a particular problem or obstacle. For **deconstructive** criticism, it is precisely around such moments of doubt or apparently unresolvable problems that reading orients itself. For **Derrida**, as for the criticism of Paul **de Man** or J. Hillis **Miller**, it is these textual gaps or stumbling-blocks to which we must pay attention.

The term is also an apt one to describe the kind of 'impossibility' of judgement which **Lyotard** identifies in the aesthetics of the **sublime** and the avant-garde, with which he identifies the **postmodern**. For Lyotard, the moment at which political judgement takes place is an aporetic one, analogous with the disjunction between the faculties of reason and imagination in the sublime, and with the avant-garde injunction to *create*, but in the absence of any rules for the production of art.

APPROPRIATION ART A term used to describe works by Sherrie Levine, Barbara Kruger, Cindy **Sherman**, Richard Prince, and those artists for whom the real has become coterminous with the image-world of contemporary social life. Levine, Sherman, and Prince were represented in the seminal *Pictures* exhibition, held at the Artists Space gallery in Lower Manhattan in 1977. The influential art critic Douglas Crimp, writing in the catalogue, waxes lyrical about artists for whom purity is defined in terms of **simulation** rather than emulation, repetition rather than originality, and confiscation rather than creation.

ARCHAEOLOGY Archaeology, the scientific study of the remains of the past, is a potent metaphor for excavations of a more subjective nature. **Freud** famously used the image of a city to picture the relation between the conscious and the unconscious. Like the city of Rome, the thinking subject is composed of many different layers of awareness and susceptibility. Destructive drives and desires may emanate from buried parts of the self, and the analyst must help the analysand to dig deep and expose repressed memories and fears to the light of waking day. Michel **Foucault** uses a similar concept to describe the investigation into the unconscious of the *épisteme*, which is shorthand for the 'epistemological field' of assumptions, expectations, values and beliefs of a society at a particular historical moment. *The Order of Things: An Archaeology of the Human Sciences* (1966), for example, seeks to uncover the formational rules and systematic shaping factors which are common to scientific **representations** of the Classical period. The **text** is an 'open site', another archaeological metaphor which refers to the necessary incompleteness of the project. So Foucault's speculations should not be read as if they were by a historian of science, but with a **postmodern** provisionality.

ARTIFICIAL INTELLIGENCE On the one hand, artificial intelligence (AI) forms a powerfully attractive motor for the artificial evolution of human reality into science-fiction; on the other, it is a research programme attracting funds from military and corporate sponsors that seeks, for the first time, to place a new, created or manufactured species of intelligent life on the earth. If this still sounds somewhat intoxicated, we need only remember AI guru Marvin Minsky discussing the possibility of real artificial intelligences: 'Of course they're possible; that's not the problem. The real problem is that the first hundred or so are going to be clinically insane.' As contemporary phenomena such as **cyberpunk** demonstrate, AI, along with **artificial life**, forms a haunting cultural threshold beyond which Frankenstein's monster already has us in his virtual grasp.

As Minsky does, however, it is also necessary to insist that these virtual monsters are also real. In AI research proper, then, there are two basic models: the first, top-down, approach seeks to develop software that can capture the core cognitive functions that define human intelligence, and thereafter to upload them into a single central processor that stands in for the human brain. Broadly speaking, this is the model pursued in the production of 'expert-systems' and the chess computers against which so many humans have pitted their wits and failed. The other, bottom-up, approach seeks to create machines that learn. Variously called 'parallel distributed processing', 'neural nets', or 'connectionism', this model allows many processors to interact in order to develop a collective response to random phenomena. Over time, such parallel machines establish pathways and **fuzzy** rules for connections in exactly the same way, it is argued, as organic, human brains do: rather than being given a set of rules and parameters as a programme that an expert system then applies, neural nets select the best from many options, so that the rules the system learns 'emerge' from its functioning.

While the top-down approach is by now all but redundant, the success enjoyed by neural nets has generated new approaches to the philosophy of mind, generally called 'connectionist' theories. Like the model of the neural net, connectivity and interaction become more important tools for the development of human intelligence than the centralized idea of the mind-brain as a whole. Perhaps, if this trend continues, the question as to which intelligence is derived from the other will be harder to pose than it currently seems, in a world that, temporarily at least, is devoid of artificial intelligences.

ARTIFICIAL LIFE Along with **artificial intelligence**, one of the two contemporary sciences of the artificial, artificial life (AL) is a truly bizarre confluence of technology, science and **simulacra**. Generating 'organisms' from algorithms, AL researchers seek not so much to model 'real life' evolutionary processes, as to extend them into the artificial environment of computer memory. Thomas S. Ray, at the Fourth International Conference on Artificial Life in 1994, suggested that his Tierra, a program that, like a digital simulation of our own primal soup, 'evolves' independent life forms in a computer, be released on to the **Internet** to 'breed' new species all over the (virtual) world. While Tierra is an example of AL *software*, AL researchers also investigate *hardware* – the construction of artificial life forms such as robots, aiming eventually at the ideal of realizing the self-replicating but abstract 'von Neumann machine' in material form – and *wetware*, the attempt to create artificial life in a test tube. AL software involves writing programs that perpetually feed back the information they produce into the production of further information, creating an informational complexity from which, it is hoped, artificial lifeforms will emerge. Key to the process, therefore, is its 'bottom up' strategy rather than the 'top down' approach initially adopted by artificial intelligence research, meaning that more emerges from AL's new, silicon-based evolutionary ecosystems than was programmed in at the start.

Aura A term associated with the German cultural critic Walter **Benjamin**. In an important essay entitled 'The Work of Art in the Age of Mechanical Reproduction' (1936), Benjamin argues that prior to mechanization, art had a non-reproductive quality which conferred upon it a unique status, or 'aura'. This aura, which signified the artwork's autonomy, had been destroyed in modern times by soulless automation. For Benjamin, the mysticism that he associates with the unique work of art has been 'withered' as a result of the machine age, and art and its artefacts have become divorced from tradition, leading to a 'liquidization of the cultural heritage'.

Auster, Paul: novelist (1947–) After producing poetry, criticism and a large number of translations of French literature, Auster, considered one of the foremost American novelists now writing, made his reputation with a series of three novels, collectively known as *The New York Trilogy* (1987). These are anti-detective fictions influenced by Beckett, French post-war experimental fiction and **postmodern** theory. All three have as their plot some kind of writer in pursuit of another, and in the second and third books, *Ghosts* (1986) and *The Locked Room* (1986), another who is an eerie double of the protagonist. The first, *City of Glass* (1985) alludes to Poe and Walter **Benjamin** in its figuring of a fragmenting self in the city. The city of glass suggests the detective's mastery of the complexity of **signs**, but presents us with the abysmal possibility that, rather than reading the city, it is a mirror-glass that merely reflects Quinn's own concerns back at him. The novels seem to be psychological studies but the fragmentation at the end of *City of Glass,* for instance, is not psychological (as it would be in many modernist novels) but **textual**: Quinn disappears when his notebook finishes.

Ghosts is the most formal of the trilogy; Blue is employed by White to follow Black. Taking notes, Blue sits in his room and watches Black writing in the building across the road. Black may be writing about him. Black may in fact be White. Again we have a tale of someone who drops out of routine existence and lets social ties fall away in pursuit of an obsession. *The Locked Room* is the most fleshed-out of the early novels and escapes the main criticism made of these works; while admiring the stylistic control, and plenitude of stories within stories, some have found these novels finally exercises in postmodern style, though getting to that 'finally' is gripping.

Auster left the self-confessed influence of Beckett, and after his distopian *In the Country of Last Things* (1987) he published in some ways his most remarkable novel, *Moon Palace*, which, in the story of Marco Stanley Fogg, continues in the quest theme of his first work. *The Music of Chance* (1990) begins as a road novel and ends as a parable about free will and, as in all his fiction, it is saturated with references to American and European literature which are part of a literary technique that teases away at the surface realism of these later novels. *Leviathan* (1992) is concerned with the political implications of public writing, and echoes some of the themes of Don DeLillo's *Mao II* (1990). *Mr Vertigo* (1994) uses the old American form of the tall tale to narrate the story of a boy who can fly. The novels after *The New York Trilogy* maintain Auster's admirable desire to avoid repeating himself, while exemplifying his continuing theme of fluid selves held together (or not) by the ability to narrate, to textualize their lives.

AUTHOR From **structuralism** through to **postmodernism**, there has been a downgrading of the author's reputation in **continental philosophical** thought, particularly in France. Roland **Barthes**'s 'death of the author' notion announced the end of the author as an authority figure responsible for the meaning of his or her work, and shifted the balance of power towards the reader. Authority figures are generally frowned upon in postmodernism, and the notion of the author as cultural icon has accordingly been challenged. There is little support among postmodernist theorists for the idea that any one individual should (or in any practical way *can*) exert control over what a **text** means, hence it is held to be pointless to seek out an author's 'intentions' (see also **death of the author**).

B

BAKER, NICHOLSON: NOVELIST
(1957–) Many **postmodernist** novels
disrupt linear narrative by burdening
the discourse with inordinate description. The books of Nicholson Baker
are classic examples of this. In *The
Mezzanine* (1990), a man's shoelace
snaps during lunch-hour in a local
office complex. While musing on why
this should happen at this particular
time, his thoughts go off on many tan-
gents: how to open a wing-flap spout
on a carton without splattering the
milk, why 'pre-bunching' is an in-
efficient way of putting on socks, and
other mysteries of minutiae. He is
eventually illumined by a paper he
discovers titled 'Methods for Evaluating the Abrasion Resistance and
Knot Slippage Strength of Shoe
Laces', published by Z. Czaplicki
in the Polish journal *Technik
Wlokienniczy*.

Baker's next book, *Room Temperature* (1990), also takes place at meal-
time. It is 3.15 on a Wednesday
afternoon, and Mike, the narrator, is
feeding his six-month-old baby, the
Bug, while his wife Patty is out at
work. As he does so, he reflects idly on
matters as diverse as nose-picking,
drawing the inside of a pillow, sucking
the tops of Bic pens, and the history of
the comma. *Vox* (1992) takes the form
of a four-hour erotic telephone conversation in which a man and a woman
exchange their most intimate fantasies
at obscene length. *The Fermata* (1994),
also descends into pornography when
the central character, Arno Strine,
finds himself blessed with the ability to
freeze time and fondle the females of
his choice. Neither of these last two
novels is as innovative as Baker's
first two.

BANVILLE, JOHN: NOVELIST (1945–)
Considered by many the foremost
living Irish novelist, Banville's work
illuminates in a critical way a series of
issues and concepts that have become
central to the criticism of contemporary writing: **post-colonialism** and
postmodernism, history as textuality,
the relationship of ethics to aesthetics,
and the nature of fiction itself. Writing
consciously from the Western edge of
modern Europe, his work has three
overlapping areas of concern. First,
there are the novels which explore the
myth of the Protestant ruling class's
'big house'. In *Birchwood* (1973), *The
Newton Letter* (1981), *Mefisto* (1986),
The Book of Evidence (1989) and
Ghosts (1993), these colonial houses
signify moral and psychological decay,
political oppression and isolation.
Second, a series of metafictional
history novels deals with the aesthetics
of knowledge: *Doctor Copernicus*
(1976), *Kepler* (1981), *Mefisto* and
The Newton Letter draw upon
Thomas **Kuhn**'s concept of scientific
revolutions in an attempt to shift the

boundaries of the history novel itself. The grand theme of these fictions is nothing less than science's invention of modern reality. Finally, *The Book of Evidence*, *Ghosts* and *Athena* (1995) use the relationship between a casual murder and a stolen painting to explore issues of judgement: artistic, critical and legal.

While finding that 'truth' may be a human construct chimes in with much postmodern philosophy, in Banville there is no simple celebration of the fact. His fictions are despairing language-games over the abyss; his second novel *Nightspawn* (1971) ends: 'I love words and I hate death. Beyond this, nothing.'

BARTH, JOHN: NOVELIST (1930–) In 'The Literature Of Exhaustion', an essay first published in 1967, John Barth made three points which now read like a manifesto for **postmodernist** fiction. The first was that traditional forms, particularly the classic bourgeois novel, were 'used-up', stale and outmoded. The second, related, point was that writers must strive to create new forms, acquiring a self-consciousness about the nature of literary language and artistic structure. His third point was that the writer still has an obligation to amuse and move the reader, speaking 'eloquently and memorably to our still-human hearts'. In his fiction from *The Floating Opera* (1956) to *The Last Voyage of Somebody The Sailor* (1991), Barth has certainly produced fiction of extreme structural complexity and formal invention. Critics are more divided about his success in moving, or even engaging, the reader.

The Floating Opera, and Barth's second novel, *The End Of The Road* (1958), both feature alienated protagonists for whom life has not only lost meaning, but simply stopped making sense. A certain glum existentialism shows the influence of Camus, but the combination of narrative trickery and occasional scatological humour points to Barth's later fiction.

The Sot-Weed Factor (1960) is Barth's masterpiece, an enormous (over 800 pages in its first edition) historical novel about the foundation of the Maryland colony. Its hero, Ebenezer Cooke, a resolutely virginal poet, and his tutor, the pansexual, protean Henry Burlingame, undergo endless picaresque adventures on the way to transcendental union with the animal and vegetable world. The story is told in a rich, part fictive, part authentic seventeenth-century English. Barth jumbles dense philosophical debate with swearing contests, snatches of journals and recipes for aphrodisiacs, without ever losing his grip on what must be the most intricate plot in English literature.

Giles Goat Boy (1966) is an equally huge and intricate work, but it lacks the vitality and humour of *The Sot-Weed Factor.* All of Barth's novels contain their narratives within elaborate framing devices, but *Giles* beats them all. No fewer than four stages come between the narrator, a young man brought up among goats and destined to the life of a mythic hero, and the reader. He dictates *The Revised New Syllabus of George Giles, Our Great Tutor* to the West Campus Automatic Computer. The computer then edits and prints the text. The hero's son further edits the computer tapes before giving them to a struggling writer, 'J. B.'. J. B. adds his amendments and then sends it to his publisher. Finally, the publisher appends a 'Disclaimer'. The central conceit is that the university becomes the universe, and the theme, like that of *The Sot-Weed Factor,* is the quest for a unifying vision, a dialectical reconciliation of the intimate and the absolute. *Lost In The Funhouse* (1968) takes experimentation a step further. A series of fourteen short 'fictions' for print, live voice and tape, it became, like *Giles* before it, a surprise best-seller. The stories continue Barth's themes – the grotesque comedy of sex and the difficulties of the storyteller in the modern age.

The three linked novellas in *Chimera* (1972) continue the investigation of myth instigated in *Giles,* dealing with the stories of Scheherazade, Perseus and Bellerophon – although each from an unusual angle; and there is a new theme, an overt feminism absent from his earlier works. The epistolary novel *Letters* (1979) again shows Barth's formal daring. Characters from earlier novels are reborn as correspondents in a tale of the usual architectonic complexity. *Sabbatical* (1982), *The Tidewater Tales* (1984) and *The Last Voyage of Somebody The Sailor* are metaphysical yarns, embodying Barth's love of sailing and, as in much of his fiction, Barth the author appears, more or less disguised.

Barth continues to publish, despite periods of intense writer's block, but his star has fallen in recent years. His formal experiments no longer seem so interesting, and his increasing focus

on the writer, and the act of creation, seems a shrinking away from his earlier grand themes. Nevertheless he remains one of the central figures in the history of postmodern fiction.

BARTHELME, DONALD: AUTHOR (1931–89) Barthelme is primarily known for his collections of short stories: *Come Back, Dr Caligari* (1964), *Unspeakable Practices, Unnatural Acts* (1968), *City Life* (1970), *Sadness* (1972), *Amateurs* (1976), *Great Days* (1979) and *Overnight to Many Distant Cities* (1983). However, he also wrote four novels: *Snow White* (1967), *The Dead Father* (1975), *Paradise* (1976) and *The King* (1989). Other works include a children's book, *The Slightly Irregular Fire Engine* (1971), and a collection of journalistic pieces, *Guilty Pleasures* (1974).

Barthelme's fictions display many of the features associated with **postmodernist** writing. He once admitted: 'As soon as I hear a proposition I immediately consider its opposite. A double-minded man – makes for mixtures.' This double-mindedness assumes many guises. For instance, his tales delight in surreal incongruities of context. In 'Me and Miss Mandible', a 35-year-old claims adjuster for an insurance company suddenly finds himself back at elementary school. His diary entries record the contrast between his cynicism and the open-eyed fun and games of the 11-year-olds. 'The Temptation of St Anthony' is posited around a similar reversal. The saint is somehow marooned in suburbia, and faced with the temptation of living an ordinary life. Many of Barthelme's stories operate on the principle of contradiction, with literary forms at variance with their contents. 'Paraguay' mimics the tone of an old-fashioned travel book, but the para-Paraguay it describes owes more to science fiction than any Baedeker guide. There are potted summaries of the country's imports and exports (silence is sold as if it were cement), its citizens (who shed their skins and share the same fingerprints), and its unusual physics (the temperature controls the inhabitants' walking speed). Other stories extrapolate from a ridiculous opening situation and exaggerate it beyond all proportion. In 'The Falling Dog', a Welsh sculptor is knocked to the ground by an Irish setter that jumps from an upper-storey window. The accident gives him ideas for new works based upon the image of the Falling Dog: plywood falling dogs like aircraft models, Styrofoam falling dogs, falling dogs the size of hummingbirds. The tale is the shaggiest of dog stories. A balloon appears over New York City in 'The Balloon'. It covers 45 blocks from north to south, and an indeterminate area from east to west. City officials are upset about the arrival of this unwelcome object on the skyline, but the citizens soon accept it. Adults scrawl on it, and children bounce on it. Some people speculate about its meaning, as if it were a work of art. So the balloon rapidly inflates from a concrete particular to something vague and abstract and full of hot air.

Barthelme's louche fictions turn their withering gaze onto the shallow indices of designer taste. Yet many of his short stories were published in *The New Yorker*, alongside advertisements for the very furnishings and fashions they satirize. As Barthelme mused on one occasion: 'People read the fiction with after-images of Rolls-Royces and Rolexes still sizzling in their eyes': another instance of postmodern double-mindedness.

BARTHES, ROLAND: CULTURAL CRITIC (1915–80) In the successive phases in his career Roland Barthes appears before us as the **Marxist** literary critic, elegantly slaying the bourgeois dragon; as a **semiologist**, carefully revealing the meanings latent in the artefacts of popular culture; as a **structuralist**, intent on a 'scientific' analysis of human society; and as a playful **poststructuralist**, celebrating the quasi-sexual pleasures of the **text**.

The most important work in Barthes' early period, and still perhaps his most influential text, is the series of reflections on contemporary French culture, originally written for the magazine *Les Lettres nouvelles* between 1954 and 1956, and published, along with a long theoretical essay in 1957 as *Mythologies*. In these essays, Barthes shows how racism, sexism and colonialism lurk behind the apparently natural and innocent. Barthes was among the first theorists to take a serious interest in popular culture, and the influence of *Mythologies* can still be seen whenever car advertisements, sport or soap operas are given the sort of critical attention more traditionally reserved for 'great' novels or the theatre.

Mythologies is an exercise in semiology, the 'science of **signs**' initiated by Ferdinand de Saussure. Semiology was one of the main strands in the great structuralist movement which dominated French intellectual life in the 1950s and 1960s, and which attempted to identify the structures which frame and govern meaningful human activities. Barthes' most sustained attempt at a full blown structural analysis is *The Fashion System* (1967). Selecting as his field the captions accompanying the photographs in fashion magazines, Barthes constructs a 'grammar' of fashion and demonstrates the different levels at which meanings are generated.

The scientific structuralism of *The Fashion System* was itself out of fashion by the time it appeared. The poststructuralism of Jacques **Derrida** and Julia **Kristeva** carried Saussure's insight into the arbitrariness of the sign to its extreme, undermining any attempt to discover ultimate meaning in the infinite play of signifiers. Barthes took these criticisms of his own methodology very much to heart, and his texts of the later 1960s and 1970s show an abrupt awakening from what he termed his 'dream of scientificity'.

The most impressive of these later works is *S/Z*, an extraordinary analysis of a short story by Balzac. Barthes demonstrates that even those texts which aspire to 'realism' are always woven from other texts, representing not a picture of reality, but a patchwork of cultural commonplaces, and second- and third-hand observations. Barthes contrasts the classic, *lisible,* or readable work, typified by the great bourgeois novels of the nineteenth century, in which the reader is a passive consumer, to the *scriptible* or 'writable' text, in which the reader becomes an active producer.

In *The Pleasure of the Text,* published in 1973, Barthes develops an 'erotics

of reading'. The contrast between the *writerly* and *readerly* encountered in *S/Z* is translated into the two types of sensation experienced by the reader: *plaisir* and *jouissance.* The text of pleasure offers the traditional joys of the classic novel: intelligence, **irony**, delicacy, euphoria, mastery and security. *Jouissance,* or ecstasy, is the shock of the unexpected, where the reader's comfort is destroyed, where language is fissured. Barthes holds out the tantalizing prospect of a text combining *plaisir* and *jouissance,* an ideal of a classic work rent by a disorienting erotic thrill, or a **modern**, avant-garde text made readable as well as shocking.

The final three texts that Barthes published in his lifetime are all profoundly personal. *Roland Barthes by Roland Barthes* (1975) is a whimsical autobiography, in which the author gently mocks his previous intellectual incarnations. *A Lover's Discourse* (1977) picks apart the language of love with an almost novelistic intensity and focus. *Camera Lucida* (1980), is both a theoretical work – a phenomenology of photography – and a very personal exploration of his relationship with his mother. In *Camera Lucida* Barthes suggests that photography gives us access to the 'real' world in a way that language cannot. We are offered a meaning beyond language, and, more than a meaning, the *truth.* This seems a complete turn around for Barthes, who had always denied the idea of a unitary truth or a fixed meaning.

Apart from *Mythologies,* Barthes is best known for his notorious 1968 essay, '**The Death of the Author**'. Barthes argues that the concept of an **author** as someone having privileged access to the meaning of a text, a meaning determined by the will of the author, has passed its usefulness. Texts are a 'fabric of quotations, resulting from a thousand sources of culture', and acknowledging the death of the author allows us to turn our attention to the reader, who is reborn as the creator of meanings.

BAUDRILLARD, JEAN: SOCIOLOGIST (1929–) Baudrillard began his career as a professor of secondary education, specializing in German social policy and literature. His first publications were essays and reviews for left-wing journals, and translations from the German of plays by Peter Weiss and Bertolt Brecht. In 1966 he began teaching sociology at University of Paris Nanterre, a position he held for over twenty years. During this period he was associated with the revolutionary left, and his work was a neo-**Marxian** critique of late-capitalist societies. In his early publications, *Le Systéme des objets* (1968), *Le société de consommation* (1970), and *For a Critique of a Political Economy of the Sign* (1972), Baudrillard began to study the part played by consumerism in the maintenance of capitalism, arguing the existence of a system of objects, which undergo a process of commodification in order to re-emerge as **signs**. These 'sign-values' are absorbed into a process of mass-production and replication which not only fulfils the needs of a consumer society, but creates the very perception of need in the first place.

With the publication of *The Mirror of Production* in 1973, however, Baudrillard began to move away from a Marxist position, arguing that Marxism has failed to conduct a sufficiently radical critique of capitalism and thus has been absorbed into the very bourgeois order it attempts to set itself against. In *Symbolic Exchange and Death* (1976), Baudrillard himself attempts to make that definitive break, in the process developing his self-appointed role as the prophet of 'the end': of economy, production and history itself. Proposing 'a "science of imaginary solutions"; that is, a science-fiction of the system's reversal against itself at the extreme level of **simulation**, a reversible simulation in a hyperlogic of death and destruction', Baudrillard envisages a **postmodern** society bound up entirely in social reproduction, or 'simulation', in which all sense of origin is lost in the play of endlessly replicating sign systems.

Baudrillard's ideas regarding simulation arise from a fascination with technology and technological processes, dating from his 1967 review of Marshall **McLuhan**'s *Understanding Media*. For Baudrillard, technology is a paradigm for postmodern society in its entirety, where, as he says in *The Ecstasy of Communication* (1983), 'the scene and the mirror have given way to the screen and the network'.

Such concepts reach their apotheosis in *America* (1988), an audacious piece of postmodern theorization which, in its combination of tourist-style photographs with Baudrillard's meditation on the 'meaning' of America, is half travelogue, half cultural analysis. He presents America as a model of a '**hyperreal**' future, where reality has entirely disappeared beneath the glossy, seductive, surfaces of simulation: 'You should not begin with the city and move inwards to the screen; you should begin with the screen and move outwards to the city.' However, in the end it is the desert, not the city, that comes to stand in this book as the ultimate symbol of the postmodern condition, 'because you are delivered from all depths there – a brilliant, mobile, superficial neutrality, a challenge to meaning and profundity, a challenge to nature and culture, an outer hyperspace, with no origin, no reference points'.

America thus also stands as an apposite example of the deliberately provocative **irony** with which Baudrillard presents his ideas. In his self-appointed role as 'intellectual terrorist' the avant-garde nature of much of his proclamations make it difficult to take them entirely seriously – although according to Baudrillard's own definition of the postmodern context, it is of course impossible to establish the 'truth' of any of the theorist's assertions, since his ideas are themselves implicated in the endless self-referential game of simulation. It is not surprising, therefore, that reactions to Baudrillard vary between claiming him as a guru for radical **postmodernity**, and castigating him for sloppy and inaccurate thinking.

Baudrillard's penchant for deliberate provocation and half-veiled irony is nowhere more apparent than in *Seduction* (1989), in which he takes issue with feminism's project to increase women's access to the sphere of the social and the political. **Seduction**, which is neither 'simple appearance, nor a pure absence, but the eclipse of presence', is equated with the feminine principle, which is in danger of being destroyed when women attempt to enter the masculine discourse of production. Baudrillard's conception of women thus appears to expose him as a male philosopher who conflates his own simplistic notions of femininity with a definition of the 'real' nature of women. Again, however, it is impossible to tell how much of this argument is intended as a genuine attack on feminism, and how much yet another postmodernist game with meaning.

BAUMAN, ZYGMUNT: SOCIOLOGIST (1925–) Zygmunt Bauman is one of the most articulate and theoretically sophisticated interpreters of modern – that is, **postmodern** – life. Before his expulsion from Poland after the Russian invasion of Czechoslovakia in 1968, Bauman was already a leading Polish sociologist. Active since 1971 at the University of Leeds, Bauman has written major studies of the post-1945 transformation of the English working class. He has also been a key interpreter of the hermeneutic tradition within sociology, the critical tradition of 'Western' or **Hegelian Marxism** and the utopian dimension of the socialist ideal.

In recent years, in a series of books concerned with the problems of **modernism** and postmodernism, Bauman has turned the spotlight on the many confusions and crises which make up the fabric of our lives towards the end of this century. A prolific writer, Bauman offers his analyses in prose that is always lucid and accessible. Bauman's *Thinking Sociologically* (1990) is a clear unfussy demonstration of what is involved in any discipline attempting to think seriously about our lives in society. It owes much of its richness and accessibility to Bauman's unparalleled grasp of the realities of contemporary life as we actually experience it. Although his learning is prodigious, even in his most far-reaching works Bauman is constantly interpreting facets of everyday life and experiences common to all, rather than simply indulging in the exegesis of theoretical texts. Bauman's compellingly readable books can genuinely serve as a 'guide to the perplexed'.

Bauman's stance is that of an interpreter of modern life, not an intellectual seeking to legislate or prescribe. Bauman's most succinct formulation of the difference between modernism and postmodernism is captured in the title of one of his shorter books: *Legislators and Interpreters: On Modernity, Postmodernity and Intellectuals* (1987). Ever since the first stirrings of modernity – in the seventeenth and eighteenth centuries – intellectuals have been tempted to identify themselves with social and political programmes which would usher in a completely new social order. Instead of grasping their flights of fancy and their critical insights as the products of a utopian imagination they have been seduced into seeing themselves as the architects of concrete, realizable utopias (a contradiction in terms). Bauman sees the chief weakness of the modernist impulse as being its refusal to live with the problems, the messiness of history. The dream of purifying history (what Marx called the leap from history into the realm of freedom) has lead to appalling programmes of social engineering – under fascism in the name of purity of race and under communism in the name of purity of class.

In *Modernity and the Holocaust* (1989), Bauman has given us a compelling interpretation of the ways in which the policies of racial murder pursued by the National Socialists in Germany expressed and exploited the achievements of modernity and cannot simply be treated as a irrational aberration. The subject is too significant and Bauman's arguments too nuanced to do justice to in summary – but he has added a crucial element to the debate. He traces the ways in which modernity made it possible for cruel things to 'be done by non-cruel people'.

Bauman has analysed specifically postmodern forms of violence – arising from the 'privatization, deregulation and de-centralization of the identity problem' – and is an acute critic of what he terms 'neo-tribal' tendencies in contemporary society.

Bauman endorses that reading of the postmodern condition which insists that we need to learn to live with the problems – and risks – of modernity. But he remains a critical spirit, committed to opposing evil and exploitation, and his books contain a catalogue of the insanities and obscenities of our contemporary life. In Bauman's terms: 'Postmodernity is the moral person's bane and chance at the same time . . . which of the two faces of the postmodern condition will turn out to be its lasting likeness, is itself a moral question.'

One of the many significant features of (post)modern life of which he is acutely critical is a process he terms 'adiaphorization' – a process that reflects the increasing distance between our morality and our deeds, and removes certain events and relationships from the domain of moral scrutiny. The term is taken from medieval scholastic debates where ideas were declared to be orthodox or heretical, or adiaphorized – declared neutral from the point of view of religious and moral dogma. Bauman traces this process in detail in *Modernity and the Holocaust* and in *Modernity and Ambivalence* (1991), and shows how the process has been exacerbated by the development of technology.

The strong concern with morality and ethics which has been developed in works such as *Postmodernity and its Discontents* (1997), *Postmodern Ethics* (1993) and *Life in Fragments* (1995) shows that a utopian impulse persists, not as a social or even theoretical programme, but as a guiding or regulative idea which keeps Bauman's unique sociological imagination constantly reflexive and critical.

BELL, DANIEL: SOCIOLOGIST (1919–)
A Harvard academic and prominent figure in the American Academy of Arts and Sciences, Bell is best known as one of the theorists of '**post-industrialism**', a notion that has had a considerable impact within **post-modern** thought. Bell's best known works are *The End of Ideology* (1960) and *The Coming of Post-Industrial Society* (1973). *The End of Ideology* has been a seminal text in the development of what has been called '**endism**': the notion that history and ideology have come to an end thanks to the twin triumphs of Western democratic politics and the economic system underpinning it, capitalism. Thinkers like Francis **Fukuyama** have been particularly influenced by Bell's

work on 'endism', a theory that has enjoyed a surge of popularity in the last decade or so with the collapse of the Soviet Union and its client states in Eastern Europe. Bell himself in his later career has become somewhat worried by the right-wing slant of much 'endist' theory; although it is worth pointing out that in its day *The End of Ideology* was vigorously attacked by left-wing critics (such as the eminent American sociologist Charles Wright Mills) who claimed that it ignored the reality of life in the Third World and helped to maintain the political status quo. For such critics, endism was merely another ideology, that of Western political liberalism, whose concern was to discourage the view that any opposition was possible.

The Coming of Post-Industrial Society, subtitled *A Venture in Social Forecasting*, suggested that we were on the brink of a new kind of information-led, service-oriented society that would replace the industrial-based model that had been dominant in the West in the nineteenth and twentieth centuries. A post-industrial society has for Bell three main components: 'a shift from manufacturing to services'; 'the centrality of the new science-based industries'; and 'the rise of new technical élites and the advent of a new principle of stratification'. Since *The Coming of Post-Industrial Society* was published, much of what Bell has forecast has indeed come to pass in the 'mass consumption' societies of the West, although, as many critics would be quick to point out, not without considerable social cost in terms of unemployment and job insecurity. Bell has, however, clearly foreseen the direction Western culture would take, and his work now looks to prefigure much postmodern thought, which has similarly emphasized the socially transforming power of information technology (see, for example, Jean-François **Lyotard**'s *The Postmodern Condition*). The need to break with the outdated narrative of **modernism**, which included within it an uncritical belief in industrial progress and exploitation of the material world, has come to be widely recognized, and in a very real sense most of the advanced Western economies could be described as post-industrial to at least some degree. Certainly, service-industries, knowledge-production, and information technology form an increasingly important part of Western life, particularly as regards wealth-creation. Whether they agree with Bell's particular vision or not, the kind of ideal society envisaged by most postmodernists is unmistakably post-industrial.

BELSEY, CATHERINE: CRITIC (1940–) Catherine Belsey is Professor of English at University College of Wales, Cardiff, where she has taught since 1975, and Chair of the Centre for Critical Theory which she founded in 1989. Belsey's critical oeuvre presents a particular commitment to exposing, attacking and undermining the way in which liberal humanism, especially as manifested in literary education, protects the interests of the ruling class. Fusing literary study with political and social struggle, Belsey thereby demands a **poststructuralist** practice which has a radical political agenda.

Critical Practice (1980), Belsey's first major work, is an introductory text which has been highly influential in changing the theoretical agenda of undergraduate literary studies. In this pithy and highly readable book, she vigorously demonstrates the critical fallacies of the Leavisite approach to literature and, taking her cue from **Barthes** and Althusser, emphasizes the potential **plurality** of the **text** and the role of the reader in the production of meaning. The **Marxist** element of Belsey's critical approach is more obviously emphasized in her seminal essay 'Literature, History, Politics', first published in the journal *Literature and History* (1983), which has re-appeared in *Modern Criticism and Theory: a Reader* (ed. David Lodge, 1988) and *Contexts for Criticism* (ed. Donald Keesey, 1994). Here she argues for the retention of canonical literature as an object for study, and also demonstrates the poverty and potentially self-defeating nature of poststructuralist theory when it is not combined with an agenda which actively advocates a politics of change.

In *The Subject of Tragedy* (1985), Belsey draws on **Foucault** and **Derrida** to investigate the emergence of the bourgeois **subject** in the early modern period and the construction of male and female within this new subjectivity. Belsey delineates the difference between the feudal subject as a subject of 'discursive' knowledge and the bourgeois subject as a subject of 'empirical' knowledge, which is author and guarantee of its own truth. The latter Belsey problematizes in its application to the female subject, who was simultaneously allotted and denied such subjectivity, being constructed as the subordinate in the absolutist marriage, yet not subordinated in other social relationships. Belsey concludes that women 'as subjects find a position in the discourses about them and addressed to them, and are consequently able to speak. But their speech is predicated on an absence which a feminism that refuses the liberal-humanist modes of self-fulfilment is able to appropriate for politics.'

Refusing to distinguish between high and popular culture, Belsey is eclectic in her choice of texts, which ranges from Everyman to the Jacobean family portrait. In *Desire: Love Stories in Western Culture* (1994), Belsey draws particularly upon the theories of **Lacan** and Derrida, and switches her focus from the construction of the subject to the **representation** of **desire**. Belsey selects a wide range of texts and genres for investigation, from Malory to **Freud** to Mills & Boon, scrutinizing the way in which love and desire have fared under **postmodernism**, and investigating the historical differences between representations of desire in medieval, early modern, postmodern and utopian texts. She explores the relationship between desire and both reading and writing, ultimately arguing that desire challenges the conventional distinction made between nature and culture.

BENJAMIN, WALTER: **CULTURAL CRITIC** (1892–1940) Walter Benjamin was born into a prosperous Jewish family in Berlin. Having failed to secure an academic position with his thesis on German Baroque Drama, he became a literary journalist. He was influenced by Ernst Bloch and Georg Lukács, and became a friend of Bertolt Brecht, whose work he championed.

Following the coming to power of the Nazis, he left Germany for France in 1933. In Paris, he worked on a project called the 'Passagenwerke' (Arcades Project), which he considered his greatest work but which he never finished. A close friend of – and important influence on – Theodor **Adorno**, his writings stand in an uneasy relation to those of the **Frankfurt School**, with which he was periodically associated (particularly while writing his study of Baudelaire, since published as *Charles Baudelaire: A Lyric Poet in the Era of High Capitalism*). Only two of Benjamin's books were published during his lifetime: *The Origin of German Tragic Drama* and *The Concept of Art Criticism in German Romanticism*. In 1940 – fleeing the Nazis – he left Paris for the Spanish border, where he committed suicide at the age of 48.

Benjamin's 1936 essay 'The Work of Art in the Age of Mechanical Reproduction' (in the collection *Illuminations*) proposes a distinction between, on the one hand, the work of art as an object with a ritual or cult value, a value gained from a specific place in space and time, and, on the other hand, mechanically reproduced work, which can have no such value. In the age of mechanical reproduction, says Benjamin, the work of art has lost its '**aura**', the perceived authenticity that comes from its being an *original*. With **modern** forms of technological representation, such as photography and cinema, not only is the work endlessly reproducible, but it makes no sense to speak of an original in the first place. This state of affairs is open to exploitation in reactionary or progressive ways, leading either to the aestheticization of politics (fascism) or the politicization of aesthetics (communism). Benjamin's ambivalence over the consequences of the new technologies for political and aesthetic representation has made this text a crucial one for later, **postmodern**, explorations of the relations between aesthetics, politics and technology.

A further ambivalence characterizes Benjamin's work as a whole: his writings oscillate between (and do not appear to reconcile) the poles of dialectical materialism and an enigmatic form of Jewish mysticism. Most evidently connected in the late essay 'Theses on the History of Philosophy', the twin allegiances of his intellectual position have in common for Benjamin the attempt to rescue a certain conception of the now, of the *Jetztzeit* ('now-time'), which is obliterated by thinking of history in terms of a progressive linear continuum. For Benjamin, the task of the historian or the critic is to see the historical moment not 'as it really was' (the project of historicism) but *blasted out of the continuum of history*, in its full potential as a moment of crisis or danger. In this he anticipates the postmodern concern with rethinking temporality and historicity.

BERLIN, ISAIAH: PHILOSOPHER (1906–97) Many people believe that where ideas or beliefs come into conflict there must be some way of either reconciling those differences or deciding between them – some higher court of appeal or overarching system. **Postmodernists** such as **Lyotard** and **Baudrillard** reject this yearning for **metanarratives** that can bring about this great reconciliation. In the place of these unifying systems, postmodernism advocates **pluralism** and celebrates **difference**. This view was given its most coherent and powerful expression not by any of the more exotic postmodernist theorists but by the rather staid, old fashioned figure of Isaiah Berlin, the great historian of ideas and defender of political liberalism.

For Berlin, the central fact of human existence is that we all want different things; our aims, aspirations, needs and desires can never be made to coincide. Berlin's 'liberalism' is based on the acceptance that society must be plural, that we cannot argue or rationalize our way out of the confusion of human values into a simpler world. To be human is to differ. Berlin's pluralism follows from his rejection of the idea that there is a single human nature. People, for Berlin, are products of the enormously complex web of influences specific to particular cultures and times, and he has always championed those thinkers, such as Vico and Herder, who have recognized this specificity. Giambattista Vico (1668–1744) was among the first to realize the imaginative leap needed to enter the minds of those living in earlier historical periods. Johann Gottfried von Herder carried Vico's insights further, emphasizing the particularity of different contemporary cultures, moulded by their separate geographies, histories, languages and myths. Berlin, although temperamentally a man of the **Enlightenment**, felt that these figures of the 'counter-Enlightenment' were a necessary corrective to the rationalist belief in the unity of mankind and the inevitability of progress.

Although, for Berlin, we are the products of our times, he retains a place for a (limited) freedom of choice for the human **subject**. In his essay 'Historical Inevitability' (in *Four Essays on Liberty* (1969)) he argues that without this freedom our concept of morality, our legal system and our view of history would have no meaning. Introducing an element of free choice means abandoning historicist, deterministic accounts of human history – there are times when the actions of great leaders have changed history, and those actions were, at least partially, the result of free choices. History therefore can have no master-plan, no fixed pattern.

Isaiah Berlin has been one of the most influential theorists of liberalism since the Second World War. It is an influence, however, felt more in the wider world of cultural discourse than among professional philosophers. His liberalism is both more humane and conceptually much richer than such neo-liberals as Friedman, Hayek and Nozick, but for that reason it came to seem a little dated in the 1970s and 1980s. However Berlin's belief in the **incommensurability** of values, his denial of the possibility of achieving the Enlightenment goal of perfect, transcultural rationality did put him in the vanguard of contemporary ideas.

BEUYS, JOSEPH: ARTIST (1921–86) Beuys, a prominent member of the Fluxus group in the early 1960s, was always outside the official spaces of high-**modernism**, which, in its rigorous opposition of art and life, endorsed the very difference Beuys wished to overcome. His practice, a mixture of performance art, Dada and

psycho-drama, was a demonstration of his belief that artistic impulses were latent in all people; that cultural expression was the purest form of social being; that art was embedded in work, play and the familiar rituals of everyday life. Thus his 'social sculpture' was meant to reveal that, as all forms of social activity expressed aesthetic qualities, art should be seen as a process rather than a form of property. These ideas formed the basis of his teaching. Having spent eleven years as Professor of Sculpture at the Kunstacademie in Dusseldorf, a period in which he became increasingly associated with an anti-modernist radicalism, he was dismissed from his post in 1972 for encouraging a programme of open admission to the academy.

Beuys's conception of art as that which originates from the primal energies of human life, a conception that tended to push art in the direction of the mythic and the archetypal, was developed by his star pupil, Anselm **Kiefer**, one of the key figures in the European form of postmodernism known as the *trans-avant-garde*.

BHABHA, HOMI K.: CRITIC AND CULTURAL THEORIST (1949–) Educated at the Universities of Bombay and Oxford, Homi Bhabha went on to become a professor at the University of Sussex. During the course of his academic career he has taught in the United States at the Universities of Princetown and Pennsylvania. His main works include *Nation and Narration* (ed., 1990) and *The Location of Culture* (1994).

Homi Bhabha's analyses of the **post-colonial** condition have contributed much to the current critical and theoretical debate. **Anti-essentialist** in his approach, Bhabha questions the notion of a 'unitary identity' with his concept of 'hybridity'; an anti-monolithic model of cultural exchange which negates the polarity of binary models of culture with elements that are, 'neither the One, nor the **Other** but something else besides which contrasts the terms and territories of both'. The alternative, according to Bhabha, is essentialized national stereotypes, constantly driven by a nostalgia for pure origins in an 'attempt to hark back to a "true" national past, which is often repre-sented in the reified forms of realism and stereotype'. He also incisively notes in *Of Mimicry and Man: The Ambivalence of Colonial Discourse* that one of the distinguishing features of a colonial relationship is what he calls 'colonial mimicry' induced in the subject race taught to imitate the dominant race. Thus the colonized is in the position of being 'almost the same' as the colonizer without being actually granted the freedoms that come with sovereignty, dominion and citizenship. Bhabha argues further for a 'discursive conception of ideology' in which ideology is multi-accentual and 'reality' is seen as *produced* by **texts** as opposed to something that is fixed or a given. In this, his work reflects **Marxist** theorists such as Althusser, **Eagleton** and Macherey; however, Bhabha's critique of con-temporary Marxist theory problem-atizes notions of 'mimeticism' and 'teleology' borrowing from **Freudian** and **Lacanian** psychoanalysis. The colonized is associated with excess and fantasy 'a site for dreams, images,

fantasies, myths, obsessions and requirements'; a discursive repository that is a function of the repression of the colonizer. Thus there is a system-atic ambivalence on the part of the colonizer towards 'that otherness that is at once an object of derision and desire'.

Bhabha's contribution to the current theoretical debate lies in his interest in the construction of identity and **sub-jectivity** from the point of view of the colonized. His critiques of **Said**, **Derrida** and **Lyotard** highlight the ways in which the colonized Other has been marginalized by contemporary **critical theory**. He further challenges the notion of the absolute **hegemony** of the colonizing power by high-lighting the way in which encounters with the colonized destabilize and interrogate notions of cultural iden-tity. Fundamentally against rigid or reductive **binary oppositions**, Bhabha's later work challenges the rigid boundaries between colonizer and colonized using a theoretical methodology that is **pluralist** and diverse, avoiding critical and theoretical exclusivity in the spirit of **postmodernism**.

BINARY OPPOSITIONS The use of binary oppositions in analysing pheno-mena is highly characteristic of **structuralism**, and one of the aspects of its methodology that is most vigorously attacked by **poststruc-turalist** critics. Thus in **Lévi-Strauss**, 'nature' and 'culture' are set in opposition to each other as mutually exclusive categories, such that given examples of human behaviour must belong to one or other category – but not both. Lévi-Strauss proceeds to run into problems with the incest taboo, which he is forced to admit *does* seem to belong to both categories. For **Derrida**, this is an admission that calls into question the whole structuralist project, the methodology of which is seen to be faulty. Poststructuralists like Derrida also consider that the principle of binary opposition (*either* one thing *or* its opposite number) depends on a notion of fixed identity that is no longer tenable; as far as they are concerned, identity is a much more fluid phenomenon than structuralists would like to believe.

BLACK CRITICISM With its emphasis on tradition, and on experience, often authenticated through the autobiographical voice, black writing seems inimical to a good deal of **postmodern** theory with its talk of the **death of the author**, the fluidity of subjectivity and of the end of history. Yet some of the most familiar critical concepts in the postmodern lexicon – marginality, **difference**, **otherness** – have given a powerful impetus to the exploration of black **texts**, though not without controversy among black scholars themselves. Black American writing is a good example of the tensions between the demands of political and aesthetic expression. Black criticism sees race as a fundamental category of cultural analysis. The publication of self-authored narratives by ex-slaves in the antebellum period was a profoundly political as well as aesthetic act. While many displayed an exuberant 'literariness', they were written as part of the propaganda war against slavery since, as a number of critics have pointed out, literacy was the principal sign of reason, a faculty

that white supremacists denied black people possessed. Art would be put in the service of politics from the Harlem renaissance of the 1920s, when critics called for a literature that would show the black race at its best, in the 1940s and 1950s by communist fellow-travellers arguing for reform and integration, and in the 1960s by black nationalists in such books as Addison Gayle's *The Black Aesthetic* (1972), which called for revolution and a cross-class alliance of black Americans. In the 1970s Gayle's essentialism and chauvinism were challenged by growing numbers of black feminist critics and by the emergence of **poststructuralist** analysis. In the postmodern world, critics still value concepts of blackness and tradition though they are no longer identified by authorial skin colour, but through the very language of the texts themselves.

BLACK HOLES Despite their being entirely hypothetical or theoretical entities, black holes remain powerfully attractive to cosmologists and astrophysicists such as Stephen **Hawking** and Roger **Penrose**. It is literally true that in order to encounter the space-time **singularities** that theoretically lie at the core of a black hole, Hawking had to join the fictional crew of the USS Enterprise (in *Star Trek*), which encounters such anomalies on a regular basis. The theory remains compelling. For all astrophysics based (as in fact all *are*) on general relativity, light is the limit velocity of the universe; nothing, in other words, travels faster than light. The first theoretical account of black holes stems from J. R. Oppenheimer's and H. Snyder's application in 1939 of the principles of general relativity to the life-cycles of stars. A black hole is a collapsing star of such mass that the velocity required to escape its gravitational field exceeds the velocity of light – which, by the principles of general relativity, is impossible. A black hole is therefore black because it emits no light, and a hole because within it all matter, and even space-time, is destroyed. Black holes are 'expected' to arise when the mass of a neutron star (not all stars will attain the violent end of the neutron star; our sun, for example, will not) reaches a density so high as to create a gravitational field so strong that even the matter-energy of which the star consists will collapse under its own gravity. Many properties stem from this. One is the notion of the 'event horizon' of a black hole: the limit point of the black hole's gravitational field. As this event horizon is approached, since light is unable to escape it, time slows to infinity until within it nothing happens: neither matter nor even space-time survives the event horizon of a black hole. Some cosmologists have hypothesized that the isolated space-time of black holes turns them, to all intents and purposes, into separate universes, each competing with others, through intense gravitation, for resources in order to realize the 'best of all possible worlds' on the evolutionary basis suggested by the fact that stars have life-cycles. It is both tempting and appropriate to suggest that the theoretical physics of black holes, a multiverse composed of timeless and spaceless, dematerialized yet physical absences, separated by unbridgeable event horizons the one from the other, provides a genuinely

physical instantiation of the **post-modern** condition.

BLOOM, HAROLD: THEORIST AND CRITIC (1930–) Harold Bloom graduated from Cornell University in 1951, and gained his doctorate at Yale, where he has taught since 1955. He is one of the most prolific of contemporary critics. His works include *A Map of Misreading* (1975), *Kabbalah and Criticism* (1975), *Poetry and Repression* (1976), *Agon* (1952), *The Book of J* (1991) and *The Western Canon* (1994). In addition, he has written over 350 introductions for the Chelsea House literary criticism series.

Three of Bloom's earliest books reconstruct Romanticism in his own image. In *Shelley's Mythmaking* (1959), he defends Shelley from the battering the poet received by the New Critics. *The Visionary Company* (1961) and *Blake's Apocalypse* (1963) assert the importance of Milton, Blake and the autonomy of the Imagination. These studies are directed against the stranglehold which T. S. Eliot held upon the literary–critical establishment at the time. Bloom allied himself with figures such as Northrop Frye, who rejected Eliot's scrupulous impressionism and embraced instead a more systematic approach to the classification of literary genres.

One of the consequences of this early work is that Bloom was concerned to describe how writers and **texts** interact through time. So in *The Anxiety of Influence* (1973), his most widely read monograph, Bloom argues that every poet is engaged in an agonistic struggle against his literary forebears. In **Freudian** psychoanalysis, the analysand must come to terms with the **Oedipal** love–hate relationship of son to father. Similarly, the poet must try to escape the gravitational pull exerted by his precursors. During this struggle, primary sources are misread and reconfigured by the later poet.

Bloom invented his own gnomic lexicon of 'revisionary ratios' to detail the psychic defences through which the poet can rebel against his forebears: *clinamen* is the deliberate misreading of an earlier work; *tessera* is the completion of an earlier poem in a different direction; *kenosis* is the discontinuity with the precursor; *daemonization* is the formation of a counter-**Sublime**; *askesis* is purging oneself of the precursor; and *apophrades* is a state in which it seems 'as though the later poet himself had written the precursor's characteristic work'.

Although this taxonomy is meant to be representative of the literary process in general, it is especially applicable to the production of **postmodernist** texts. Authors as diverse as Kathy **Acker**, John **Barth**, Italo **Calvino** and Umberto **Eco** are only too well aware that everything has already been written before them. Indeed, Barth coined the term 'literature of exhaustion' to denote the condition of 'used-upness'. Faced with this belatedness, the postmodernist novel typically misreads a previous novel or novels. Acker's *Great Expectations* (1978), Barth's *Sot-Weed Factor* (1960), Calvino's *Invisible Cities* (1972) and Eco's *The Name of the Rose* (1984) can all be usefully studied in terms of their relation to prior texts.

Bloom's emphasis on misreading was congenial to members of the **Yale** School of **deconstruction**, such as Geoffrey **Hartman**, Jacques **Derrida**, and J. Hillis **Miller**.

BODY WITHOUT ORGANS A term used by **Deleuze** and **Guattari** to describe all those forces that hinder the free expression of **desire** and **libidinal** energy. For the authors, the body without organs (which they also refer to as 'the body without an image') is sterile and unproductive, and they identify it with the forces of repression in society. Capital, for example, is to be regarded as the body without organs of the capitalist, which appropriates the production of individual **desiring-machines** (in this case wage labourers) for its own ends. Production (a term encompassing the expression of desire and libidinal energy) is a positive force for Deleuze and Guattari, and bodies without organs are to be resisted because they restrict its range while channelling what is left into their own projects (the creation of profits for themselves, for example).

BOFILL, RICARDO: ARCHITECT (1939–) Claiming the title of 'the Jimi Hendrix of architecture' early in his career, Bofill has more in common with psychedelic fantasy album cover art. His idiosyncratic architecture is a strange overgrown classical encrustation – Corinthian columns pumped full of steroids. It is an aesthetic that is grotesque and surreal – monumental façades decorated with massively over-scaled columns concealing modern apartment complexes. Recalling a European tradition of fascist architecture and grandeur associated with Napoleon, Hitler and Franco, and an affinity with the conscientious 'mad genius' of fellow Catalans Gaudi and Dali, Bofill found admirers among French property developers. His heroic and triumphalist containers of luxury apartments encrusted with concrete baroque ornament appealed to the imagination of the French homeowners in a way that **modernist** equivalents failed to. His scheme for the Palace of Abraxas, in suburban Paris, invents itself as a ten-storey circular theatre, enclosing an area of public space while internally, fluted one-way mirror columns rise up the façade. Les Arcades du Lac, another Parisian housing scheme, features strange interpretations of Doric columns which house new programmes such as stairways or bathroom blocks.

Bofill's freewheeling use of classical iconography is made all the more weird by its lack of **irony**. These are buildings that fail to engage with their own absurdity. Though full of contradictions and complexities, it is an architecture completely engrossed in and enamoured with its own grandeur.

BOURDIEU, PIERRE: SOCIOLOGIST (1930–) One of the key claims in the debate over **postmodernism** is the assertion that the distinction between high and low culture is becoming increasingly blurred. This collapse in cultural certainty has brought about a rethinking of traditional ideas of cultural value. The turn to questions of value has witnessed a growing interest in the work of the French sociologist Pierre Bourdieu. He argues that distinctions of 'culture' (whether understood as **text**, practice or way of living) are a significant aspect in the struggle between dominant and subordinate classes in society. He shows how arbitrary tastes and arbitrary ways of living are continually transmuted into **legitimate** taste and the only legitimate way of life. The 'illusion of "natural distinction" is ultimately based on the power of the dominant to impose, by their very existence, a definition of excellence which [is] nothing other than their own way of existing'. For Bourdieu, 'taste classifies, and it classifies the classifier'. We are classified by our classifications and classify others by theirs. While such strategies of classification do not in themselves produce social inequalities, the making, marking and maintaining of them functions to legitimate such inequalities. Taste is a profoundly ideological discourse; it functions as a marker of 'class' (using the term in the double sense to mean both socio-economic category and a particular level of quality). The consumption of culture is, ultimately, he claims, 'predisposed . . . to fulfil a social function of legitimating social **difference**'.

Bourdieu's work on culture is underpinned by his view of education. He argues that the education system fulfils a quite specific function: to legitimate social inequalities which exist before its operations. The cultural tastes of dominant classes are given institutional form and then, with deft ideological sleight of hand, their taste for this institutionalized culture (i.e. their own) is held up as evidence of their cultural, and ultimately social, superiority. Distinction is generated by learned patterns of cultural consumption which are internalized as 'natural' cultural preferences, and interpreted and mobilized as evidence of 'natural' cultural competences, which are ultimately used to justify forms of class domination. To understand this fully we need to understand how Bourdieu distinguishes between three types of capital: economic, social and cultural. In capitalist societies economic capital in the form of money, property, etc. is able to buy access to cultural and social capital. Hierarchies openly based on the accumulation of economic capital are vulnerable to challenge. Cultural and social capital is able to conceal and legitimate economic domination by reproducing it in the form of cultural and social hierarchies.

Bourdieu's purpose is not to prove the self-evident, that different classes have different lifestyles, different tastes in culture, but to identify and interrogate the processes by which the making of cultural distinctions secures and legitimates forms of power and control rooted ultimately in economic inequalities. He is interested not so much in the actual differences, but in how these differences are used by dominant classes as a means of social reproduction. His project is to (re-)locate 'value' in the world of everyday experience, to suggest that similar things are happening when I 'value' a holiday destination or a particular mode of dress, as are happening when I 'value' a poem by T. S. Eliot or a song by Oasis or a photograph by Cindy **Sherman** or a piece of music by Philip **Glass**. Such evaluations are never a simple matter of individual taste; cultural value operates both to identify and to maintain social difference and sustain social deference. From this perspective, the much heralded postmodern collapse

of standards rehearsed (almost weekly) in the so-called 'quality' media, may be nothing more than a perceived sense that the opportunities to use culture to make, mark, and maintain social distinction are becoming more and more difficult to find, as Pavarotti tops the charts, Górecki outsells most of the acts on *Top of the Pops*, and Premier League football becomes, in many instances, as expensive as ballet or opera.

BRAIDOTTI, ROSI: FEMINIST PHILO-SOPHER AND CULTURAL THEORIST (1954–) Born in Italy, Braidotti was raised in Australia, wrote her doctoral dissertation in French at the Sorbonne, and is now Professor of Women's Studies at the University of Utrecht. Her first book, *Patterns of Dissonance* (1991), was written in French, translated, then extensively rewritten in English, becoming 'a translation without originals'. This self-description as a 'subject in transit', a thinker with 'no mother tongue, only a succession of translations, of displacements', is crucial in Braidotti's articulation of a **postmodern** feminism.

Patterns of Dissonance analyses the relationship between philosophy and feminist theory, arguing that postmodern French philosophers such as **Foucault**, **Derrida** and **Deleuze** have responded to the contemporary 'crisis' of the rational subject by embracing 'the feminine'. This metaphorical embrace, however, goes hand in hand with a renewed exclusion of women from philosophical discourse. Against this, Braidotti sets feminist critiques of rationality and its relation to sexual **difference**. Feminist theory, she argues, insists on the embodied and therefore sexually differentiated nature of **subjectivity**. The feminist theorist *speaks as* a woman, so that theorizing is reconnected to its roots in the body and in **desire**, and incorporates both an ethics and a politics. Embodiment does not, however, mean 'essentialism'. Braidotti's embodied female subject is not a fixed and monolithic essence but the site of multiple, complex and potentially contradictory sets of experiences. Her knowledge is situated and partial; her identity simply a map of where she has already been. She is therefore 'nomadic', a concept developed in *Nomadic Subjects* (1994). The nomad is both situated (hence interconnected) and in movement, with a critical consciousness which resists incorporation. As such, she becomes a metaphor for Braidotti's vision of a postmodern feminism, which can counter the pessimism of postmodern philosophy by embracing its emphasis on the fragmentary nature of identity, while retaining a politics, and an ethics, of sexual difference.

BRYARS, GAVIN: COMPOSER (1943–)
While studying philosophy at Sheffield University, Bryars played jazz double bass in his spare time, exploring free improvisation. As well as gaining a considerable reputation as a jazz performer, he was a founder member of the Portsmouth Sinfonia. This experimental ensemble that undertook anarchic reinterpretations of standard orchestral concert pieces, consisted mainly of amateurs and gained a certain cult status.

Early pieces such as *Jesus' Blood Never Failed Me Yet* show an indebtedness to the repetitive **minimalist** techniques of American composers such as **Reich** and **Glass**. Bryars has written for a variety of instrumental forces. He has composed orchestral pieces (such as *The Green Ray* (1991)), Choral works (*On Photography* (1983)) and many pieces for his own ensemble (such as *The Cross Channel Ferry* (1979) and *Viennese Dance No. 1* (1985). This ensemble was formed in 1979 and tours extensively.

His first opera, *Medea*, a five-act work that was directed and designed by Robert Wilson, was first performed by Opéra de Lyon in 1984. Bryars' music has also been used by choreographers. *Sub Rosa* (1986) was used by William Forsythe for the Frankfurt Ballet's 'Slingerland' and *Four Elements* (1990) was commissioned by the Rambert Dance Company for a ballet by Lucinda Childs. Bryars is also Professor of Music at Leicester's De Montfort University and Musical Associate at the Leicester Haymarket Theatre.

BUTLER, JUDITH: FEMINIST SOCIOLOGIST AND PHILOSOPHER Butler's work centres primarily around the interrogation of gender identity. In her most widely read publication, *Gender Trouble: Feminism and the Subversion of Identity* (1990), she maintains that feminist theory and politics build their agendas upon an unquestioned assumption that women, purely because of their shared femaleness, share a common identity which cuts through differences of race, class and sexual preference. However, Butler, far from regarding gender identity as 'natural', redefines it as a discourse which is both constructed and maintained by society.

Butler also argues that feminist theorists such as Luce **Irigaray** are misled in their attempt to posit the existence of a female sexuality which exists independently of the phallocentric order, for 'if sexuality is culturally constructed within existing power relations, then the postulation of a normative sexuality that is "before", "outside" or "beyond" power is a cultural impossibility and a politically impractical dream'.

For Butler, any consideration of identity cannot be carried out independently of the interrogation of gender, since gender is the foundation upon which the concept of identity itself is based. In other words, **subjects** only become intelligible when defined in relation to accepted categories of gender. She uses the term 'compulsory heterosexuality' to describe the institution which maintains the coherence of gender identity through persistent reference to the fixed opposition male/female, in which each category is defined through its difference to the other; a distinction which is consolidated through heterosexual practice.

The system, therefore, conceals its own status as construction by presenting the heterosexual dualism as 'normal', 'natural' and 'right'. Nevertheless, however convincing it might be, the construct is not seamless, and its maintenance is far from effortless. Instead, Butler defines gender constructions as 'performances' or 'fabrications', perpetuated by the repeated inscription of gendered 'acts, gestures and enactments' upon the surface of the body. The illusion has to be constantly maintained, however, in order to conceal the fact that it 'has no ontological status apart from the various acts which constitute its reality'.

This performative aspect of gender becomes, for Butler, the means by which its claims to be expressive of 'true' identity can be questioned. While it may be impossible to construct a notion of sexual identity outside this framework, it is possible to find opportunities to expose the regulatory aims within the apparatus of 'gender' from within its margins, by looking at gender identities which do not conform to the heterosexual norm. Homosexual, lesbian or bisexual practices all pose an implicit challenge to the fixed male/female opposition by demonstrating a multiplicity of different ways in which that dualism can be reconfigured.

In *Bodies That Matter: On the Discursive Limits of 'Sex'* (1993) Butler turns to the body of the drag queen as a particularly fruitful source for such subversive readings of gender. Although it can certainly be used in the service of the norm, the parodic nature of the drag act – which ostentatiously appropriates the paraphernalia of femininity or masculinity, then inscribes it upon the 'wrong' body – has the potential to initiate a 'reverse' reading of gender codes, exposing 'the understated, taken-for-granted quality of heterosexual performativity'.

C

CALVINO, ITALO: NOVELIST (1923–87)
Italo Calvino was born in a Cuban
village to Italian parents and was
brought up in San Remo. He fought
for the resistance movement during
the Second World War, and after the
conflict wrote a doctoral thesis on
Conrad at the University of Turin. He
entered publishing, and remained
with this career even after settling in
Paris. He stayed in France until his
return to Italy in 1980, where he died
seven years later.

His early fictions were coloured by
his left-wing politics and neo-realist
aesthetic. His first novel, *The Path
to the Nest of Spiders* (1947), for
instance, is an adventure story in
which fourteen-year-old Pin mingles
with the partisans during the war.
Many of the short stories in *Adam,
One Afternoon and Other Stories*
(1949) are realistic, too, although elements of fantasy are also prominent
in this collection. He will be remembered most, however, for his experimentation and bold storytelling gifts.
In *If on a Winter's Night a Traveller*
(1979), for instance, he adopts the
second-person narrative viewpoint.
To complicate matters further, the
addressee is a Reader engaged in the
process of reading. Initially the
Reader is reading Calvino's book. The
Reader soon discovers, however, that
his book is faulty and repeats the first
chapter several times. So the Reader
returns the book, only to discover that
the new copy presents a completely
different narrative altogether. In the
bookshop, the Reader comes into
contact with the Other Reader, Ludmilla, the female counterpart of the
male 'you'. The narrative then alternates between two distinct levels: one
concerning the relationship between
the two Readers, the other revolving
around a variety of first chapters –
each in a different style – which the
first Reader 'reads' in his replacement book.

This subtle and sinuous text is Calvino's masterpiece, and crystallizes
many of the techniques and themes
that made him into one of the
consummate **postmodernist** writers.
First, there is the interest in the
permutation of plot and content.
Other works that play games of
combination include *The Castle of
Crossed Destinies* (1969), which is
based on a set of tarot cards, and
Invisible Cities (1972), in which
Marco Polo describes to Kubla Khan
the various cities he has visited within
his empire. Second, there are the
experiments with generic conventions. His early novels *The Cloven
Viscount* (1952) *The Baron in the
Trees* (1957) and *The Non-Existent
Knight* (1959) merge fantasy and
romance deftly. Science-fiction is
explored in *Cosmicomics* (1965), in
which the origins of the universe are

209

observed by a life-principle called Qfwfq, and *t zero* (1967), where abstract **binary oppositions** such as chaos and order are personified. Many of Calvino's short stories are based on motifs from folk-tales and fables. Third, despite his bent for philosophical and theoretical speculation, each of Calvino's fictions is grounded in a commitment to the enrichment of human values and the redemptive power of love. John **Barth** once compared writing to love-making; passion without virtuosity is clumsy, while virtuosity without passion is cold and clinical. Calvino's triumph is that he demonstrated both passion *and* virtuosity in his work.

CARTER, ANGELA: AUTHOR (1947–92) Angela Carter is now widely accepted as one of the most innovative writers of recent years. Along with Salman **Rushdie**, she is often classified as an English exponent of **magic realism**. Although she is best known for her novels and short story collections, in the course of a prolific career she also established herself as a journalist, reviewer, playwright and cultural commentator.

Carter wrote her first novel, *Shadow Dance,* while studying for a degree in English at the University of Bristol. Published in 1966, a year after her graduation, it immediately established the salient characteristics of her work. Written in an elaborate, ornate, prose style, the novel recasts the world of provincial 1960s bohemia as Gothic narrative, and its fascination with costume, theatrics, and insane states and situations follows **postmodernism** in asserting the fluidity and malleability of the

subject, which is not born so much as constructed. It was closely followed by *The Magic Toyshop* (1967), for which Carter won the John Llewellyn Rhys Memorial Prize, *Several Perceptions*, which gained her the Somerset Maugham Award for 1968, *Heroes and Villains* (1969) and *Love* (1971).

Carter used the money from the Somerset Maugham Award to travel to Japan, where she lived until 1972. She earned her living by writing articles for the periodical *New Society,* many of which chronicle her experience of cultural alienation. During her time in Japan she also wrote the short stories collected in *Fireworks* (1974), as well as the novel *The Infernal Desire Machines of Doctor Hoffman* (1972), a piece of macabre fantasy which was heavily influenced by surrealism.

Later, Carter also credited Japan with inspiring her conversion to feminism; although it was characteristic that on her return to England she immediately began work on a controversial study of the work of Marquis de Sade. *The Sadeian Woman,* which was eventually published in 1979, has been condemned by some feminist critics, Andrea Dworkin among them, as an inexcusable defence of pornography. Carter's next novel, *The Passion of New Eve* (1977), written while she was still researching de Sade, exploits the tension that arises from the attempt to combine a feminist analysis of oppression with a continued fascination with the extremities of **desire**.

However, it was Carter's collection of rewritten fairy tales, *The Bloody Chamber* (1979), which aimed to uncover the latent subversive potential of familiar nursery stories, that was primarily responsible for bringing her work to the attention of a wider audience. As well as the book itself, her version of the tale of Little Red Riding Hood, 'The Company of Wolves', was rewritten by Carter herself as a radio play (1980) and also as a screenplay for a film directed by Neil Jordan (1984).

In the final years of her life she produced her two great novels, *Nights at the Circus* (1984), whose central character is a winged trapeze artist, and *Wise Children* (1991), which is not only a carnivalesque romp through a medley of Shakespearean allusions, but also – given that Carter died less than a year after its publication – an uncannily prescient contemplation of the inevitability of ageing and death. A collection of Carter's criticism, *Expletives Deleted,* was published posthumously in 1992, and a final collection of short stories, *American Ghosts and Old World Wonders,* appeared in 1993.

CATASTROPHE THEORY Apocalyptic similarities with **chaos theory** notwithstanding, catastrophe theory shares little with the latter beyond both implying, through their names, that mathematics at the end of the twentieth century has become a technical code devoted to the analysis of some glamorously crash-and-burn apocalypse. Invented by mathematical 'sorcerer' René **Thom** in *Structural Stability and Morphogenesis* (1972) there is in fact little catastrophic about the theory. Instead, the overt strategy of catastrophe theory is to demonstrate a formal, mathematizable continuity between states in a dynamical system despite gross apparent discontinuities between those states. An ice-age, for example, does not appear to be part of the mesh of interconnected systems of life on a temperate earth, but rather its end. Catastrophe theory seeks to demonstrate that what appear to be catastrophes that change everything are, at the level of mathematical form – *morphogenetically* – profoundly continuous. A catastrophe is not the end of a system, but an inherent, predictable and mathematizable component of it. So stated, emphasizing continuity over discontinuity, catastrophe theory seems anything but **postmodern**; it is paradoxical, then, that Jean-François **Lyotard** derives some of the more celebrated theses of *The Postmodern Condition* (1979) from this body of theory. Just as, for example, Lyotard famously insists that '**postmodernity** is incredulity towards **metanarratives**', so Thom declares that 'the era of grand cosmic synthesis is at an end' and that science can no longer be characterized as the investigation of the ultimate nature of reality. Accordingly, catastrophe theory recognizes the impossibility of the quantitative global model aspired to by Euclidean geometry, and frames its analyses within the local parameters of the dynamical system under study. Catastrophe theory's emphasis on formal continuity is therefore both local and abstract, the sequence of models amounting to nothing more than 'the play of pure forms' – morphogenesis. Following this abstract line, catastrophe theory thus broaches territories long since barred to mathematics, including sociology, linguistics and **semiotics**, so that it feeds directly into the arenas where postmodernism is currently contested.

CHAOS THEORY A chaotic system is one that shows a sensitive dependence on initial conditions. If chaos theory can be said to have a beginning, it was the discovery by Edward Lorenz in 1960 that tiny errors in equations he was using to model weather systems resulted in enormous and apparently unpredictable variations in the outcome of the equations. The consequences of this seemed fatal to any attempt to make long-term weather forecasts – minute differences in the initial conditions could mean the difference between flood and drought. This has become known as the butterfly effect – the flapping of a butterfly's wings in China could create a causal chain the final outcome of which is a hurricane in Indonesia.

Postmodernists have embraced chaos as a counter to the expansive truth-claims of science. Chaos seems, superficially, to throw an element of uncertainty into the activity of the material world: it has been argued that it would require a computer bigger than the universe itself to predict the behaviour of all the chaotic systems it contains.

This is, however, to ignore the constructive side of chaos theory. When data from chaotic systems are plotted, complex but recognizable patterns emerge – the consequence of what are known as strange attractors. These patterns in chaotic behaviour make it possible to make short-term predictions and to predict general trends. The quest to find order in chaos has led to the creation of

another new field – the science of complexity.

Chaos theory has been used to help explain the baffling orbits of certain satellites, to understand fluctuations in animal populations, to track the movement of the market and to model the beating of the human heart. There are, however, those who claim that there has been precious little real achievement to justify the hype.

CHORA In Plato's *Timaeus,* chora is the unnameable, unstable receptacle existing prior to the nameable form of the One. Generally, in **postmodern** usage, chora designates a site of undifferentiated being, connoting the experience of continuity with the maternal body as an infinite space. Specifically in Julia **Kristeva**'s work, chora specifies the presignifying traces which underlie and at times break through the order of signification. Hence the shared bodily space of mother and child resists **representation**, yet is experienced as **desire**, the uncanny or the mystical. The chora as maternal desire threatens to destablize the finite unity and autonomous identity of the **modern** 'man'.

CIXOUS, HÉLÈNE: AUTHOR AND CULTURAL THEORIST (1937–) Cixous is one of the leading figures in recent French feminist thought, and is usually identified, along with such as Luce **Irigaray**, with what has come to be known as **difference feminism** (although she herself rejects the description of 'feminist', and is not as radical in her concept of difference as Irigaray proves to be). Within France itself Cixous is also well known as the author of experimental fiction, including works for the theatre.

Cixous is a strong advocate of women's writing (*l'écriture feminine*), arguing that 'Woman must write her self: must write about women and bring women to writing', on the grounds of a perceived sexual difference. For Cixous, 'a woman's instinctual economy cannot be identified by a man or referred to a masculine economy': a claim that has led to her being accused by some critics of biological essentialism. However, she has been careful to make it clear that *l'écriture feminine* is not to identified with women alone. It is to be seen instead as a form of writing that challenges existing linguistic conventions (which are the product of a particular kind of patriarchal society), with the ultimate aim of breaking down repressive cultural structures. Thus Cixous can cite Jean Genet as an example of the *l'écriture feminine* approach. Given the heavily patriarchal nature of the society in which we live, however, it is likely that most practitioners of *l'écriture feminine* will in fact turn out to be women; although it should be regarded overall as an essentially tactical exercise designed to correct certain social wrongs, rather than a marker of difference between the sexes.

Cixous provides further arguments against biological essentialism when she writes in *The Newly Born Woman* (co-written with Catherine Clement, 1975) that it is at least possible to imagine a radical change in cultural organization, such that 'what today appears to be "feminine" or "masculine" would no longer amount to the same thing'. She speculates that such a change could then lead to existing notions of gender difference being replaced by 'a bunch of new differences'; although exactly what those might be, it is extremely difficult to say from our current cultural vantage point.

COMMUNICATIVE ACTION Communicative action is a form of interaction whose success depends on the hearer responding with a 'yes' or 'no' to the validity claim raised with a given utterance. Jürgen **Habermas**'s theory of communicative action derives from speech-act philosophy, sociolinguistics and, in particular, from the idea of conversational implicature. The latter idea refers to what is implied in speech as opposed to what the same words in a written sentence might logically imply. What is implied by the rich context of speaker meaning cannot be ignored by or replaced with abstract rules of logical implication. The anti-positivism of conversational implicature reinforces both a pragmatic concern with the rich context of meaning, of beliefs and goals, from which individuals speak and a **Kantian** concern with universal rules. A **postmodern** critic would question the success of communicative action insofar as the concrete differences of marginalized persons are ignored or erased by the public realm of discourse. A relevant postmodern defence would have to demonstrate that the obligations implicit in communicative action demand – universally – inclusion of and openness to the other.

COMPLEXITY THEORY The world is full of complex systems, from the internal structure of single-celled organisms to the working of the stock exchange. Complexity theory has attempted to define these 'self-organizing' systems, and then to find the general principles that underlie them, with the goal of producing a unified law of complexity. Although the search for a unified law betrays a deep-seated reductionist bias, there is also a counterbalancing holism in that the behaviour of complex systems cannot be simply deduced from their constituent parts. Complexity therefore calls for new principles, new modes of analysis.

Although there is no consensus among researchers, the nearest thing to a common definition of complexity involves the 'edge of **chaos**' hypothesis. The distinguishing feature of complexity, in this view, is high informational content, and informational content is maximized in systems that exist at the border between highly stable states (crystalline structures, regular planetary orbits) and chaos.

Complexity theorists typically spend their time producing computer models of natural behaviours. Shapes squirm and wriggle across computer screens in **simulations** of bacteria or antelope, struggling for survival, competing for resources in harsh environments, evolving, dying. This '**artificial life**' research attempts to find the simple laws that generate both the complexity and the emergent order. Researchers argue that if you can create complex behaviour in a computer from a small number of simple rules, the corresponding behaviours in the 'real' world must equally be the product of a small number of simple rules. If it is countered that

there is a fundamental difference between real-world organisms and the blips on a computer screen, complexity theorists tend to suggest that the parallels are so close that the 'virtual' organisms should be granted the same status as their flesh and blood cousins. This blurring of real and virtual worlds is, of course, very **postmodern**.

CONTINENTAL PHILOSOPHY Philosophy in Europe (particularly in France and Germany) has been felt by many to have developed in a radically different way in modern times from that in the English-speaking world, and the term 'continental philosophy' has increasingly come to be applied as a way of differentiating it from what is taken to be the philosophical mainstream. Many would date continental philosophy back to **Kant** (in particular to his *Critique of Judgement* and its theory of the **sublime**), but in a more recent sense it refers to movements such as phenomenology, existentialism, **structuralism**, **poststructuralism**, **postmodernism**, and **difference feminism**. **Husserl** and **Heidegger**'s phenomenology is one of the critical influences on later twentieth-century continental philosophy (nearly every major poststructuralist and postmodernist thinker acknowledges their influence), which has also drawn freely on such intellectual traditions as **Marxism** and **Freudianism**, and such maverick philosophical figures as **Nietzsche**.

The English philosopher David Cooper has usefully defined continental philosophy as having the following major concerns: (1) cultural critique; (2) concern with the background conditions of enquiry; (3) 'the fall of the self' (that is, a loss of belief in the notion of a unified personal identity or **subject**). Although such concerns can also be found in the work of English-speaking philosophers, they hardly ever dominate debate they way they do on the Continent, where they recur obsessively in the work of such recent figures as **Foucault**, **Derrida**, **Deleuze** and **Lyotard**.

Although it is identified with French and German thought, it is nevertheless possible to be defined as a continental philosopher outside those traditions – the American philosopher Richard **Rorty** being one such example. Continental philosophy is to be regarded as a particular 'style' or 'mood' of philosophical discourse rather than a specific cultural or national tradition as such.

COOVER, ROBERT: AUTHOR (1932–)
Robert Coover has published several short story collections, including *Pricksongs and Descants* (1969), *In Bed One Night and Other Brief Encounters* (1983) and *A Night at the Movies* (1987). His novels include: *The Origin of the Brunists* (1966), *The Universal Baseball Association* (1968), *The Public Burning* (1977), *Spanking the Maid* (1982), *Gerald's Party* (1986) and *Pinocchio in Venice* (1991). Coover's works are influenced by Latin American magic realism. He produces what Salman **Rushdie** calls 'matter of fact descriptions of the outré and bizarre, and their reverse, namely heightened, stylised versions of the everyday'.

In *The Universal Baseball Association*, J. Henry Waugh, a lonely accountant, devotes most of his spare time to a fantasy table-top baseball game. The Association is regulated by dice, and trouble looms when his star player Damon Rutherford is killed by a wild pitch. Waugh is warped by feelings of revenge. He alters the dice in a later game and 'murders' the pitcher, Jock Casey. In the last chapter of the book the base-ball world breaks completely free of its creator (whose initials, J. H. W., suggest some obvious biblical parallels with Jahweh). The players autono-mously commemorate 'Damonsday', several generations after the deaths of Rutherford and Casey.

In a similar manner, Coover de-mythologizes two religious episodes in the short stories 'The Brother' and 'J's Marriage' from *Pricksongs and Descants*. In the first story, Noah is mocked by his brother for building an ark to save the animals from the flood. The narrator's slack punctu-ation and modern American idioms sink the pomposity of Noah's mission. Even so, his boat stays afloat. In 'J's Marriage', a couple undergo several rites of passage (courtship, matri-mony, the birth of their first child): nothing startling in that, perhaps. The husband, however, is no ordinary Joe: he is the carpenter Joseph, his wife is the Virgin Mary and his child Jesus Christ. The immaculate conception and nativity are unfamiliar when framed through the perspective of a husband who knows that his marriage has not been consummated.

The literary form most persistently mimicked by Coover is that of the fairy tale or fable. The opening story of *Pricksongs and Descants*, 'The Door: A Prologue of Sorts', injects a heady fix of sex and violence into the stories of Little Red Riding Hood and Jack and the Beanstalk. This is Grimm revised by **Freud**. In 'The Magic Poker', a caretaker's son spies upon two sisters as they visit a remote island. The girls find a wrought-iron poker in the grass, a primal scene returned to many times. In some action replays it is Karen who finds the poker, in others it is her sister. When the poker is kissed, it sometimes turns into a handsome man, or remains its rusty self.

Like Zeuxis in the Greek myth, who painted grapes so lifelike that birds pecked at them, Coover is fascinated by the interface between art and reality. And like Parrhasius, whose curtain on a canvas fooled Zeuxis into thinking it was an actual cloth cover, Coover loves nothing better than to play games with frames.

COUPLAND, DOUGLAS: NOVELIST AND JOURNALIST (1961–) In 1988, after training as a sculptor and in business management, Coupland wrote an article for a Vancouver magazine on a group of young, disaffected, over-educated and underachieving twenty-somethings he called '**Generation X**'. The following year a publisher asked him to expand this into a sociological guidebook. However, Coupland wrote a novel instead, the extremely successful *Generation X* (1991). It became one of the most influential books of the year and gave birth to thousands of newspaper articles debating Coupland's chapter titles ('Dead at Thirty, Buried at Seventy') and discussing the coinages and definitions which peppered the margins

of his book ('A "McJob": a low pay, low status, no future job in the service sector'). The depressing statistics that form the final chapter give empirical support to the characters' reading of the world around them – while everyone now may own a TV set, this post-boomer generation are the first Americans since the Second World War to be worse off than their parents.

Generation X, Shampoo Planet (1992) and especially the short stories in *Life After God* (1994) echo Thoreau in looking to nature to invest the world with meaning. Even in the more upbeat *Microserfs* (1995) Coupland's characters live in a belated, **postmodern** world which has seen the arrival of **Fukuyama**'s 'end of history' – the empty triumph of capitalist democracy in which his characters keep banality at bay only through a shoulder-shrugging irony.

CRITICAL THEORY Critical theory is a methodology most closely associated with the **Frankfurt School** of social and political thinkers. The term itself does not designate a uniform or unified approach to social and political phenomena, and has been variously deployed by its leading practitioners. Nevertheless, underneath the differences that exist in the thought of **Adorno**, **Horkheimer**, **Marcuse** and, most recently, Jürgen **Habermas**, critical theory is most closely associated with **Marxist** philosophy. Critical theorists apply their method to the dominance of capitalism in advanced industrialized societies in Western Europe and the United States, and to the development of Marxism in the former Soviet Union and Eastern bloc. The philosophical base of critical theory is neo-**Hegelian** and can be found in the works of the Hungarian Marxist Georg Lukács. Lukács's debate with Adorno and Brecht in this period regarding the nature of **modernism** demonstrates the diversity of opinion in the Marxist tradition regarding the role of aesthetics in modern life. Critical theorists such as Adorno recognize that culture is an industry, though some aspects of art are autonomous. The historical high point in the work of critical theorists is the period between 1950 and 1970, when the critique of positivism (a particularly strong form of empiricism associated with Auguste Comte) led by Adorno and Horkheimer concluded that positivism does not lead to a realistic interpretation of social events. In this respect critical theorists recognize that economic determinism and historical materialism do not provide a convincing total critique, and stress instead the relationship between structure and agency, with the objective and subjective reflected in social conditions.

CULTURAL MATERIALISM Cultural materialism is the term used by critics Jonathan **Dollimore** and Alan **Sinfield** to describe their work (and that of like-minded critics). They argue that culture is inseparable from its conditions of production and reception in history. The term was originally coined by Raymond Williams in the early 1980s to describe 'the analysis of all forms of signification . . . within the actual means and conditions of their production'. Cultural materialism's 'key axiom', as Sinfield calls it, is 'culture is political'. For Dollimore 'there is no cultural practice without political significance'. Their method of analysis takes the form of politically engaged and theoretically informed close readings of, for example, Shakespeare's plays, which would take issue with more conservative readings that make the dramas vessels of universal, timeless values. In this respect cultural materialism is akin to American new historicism, though this is a more pessimistic method of analysis that looks to **Foucault** rather than to **Marx**, and suggests, as many postmodern critics do, that 'subversion' in Renaissance drama is finally contained and may have been a ruse of power to consolidate itself all along. Dollimore finds this work 'salutary', but argues that to contain a threat by rehearsing it at least gives it a voice.

CULTURAL RELATIVISM Perhaps the first explicit statement of the concept of cultural relativism occurs in Book III of *The Histories* when Herodotus observes that we all follow the customs of the society into which we are born, and that, as a consequence, all such customs should be respected. The following two thousand years saw that principle sadly neglected. While it might be acknowledged that other cultures operated with different value systems, it remained the orthodox view in Western culture from late antiquity to the nineteenth century that alien cultures (African, Oriental, Native American) could be judged from the vantage point of Western 'rationality'.

A fully developed theory of cultural relativism had to wait until the rise of modern anthropology in the early twentieth century. A number of American anthropologists began to attempt to understand non-Western cultures 'from the inside'. The proper investigation of other cultures came to involve a complete immersion in the values, traditions and beliefs of those cultures. Other societies came to be seen as self-contained, self-validating 'organic' forms. The corollary of this was a thoroughgoing moral relativism: what is right or wrong is defined within each culture, and there is no objective position from which two different cultural/moral systems might be assessed.

CULTURAL STUDIES The object of study in cultural studies is not culture defined in the narrow sense, as the objects of aesthetic excellence ('high art'), but culture understood as the **texts** and practices of everyday life. This is a definition of culture which can embrace the first definition, but also, and crucially, it can range beyond its social exclusivity, to include the study of popular culture.

Cultural studies insists that to understand a cultural text or practice we must always locate it in relation to the social structure and its historical contingency. Although constituted by a particular social structure with a particular history, culture is not studied as a reflection of this structure and history. Culture's importance derives from the fact that it helps constitute the structure and shape the history. Capitalist industrial societies are societies divided unequally along ethnic, gender and class lines. Culture is one of the principal sites where these divisions are established and contested.

People *make* culture from the repertoire of commodities supplied by the culture industries (film, television, music, publishing etc.). Making culture ('production in use') can be empowering to subordinate and resistant to dominant understandings of the world. But this is not to say that it is always empowering and resistant. To deny that the consumers of popular culture are cultural dupes is not to deny that the culture industries seek to manipulate. But it *is* to deny that popular culture is little more than a degraded landscape of commercial and ideological manipulation imposed from above in order to make profit and secure ideological control. To decide these matters requires vigilance and attention to the details of the production, distribution and consumption of culture. These are not matters that can be decided once and for all (outside the contingencies of history and politics) with an élitist glance and a condescending sneer. Nor can they be read off from the moment of production (locating meaning, pleasure, ideological effect etc. in, variously, the intention, the means of production or the production itself); these are only aspects of the contexts for 'production in use', and it is, ultimately, in 'production in use' that questions of meaning, pleasure, ideological effect etc. can be (contingently) decided.

CYBERPUNK Cyberpunk is a term loosely applied to a variety of recent science-fiction. It was first used by critics to describe William **Gibson**'s influential science-fiction novel *Neuromancer* (1984) and then such writers as Bruce Sterling, John

Shirley, Pat Cadogan and Elizabeth Vonarburg, who present a grimly commodified dystopian future. Stylistically, cyberpunk is an eclectic collage of influences, among them *Blade Runner*, William Burroughs, Thomas **Pynchon**, Raymond Chandler, *film noir* and the 'psychological' sciencefiction of late 1960s counter-culture: J. G. Ballard, Philip K. Dick and Samuel Delany. 'Cyber' comes from control and communications systems and 'punk' from the relative youth of the writers and their indebtedness to popular music and TV. Cyberpunk is interested primarily in the interface (a favourite word) between humans and new technologies such as '**virtual reality**', cloning, and in the psychological and philosophical consequences of the blurring of such distinctions as human/machine and illusion/reality. Seen as quintessentially **postmodern** by many critics, the world of cyberpunk is a bleak **Baudrillardian** one of **simulation**, where image and reality have imploded. However, many women writers have been drawn to the genre to explore, through the virtual disembodiment of **cyberspace**, different constructions of gender and gender relations.

CYBERSPACE Take the mouse on your computer. Remove a document from a file and throw it away. Once upon a time you would have typed DOS (disk operating system) instructions to do this. The graphic user interface (GUI) which spatializes the process is a version of cyberspace, a virtual space that exists nowhere and is made of millions of pieces of information. It is where your money is.

What if you could put on a certain kind of headset and could dissolve the distinction between you and your computer, entering the information site through your mind? And what if more than one of you could enter the (non-)space and could interact? This is the premise of *Neuromancer* (1984), William **Gibson**'s hugely influential **cyberpunk** novel. Gibson invented the term 'cyberspace' in the novel and describes it as 'a consensual hallucination experienced daily by billions of legitimate operators in every nation. A graphic representation of data extracted from the banks of every computer in the human system. Unthinkable complexity.' Cyberspace is a non-space that is everywhere and yet nowhere. This space exists: it is called the **Internet**, the decentralized and global network of networks. We do have interaction: it is called a multi-user domain (MUD). We can make porous the human/machine interface: it is called **virtual reality**. All that makes Gibson's book science-fiction is the nature of the interface, which is of an interactive complexity we have not as yet achieved. Cyberspace is a world of **postmodern simulation**, where image and reality, human and machine implode, become porous. While for some, cyberspace throws up profound epistemological and ontological problems, for many the democracy of the Internet is a potential liberation, not least from the sexual, racial and bodily identities they live with in the corporeal world.

CYBORG The term cyborg was first coined in 1960 by Manfred Clynes, a research space scientist.

A combination of 'cybernetic' and 'organism', it is used to describe a hybrid being who is half-human, half-machine. Cyborgs have been a staple motif in science-fiction since the 1920s. However, they have gained a new position in the popular imagination since the success of such cult films as *Terminator* (1984). Beneath its playing out of familiar macho fantasies, *Terminator* also communicates the anxiety inherent in the concept of the cyborg, whose technological modifications, combined with the emotionlessness of a machine, make him an invincible instrument of destruction. In its iconic role, therefore, the cyborg acts as a symbol of the fear that humanity itself is in danger of becoming entirely absorbed into a wholly technological future within which the machine becomes the paradigm by which the organic itself functions.

On a more mundane plane, however, cyborgs already exist, for mechanical body-parts are now routinely used as a replacement for human organs, joints and limbs. For **postmodernist** techno-theorists such as Donna **Haraway**, it is these less-dramatic manifestations of the cyborg that demonstrate that a future in which the boundaries between the organic and the technological are being transgressed every day, is one we already, inescapably, inhabit.

D

DEATH OF THE AUTHOR Roland Barthes's notion of the death of the author is one of the rallying cries for **poststructuralism** in its insistence that the author is not to be regarded as the final arbiter of a **text**'s meaning. In Barthes' view, **authors** had come to be considered as authority figures, thus placing the reader in an inferior position. He called for the death of the author (more precisely, the death of a certain conception of the author, the author as authority figure) in order to free the reader to be creative. Reading was no longer to be considered a passive process, but instead an active one in which the reader was fully engaged in the production of textual meaning. The birth of the reader, as Barthes put it, was to be achieved at the expense of the author. The major thrust of Barthes's attack is against the modern tendency to treat authors as cultural icons (the Author rather than the author, with the capital 'A' signalling the importance accorded this figure), rather than authorship as such, and the death of the author is an implicitly anti-traditional notion much in keeping with the liberationist tenor of the 1960s when it was devised.

DEATH OF MAN (DEATH OF THE SUBJECT) Michel **Foucault** is somewhat notorious for proclaiming the death of man (for which we are to read the death of a particular conception of man), and this politically-charged idea is certainly prevalent in **poststructuralist** and **postmodernist** thought. (Another way of putting this is to speak of the death of the 'subject'.) In Foucault's view, man is a recent, and not particularly noteworthy, invention that will be erased by the passage of time. His target is the humanist conception of man (the dominant one in the West for the last few centuries), where the individual is regarded as the focal point of the cultural process. Earlier versions of the notion can be found in **structuralist** thought, with Claude **Lévi-Strauss** providing one of the best-known examples: for Lévi-Strauss it is the system, not the individual, that is of importance. Structural **Marxism** too, with its emphasis on the critical role played by institutional structures in determining the ideology of Western society, assumes the death of man as a starting point for its cultural analyses, which it openly declares to be anti-humanist. Critics of this movement have spoken of it as giving us 'history without a subject'.

DECONSTRUCTION Deconstruction is a term coined by the French philosopher Jacques **Derrida** in the late 1960s to offer a mode of reading which is attentive to a **text**'s multiple meanings. Rather than attempting to find a true meaning, a consistent point of view or unified message in a given work, a deconstructive reading *carefully teases out*, to use Barbara Johnson's words, 'the warring forces of signification' at play and waiting to be read in what might be called the textual unconscious. As a mode of reading, then, which exposes a text's internal differences and attends to its repressed contradictions or inherent vulnerabilities, its strategy is also interventionist, and as such, despite many a claim to the contrary, deconstruction is political. This is not only because of the ways in which a deconstructive reading can turn a text's logic against itself by showing how the logic of its language can differ from and play against the logic of its **author**'s stated claims, but also because deconstructors tend to seize on the inconsistencies, inequalities, or hierarchies which are expounded or glossed over either by a text, by a whole discourse, or even by an entire system of beliefs. For instance, the structure of hierarchy which Derrida sees implicit in the minds of '**binary oppositions**' which have traditionally informed, organized and ranked Western thinking, and have therefore led us to value a concept such as 'order' more highly than its opposite, '**chaos**', makes it imperative for Derrida to re-examine other such binary couplets. What the privileging of one term over and above the other (such as good over evil, light over dark, reason over emotion, male over female, master over slave, model over copy, original over reproduction, literature over criticism, high culture over popular culture, etc.) reveals is that the preference for one term

always works at the expense or exclusion of the **other**, subordinated, term. **Difference feminists** have drawn on this kind of analysis to question not only the position of women *vis-à-vis* men, or the subaltern *vis-à-vis* the Westerner, but moreover to deconstruct the very system of conceptual opposition which has enabled, and still perpetuates, such metaphysical and ideological values in Western society. Deconstruction then is the very means, Derrida suggests, by which to expose, reverse and dismantle binary oppositions with their hierarchies of value; that is, to render untenable the logic which, while pitching one term against the other, fails to recognize that each term both *differs* from and *defers* to the other term (Derrida's '**différance**' captures both senses of this movement simultaneously), and thus also fails to acknowledge that even though 'good', for example, is distinct from 'evil', as the privileged term 'good' also depends for its meaning on its association with *its* subordinate opposite, 'evil'. This suggests not only a degree of contamination between opposite terms, 'each' a kind of trace of the other, but concomitantly also indicates the impossibility of ever maintaining a clear-cut division in the form of an opposition, hence pointing up once more the unstable nature of meaning.

DELEUZE, GILLES: PHILOSOPHER (1925–95) Until his death in 1995, Deleuze was Professor of Philosophy at University of Paris-VIII at Saint-Denis. Michel **Foucault**'s extravagant claim, in a review of two of Deleuze's driest and most complex books, that 'one day this century will be known as Deleuzian' sits ill at ease with the relative infrequency, when compared to thinkers such as Foucault himself, with which Deleuze's name is currently heard in discussions of our '**postmodern** condition'; but there are perhaps reasons to think that his reviewer's prognosis will be borne out not in this but the next century. In part this is due to the incredible range of Deleuzian thinking, adopting literature (writing extensively on, for example, Proust, Beckett, Melville and Lovecraft) and cinema as ways of thinking rather than objects for philosophical or theoretical study, while practically reinventing the history of philosophy according to its heretics and outcasts, rehabilitating Lucretius, Hume, Spinoza, **Nietzsche** and Bergson against the post-war French canon of **Hegel**, **Husserl** and **Heidegger**.

Ultimately, however, Deleuze's principal contribution is perhaps his consistent experimentation with re-engineering new concepts to propel philosophy beyond the human frame, a concern he carried through from *Difference and Repetition* (1968) to *What is Philosophy?* (1991). Thus time becomes 'deep' or geological, rather than lived or phenomenological, and the species-barriers that perpetuate anthropocentric thinking about mineral, animal and – crucially – *machinic* life inevitably break down as the thought augments its scale and reorients its detail towards the vast mineral and chemical vortex of life in geological time. The figure of man is not so much a sketch in sand washed away by incoming tides as it is a minuscule tyrant bearing down upon the 'image of thought'. While this scale might tempt us to think of the individual subject, following terms invented in Deleuze and **Guattari**'s two-volume *Capitalism and Schizophrenia: Anti-Oedipus* and *A Thousand Plateaus*, as 'molecular', the real problem is derived from its 'molar' form. Molecularity has nothing to do with scale, but, as in chemistry, with the gravity or force of molecular bonds that keep them in orbit around a stable centre, just as thought revolves around the human. Molecular thought thus follows the unstable and eccentric or 'deterritorializing' trajectories of minor particles or flows, much as Deleuze treats the history of philosophy. The infamous '**desiring-machines**', claimed in *Anti-Oedipus* to be 'real machines, not imaginary ones', that industrialize the psychoanalytic category of the unconscious, to make it into a machine that produces reality rather than merely dream or fantasy, thus conjoin the molecular flows of money in advanced capitalism with the flows of desire in schizophrenia. Both flows, at their most eccentric, 'deterritorialize' the terrains in which they invest: capital has no love of institutions, just as schizophrenia refuses to understand delirium as a bad representation of reality, but as reality intensified.

While machines already take centre stage in Deleuze's 'theatre of philosophy' in the early 1970s, machinic thinking assumes greater complexity in *A Thousand Plateaus*. In particular, the idea of the 'machinic phylum' allows technology to be viewed from the evolutionary perspective of, as Manuel de Landa put it, a 'robot historian contemplating how it got

223

there'. In effect, Deleuze challenges biology, the 'logic of the living', as to the strange prejudice it maintains for carbon- over silicon-based life, and it is a further confirmation of the far-sightedness of his wildest work that such issues come into sharper focus as we witness the innumerable scientific, philosophical and cultural shifts attendant upon what is often glibly dismissed as a millennial fascination with the chaotic nature of technological advance.

DELILLO, DON: NOVELIST AND PLAYWRIGHT (1936–) If you met the Pope, how would you recognize him? From his image on the TV screen. In DeLillo's fictional biography of Lee Harvey Oswald, *Libra* (1988), the crowd gathers at Love Field in 1963 to see the arrival of John F. Kennedy. They are gratified that the president 'looked like himself'. In other words, for them his authenticity is guaranteed and confirmed by his image in the media. We are at the moment, as DeLillo writes in *The Names* (1983), 'when the image has seeped into the texture of the world'. For Oswald, Kennedy's image is a vision of plenitude and he tries to hollow out an identity for himself in relation to that seductive image. Oswald's assassination attempt is planned imagining how his own death will play in the media. In *White Noise* (1985) the simulation of events takes precedence over the events themselves. In DeLillo's ten novels, from *Americana* (1971) to *Mao II* (1991) we enter the **postmodern** realm of **simulation** and **hyperreality**, a fallen world in which reality is profoundly mediated by electronic information systems. When

did this fate befall us? DeLillo's first novel, *Americana,* concludes in Dealey Plaza, where J. F. K. was shot. Kennedy's assassination gave DeLillo his theme: the assassination was not the moment when America lost its political innocence and darkness triumphed over light (as it is in Oliver Stone's film *JFK* or in the work of Arthur Schlesinger Jr, where the Kennedy era was a kind of modern Camelot), it was the moment when it became clear that **representation** had been divorced from reality.

The only extant filmic evidence of the Kennedy shooting is the famous Zapruder footage. But, like a dream-text, this amateur film is profoundly 'overdetermined' by the number of interpretations it has produced. It will not yield up a singular meaning, rather it provides evidence for a wide range of readings. Its relationship to reality is disturbingly problematic. For DeLillo, this was the significance of the assassination of the first 'TV president'. As *Libra* has it, the Zapruder film signifies 'an aberration in the heartland of the real', the symbolic moment when it appeared that reality and its representation became somehow divorced. In his essay 'American Blood' (*Rolling Stone* (1983)), DeLillo writes of the assassination that 'we seem from that moment to have entered a world of randomness and ambiguity . . . the physical evidence contradicts itself, the eyewitness accounts do not begin to coincide'. The Zapruder film is our 'major emblem of uncertainty and chaos', and with this goes 'the public's growing belief in the secret manipulation of history'. In DeLillo's paradoxical world of both conspiracies and chaos, his characters feel both manipulated by larger forces and appalled by life's lack of pattern and meaning. Like Oswald, they attempt to create meaning from whatever materials they have. For the reader, what redeems the bleakness of the fiction is the immense energy of the plotting and line-by-line brilliance of the writing itself.

DE MAN, PAUL: CRITIC (1919–83) Originally from Belgium, de Man was until his death Professor of the Humanities at Yale University, and thus an occupant, together with **Bloom**, **Hartman** and **Miller**, of what Frank Lentricchia has called the 'critical house of ill-fame', or what is otherwise referred to as the **Yale School** of criticism. Perhaps its most rigorous **deconstructionist**, and certainly its most notorious personality, given the revelation after his death of his collaborationist and anti-semitic wartime journalism during the Nazi occupation of Belgium, de Man is best known for his work on the relation between literature and philosophy, with his insistence in *Allegories of Reading* (1979) that philosophy might well be 'an endless reflection on its own destruction at the hands of literature'. Since rhetoricity characterizes all language, philosophical writings are also marked by a literariness, and thus not exempt (although their **authors** would seem to deny this or are simply blind to it) from the disruptions, ambiguities and indeterminacies of meaning that literary **texts** are in the business of playing on. Undermining the claim therefore that philosophical or critical works, unlike literary texts, can reliably transfer a meaningful content, are able to transmit knowledge coherently and truthfully, de Man illustrates that tropes and metaphors, precisely because they are operative in all writing, put an unsurmountable obstacle in the way of readers, not only highlighting the limits to intelligibility but also making understanding an error-prone enterprise.

For de Man, the paradigm case of such compound errors as, he claims, inevitably occur in reading and in literature, he calls **aporia**, which literally means 'lack of means'. Language lacks the means to say anything univocally: a text will always say something other than what it seems to, creating an unresolvable undecidability, hence aporia, between conflicting or contradictory readings. This is why rhetoric perpetually presents the threat of misreading, and why de Man warns us that the impossibility of reading, an 'unreadability' that is not a product of the reading, but inheres in the text itself, should not be taken too lightly.

De Man's own method of reading thus seeks out those instances in a text that resist understanding, and which have, he demonstrates in *Blindness and Insight* (1983), resisted other critics' understanding, despite their misguided efforts to the contrary, as such frustrating their attempts to master, or gain a total insight into, a given text. Even **Derrida**, de Man illustrates, in his attempt not so much to master Rousseau, but to outwit the master with deconstruction, falls victim to de Man's analyses of Rousseau's text, which shows that the master had already deconstructed himself, long before the upstart Derrida came on the scene of writing.

Derrida's blindness to Rousseau's auto-deconstructing text proves to be his greatest insight: proving de Man's point that great works, whether literary as Miller also claims, or philosophical as here, *deconstruct themselves*. What follows from de Man's insights then, is that the whole history of criticism is nothing other than a history of *its* own errors and blindnesses.

DERRIDA, JACQUES: PHILOSOPHER (1930–) After initially training in literature in his home country of Algeria, Derrida was led by an increasing interest in philosophy to France where he took up a place at the Ecole Normale Supérieure. Now Director of Studies at the Ecole des Hautes Etudes en Sciences Sociales in Paris and Professor of the Humanities at the University of California, Derrida is best-known for his work on the relation between thought and language with its playful interrogation of the borders between philosophical and literary writing.

Derrida's most influential books, published between 1967 and 1972, reread major figures of the **continental** tradition of philosophy from Plato to **Heidegger**, to expose what he calls their **logocentrism**. As a system of thought which continually strives to go back to origins, find centres, fix points of reference, certify truths, verify an **author**'s intentions, or locate a **text**'s core of meaning, it is perhaps best encapsulated in the biblical phrase 'in the beginning was the Word [the *logos*]', with its concomitant faith in God, the Self, and the Order of the Universe, and its tendency to privilege the singular and definitive over the multiple and in-determinate. What Derrida seeks to undermine in common with other **postmodernists** is the metaphysical certainty not only that a unique 'I' behind any utterance guarantees a consistent, totally conscious, and rational point of view, or that a unified meaning might be traced back to an originary intention, but also that graphic modes of **representation**, be they in words or images, directly refer to a pre-existent reality. Precisely because concepts such as reality, consciousness, intentionality and purpose are so deeply embedded in Western thinking, as well as in language, and yet go unacknowledged, it is imperative, he contends, to question the assumption that word and world coincide, or that word and deed are one.

By paying attention to the ways in which philosophers use language, seizing for instance on their use of metaphor, Derrida illustrates that figurative devices are operative in all writing, be they literary or philosophical, and that pure thought furthermore, despite philosophers' claims to the contrary, is never independent from its mode of expression. Thus, language can give away either an underlying belief system that remains unconscious to the writer's intention (not unlike the **Freudian** slip), or show up a hitherto unrecognized rupture in a text's logic; which is why linguistic ambiguity, once exposed, does not merely highlight that meaning cannot be determined, but can uncover a whole nest of contradictions in the reasoning of those who profess themselves to rely on such concepts as reason and unitary demeaning for the coherency of their argument. The Greek term *pharmakon,* for instance, which means both 'cure' and 'poison', and is used by Plato in its latter sense as a metaphor to describe writing, is such a point in case for Derrida in *Dissemination* (1972; English translation 1982). Plato distrusts writing because he sees it as a mode of communication which is always open to reinterpretation and hence distortion in the absence of the originary speaker, leading him to rank it inferior to living speech, which he sees as potentially able to disclose true meaning, im*mediate*ly and un*mediate*d by the dead weight of the written word. Consequently, Plato associates the written word with 'poison', and merely deems it as a 'cure' in the sense that in recording speech it can act as a remedy for the potential weakness of memory. Despite carefully contextualizing the term as to its specific sense whenever it is used in the *Phaedrus* to avoid possible confusion or ambiguity, Plato's aspiration to the purity of philosophical discourse is continually spoilt by the resonances that the word's multiple and contradictory meanings have in his text. What Derrida does then is to prompt Plato's text to refute its own logic, less by pointing to lapses in its author's argumentation or thinking, than by unravelling how the text's language actually works against its stated intentions.

Derrida's close readings therefore attend to those processes *always already* operative in a text, which unknit its ideal unity. The movement by which such processes are brought into play is what Derrida calls **deconstruction**. Working only with the resources presented to it by the text under study, a deconstructive reading displays just how much textuality is always a network of unfinished meanings, with 'each' text differing from itself, for which he coins the term '**différance**', and 'each' text a trace of, and endlessly referring to, other texts, which invokes **Barthes'** term **intertextuality**. While arguing that a text is 'no longer a finished corpus of writing, some content enclosed in a book or its margins', Derrida's writing also, however, performs what it states. The arguments in *Of Grammatology* (1967; English translation 1976), perhaps his major book to date and also one of his more 'analytic' works to generalize deconstruction's principles, are brought into a more productive frame in a later more 'synthetic' work such as *Glas* (1974; English translation 1986); which, by knitting together commentary and citation from **Hegel's** and Genet's writings not only blurs the boundaries between philosophy and literature, but also creates a new kind of textuality. As if anticipating **hypertext**, *Glas's* typography undoes the linearity of writing, transgresses the borders of text and puts into question the very form of the book.

DESERTIFICATION In his book *America* (1986), Jean **Baudrillard** argues that the desert constitutes some kind of a model for **postmodern** existence. The desert represents existence stripped down to its basics ('No desire, the desert'), which is how Baudrillard thinks the self should be. There is something of a Zen-like quality to the notion, in that desertification is a state beyond value judgement, where meaning has disappeared and we are mere passive observers of events. The desert has the character of the **sublime** for Baudrillard in this respect, being the point at which reason and discourse reach their limits and a more elemental, visceral response takes over.

DESIRE In **postmodern** thought, desire represents all those libidinal drives in the individual that subvert the power of reason. The conception derives from **Freud**, whose studies had emphasized the hidden part of human nature in the subconscious, of whose workings we were at best only dimly aware, but which were often able to override our conscious, rational intentions.

For most postmodern thinkers, desire is what Western culture has been concerned to suppress for the last few centuries on the grounds that it represents a threat to social order and institutional structures. Thus for **Deleuze** and **Guattari** modern psychoanalysis was an exercise in social control, the objective of which was to curb desire and to make individuals conform to an authoritarian social system. The schizophrenic, who frustrated the attentions of the psychoanalyst, turned into an ideal type for them as a result. **Foucault** argued that sexual desire in the modern world had been restricted to one socially acceptable, and also heavily policed, type, that of heterosexuality within marriage – a cultural trend that marginalized, and in some cases criminalized, most other forms of sexual expression. Once again the goal was control of the individual's actions at a basic level. **Lyotard** attacked rationalist-oriented theories

such as **Marxism**, which allowed no scope for desire, or '**libidinal economy**' as he dubbed it. In each case, to champion the cause of desire was to criticize the culture in which we live, given that this culture was, in general, concerned to limit the free expression of desire in the name of authoritarian norms of conduct.

The general turn away from reason in postmodern thought has involved a corresponding commitment to desire, which has become a key strategy in the subversion of **modernity** and its allegedly authoritarian systems. Desire represents an implicitly antiauthoritarian force for the postmodern movement.

DESIRING-MACHINE Individuals constitute desiring-machines in **Deleuze**'s and **Guattari**'s terminology. In *Anti-Oedipus* (1972) they argue that we have transcended such traditional categories as man and nature, and are now in a society that consists of various kinds of 'machines' – for example, desiringmachines, producing-machines and schizophrenic-machines. It is the point of modern psychoanalysis (summed up under the blanket heading of **Oedipus**) to repress desiring-machines and, indeed, the expression of **desire** in general. The desiring-machine is driven by **libidinal** energy rather than reason, and lacks the unity normally associated with individual identity in Western culture. It is therefore seen by the ruling authorities as a threat to social order.

DIFFÉRANCE Différance, a term coined by Jacques **Derrida**, both signals how language works and is also another term for the manoeuvres and movements of **deconstruction**. As a descriptive term, Derrida uses it to illustrate, following the Swiss linguist Ferdinand de Saussure, how any word always depends for its meaning not on its natural bond with the real, as if it were its stand-in, but on its association with other words along a whole chain of significations, to which it refers but also from which it is different, thus indicating perpetual movements as well as potential slippages of meaning in language. As a neologism, created from the French verb *différer* which means both 'to differ' and 'to defer', différance, referring to both senses simultaneously and therefore deliberately ambiguous, demonstrates that language is always indeterminate, and that meaning is always undecidable and thus endlessly deferred. As such, différance not only describes linguistic functions, it also performs them. As an interchangeable term for deconstruction it also, however, fulfils another function. While undermining any sense of unity, it can never just simply be conceived as its opposite; for, to conceive of différance in op*position* to another term, such as unity, would be to fix it in a certain *position* and thus curtail what characterizes it: suspension, movement, deferral. Thus, as its very operations illustrate, it is an alternative term for both unity *and* difference.

DIFFERENCE Difference, as a term in **deconstruction** and **poststructuralism**, signals that a **text** is not an ideal unity, but always subject to indeterminacies inherent in language, which resist interpretive closure of meaning, thus illustrating that although there is a difference between texts, there is also difference within 'one' text. While **postmodernism** tends to celebrate difference, schools of thought following **Hegel** seek to overcome it. Thus, for Hegel difference is something to be mediated, which results in the dialectical synthesis between two terms in an opposition, to produce an altogether new and different third term. For **Derrida**, on the other hand, to overcome difference is to subsume two opposing terms in one fusion, reduce them from two into one, without preserving their radical alternativity from, or difference from, each other, without respecting each 'one' in its 'many-ness'. For this reason, Derrida suggests as a third term, the notion of **différance**, which as an alternative to both unity and difference, is always marked by an excess, resisting the pull to be unified, to be assimilated into one. Derrida's suspicions in *Altérités* (1986) of the Hegelian tendency to gather and fuse that which is dispersed is a reaction to, as he sees it, the dangerous willingness of thinkers such as **Habermas** either to find or to impose unity or consensus, respectively. In common with **Lyotard**, he believes that to force agreement where there is disagreement, to will consensus where there is dissent, is also to level difference, to efface otherness, and to eliminate multiplicity.

DIFFERENCE FEMINISM A highly contentious concern with **difference** is one of the contemporary characteristics of **postmodern** thought. A similar concern also emerged in the 1970s from the practical domain of an emergent feminist politics. Within the second wave of feminism, difference came to signify all the theoretical complexities arising from the socio-logical observation that women do not possess a uniform social identity. Postmodern thought and difference feminism come together in a fragile alliance: both recognize the practical and epistemological significance of women being variously situated, like men, in a network of many dimensions of identity and power.

However, in the context of feminist psychoanalytic theory 'difference' is used in a narrower sense: it signifies specifically male–female sexual differ-ence. Unlike a feminist psycho-analytic ethics of sexual difference, difference feminism represents a decisive split within feminism itself over the exclusionary dominance of a white, middle-class perspective. Yet this split raises the hope that a new sort of feminist politics will strive for solidarity without doing violence to the intricacies of social identity, the goal being a transformation of the politics of gender in becoming aware of various relations of oppression.

Difference here is not a description of the attributes of a group, but a function of the relations between groups, intending emancipation rather than exclusion. A positive sense of group difference is emancipatory insofar as it is a creation, and not an assertion, of a singular identity given with certainty by experience. The group 'women' has overlapping experiences with such group differences as race, class, religion and ethnicity. To pre-serve difference without creating new entrenched forms of identity, differ-ence feminists articulate a politics in which the meaning of difference itself becomes a terrain of political struggle.

DIFFEREND In Jean-François **Lyo-tard**, a differend is a dispute that arises when each party is employing a form of language (or discourse) **incommensurable** with the other. Thus an employee being exploited by an unscrupulous employer cannot find redress from that employer in a court set up according to the laws of a society which specifically sanctions economic exploitation of employees by employers. The dispute is irre-solvable, except in the sense that one party can use its greater power to enforce its will on the other (as happens, for example, in colonial situations). Differends are, there-fore, normally suppressed by means of brute power, but Lyotard wants them to be acknowledged, and not taken advantage of by the stronger party. It is the duty of philosophers to help the weaker parties to disputes to find the language (or '**phrase-regime**', as Lyotard refers to it) in which their grievance can be framed. In a geopolitical sense, recognizing the differend would mean acknow-ledging the rights of exploited peoples and minority groups to be heard (acknowledging the claims to land ownership of the native peoples in North America or Australia, for example), and in general backing away from 'solutions' to political problems based on the mere exercise of power.

DISCOURSE ANALYSIS Discourse analysis is the study of the use of language as it flows or unfolds, as opposed to the rather atomistic sentence-based focus of stylistics or traditional linguistics. It is associated primarily with the philosopher H. P. Grice, who stressed that speakers make sense of utterances because they are embedded within a hinterland of assumptions and expectations about what speech is and how it functions. Every community shares a body of knowledge which is implicitly activated by any one semantic exchange. This body of knowledge shapes the norms of intelligibility which will determine whether or not a statement is perceived as true, clear and relevant.

Grice was influenced by J. L. Austin, who distinguished between two main types of utterance in *How to Do Things with Words* (1962). A performative speech-act performs an action, such as naming a ship. A constative speech-act is a simple statement of fact, such as 'This is a big ship'. While constatives can be true or false, truth criteria are not applicable to performatives: they can only succeed or fail. What, then, determines the success of a performative? Austin's answer was: context. It is the surrounding social frame that governs appropriateness or 'felicitousness'.

Austin was at pains to separate ordinary language from what he called the 'parasitic' uses of language to be found in fiction, poetry and drama. He argued that these utterances were never intended to succeed or fail in relation to the performance of an action, and so should be treated as exceptions to the rule. A challenge was made to this model by Jacques

Derrida in his paper 'Signature, Event, Context', delivered at a French colloquium in 1971. Derrida disputes that context is sufficient to ground a performative utterance. Indeed he claims that speech is parasitic upon writing. The iterability of the written word through print undermines the power of context to make sense of utterances by referring to a located speaker.

DISSEMINATION As outlined in the book of the same name by Jacques **Derrida** (1972), dissemination is a method of reading involving the **deconstruction** of certain highly influential texts in the Western philosophical tradition – such as Plato's *Phaedrus*. The concern, as so often in Derrida's work, is with challenging the view that speech is privileged over writing; the latter being a standard assumption of discourse in the West. The *Phaedrus* takes the customary Platonic form of a dialogue, in which Socrates listens to a speech written by Lysias which is in the possession of Phaedrus. In his response to Phaedrus, Socrates relates the story of Theuth, the inventor of writing. Much of Derrida's discussion turns on the term 'pharmakon', which Plato uses to refer to writing, and which has been variously translated as both poison and remedy. Derrida points to the deeply ambivalent nature of the term, and from this demonstrates that in his condemnation of writing Socrates borrows from the very tools he disparages, thus undermining his arguments.

DOLLIMORE, JONATHAN: CRITIC (1948–) Dollimore is a professor of

English in the School of English and American Studies at the University of Sussex. Through his own publications and through his editorial work with his Sussex colleague Alan **Sinfield** he is one of the leading exponents of '**cultural materialism**', the most significant development in Renaissance studies in the 1980s. The term is taken from the work of cultural critic Raymond Williams and means, very broadly, a politically engaged, materialist analysis of culture. Dollimore is an acute commentator on new developments in the field, where his sympathy to (but political difference from) **postmodern** theory can be seen most clearly. He also has been influential in the theorization of lesbian and gay studies. Dollimore's early research, which appeared as *Radical Tragedy* (1984), was an exploration of the relationship between subjectivity, power and ideology in the early modern period. As a materialist, Dollimore takes the view that there is no essential, irreducible self that exists before entering social relations. The human self is a construct. 'Idealist' criticism, which believes in transhistorical truth, elides or erases cultural, racial and sexual **difference**, the very subjects of Dollimore's attention.

For Dollimore, objectivity in cultural analysis is a chimera; all cultural practice has a political dimension. **Texts** do not simply reflect reality; they play a part in the making of meaning. Using insights from postmodern **continental** theory and the close-reading techniques of ideological critique, Dollimore sees texts as sites of political and ideological struggle where the critic should attempt to locate the text's 'internal dissonance', what Pierre Macherey describes as the text's difference from itself. Dollimore makes the suggestive point that often the culturally peripheral turns out to be symbolically central and this has led him to examine the way such groups are represented in texts. He uses this insight as a way of exploring, for instance, the role of the prostitute in Shakespeare's *Measure for Measure*. While his politically committed interest in 'the subordinate, the marginal, the excluded and displaced' chimes in with the interests of radical postmodernist critics, 'marginal' figures are not simply celebrated. Not for Dollimore 'the too convenient appropriation' of them in an ahistorical way nor 'the identification with the process of victimization rather than the victims'. In Jacobean drama the prostitute, the 'sodomite', and the transvestite are not postmodernists *avant la lettre;* as they appear in some recent radical criticism. Dollimore finds in Jacobean tragedy 'not a vision of political freedom so much as a subversive knowledge of political domination'. Dollimore's work avoids the politically empty valorization of 'subversion'; 'nothing is intrinsically subversive independent of its articulation and context'. In *Sexual Dissidence* (1991), Dollimore takes as his title a technique for the gender-related unsettling of such oppositions as dominant and subordinate which has similarities to the work of Eve Kosofsky Sedgwick, whose work, along with Dollimore's, has had a shaping influence on recent '**queer theory**'.

DOUBLE CODING Double coding, according to Charles **Jencks**, describes a defining characteristic of **postmodern** architecture. In *The Language of Post-Modern Architecture* (1977) he describes double-coding as 'the combination of modern techniques with something else (usually traditional building)'. Among the many examples Jencks uses is British architect James Stirling's addition to the Staatsgalerie in Stuttgart. While obviously a contemporary building, it echoes and plays with past art and architecture, including classical and pop art. Jencks sees this kind of postmodernist building as a way of opening up the minimalist language of **modernism** to history, context and **difference**. During the 1980s, Jencks expanded his theory of double coding into other areas of culture. In art, Jencks sees the return of **representational** painting, self-conscious allegory, eclecticism and hybridity as signs of ubiquitous postmodern double coding. In fiction, Jencks admires writers who neither repudiate nor slavishly imitate the experimental modernist writers of the early years of the century, but who, like John **Barth** and Umberto **Eco** for instance, give us the traditional pleasures of plot and work on a number of other levels too. Theories of postmodern fiction such as Linda Hutcheon's 'historiographical metafiction' have put Jencks's concept to interesting use.

E

EAGLETON, TERRY: WRITER AND CRITIC (1943–) Eagleton is Wharton Professor of English at the University of Oxford. A dramatist and novelist, he is best known as the leading **Marxist** literary critic writing in Britain. His work is marked by a critical engagement with continental **critical theory** and he has produced popularizing works from *Marxism and Literary Criticism* (1976) to *Literary Theory* (2nd edn 1996), detailed studies of canonical authors such as Shakespeare in *Shakespeare and Society* (1967) and Samuel Richardson in *The Rape of Clarissa* (1982) as well as a Marxist reading of the history of aesthetics, the remarkable *Ideology of the Aesthetic* (1990). One of its most cogent critics from the left, he has argued against most aspects of **postmodernism**, from his 1985 essay in *New Left Review*, 'Capitalism, **Modernism**, Postmodernism', to his most fully worked out response, *The Illusions of Postmodernism* (1996). Here he examines a series of oppositional pairings familiar to postmodern thinking, such as identity/**difference** and nature/culture, which Eagleton sees in the light of the debate over universals and particulars. Eagleton acknowledges that postmodernism has allowed us to re-evaluate our conception of the relations between power, **desire**, identity and political practice and, at its most militant, has lent a voice to the humiliated and reviled. In doing so it has threatened to shake the imperious self-identity of dominant political systems to their core. It has produced, in the same breath, an invigorating but paralysing scepticism that valorizes a whole series of concepts ('difference', 'culture', 'subversion', 'marginality') in a formalistic and ahistorical way, lining them up against such scare-words as 'identity', 'nature' and 'universality'. His main charge is that postmodern art and thought acquiesces 'with the appalling mess that is the contemporary world'.

First, identity/difference: using the postmodern concept of 'difference', a large number of marginalized groups have found a political voice. For Eagleton, socialism goes further and wants to see the emancipation of difference at the level of human mutuality and reciprocity. This raises the much discussed topic of subjectivity and its decentring or destabilizing in postmodern thought. While the questioning of the self-identical **subject** of Western thought is valuable, it is not postmodernism that has most effectively destabilized the humanist subject, but advanced capitalism. The most anti-élitist force in contemporary society is the marketplace itself, which buries all distinctions and gradations beneath the abstract quality of exchange-value. Furthermore, the **deconstructed** subject of postmodern discourse is capable of various subversions of the dominant social values, but is incapable of the emancipatory goal transforming society in any meaningful way. Rebellion could not succeed if human agents were not provisionally self-affirmative and self-identical enough to carry it through. For Eagleton, you need an idea of a human subject unified enough to take significantly transformative action. He suggests that a reasonably secure identity, as opposed to a paranoiacally cohesive one, is a necessary condition of human well-being and it is morally irresponsible of some postmodernists to deny this. Difference cannot flourish under forms of exploitation; to combat those effectively requires a notion of humanity which is necessarily universal.

Second, universality/particularity and nature/culture: **Enlightenment** philosophers argued a radical, universalist case for equal rights: everyone is entitled to freedom, autonomy, justice and political equality because we are equally individuals and share a common human nature. While postmodernism, sceptical of overarching, universalizing theories of history and the human self, sees not nature here, but culture, Eagleton sees postmodernism as a form of 'culturalism' because it refuses to recognize that what different ethnic groups have in common socially and politically is more important to their emancipation than their cultural differences, which postmodernism drastically underestimates. There are no 'noncultural' human beings not because

culture is all there is to us, but because culture belongs to our nature. Postmodernism's glamorization of the 'marginal' and suspicion of centres of power and authority forbids it conceiving of a majority political movement, such as Solidarity in Poland or the African National Congress. Finally, postmodern thinking overlooks the fact that capitalism is formidably resourceful and also spectacularly unsuccessful in providing adequate resources for the majority of the world's population. Postmodernism and **post-Marxism** are responses, paradoxically, to a power structure more 'total' than ever. This 'total' system, however, is not homogeneous. Eagleton argues that postmodernists suffer from 'holophobia', a fear of totality; and not looking for totality is code for their main mistake; not looking for capitalism, the very thing that stands in the way of human freedom.

ECO, UMBERTO: AUTHOR AND THEORIST (1932–) An intriguing feature of **postmodernism** is the desire for theorists to practise what they preach, and for artists to preach what they practise. One need only think of the literary pretensions of **Derrida**, or the philosophical leanings of artists such as Richard Long, to prove that this is so. It is this blurring of the boundaries between distinct discursive zones that makes Umberto Eco such a pivotal figure on the contemporary scene. He is a writer who is equally at ease in low or high culture. He worked as an editor for *Radiotelevisione Italia* between 1954 and 1959, and has written extensively for Italian newspapers and magazines, including *La*

Stampa and *La Repubblica*. The best of these pieces are collected in *Misreadings* (1993) and *How to Travel with a Salmon* (1994). Currently Chair of **Semiotics** at the University of Bologna, he has published as an academic a formidable array of volumes on literature and linguistics, including *The Role of the Reader* (1981), *Faith in Fakes* (1984) and *The Limits of Interpretation* (1990).

Eco's doctoral dissertation at the University of Turin was on theologian Thomas Aquinas, and he has pursued his interest in medieval matters throughout his career. This is not surprising, as there are many parallels that link the Middle Ages with the postmodern moment. Both are periods of in-betweenness, interim states defined in terms of the historical eras they succeed and anticipate. Both are fascinated with the stacking of layers of meaning and the interpenetration of different worlds of meaning.

Such parallels are probed with great dexterity in Eco's worldwide best-selling novel *The Name of the Rose* (1984), which is simultaneously a murder mystery and a semiotic mystery. The murder plot concerns a Benedictine monastery in northern Italy, where an important meeting is scheduled in 1327 between two rival factions of the Franciscan order who espouse or oppose the vow of poverty. Against this rich historical backdrop (created by many lucid and learned passages of exposition by Eco), several murders take place, beginning with a young monk who is found at the bottom of a cliff. William of Baskerville investigates these crimes with a novice called Adso, who plays Watson to William's Holmes. The

semiotic plot centres around the monastery library, which seems to provide the vital clue for the murderer's motive. The library is also a labyrinth, and Eco acknowledges his debt to the postmodernist Argentinian writer Borges for this image of hermeneutic intricacy through the character of the blind librarian, Jorge. The solution to the crimes involves Aristotle's famous lost book on comedy, which threatens the power of the church by advocating humour as a corrective to tragic self-importance.

Eco's working title for *The Name of the Rose* was *The Abbey of the Crime*, an altogether inferior title, as it directs the reader to a very particular detective-fiction mindset. The actual title, on the other hand, suggests many possible interpretations based upon the complex symbology of the rose. The contrast between these two titles is therefore a good illustration of Eco's distinction between closed and open **texts**, which he makes in *The Open Work* (1989).

If *The Name of the Rose* is destined to be remembered as the quintessential postmodernist novel, Eco's subsequent fictions – *Foucault's Pendulum* (1989) and *The Island of the Day Before* (1995) – haven't quite attained the same dizzying heights of academic and popular acceptance. There is, however, at least one of Eco's non-fictional statements which has already achieved canonical status as a definition of postmodernism itself. Here it is, quoted in full, from *Reflections on the Name of the Rose* (1985):

> I think of the postmodern attitude as that of a man who loves a very cultivated woman and knows that

he cannot say to her, 'I love you madly', because he knows that she knows (and that she knows that he knows) that these words have already been written by Barbara Cartland. Still, there is a solution. He can say, 'As Barbara Cartland would put it, I love you madly.' At this point, having avoided false innocence, having said clearly that it is no longer possible to speak innocently, he will nevertheless have said what he wanted to say to the woman: that he loves her, but he loves her in an age of lost innocence. If the woman goes along with this, she will have received a declaration of love all the same.

This passage summarizes many of the key attributes of postmodernism: its knowing **irony**, its penchant for quotation, its flirtation with popular culture and its playful **polysemy** or **plurality** of sense.

EISENMAN, PETER: ARCHITECT (1932–) Eisenman produces a brand of dry expressionist architecture, a version of **deconstructivism** that perversely refuses to enjoy its formal gymnastics. His is an architecture that stresses the alienation that architecture forces on its occupiers. Many of his obsessions are revealed in his early House series (1–9) – where incidents occur within the exasperated formalism such as splitting of the marital bed into two, with a thin gap that separates the two halves, a void above the living space, or a structural column grid that is engineered such that one column does not quite meet the ground. He seems to revel in the difficult, the obscure, and the pointless – things that architecture has consistently tried to ignore

and exclude – banality and unfriendliness. His own (well-publicized) psychoanalysis has helped him produce an architecture that is both self-obsessed and self-loathing. His buildings attempt to undermine themselves, twisting logics of structure, geometry and order. They are exercises intended to problematize architectural practice – marking out the unresolvable complexities inherent in the contemporary making of buildings. It is the constant formal manipulations of the sparse and abstract language of high **modernism** rather than its contamination with other codes that provides the ground for his work. Whether aligning the axis of the Wexner Arts Centre with the flightpath into Columbus, Ohio Airport or aligning the Social Housing IBA five degrees off the city grid, his points of reference are deliberately placed beyond the grasp of the buildings' users.

ELLIS, BRET EASTON: NOVELIST (1964 –) On the publication of his first novel in 1985 the 21-year-old American author, like Lord Byron before him, awoke to find himself famous. While his three novels, *Less Than Zero* (1985), *The Rules of Attraction* (1987) and *American Psycho* (1991), are not **postmodern** in form, they, along with his book of linked stories *The Informers* (1994), detail the lives of the young affluent whites who consume postmodern culture, those whom Jean-François **Lyotard** describes as 'wear-[ing] Paris perfume in Tokyo and "**retro**" clothes in Hong Kong; knowledge is a matter for TV games'. *Less Than Zero* describes an 18-year-old's round of

THE ICON CRITICAL DICTIONARY OF POSTMODERN THOUGHT

parties, visits to friends, drink and drug abuse, but also ambitiously used the 'blank generation' as a metaphor for a philosophical emptiness registered in the book's title.

The anger many felt at Ellis's non-judgemental tone turned incandescent on the publication of his black comedy *American Psycho,* the self-narrated tale of the ultimate consumer; a cannibalistic Wall Street yuppie serial killer. The narrator, however, is an extremely unreliable fantasist. We are never offered any psychological explanation of the narrator's actions, so the novel's exhaustive and exhausting catalogues of consumer goods, sexual positions and torture become indices of a whole social layer's alienation and commodity fetishism. *Less Than Zero* begins 'People are afraid to merge on the highways in Los Angeles', echoing E. M. Forster's liberal plea 'only connect'. Here, though, in Ellis's affectless, postmodern world, there is little hope that such connections could be made.

ENDISM Endism refers to the various theories circulating in the late twentieth century proclaiming the end of phenomena such as history. Francis **Fukuyama** is somewhat notorious for arguing that the collapse of communism signals the end of history in the sense that liberal capitalism has now won the global political struggle, and that henceforth it is the only viable political system. Daniel **Bell** had earlier proclaimed that we had moved beyond industrialization to what he called a '**post-industrial**' culture, an idea that influenced thinkers like Fukuyama. Jean **Baudrillard** fits

into this developing tradition of endist thought, being happy to abolish history, because, as one of his typically provocative arguments puts it, if we are only alienated *in* history, then the end *of* history must constitute the end of our alienation. **Postmodernism** in general is somewhat ambivalent about endism. On the one hand, postmodernist thinkers are fond of claiming that we have passed over a watershed to a new kind of cultural formation; on the other, postmodernism is often a self-conscious dialogue with the past, in the sense of a recovery of older artistic forms (novelistic realism, figurative painting, pre-**modernist** architecture, etc.) or ideas (the '**sublime**', for example).

ENLIGHTENMENT PROJECT Historians use the term 'the Enlightenment' to refer to the 'long' eighteenth century which stretches from England's 'Glorious Revolution' (1688) to the outbreak of the French Revolution (1789). But the Enlightenment was not only a historical period; it was also an intellectual project brought into focus by the group of French intellectuals – the *philosophes* – involved in the publication of the *Encyclopédie,* edited by Denis Diderot over a period of twenty years from 1751. The ideals of this group were increasingly shared by educated men and women across the globe.

To understand the relevance of what is repeatedly referred to in **postmodernism** as the 'Enlightenment project', it is vital to distinguish between a critical, often polemical, element and its more progressive, constructive and sometimes prescriptive developments.

Enlightenment was defined as the project of dispelling darkness, fear and superstition; of removing all the shackles from free enquiry and debate. It opposed the traditional powers and beliefs of the Church (branded as 'superstition') and raised questions of political legitimacy. All received or traditional notions, and social relations, were to be made subject to the scrutiny of the public, and therefore, collective – or inter-subjective – use of 'reason'. The comparatively liberal social arrangements which characterized politics and commerce in eighteenth-century England were one important model or inspiration for Enlightenment thinkers. The other was the fantastic achievements of science and technology, in the wake of Newton's scientific revolution. This was the epoch which first came to terms with extensive and tangible improvements in many areas of life affected by the application of science, giving rise to the dream of a world radically improved, ordered, engineered, mastered. The idea of the improvement of the human race, and of 'moral progress', was born. The desire to master nature developed into the dream of mastering society and history. The dark, nightmarish side of this dream was analysed by **Adorno** and **Horkheimer** in *Dialectic of Enlightenment* (1947), whose opening reads: '[T]he Enlightenment has always aimed at liberating men from fear and establishing their sovereignty. Yet the fully enlightened earth radiates disaster triumphant.'

One shorthand way to define postmodernism is as the end of the Enlightenment dream of mastery and a definitive improvement to human society through knowledge and technology. In recent years the eighteenth century has become the focus of intensive historical research. The results, recorded in fascinating biographies and penetrating monographs, could go a long way to correcting the caricature of the Enlightenment which the 'postmodernism' debates have tended to circulate. The eighteenth century saw traditional certainties dissolve. Even the most optimistic thinkers were plagued by doubt and even despair. It was a time of constant experimentation, not of complacent self-confidence.

ENO, BRIAN: MUSICIAN AND ARTIST (1948–) 'Eno', as he himself is keen to point out, is an anagram of 'one'. He has more than one role, however: he is a rock musician, producer, painter, video artist, designer of perfumes and wallpaper, business consultant and all-round lateral thinker. Like John Lennon of the Beatles, Pete Townshend of the Who and Ray Davies of the Kinks he studied at art school, completing his foundation studies at Ipswich (1964–66) and graduating from Winchester with a Diploma in Fine Art (1969). His tutors at these institutions (including Tom Phillips, the **postmodern** multimedia artist) exposed him to many radical ideas. Hence Eno's first musical venture involved recording a metal lampshade as it is struck by various objects and playing it back at altered speeds. The minimalism of Steve **Reich** and Philip **Glass** convinced Eno that music could be made with the simplest of materials and that process was more important than product.

Eno achieved celebrity as synthesizer player with the glam-rock band Roxy Music in the early 1970s, although this was thanks to his elaborate eye make-up and extravagant feather boas rather than his keyboard skills (indeed, in 1970 he privately printed a pamphlet called *Music for Non-Musicians*). He left the band to pursue a successful solo career, and albums such as *Here Come the Warm Jets* (1973) and *Before and After Science* (1977) were hailed for their experimental verve and quirky lyrics. Lines such as 'Dalai Lama lama puss puss / Stella maris missa nobis / Miss a dinner Miss Shapiro / Shampoo pot-pot pinkies pampered' ('Miss Shapiro') ensured that Eno never topped the charts.

Eno's main instrument is the recording studio itself, where he can manipulate traditional instruments beyond recognition and create unusual electronic sounds. He often works collaboratively (Talking Heads, David Bowie, Cluster) or as producer (U2, Devo, James), where his role is that of *provocateur*. He loves to push people into places they don't want to go, often with the aid of a set of cards he devised with Peter Schmidt called 'Oblique Strategies'. These instructions are meant to inspire novel solutions to old dilemmas. Some prompt a consideration of the situational frame, e.g. 'Assemble some of the elements into a group, and treat the group'. Others offer specific advice such as 'Go outside – shut the door' as a means of introducing discontinuity into the compositional activity.

Eno's most challenging work has been concerned with finding new ways of listening to music. He updated Erik

Satie's concept of 'furniture music', music which could be ignored or listened to at whim, with a series of so-called 'ambient music' pieces between 1978 and 1982. The dense textures and environmental sensitivity of *Music for Airports* (1979) and *On Land* (1982) are very different from supermarket Muzak, though. Ten albums released on Eno's Obscure Records throughout the 1970s showcased some of Britain's foremost postmodernist musicians: Gavin **Bryars**, John Cage, Michael **Nyman** and the Penguin Café Orchestra. This was music that plainly could not be ignored or listened to without full attention.

ERASURE Erasure is a **deconstructionist** technique whereby a word or term is used but what it commits one to (its meaning, as well as the theory of meaning lying behind it) is denied, or, as Jacques **Derrida** puts it, placed 'under erasure' (*sous rature*). This enables Derrida to claim that he can use the language of Western philosophy without that use committing him to a belief in its concepts or any of its principles. The practice is derived from Martin **Heidegger**, who in *Zur Seinsfrage* used the word 'being' with a line drawn through it, in order to signal that he wished to preclude being drawn into debates about the concept, since that would imply his acceptance of Western philosophy's metaphysical assumptions about being. Erasure is one of the ways Derrida attempts to answer what has become a standard criticism of his work: that he relies on language to put his arguments across, while simultaneously claiming that language is unstable and meaning indeterminate. Critics have pointed out that Derrida's critique of language could not be understood unless language and meaning *were* at least relatively stable. Seen from that latter perspective, the technique of erasure is something of a confidence trick.

ÉVÉNEMENTS In May 1968, the *événements* (the '**events**') shattered the banal peace of urban Paris. While they may not have achieved the overthrow of de Gaulle's government – although, but for the intervention of the unions, they might well have done so – they *practised* the revolution of everyday life along the object of the theoretical forecasts and personal dreams of many unorthodox Communist Party members and **Marxist** theoreticians. Following the arrest of the activist leaders of the National Committee for Vietnam, students at the University of Paris formed the 22nd March Movement, and under the emerging leadership of Daniel Cohn-Bendit occupied its Nanterre campus and vociferously condemned the education regime as a factory for turning out the bureaucrats of everyday life. Similar occupations and demonstrations followed in Dijon, Nice, Aix, Montpellier and Nantes. Meanwhile, union unrest was also growing, with the major unions rejecting government pay policy and sparking protest marches and strikes throughout the country. The unions themselves, however, begin to condemn the activist tendencies of both the workers and the students, opening up the rift between the protesters and their union representatives that would eventually see these populist

movements caught in a government–union axis. The spark came when, on 3 May 1968, the Paris riot police, the CRS, surrounded and sealed Nanterre before bombarding the campus with tear gas and invading it. The French Communist Party (PCF) meanwhile condemned the student occupations (although Lefebvre, for example, supported them), prompting a final break between the students and the left-wing political parties. This break is decisive for the widespread sense of the failure of the Marxist project, since its PCF vanguard effectively colluded with the government and the unions to bring an end to the *événements*, rather than supporting their revolutionary aims. For the first time, decisively for the politics of **postmodernism** in France, Marxism was revealed as a bureacratic machine for the suppression rather than the advancement of revolution.

Following a massively successful general strike, the workers, students, the angry and the dissident intellectuals of the **Situationist** International took over the streets of Paris. After a month of barricades and immediate revolution, the government forces eventually put down the insurgents while the trade unions swiftly negotiated a return to work. The *événements* nevertheless mark the closest a modern, First-World state has come to complete dissolution at the hands of popular revolution.

EVENT Jean-François **Lyotard** refers to an 'event' as the change in perspective that takes place after a particularly significant cultural occurrence. The most frequently cited example of this in Lyotard is Auschwitz, which he argues irrevocably altered our perception of human nature and the world in which we live (Theodor **Adorno** had also spoken of the impossibility of writing poetry after the facts of Auschwitz had become known). The 1968 *événements* in Paris are another example of an event which irrevocably altered the world view of a specific social group, in this case a whole generation of French intellectuals. What was shattered was that generation's belief in the moral supremacy of **Marxism**, as enshrined in the French Communist Party (PCF). The collusion of the latter with the forces of the state in bringing down the alliance of workers and students that had briefly challenged the state's authority, was felt by many French left-wing intellectuals, including Lyotard, to have compromised Marxism to the point where it had lost all credibility. Lyotard speaks of the need to be 'open' to the event, meaning to be able to approach new experiences without bringing with us the prejudices of outmoded theories such as Marxism.

F

FEDERMAN, RAYMOND: NOVELIST
(1928–) Raymond Federman was
born in France. In 1940 virtually
his entire family were sent to concentration camps. He himself only
narrowly escaped because his mother
bundled him into a closet before
the Nazis came. After the war he
emigrated to the United States, and
established himself as a **postmodernist** writer in the 1970s. His
startling works *Double Or Nothing*
(1971) and *Take It Or Leave It* (1976)
are examples of 'concrete prose',
novels whose typographical appearance is as important as what they say.

Double Or Nothing uses many
iconic designs, where the words on
the page are arranged into a shape
imitative of what they describe. So the
word PLUNGING falls down the page;
the word ROLLS is spaced out like a
bread bun; and a ship is welded out of
the words THE CALL OF THE OCEAN and
ATLANTICPACIFIC. Federman also uses
abstract shapes, in which there is no
necessary relation between the design
and the words that compose it.
Entire pages are typed as an hour-
glass, a zigzag or an L-configuration.
Federman's 'spatial displacement of
words' continues in *Take It Or Leave
It*. These language games force a split
between sound and sense, **text** and
subtext, the materiality of the book
and its meaning. At the heart of these
books, and others such as *The Voice*
in the Closet (1979) and *To Whom it*
May Concern (1990), is a silence, the
untellable story of his own personal
Holocaust experiences.

Federman has also theorized his
literary practice, and in 1991 at the
Stuttgart Seminar in Cultural Studies
he (cheekily) announced the death of
postmodernism.

FEYERABEND, PAUL: PHILOSOPHER
OF SCIENCE (1924–94) Paul Feyerabend was, along with Karl Popper
and Thomas **Kuhn**, one of the
twentieth century's most important
philosophers of science. Although he
did not call himself a **postmodernist**,
and indeed the dialogue in which he
took part began not with **Lyotard**,
Foucault and **Baudrillard**, but with
the pre-Socratic Greek philosophers
of the fifth century BC, both Feyerabend's relativism and his irreverent,
gadfly style of discourse set up a
profound resonance with postmodernism. In his three major works,
Against Method (1975), Science in a
Free Society (1978) and *A Farewell to*
Reason (1987), Feyerabend battles
against two related ideas: first, that
there are objective truths, scientific,
political or moral, 'out there' in the
world and second, that there is one
method for discovering those truths.

Feyerabend was influenced by
Thomas Kuhn's historicist approach
to science and, later, by Michel

Foucault's '**archaeology** of knowledge'. Underlying his view is a passionate commitment to relativism, to the argument that truth is always truth *for* someone. Different groups, separated by history, geography or ideology see the world in very different ways. Often those world views will have little or nothing in common. For an objectivist, there must be a way of either reconciling differences or deciding between them. For Feyerabend, on the other hand, 'we should simply accept different world views as **incommensurable**'. This has led Feyerabend into some rather strange company. He has argued that as there is simply no common ground between the Creationist and Darwinian views of the origins of humankind they should be taught in schools on an equal basis.

Much of Feyerabend's work can be seen as an answer to the enormously influential philosophy of science of Karl Popper. In his major work, *The Logic of Scientific Discovery,* Popper argued that a scientific hypothesis could never be proven to be absolutely true. We might observe a thousand white swans but that can never prove beyond doubt the theory that all swans are white. On the other hand, the first black swan observed conclusively 'falsifies' the theory. From this basic insight, Popper argued that scientists should spend their time concocting new and radical theories which they then endeavour to disprove. Science progresses, on this model, through a series of conjectures and refutations, driven by imaginative leaps made by great scientists. Although positive truth remains illusive in Popper's theory,

he nevertheless retains a realist, objectivist position: there is a real world out there, and the scientist's job is to reveal it.

In *Against Method* (1974) Feyerabend rejects the realism and objectivism of Popper's falsificationism, as he rejects all other positivist and empiricist views of science. Feyerabend argues that scientists have, at different times, made use of many different methodologies often importing concepts and approaches from other, non-rational, spheres. Without this heterogeneity, there would have been no 'progress'. All too often a marginal theory, rejected by the scientific establishment, has proved to be more successful than its more popular rivals. In consequence, science needs **pluralism**, not the exclusiveness inherent in the falsificationist approach. As he puts it: 'There is no single rule, however plausible, and however firmly grounded in epistemology, that is not violated at some time or other.' Rigid definitions of what scientists *should* do simply do not fit what real scientists actually do.

Feyerabend rejects the 'big' science of massive, government-funded schemes (nuclear power, space programmes, the Human Genome Project). Following Foucault, he interprets these as simply a matter of power, exerted by élites in order to regulate and control. In its place, he suggests that science should be a way of solving local problems, or of promoting the wealth and well-being of the general community.

Feyerabend's radical politics, brilliant lecturing style and accessible writing always made him more popular with students than with professional philosophers, who tended to regard anyone who took Voodoo as seriously as **quantum mechanics** as, at best, irresponsible.

FITKIN, GRAHAM: COMPOSER (1963–) Fitkin has continued and developed the **minimalist** tradition that was laid down by **Reich** and **Glass** in the 1960s. His music, which contains many of the minimalist distinguishing features such as pulse, tonality, repetition and rhythmic complexity, does not rely on process or large-scale cyclical structures. Instead, Fitkin likes to play with process and narratives, fragmenting them, and to juxtapose seemingly disparate musical elements.

Having graduated from Nottingham University he studied with Dutch composer Louis Andriessen in The Hague before returning to the UK in 1986. While he has written orchestral pieces (such as *Length,* composed while working in association with the Liverpool Philharmonic Orchestra) and pieces for large ensemble (such as *Cud,* written for the John Harle Band), the piano and piano ensembles have provided Fitkin with constant fascination. He believes that their neutrality of timbre allows the composer to escape from the distractions of orchestral colour and to focus on the more crucial musical parameters of structure and rhythm. Pieces such as *Sciosophy* were written for his own ensemble, The Nanquidno Group (four pianists sitting at two keyboards), while *Log, Line* and *Loud* were commissioned by the six-piano ensemble, Piano Circus. While the influence of Reich, Glass and

Andriessen is evident in Fitkin's music, so too is that of rock, jazz and Latin-American music.

FOUCAULT, MICHEL: PHILOSOPHER, HISTORIAN AND CULTURAL CRITIC (1926–84) Michel Foucault was perhaps the single most influential theorist to have emerged from the transformation of the great post-war **structuralist** programme into the **postmodern** theoretical world. More even than his contemporaries Roland **Barthes** and Jacques **Derrida**, Foucault has inspired whole schools of thought, moulding philosophers of science, literary critics, sociologists and cultural historians to his own distinctive form of **discourse analysis**. Whenever the term 'discourse' is mentioned, whenever a reference is made to 'the body' as an object of control or coercion, we find Foucault's ghostly presence.

Foucault's oeuvre consists of a series of historical investigations into particular institutions, or 'discourses'. A discourse, for Foucault, is the matrix of **texts**, the specialized languages and the networks of power relations operating in and defining a given field. He returns always to the relationship between power and knowledge which, for Foucault, amount to very much the same thing.

The first of Foucault's major studies, *Madness and Civilization* (1961), examines the treatment of the insane from the end of the Middle Ages, a period of relative freedom, through the 'great confinement' of the Age of Reason, to the superficially more enlightened policies adopted towards those who were now considered mentally ill after the French Revolution. *The Birth of the Clinic* (1963) is a similar '**archaeological**' project, focusing on the new type of observation, or 'gaze' that began with the first modern teaching hospitals, attended by the bedside physician, the eyes through which the state monitored its subjects' health. *The Order of Things* (1966), which established Foucault's critical reputation, and became a bestseller in France, is a more general study of how, from the seventeenth century, the disciplines of psychiatry, medicine, biology, linguistics and economics came to define their 'proper' subjects, carving the world into ordered, controllable units, fixing each into a rigid structure.

Foucault defined the methodology governing these early works in *The Archaeology of Knowledge* (1969). In distancing his approach from that of conventional historians Foucault leans heavily on the concept of discontinuity. For the traditional historian, discontinuity was both 'the given and the unthinkable': the past is made up of innumerable instances – 'decisions, accidents, initiatives, discoveries' which the historian must annihilate by moulding them into a continuous narrative. In contrast Foucault stresses the fact that certain forms of knowledge (about the human mind and body, about biology, politics or language), after periods of stability in which the fundamental processes of a discourse remain largely unquestioned, undergo rapid transformations. During these transformations (which sound uncannily like Thomas **Kuhn**'s '**paradigm shifts**') there is not only a change in the content of a discourse, but also a

fundamental change in what might count as knowledge itself.

The most radical and unnerving of Foucault's claims is that the very concept 'man' was the creation of a unique set of historical contingencies, a consequence of certain relationships of power, a figment of discourse. By 'man' Foucault means the (by his account) relatively modern idea of man as a self-contained rational agent, that knowing subject assumed by rationalists, and triumphant in the French Revolution. And if, as he claims, we can trace the moment that 'man' came into existence, so we can predict his end. And with the **death of man**, so might perish the urge to classify, dominate, exclude and exploit, which derives from that idea, and that has caused such havoc in our modern age.

In *Discipline and Punish: The Birth of the Prison* (1975), Foucault describes the transformation from the brutal treatment of criminals under feudal regimes to the more diffuse, and yet more effective, forms of social control in modern society. Jeremy Bentham's 'Panopticon' (a design for a penal institution in which prison cells were arranged around a central watchtower) becomes a metaphor for these insidious forms of policing. Never knowing for certain at any time whether or not they were subject to the penetrating gaze of the guard, the prisoners come to regulate their own behaviour.

Foucault's last great project, unfinished at his death, was *The History of Sexuality*. In the first of the three published volumes he seeks to undermine the 'repressive hypothesis', the commonly held belief that the freedom of discussion about sex in the modern age represents a radical and positive departure from the Victorian world of repression and silence. Foucault argues that, on the contrary, the Victorian age saw an acceleration in the multiplication of discourses aimed at delineating, explaining and ultimately controlling sexual behaviour. The modern 'sciences of sex', including psychoanalysis, are simply the continuation of the will to power in the form of the demand to know. The second and third volumes, *The Use of Pleasure* and *The Care of the Self* (both published in 1984), present a series of fascinating case studies showing how sexual behaviour developed from the classical obsession with boy love to the early Christian concern with marriage and heterosexual relations. If he does little to advance the argument of the first volume, Foucault at least gives ample evidence to demonstrate his case against the view that there is anything inherently 'natural' about any particular form of sexual intercourse: sexual relations are always governed by complex codes, strict rules about what can and cannot be done.

Foucault's brand of political activism was closely allied to his intellectual position. After an early flirtation with orthodox **Marxism**, he came to believe that the grand causes and class-based politics advocated by the traditional left in France were as oppressive as the bourgeois establishment they wished to overturn. In places of these meta-issues, Foucault advocated a local, small-scale but tenacious resistance to power. Perhaps the spirit of Foucault's politics is best caught by today's eco-warriors, rejecting as they do traditional forms of political debates, relying rather on causing disruption, challenging the power of the state and big business, and getting stoned.

FRACTALS Fractal geometry, a field invented by Benoit **Mandelbrot**, builds on work begun but discontinued at the turn of last century by the French mathematicians Henri Poincaré, Pierre Fatou and Gaston Julia. Both Mandelbrot and Julia have fractal sets named after them, sets that have served as a cultural icon of **chaos**. There are three basic types of fractal: linear self-similar (or 'self-repeating'), random self-similar, and fractal or 'chaotic' attractors. The first is best illustrated by a phenomenon known as a 'Sierpinski gasket': take a triangle and subdivide its area into smaller triangles. Following this first subdivision, repeat or 'reiterate' the operation on these smaller triangles, and so on *ad infinitum*. Such a figure is linearly self-similar because each part of the object is exactly like the whole from which it is derived. Random fractals are found in natural phenomena such as coastlines, mountains and clouds. One of Mandelbrot's earliest explorations of what he then called 'fractional dimension' was entitled 'How Long is the Coastline of Britain?' (1967). His paradoxical thesis in that paper is that since a coastline is not a pure curve but a random series of indents and excrescences, the coastline does not have a line that can be measured, but an infinite series of fractional dimensions that cannot be finally measured. If we regard a coastline from the air, it appears jagged and random. From ground level, a different dimension of randomness is revealed. Microscopically, the randomness is different again, and so on. Hence the various dimensions of randomness revealed by studying coastlines, clouds and mountains are randomly self-similar, since each dimension repeats randomness, but repeats it differently. Third, chaotic fractals, such as the Mandelbrot set itself, model the behaviour of complex systems. Such systems are really chaotic rather than self-similar since each iteration reacts upon the previous one to produce endless bifurcations. The figure produced by the Mandelbrot set, the most familiar image of chaos, consists of a series of 'blobs' each of which repeats the core blob from which the set starts. With each fractal iteration of the blob, however, a new fractal dimension is produced that does not resemble the whole. This system is therefore complex, both linearly self-similar and random, depending upon which fractal dimension of this non-linear, dynamical system is studied.

FRAMPTON, KENNETH: ARCHITECTURAL THEORIST, CRITIC AND HISTORIAN (1930–) Frampton is undoubtedly one of the foremost architectural commentators of his generation. The author of countless introductions to architectural monographs, he is best known for two publications: *Modern Architecture, a Critical History*, is probably the most widely read primer for architectural students in print; and the essay 'Critical Regionalism', first published in *The Anti Aesthetic* (ed. Hal Foster (1983)) and reprinted in later

editions of *Modern Architecture*, is perhaps his most influential contribution to architectural theory.

Frampton's sympathies are essentially **modernist**. However, his support for 'the unfinished modernist project' is inflected with a critique of the postivist mainstream of architectural modernism derived from the existentialist phenomenological schools of **Heidegger** and Ricoeur. This is most clearly expressed in his promotion of architectural tectonics, that is, the palpable display of the poetics of actual construction, as the primary means of disclosure of authentic architectural meaning. It is also made manifest in his rejection of the universal culture implied by utopian **modernism** which forms the basis of his theory of critical regionalism – a doctrine which, while supporting modernist aesthetics, seeks to resist the homogenization inherent in late-capitalist culture via recourse to the development of local traditions. As such, he is firmly opposed to the architectural manifestations of mainstream **postmodernism** which, by giving precedence to imageability via engagement with **semiology** and other forms of secondary signification, stand in opposition to the primary tectonic architectural culture that Frampton propagates.

FRANKFURT SCHOOL The Frankfurt School of Social Research, founded by Max **Horkheimer** at the University of Frankfurt, comprised such well-known figures as Theodor **Adorno** and Herbert **Marcuse**, as well as Horkheimer himself, and, on the fringes of the School, the cultural critic Walter **Benjamin**. The School relocated in America after the Nazi takeover in 1933 had caused its members, basically Marxist in orientation, to leave Germany. While Adorno returned to Germany after the Second World War, Marcuse remained in America, where he became an inspiration to the student protest movement that grew up in the 1960s. The school is famous for developing the method of analysis called '**critical theory**', which until the rise of **structural Marxism** in the 1950s and 1960s was arguably the dominant form of critique in what has come to be known as Western Marxism. Western Marxism, as borne out by the work of the members of the Frankfurt School, tended to be more interested in philosophical and aesthetic matters than economic ones: the latter being the province of Soviet theorists. Critical theory seeks to uncover the underlying power relations within cultural phenomena. Thus in works like *Dialectic of Enlightenment* (1947), Adorno and Horkheimer argue that the so-called '**Enlightenment project**' (the commitment to the liberation of mankind from material deprivation and political oppression) has become a myth that sustains the cultural status quo, leading to the subjugation of the individual within a repressive mass culture.

Adorno's later work, with its stress on '**negative dialectics**' (the insistence that dialectical processes never resolve themselves into a final synthesis where problems are completely overcome), is often seen to prefigure **deconstruction** as well as **post-Marxism**. Marcuse, too, ultimately moved away from the tenets of classical Marxism in his later career,

when he became a champion of the new social movements that sprang up in the 1960s.

FREUD, SIGMUND: PSYCHOANALYST (1856–1939) Sigmund Freud was born in Freiburg to a Jewish family. When he was three the family moved to Vienna where Freud spent most of the rest of his life. Fleeing Vienna in 1938, he died not long after in London. Initially as a neurologist but ultimately as a psychologist Freud studied human motivation. His psychoanalytic writings apply not only to neurotic behaviour but to all human endeavours. Changes in Freud's views constituted a complex catalyst for the reception of his various ideas, allowing the Freudian legacy of concepts to be developed in a variety of ways by modern and **postmodern** theorists. Freud's most central concept of the unconscious changed with the metapsychology – i.e. the theory about the structure of psychic reality. At any one time Freudian metapsychology determined the models – or 'topographies' – used for describing and interpreting the unconscious.

Freud's concept of the unconscious distinguishes psychoanalysis from other psychologies. The unconscious has an energy, logic and ethics of its own, radically incongruent with the contents of consciousness. It is rooted in unavowable and unavowed **desires** which have undergone repression such that their content remains cut off from consciousness. Consciousness expends energy to bar knowledge and memory of such desires from itself. The full complexity of Freud's concept becomes manifest in a first and second topography. These topographies constitute descriptive models for locating the unconscious and repression in terms of spatial and temporal divisions. A division which appears in both topographies is that between, on the one hand, consciousness and what it is permitted to know and, on the other hand, the unconscious.

In 1895 Freud developed a first topography which contained three systems: the conscious, the preconscious and the unconscious. A censorship exists between the unconscious and the preconscious and conscious. This censorship prevents ideas of one system from moving to another or both others. In 1923 Freud introduced a second topography as the model of intrasubjective relations which function within the psychic apparatus: the ego, id, and superego enter into relations with each other. The superego becomes the forces of repression; the id the places of repressed desires; the ego balances the demands of the other two, while remaining responsible to external reality.

Both topographies are marked by the censorship which constitutes the barrier to the unconscious. An initial censorship – or repression – of the child's incestuous desires has the crucial role of constituting the unconscious. This original repression has as its object the **Oedipus** complex; and derivative repressions are in some sense based upon the images and desires of the initial censorship, explaining the infantile nature of the unconscious. The repressed remains an idea that is charged with a certain amount of energy; the act of repression cuts the energy off from the idea.

Freud's first topography also employs an interpretative model called 'the energetics' as opposed to 'the hermeneutics' of the second topography. The energetics names Freud's use of an anatomical, quantitative model, while his later hermeneutics is built upon to a symbolic, qualitative model of interpretation. Giving Freud's project its scientific distinctiveness, the energetics employs a naturalistic language of energies or organic forces. In contrast the second topography uses hermeneutics to read a symbolic language of double meanings. So Freud's accounts of desire and sexuality treat language in both naturalistic and symbolic terms. If the former terms are used then expressions of sexual desire should be read as directly referring to psychic forces. If the latter terms are employed, then the analysand's statements conceal unconscious meanings which the analyst must interpret as symbols representing the duplicity of desire. These different models of interpretation imply that the unconscious cannot be merely equated with the latent meaning of consciousness.

Freud does not replace his energetics with hermeneutics. Instead, alongside his interpretation of the double meanings of symbols, Freud continues to discuss affects – of rage, envy, love, hate – in terms of the energies which are organized as a natural science like physics. These energies are simply on a separate level of psychic organization from the symbols of desire. The continuing relevance of an energetics means that psychic reality remains linked with the material reality of energies and forces.

Although no agreement exists on any Freudian discovery, Freud's influence is immeasurable. His impact upon contemporary theory is part of the larger climate of postmodern uncertainty and ambivalence, while the disagreement concerning his ideas is compatible with the general environment of postmodern fragmentation. Notwithstanding disagreements, Freud's theories about the unconscious have had a fundamental influence upon postmodern theorizing, especially theories of desire.

FUKUYAMA, FRANCIS: POLITICAL THEORIST (1952–) Fukuyama was propelled into prominence by the controversy with which his book, *The End of History and the Last Man* (1992) was greeted. This presented one of the first philosophically ambitious interpretations of the collapse of Soviet-style communism in 1989. Unfortunately Fukuyama's philosophical capacities were no match for these ambitions. Commentators were astounded by the audacity of Fukuyama's thesis: that with the fall of the Berlin Wall, the logic of history had finally been worked out; that history had come to its logical conclusion in the triumph of the twin principles of liberal democracy and the market economy.

Fukuyama studied in Paris with Jacques **Derrida** before becoming an official in a remote corner of the US administration. His book is a rather trite and superficial treatment of the (Hegelian) notion that there are principles or ideas at work in history. In **Hegel**'s attempt to sketch a world history of *Geist* (spirit or intellect), a key dynamic is the struggle to recon-

cile the principles of freedom and recognition. In a series of lectures in Paris in the 1930s, Alexandre Kojève provided a radical reading of Hegel's *Phenomenology of Mind* based around a passage in which Hegel details the dialectic of master and slave. Fukuyama's 1992 book was thus recycling Kojève's deduction of the idea that the logic of history had, in principle, come to an end. Although Fukuyama has half a century's worth of further examples and historical development to draw on (and to explain), his is a depressingly superficial treatment of history. But the timing of his book made his notoriety inevitable. The crisis in one superpower (what was the USSR) allowed Fukuyama to construct a historical perspective entirely circumscribed by the perspective of the other. Inevitably Fukuyama was read, by friend and foe, as giving a Hegelian, postfacto justification to the USA–Western Europe axis. In countless interviews and commentaries Fukuyama had to explain that his account applied not to the real, painful historical conflicts going on around the world but only to the logic of the ideas which have *so far* played a crucial role in the history of the advanced or industrial world.

Fukuyama's major subsequent publication, *Trust*, is a contribution to an important contemporary theme, but lacking the overwhelming topicality of *The End of History*, it has had little resonance.

FUZZY LOGICS Otherwise known as 'vague' or 'multivalent' (many-valued), fuzzy logics have been developed since the 1920s, when Jan

Lukasiewicz, a Polish logician, formalized a continuum of possible states. Lukasiewicz's impetus came from Werner Heisenberg's uncertainty principle, which postulated that no observer can measure both the position and the velocity of a given electron. In other words, the more precisely the electron's velocity is delineated, the more vague its position becomes. **Quantum mechanics** therefore demanded a more flexible mathematical model not in order to resolve the uncertainty, but, on the contrary, to account for it. More recently, fuzzy logics have found a niche in **artificial intelligence** research, where neural nets 'grow' fuzzy rules from fuzzy data, rather than computers getting it wrong with unerring precision. Fuzzy logics allow computers to learn rather than simply to act upon preprogrammed instruction, exactly in the way that humans learn within a context of real-world fuzziness: humans do not act in accordance with formal rules so much as by approximation and adjustment. Thus Bart Kosko's *Fuzzy Thinking* contrasts the fuzziness of everyday life with the artificial, black-and-white,

1 or 0, binary world long championed by science and philosophy, and even goes so far as to suggest that fuzziness has a history repressed by the avatars of precision that, since Aristotle, have acquired an unshakeable prestige under Western science. The logical basis of such models of scientific certainty ('true or false', but not both), was formulated by Aristotle in the fourth century BC as the law of the excluded middle, which states that a thing cannot be both x and not-x at the same time. In reality, of course, things are frequently x and not-x: a half-eaten apple. At what precise point, for example, does a half-eaten apple cease to be an apple; at what point does the apple cease to be red and become not-red? Fuzzy logics therefore replace the two-value abstractions (black or white, x or not-x) of the law of the excluded middle with a multivalent, 'fuzzy' principle of '*both x and not-x*'. What this means in practice is that precise, quantitative points are replaced by qualitative shifts, a phenomenon that, according to many mathematicians, aligns fuzziness with, for example, the new mathematics of **fractal** objects.

G

GATES, HENRY LOUIS, JR.: CRITIC
AND EDITOR (1950–)   Gates is Chair
of the African-American Studies
Department at Harvard University
and, along with Houston Baker Jr., is
the most prominent male theorist of
African-American literature of his
generation. He was one of the first
critics to use the insights of **continental** theory to examine black **texts**.
He has argued, in such books as
Figures in Black (1987) and especially
in *The Signifying Monkey* (1988), that
black American writing deserves to
be, and allows its most distinctive
forms to show when, examined
through close readings that are alive
to their structural, rhetorical and
deeply figural nature. Gates is also an
influential editor and cultural commentator; he has recently overseen
the publication of the mammoth,
path-breaking *Norton Anthology of
African American Literature* (1997)
and is general editor an important
series of reprints, *The Schomburg
Library of Black Women Writers* (1988
onwards). In *Loose Canons* (1992),
he eloquently defends the concept of
multiculturalism. He has recently
reflected on his own relationship to
his past in a highly praised autobiography, *Colored People* (1994).

Gates's work is meditation, not just
on what **postmodern** theory can have
to say about black writing, but crucially, on what these texts already

know about the nature of signification. Furthermore, he asks whether
it is legitimate to translate theories
drawn from a literary tradition that
has often represented blacks as
barely human. The sceptical **anti-
essentialism** of much of postmodern
theory with its destabilizing of
authorship and subjectivity would
seem to be unpalatable to the black
American tradition of unearthing the
repressed black voice in the face of
slavery and its historical consequence: racism. Gates has a number
of responses to these questions. First
he argues that '*any* tool that enables
the critic to explain the language of a
text is an appropriate tool, for it is
language, the black language of the
black text that expresses the distinctive quality of our tradition.' Second,
he would say that celebrating the
discovery of hitherto forgotten black
writers does not mean that these
authors in any way determine the
meanings that may be read into their
work.

In fact the creative rereading of
the black tradition is at the heart of
Gates's own theory of African-
American literature worked out at
length in *The Signifying Monkey*. The
kernel of this theory can be found in
his 1983 essay 'The Blackness of
Blackness'. Gates suggests that one of
the distinguishing features of black
American writing is 'saying one thing

and meaning something quite other', a technique of survival developed by black slaves. Gates's term for this is 'signifyin(g)', which refers both to the African-American tradition and to the influential Swiss linguist Saussure. 'Signifyin(g)' is a term that has been in the black vernacular for more than 200 years and refers to the ability to parody, reverse and revise another's language. Gates pursues the concept from Africa and the Caribbean through to contemporary black writing. A number of critics, especially black feminists, feel that Gates dispenses too quickly with the notion of black identity (which for postmodernists is a social construct) and find his theory of the black text too narrow. However this may be, Gates does not want to read off a benighted black text using a postmodern template; he wishes to explicate black writing in a way that 'changes both the received theory and received ideas about the text'.

GEERTZ, CLIFFORD: ANTHROPOL-OGIST (1926–) A distinguished academic who has held posts at the University of Chicago and the Institute for Advanced Study at Princeton University, Geertz's work has helped to found the discipline of 'cultural anthropology'. Cultural anthropology rejects the ethnocentrist assumptions built into much anthropological enquiry, and attempts to reach an understanding of a culture (as in the case of Geertz's fieldwork studies in Indonesia and North Africa) rather than just provide a description of it.

Geertz is concerned to interpret cultures through a study of the contexts in which human actions occur

such that they become endowed with meaning. This is his so-called 'thick description', as outlined in his highly influential book *The Interpretation of Cultures* (1973), in particular in the essay 'Thick Description: Towards an Interpretive Theory of Culture'. 'Thin description', on the other hand, fails to provide any real interpretation of the culture in question, but contents itself with cataloguing its objective features. The **structuralist** anthropology of Claude **Lévi-Strauss**, with its desire to find common objective features across cultures, would be an example of the latter type.

Geertz is anti-ethnocentrist, believing that anthropological enquiry all too often involves an implicit assumption of the superiority of the anthropologist's own culture, or at the very least uses his/her own culture as a reference point to explain how other cultures operate. This anti-ethnocentrism, with its insistence that no one culture should be privileged in terms of interpretation, aligns Geertz with **postmodernism** and its commitment to **pluralism**, as does his conception of culture as a series of **texts** whose semantics need to be unravelled before we can understand how their meanings are created.

The postmodern tendency to regard culture as a series of narratives, none of which should be considered to have a privileged claim on our attention, and which need to be understood in terms of their rhetorical strategies, has obvious similarities to the approach of Geertz. In *Local Knowledge* (1983) Geertz has reiterated his opposition to 'grand theories', as well as his commitment to pluralism, thus bringing him into the general orbit of postmodern thought where grand theories (or '**grand narratives**' as Jean-François **Lyotard** calls them) are viewed with scepticism and even outright hostility because of their authoritarian pretensions. The impact of cultural anthropology has been felt across the human sciences, with interpretive theories such as **new historicism** drawing inspiration from Geertz's methods, as in the case of Stephen **Greenblatt**'s analyses of Renaissance literary culture.

GENEALOGY Genealogy denotes the tracings of the origin of a phenomenon, and is associated principally with **Nietzsche**. Whereas **Kant** had looked for the conditions of knowledge and asked, 'how is x possible?' Nietzsche wished to add a second question to this, namely, 'why is x necessary?' Genealogy is therefore an investigation into the combined possibilities and necessities of a form of life. Nietzsche's most sustained exploration into origins is *Toward a Genealogy of Morals* (1887). Here he tracks the formation of notions of 'good' and 'bad', and 'good' and 'evil', and the corresponding states of responsibility, guilt and bad conscience which usually accompany those terms. Nietzsche's project is not primarily etymological. Rather, he is careful to stress that the evolution of a thing is not directed towards a single purpose, but is subject to changing pressures and circumstances. More recently, **Foucault** has engaged extensively with the work of genealogy. In *Discipline and Punish* (1975), he presents a history of how Western society has dealt with crime. He illustrates a shift from practices involving bodily mutilation and public humiliation, common at the time of Shakespeare, to punishments since the eighteenth century involving incarceration or financial reparation. Again it is the non-continuities and complex transactions between institutions and their discursive power that are highlighted.

GENERATION X Asked by a publisher to write a guide to the twenty-something generation, Douglas **Coupland** turned in a novel, the phenomenally successful *Generation X* (1991), noted for capturing the mindset and language of privileged, young 1990s Californians. A good deal of the novel's energy comes from the marginalia – a whole series of *Zeitgeist*-defining neologisms, asides and summaries which generalize the main characters' experience. Generation X-ers are young, well-educated, under-employed post-babyboomers who despise the corporate ideology of the 1980s, but have little to put in its place. In this vacuum, they affect a **postmodern** superficiality, an all-pervasive 'knee-jerk **irony**', spending their time practising an ironic form of cultural snobbery by one-upping each other with knowledge of TV trivia ('obscurism') when not doing low-pay, low-esteem, no-future, service-sector work ('McJobs'). They get by through personally tailored but wildly uninformed philosophico-religious beliefs ('Me-ism') and settle for 'lessness' – reconciling themselves to diminishing expectations. If, for some, these modes of living disguise a romantic longing for a form of authentic experience often associated in classic American literature with nature, then other X-ers might say (if they would admit to reading him): 'Nature? How *Ralph Waldo Emerson*.'

GIBSON, WILLIAM: NOVELIST (1948–) After publishing a number of distinguished short stories in the early 1980s, Gibson made the most spectacular debut in recent science-fiction history with *Neuromancer* (1984), winning the two major science-fiction awards. What made it different from other science-fiction was its style, an eclectic pastiche of influences, among them *Blade Runner,* William Burroughs, Thomas **Pynchon**, Raymond Chandler, *film noir* and the 'psychological' science-fiction of late-1960s counter-culture, J. G. Ballard, Philip K. Dick and Samuel Delany. The self-consciously 'pulp' plot and the glittering, allusive surface of the prose led to it being called '**cyberpunk**'. 'Cyber' comes from control and communications systems and 'punk' from the relative youth of the author and his indebtedness to the sensibility found in the music of the Velvet Underground and garage punk bands. *Neuromancer* is a classic 'caper' novel which assembles a group of experts to break through the defences of a big business information system. It is concerned primarily with the interface between humans and new technologies such as **virtual reality** and cloning, and in the psychological and philosophical consequences of the blurring of such distinctions as human/machine and illusion/reality. Seen as quintessentially **postmodern** by many critics, the

world of cyberpunk is a bleak **Baudrillardian** one of **simulation** and the **hyperreal**, where image and reality have imploded.

For Gibson (who invented the term), **cyberspace** is 'a consensual hallucination experienced daily by billions of legitimate operators in every nation. A graphic representation of data extracted from the banks of every computer in the human system. Unthinkable complexity.' Cyberspace is a non-space that is everywhere and yet nowhere. Night city, where most of the action takes place, is memorably described as 'a deranged experiment in social Darwinism, designed by a bored researcher who kept one thumb permanently on the fast-forward button'. Gibson develops this theme in more detail in the two novels that follow, *Count Zero* (1986) and *Mona Lisa Overdrive* (1988). 'Simstim', 'meat puppet', 'prosthetic limbs', 'cranial sockets', 'mimetic polycarbon'; the three novels are obsessed with the porous nature of the human body/technology interface and the ways the body can be both extended and transformed. *The Difference Engine* (1990), written with Bruce Sterling, is a remarkable alternative history involving Babbage's invention of an early computer. Arguably his best work, the melancholy *Virtual Light* (1993) is a near-future tale concerned with the inhabitants of a shanty town under the Golden Gate bridge and is a much more downbeat, socially concerned piece. *Idoru* (Japanese for 'Idol', pronounced in English: 'I adore You') (1997) involves a 'female personality construct'. Its Japanese setting returns Gibson to his most popular landscape. After fifteen years of publication in a field that quickly sees careers go by the wayside after initial critical and commercial success, Gibson's fiction is still among the most original and influential science-fiction around.

GIDDENS, ANTHONY: SOCIOLOGIST (1938–) Giddens is probably the best known British sociologist. Throughout an academic career that began in the early 1960s and which has seen him progress from lecturer at the University of Leicester via Professor of Sociology at Cambridge to Director of the London School of Economics in 1997, Giddens has consistently struggled with some of the central theoretical concerns of sociology. In his early work he made an extensive contribution to the interpretation of the classical sociological texts including books on Weber, Durkheim, social class, and a three-volume critique of historical materialism.

He is perhaps best known for his concept of *structuration*, which is an attempt to resolve one of the basic dilemmas of social theory. Sociology has classically been divided between those who are closer to a macro perspective and those who are closer to a micro one. To put this another way, writers have provided social explanations which either give greatest emphasis to the importance of active individuals and human agency (*action theories*) or to constraining social structures and institutions (*structural theories*). Giddens suggests that it is essential to bridge this simplistic duality and argues that human beings always have the capacity to change their social circumstances, even if these are limited by specific social contexts. He has been applauded for the detailed and meticulous way in which he has analysed preceding theories and synthesized these to support his ideas. This is in contrast to work of more radical writers who have rejected all that has gone before and filled the resulting vacuum which they have created, with a new, but ungrounded orthodoxy. Giddens is a theorist of the middle ground and in his most recent works he has tried to come to terms with the challenge of **postmodern** theory. In doing this he has continued to try to hold the same theoretical space.

In advocating the case for the decline of **metanarratives** and describing a world in which our identities essentially reside in our capacity to shop, postmodern theorists have variously claimed the end of history, of sociology, and of all certainty. Critics of postmodern perspectives have pointed to their inherent theoretical helplessness and nihilism. While some of these writers simply wish to see a return to the old ideas, Giddens characteristically holds the middle ground. He incorporates concepts from both sides of this divide calling the contemporary epoch 'late' or 'high' modernity.

He agrees with the theorists of **postmodernity** that massive changes have occurred in the late twentieth century which have led to a restructuring of social experience, identity and knowledge. However he does not agree that these changes constitute a complete break with modernity. Giddens develops the concept of reflexivity beyond its previous usage.

He suggests that contemporary life is characterized for the individual by more than a simple capacity to reflect upon the self. Instead he argues that in late **modernity** it is the process of reflection itself which has become the topic for reflection. This fits with the self-consciousness and **irony** of postmodernism and illustrates the extent to which the self has also become a reflexive project. It also builds a link for Giddens back to his earlier concerns with the connections between social identity and social structure. This provides us with the paradox that the only security that we can find in contemporary life is the certainty that everything is uncertain.

Giddens explores the idea of the self further when he considers the basis of intimacy in contemporary life and attempts to describe and explain the shifting patterns of marriage and personal relationships. He argues that human relations are *unhooked,* lacking traditional linkages with the rules and patterns of family, community and reproduction. Interaction is person centred and based upon the fulfilment of individual need. We therefore feel that we are at liberty to move on when those needs are no longer adequately met. There are echoes here of the spirit of postmodern consumption applied to love and marriage.

Giddens has maintained a constant set of interests throughout his academic writing. His latest work attempts a synthesis of some of the central issues of contemporary experience. He continues to explore the interdependence of the individual and social structure by emphasizing the twin themes of security and danger

and of risk and trust. He agrees that life in the late twentieth century is precarious, but leaves space for the individual to be rather more than a mere fashion victim. Even if we do choose to collude with the imperatives of corporate capitalism, at least we can also reflect upon them. The central aim of the self in high modernity is to escape the trap of becoming fixed. We have to keep moving.

GILBERT AND GEORGE: ARTISTS (1943– , 1942–) Tradition, custom and ceremony are entangled in Gilbert and George's monumental art, which first came to prominence in the late 1960s in the form of 'The Singing Sculpture'. Combining pre-war popular culture with performance art, the work comprised Gilbert and George dressed in anonymous business suits singing Flanagan and Allen's 1932 song 'Underneath the Arches'. In these all-day performances, which were enacted in Europe, Australia and the USA between 1969 and 1973, the robotic nature of the 'act' would be reinforced by their machine-like movements. Referring to their show at New York's Sonnabend Gallery in 1971, Robert Rosenblum claimed that such work, at once '**ironic** or nostalgic' and '**postmodernist**', was an unclassifiable combination of the 'ephemeral and permanent, the human and the mechanical'.

By the 1970s other critics could see such practices as postmodern because they signalled the emptiness of late **modernist** minimalist sculpture and deflated the 'virile' rhetoric of much performance art. Examining the blankness of the 'singing sculptures' it was possible to assert that modernist creativity had been replaced by mechanical anonymity: instead of carving, building and making things Gilbert and George played out the endless inertia of late modernist art by becoming metallic mannequins; and in the rigidity of their performances could be found confirmation of the 'lifelessness' of late-modernist sculpture.

This strange combination of the avant-garde and the antiquated – of 'shock' subject-matter and traditional iconography, of alienation and celebration – has been a feature of all their subsequent photo-based productions, the most recent of which are organized around dramatic polarities of light and dark, vitality and stasis. Deploying the techniques of commercial photography, the works in *Crusade* (1982), *Modern Faith* (1983), *The Believing World* (1984), *New Moral Works* (1985) and *The Cosmological Pictures* (1989), contain echoes of pop art, Christian art, Soviet socialist realism, and advertising, all of which are played out in compositions where Gilbert and George, resembling middle-class versions of Morecambe and Wise, preside over 'heraldic' landscapes festooned with melancholic or taciturn teenage boys. If this camp cornucopia is a rejection of the visionary or utopian nature of modernism, it still embraces the aesthetics of redemption: in place of the artist as the difficult outsider creating 'dense' or 'difficult' art, the artist knits together historical and contemporary sources to construct a homoerotic postmodern religion of the self.

In *The Cosmological Pictures* a kind of kitsch fecundity replaces the filmic bleakness of their early black and white imagery; and by deploying the constructed and collaged style associated with American postmodernism, formal repetition is animated by dramatic contrasts of scale and through the juxtaposition of natural forms, many of which glow with vivid and vibrant colours. These exercises in Technicolor are augmented by the domination of the frontal plane, where figures loom in the manner of the designs found in the stained glass windows of medieval churches. However, if the poses of the figures connote devotion, submission and reverence, the intensity of the lighting, the kitsch quality of the coloration, and the theatrical nature of the facial expressions announce the impossibility of solemnity and disbelief in the rituals, systems and ceremonies which are enacted by the artists and their retinue. These standing, reclining, crouching or kneeling figures are condemned to repeat the actions of narratives that have disappeared. This is art apart: we find the postures and gestures associated with Michelangelo, Blake and Munch, but narrative content is buried beneath the self-emptying repetition of tacky Gothic subjects, camp angels clothed in the Day-Glo colours of comics, and environments which conflate the kitsch and the uncanny through the facial expressions of figures, many of whom appear to be watching horror films. It would seem, then, that in this form of postmodernism the transcendental verities of modernist art have been replaced by a contradictory art that is hermetic and popular, theological and ironic, animated and blank.

GLASS, PHILIP: COMPOSER (1937–)
Glass has played a key role in the development of **minimalist** music. He received a rigorous formal education in music but was inspired by non-Western musics as well as other composers of minimalist music (such as his one-time colleague, Steve **Reich**). His career has been characterized by collaboration both with a diverse selection of musicians and with people from other artistic fields. Studying piano, flute, violin and theory from a young age he determined to become a composer and moved to New York to study at the Juilliard School (1956). He then took private composition lessons with a number of composers in America before moving to Paris to study with the renowned teacher Nadia Boulanger. Here, as well as undertaking a rigorous study of nineteenth-century harmony, he was fortunate enough to meet and work with the world famous Indian sitar player Ravi Shankar. Thus began a lifelong interest in and study of the music and aesthetic principles of other cultures. Following a period of research in India, North Africa and Tibet, Glass moved back to New York to begin synthesizing his influences into his own unique musical voice.

Serialism – the technique of treating each of the twelve notes of the chromatic scale with equal weighting and thus ensuring that the music never settles into any one key – had become the norm in serious concert music. Glass, while being trained in the serial technique of composition, was quick to reject it, claiming it was élitist, academic and old-fashioned. His work as a performer with Steve

Reich's ensemble, coupled with his knowledge of non-Western forms, inspired him to develop his own techniques of composition. His early works, such as *Two Pages* (1968) and *Music in Fifths* (1969), could stay not only in the same key but on the same chord for long periods, drawing their interest from the dimensions of rhythm and structure. His music used structuring principles (such as additive process – whereby notes are systematically added to a repeated motif increasing its length and altering the underlying metre of the music – and cyclical structure) which were derived from Eastern musics, while the surface level utilized the more familiar Western scales and arpeggios.

In addition to setting up his own ensemble (which he did in 1968) Glass, who had always had a love of the theatre, wrote a number of collaborative music-theatre works, the first three of which, *Einstein on the Beach* (1976), *Satyagraha* (1980) and *Akhnaton* (1984), form a trilogy.

Glass, perhaps more than any other twentieth-century composer, has continually worked to break down the barriers that rigidly separate 'high' and 'low' art. Many of his collaborations have been with artists from rock, popular and non-Western traditions. In *Songs from Liquid Days* (1986) he worked with a number of popular songwriters including Paul Simon, David Byrne and Suzanne Vega. The songwriter provided the lyrics, which Glass then arranged and set to music. In the late 1980s Glass collaborated with the African composer Foday Musa Suso to produce the music for Jean Genet's stage work *The Screens*. Although Glass had been deeply inspired by the music of Ravi Shankar while working with him in the 1960s, it was not until 1990 that the two were able to collaborate again. The project, which produced a CD recording entitled *Passages*, involved each composer writing a piece based on a theme supplied by the other. Another notable collaboration has been that of Glass's hugely successful *Low* symphony (1992). This three-movement work for full orchestra was inspired by the David Bowie and Brian **Eno** album, *Low*, of 1977 which, being a collection of songs and instrumental pieces, provided Glass with the themes on which to construct the symphony. The *Heroes* symphony (1997) again draws on a Bowie and Eno album of the 1970s.

As with his contemporary Steve Reich, Philip Glass's work has been largely shunned by the (essentially **modernist**) music establishment. Again like Steve Reich he solved this problem in the early days by writing a large proportion of his material for his own ensemble and forging a new audience away from the traditional concert halls. Glass has been hugely inspirational, not only to many younger composers of 'classical' concert music, but also to the producers of ambient, house and dance music.

GRAMMATOLOGY The term 'grammatology' first came to prominence with the publication of Jacques **Derrida**'s *Of Grammatology* in 1967, and describes a science of writing that puts into question the inherent value of the linguistic **sign**. Derrida's use of the term is part of a critique of Western philosophy for giving precedence to speech over writing.

Western philosophical discourse is held to be committed to phonetic writing, the kind of writing that attempts fully to represent speech. Grammatology as a science of writing is part of a general tendency in Derrida's work to redress this balance. Central to this process is the refutation of the **structuralist** notion that signifier and signified form an organic unity. Speech is regarded as an original **presence** in structuralist linguistics and writing an invasion of purity. **Logocentric** writing (the reproduction of the phoneme or the voice), is distinguished by the grammatologist from *écriture*, or grammatological writing, which is concerned with characterizing those actions that create language. Following Derrida, the grammatologist argues that 'there is nothing outside the **text**', and that language is open to myriad interpretations that continually defer meaning. This involves a rejection of the possibility of an absolute truth fixed by a transcendental signifier. Such a position has affinities with the **postmodern** dismissal of **grand narratives**.

GRAND NARRATIVE Jean-François **Lyotard** described as grand narratives theories which claim to provide universal explanations and trade on the authority this gives them. An example would be **Marxism**, which processes all human history and social behaviour through its theory of dialectical materialism. According to dialectical materialism all human history has been the history of class struggle, and it denies the validity of all other explanations, laying sole claim to the truth. The ultimate goal of human history is the 'dictatorship of the proletariat', where class struggle has been eliminated for the common good and individuals are no longer exploited. Most religions offer a similarly all-embracing explanation of human history to fit their particular schemes. Lyotard's contention is that such schemes are implicitly authoritarian, and that by the late twentieth century they have lost all claim to authority over individual behaviour. It is part of living in a **postmodern** world that we no longer can rely on such grand narratives (or '**metanarratives**'), but must construct more tactically oriented '**little narratives**' instead if we wish to stand up against authoritarianism. In Lyotard's view, we have now seen through grand narratives and realized that their claims to authority are false and unsustainable.

GREENAWAY, PETER: FILM DIRECTOR (1942–) Greenaway is best known for an oeuvre of over thirty films that display a unity of art and literature. These films are characterized by rich cinematography and experimental structure providing 'opportunities to play with images, to play with words, to play with their interactions'. Since 1978 the **minimalist** composer Michael **Nyman** has written all the scores for Greenaway's films.

Greenaway's early works reflect a sustained interest in system and structures. *Windows* (1976), *A Walk Through H* (1978) and *H is for House* (1978), show a preference for a formalist application of letter or number frameworks that self-consciously reference the process of making films such as *The Draughtsman's Contract*

(1982) explore systems in a more overtly **semiotic** fashion and suppress their early minimalist manifestations for a context that revels in the excessive and extreme, the cannibalism of *The Cook, the Thief, his Wife and her Lover* (1989) being a prime example. These films reflect Greenaway's move into **postmodernism**. From the 1980s his work is increasingly underscored by a concern with **intertextuality** and eclecticism in both the structure of his films and the characterization of their leading players. *The Draughtsman's Contract* appropriates the seventeenth century, *The Belly of an Architect* (1987) draws upon another's history, the French eighteenth-century architect Boullée, to provide a cross-temporal search for self in the main character. Greenaway forgoes psychological characterization, however, for a postmodern revival of allegory, speaking of his characters as '*ciphers . . . to hold a weight of allegorical and personifying meaning*'.

Greenaway's concern to extend the boundaries of cinema in parallel with such developments in art and literature gave his early films an exclusively art-house audience. However the spectacle and excess of films such as *The Cook, the Thief, his Wife and her Lover*, and the attraction of leading actors such as Sir John Gielgud in *Prospero's Books* (1991) and Ewan McGregor in *The Pillow Book* (1996), have gained him a more mainstream audience without compromising on style.

GREENBLATT, STEPHEN: LITERARY CRITIC (1937–) Greenblatt is the central figure in American '**new historicism**', a term which he coined in 1982. New historicism is rooted in a conviction that the American theoretical orthodoxies of the 1970s, notably **deconstruction**, were as ahistorical in their methodologies as the critical schools – new criticism and myth criticism – which they challenged and replaced. Greenblatt rejects criticism which addresses an artwork as a self-sufficient object divorced from its historical contexts and cultural antecedents. However, addressing literature in its historical context is nothing new; what distinguishes Greenblatt from more traditional historicist criticism is his problematizing of its division between literary foreground and political background. In addition, Greenblatt borrows from sources alien to traditional historical criticism: anthropology (notably **Geertz**), **Lacanian** neo-**Freudianism**, and, in particular, **Foucault**. Greenblatt, following Foucault, foregrounds the concept that 'history' is itself **textually** mediated, and problematizes the mimetic model of previous historicist criticism which viewed a text as simply reflecting the history around – and thus still outside – it. **Representations** are not simply the products of an age; they are themselves productive, engaging with and often subsequently altering the forces that brought them into being. Nor is history the stable and incontrovertible backdrop to the work of literature assumed by monological historical scholarship. Non-literary texts are not simply neutral transcriptions of reality; instead, historical fact and experience are available to us only in 'textual traces', with all the concomitant rhetorical strategies which characterize textuality.

Renaissance Self-Fashioning (1980) takes issue with the presuppositions of new criticism's close-reading techniques. Art cannot pretend to autonomy, and textual traces are 'self-consciously embedded in specific communities, life situations, structures of power'. Simultaneously, Greenblatt rejects reductive generalizations about his authors' relationship to their culture. Shakespeare's plays, for instance, do not offer a 'single timeless affirmation or denial of **legitimate authority**'. Renaissance society was not homogeneous and its literature enacts its ideological struggles. Renaissance literary works are not 'a stable set of reflections of the historical facts that lie beyond them'; they are 'places of dissension'. Despite the repudiation of the ahistorical orientation of much **postmodern** thought, his work owes much to deconstruction, borrowing some of its terminology ('origins', 'rupture', 'inscription', and so on) and arguing that there is no grand originating consciousness available in literary works, which have no 'central, unwavering authorial presence'. *Renaissance Self-Fashioning* addresses the concept of the construction of identity, and its ideas are often heavily influenced by deconstructive notions of human subjectivity. For instance, Othello's self-fashioning is seen as discursive, produced by external rhetoric; his innermost self is dependent upon 'a language that is always necessarily given from without and upon representation before an audience'.

Shakespearean Negotiations (1990) employs Foucault's genealogical methodology, refusing to privilege canonical Renaissance literature and dwelling upon what Greenblatt calls writings from the 'borders'. This strategy raises issues of canonicity, politicizes major/minor literary argument and, in particular, problematizes orthodox historiography. Greenblatt, like Foucault, is unafraid of connecting supposedly non-literary historical texts with the literary artefact – a legitimate strategy if history is available to us only in the form of narrative. For instance, 'Fiction and Friction' uses an anecdote about transvestism in the 1580s to initiate a reading of *Twelfth Night*. Such juxtapositions have become mannerisms in new-historicist writing, but form an 'anecdotal historiography' which repudiates, to use **Lyotard**'s term, the **grand narratives** of orthodox historiography. *Shakespearean Negotiations* is also Foucauldian in its concern with power, especially in its close attention to the concepts of subversion and containment. Greenblatt examines how ideologies 'co-opt' subversive discourses, thereby assimilating or neutralizing them. The gloomy message for the radical is that subversive voices are 'produced by and within the affirmations of order; they are powerfully registered, but they do not undermine that order'.

Marvellous Possessions (1992) examines how selfhood is frequently constructed by the identification of an (often demonic) other. Addressing encounters between Europeans and the inhabitants of the New World, Greenblatt discerns an initial sense of 'wonder'. This leads to a crisis of representation; how does one address the absolutely other? Colonialists rename, transform and appropriate in a strategy of terroristic estrangement. The **other** is made an alien object, a thing that can be either destroyed or subtly incorporated and contained through linguistic colonialism.

Greenblatt's work has set the tone for the new-historical strand within contemporary literary theory. He has been highly influential as a propagandist for Foucault in American academe, and his work is central to the new brand of Renaissance studies which began to reclaim the critical high ground from Romanticism during the 1980s.

GREENS (GREEN MOVEMENT) The increasing threat to the environment posed by modern industrial and technological processes (resulting in, for example, the creation of holes in the ozone layer) has led to the formation of pressure groups to resist, and, if possible, arrest this cultural trend. Collectively, such groups have been dubbed the 'Greens', and have had a significant impact on Western culture. It is not just the processes that the Greens have called into question, however, but also the socio-economic and political systems they derive from, with their seemingly insatiable demand for technological progress and ever-higher levels of consumption. Although they have enjoyed a certain amount of success in local and national elections across Western Europe, the Greens function most effectively as a pressure group. In this latter guise they have managed to make most of the continent's major political parties and public institutions pay at least lip-service to Green principles, such as the need to protect the environment by restricting car usage and controlling the disposal of industrial waste. The Green Movement can be regarded as **postmodern** in its generally sceptical attitude towards progress, as well as in the way that it cuts across existing political party lines to challenge the prevailing power structures in Western society.

GUATTARI, FÉLIX: PSYCHIATRIST, PHILOSOPHER AND POLITICAL ACTIVIST (1930–92) A psychiatrist at La Borde clinic and rebellious student of **Lacan**, Guattari presaged much of what was to become, in the 1960s, the anti-psychiatry movement most closely associated, in the English-speaking world, with R. D. Laing. Guattari is best known, however, as a prolific philosophical writer and political activist, collaborating with Antonio Negri and the Italian autonomia movement and, more famously, Gilles **Deleuze**, in whose company he wrote *Capitalism and Schizophrenia 1: Anti-Oedipus,* which defined the philosophical terrain of **post-Marxist** French intellectual life following the *événements* of May 1968. His later work, taking its lead from the second volume of *Capitalism and Schizophrenia: A Thousand Plateaus,* turned increasingly towards the sciences – especially molecular chemistry, physics and geology – in works such as *Chaosmosis* (1992), and established *Chimères,* a journal to which philosophers and social theorists such as Deleuze and Paul **Virilio**, as well as scientist-philosophers such as Ilya Prigogine and Francesco Varela, contributed. What Guattari drew from this rich,

hybrid background, however, in line with his long-term political commitments, were ways to remodel political and real-life selves according to self-organizing, 'minoritarian' clusters that emerge, as it were, from the 'ground up' to create new political trajectories. Avoiding – and indeed, regularly attacking – the strait-jacketing dogmas of political movements left and right that impose and reinforce 'top down' or 'molar' subjectivities through mechanisms of internal policing or 'self-criticism', Guattari therefore attempted, with Antonio Negri in *Communists Like Us* (1990), to rehabilitate a form of communism that emphasized the immediacy of the production of subjectivity from actions rather than, as **Marx** did, emphasizing the destruction of a pre-existing 'natural' subjectivity under capitalism. While viciously critical of 'the **postmodern** dead-end', Guattari has perhaps contributed to some of its major themes, but has brought a political edge to them that many refuse to recognize.

GYNOCRITICISM Coined by the American literary critic Elaine Showalter in 'Towards a Feminist Poetics' (1979), gynocriticism denotes a feminist critical practice which focuses on women as both the recipients and the producers of **texts**. Showalter outlines its ultimate intent as being 'to construct a female framework for the analysis of women's literature [and] to develop new models based on the study of female experience'. An important element in this project is the recovery of a tradition of female authorship, an endeavour with which Showalter became particularly identified following the publication of *A Literature of Their Own* (1978), which brought to light a hidden history of women's publications which had been largely obscured by a literary canon dominated by male **authors**. As the title of Showalter's book itself indicates, one of gynocriticism's most important foremothers is Virginia Woolf, who in *A Room of One's Own* (1929), similarly called for the necessity of recovering a record of women's 'infinitely obscure lives'.

Gynocriticism forms the cornerstone of the 'Anglo-American' school of feminist thought, which appeals to the notion of a collective female experience, unproblematically founded on the concept of a unified **subjectivity** capable of being rendered apprehensible through language. It is therefore open to question from those critics influenced by French **deconstructive** theory, who interrogate the very basis upon which such assumptions are made.

H

HABERMAS, JÜRGEN: PHILOSOPHER AND SOCIOLOGIST (1929–) Habermas is one of most important figures in German intellectual life today. Many consider him the most important sociologist or social theorist since Max Weber. Between 1956 and 1959 he worked as assistant to Theodor W. **Adorno**, although it is only since the 1980s that Habermas has offered any systematic account of the relationship (which is anything but straightforward) of his own work to that of the earlier generation of '**critical theorists**' (see '**Frankfurt School**' on page 248). In 1964 he was made Professor of Philosophy and Sociology at the University of Frankfurt and in 1971 he became co-director of the newly created Max Planck Institute for the Study of the Conditions of Life in the Scientific-Technical World. Habermas has been a key figure in directing and co-ordinating various research programmes and has influenced a wide range of empirical and historical studies.

Habermas's own writings have included a whole series of painstaking critiques and reconstructions of the classics of sociology and philosophy. His early work was placed under the heading of a 'reconstruction of historical materialism'. In it Habermas sought to mobilize all the intellectual resources of the twentieth century in order to redeem the nineteenth-century project of a science of society. In *Knowledge and Human Interests* (1968), Habermas addresses the insight that interests inevitably play a role in determining the nature and shape of sociological (and indeed other scientific) investigation. He sets out to combat the relativist implications of this notion by establishing the constructive, guiding role of 'knowledge-constitutive interests'. As Habermas's enormously ambitious programme of synthesis and criticism has taken shape, communication and discourse are the themes that have come to occupy the foreground. Habermas has drawn widely on empirical studies in sociology, anthropology, linguistics and psychology, but always with the aim of providing a modern, up-to-date version of 'human nature' as the basis for the progressive development and evolution of society. Habermas's work is justly claimed – by friend and foe – to be in direct continuity with traditions in social philosophy that stretch back to the beginnings of the **Enlightenment**.

When **Lyotard** wrote *The Postmodern Condition: A Report on Knowledge* (1979) Habermas was made its main target. Throughout the work, Habermas's ambitious theoretical constructs are taken to be one more (rather abstract and general) **grand narrative**. Lyotard objected in particular to Habermas's adherence to the need to 'unmask' ideology and his insistence on evaluating social relations in terms of their contribution to some future better state of society.

Habermas's immensely elaborate theoretical constructions offer a highly nuanced treatment of levels of discourse and of the interrelations between the various structures and behaviour patterns that make up society. But Habermas is condemned by his **postmodern** critics for maintaining a connection – however mediated – between questions of **legitimation** in science and the issue of legitimacy for political institutions. For Habermas the question of 'in the name of what?' retains its primacy when reflecting on how and why social relations become criticizable. Habermas's answer involves the notion of a potential (or ideal) consensus. Serious engagement with Habermas's work involves being very precise about the methodological or epistemological status he assigns to such very abstract notions. But in contemporary academic polemics such subtleties often go unobserved.

Habermas's whole theoretical project is rejected by Lyotard as the unacceptable remnant of a 'totalizing' philosophical tradition and as the valorization of conformist, when not 'terrorist', ideals of consensus. Being singled out for special treatment by postmodernism, Habermas has returned the compliment and offered a sustained critical engagement with his critics and with what he sees as the irrationalist, nihilist and neo-conservative tendencies within postmodernism. Habermas has been consistently sceptical of its inflated claims and deeply suspicious of its extreme scepticism. Habermas's most sustained and substantial treatment of what he sees as the flaws and dangers of postmodernism is presented in his twelve lectures on *The Philosophical Discourse of Modernity* (1985).

Habermas's mentor, Adorno, had held that there was a fundamental flaw in the logic of modernity and that its ineluctable destiny was to give rise to domination. For Habermas there is no historical necessity involved in domination in the modern world of specific forms of *Zweckrationalität* (instrumental reason). He maintains the conviction that a humane collective life depends on the vulnerable forms of innovation-bearing, reciprocal and unforcedly egalitarian everyday communication. Habermas's constant reformulations of his basic inspiration have made clearer his affinity to central themes of American pragmatist tradition. Like C. S. Pierce, Habermas's immense theoretical efforts live off the vision that society is a self-corrective critical community of enquirers without any absolute beginning or finality.

HALLEY, PETER: ARTIST (1953–) Emerging as an important player in **postmodernist** critical practice in the early 1980s, Halley was the most significant force in the New York **neo-geo** or **simulationist** movement, reading the formal qualities of **modernism** through his understanding of the theories of **Foucault** and **Baudrillard**. In place of the serene symmetry or asymmetric purity of classic modernist abstraction, throughout the 1980s Halley imprisons his geometry in unhomely and bleak compositions. There is nothing lyrical, elegant or luminous about such paintings. If he deploys some of the trademarks of transcendental abstract expressionism – the epic sense of space, the dramatic fields of colour and a compositional register that suggests the **sublime** – there are no traces of the metaphysical in his work. Exhilaration has been replaced by alienation in Halley's anonymous abstract simulations. 'Notes on Painting', an influential essay from 1983, explains his strategy:

> Even though my work is geometric in appearance, its meaning is intended as antithetical to that of previous geometric art. I have tried to employ the codes of minimalism, Colour Field painting and Constructivism to reveal the sociological basis of their origins. Informed by Foucault, I see in the square a prison; behind the mythologies of contemporary society, a veiled network of cells and conduits.

Halley finds in the pictorial logic of geometric art the spatial order of the Panopticon, the nineteenth-century prison model organized around an all-seeing centre from which radiate cells and chambers. Following Foucault, Halley finds in the Panopticon a new geometry of power in which vision becomes a regime of control, a form of authority that is applied to a multiplicity of institutional and bureaucratic spaces. From this he goes on to assert that at all levels of articulation, geometric structures are entangled in the disciplinary and organizational logics of a social system based on surveillance, visibility and spatial order.

Because Halley believes that modern art has been entirely assimilated into the workings of a global technocratic culture, his neo-geo or simulationist works are not so much paintings as models of paintings: they register the flows of power, knowledge and information in postmodern economies; they affirm that experience of the world is produced by simulations and duplications of life. Baudrillard, horrified that anyone could attempt to use his ideas by producing an 'iconography' of simulation, denounced Halley's project. However, as can be gathered from his interest in surveillance, Halley has always been more interested in the writings of Foucault. Leaving aside Baudrillard's justifiable claim that it is impossible to represent simulation, we might add that, even if this were possible, why does Halley believe that such **representation** would be 'critical' of simulation? Halley would argue that although it may be impossible to produce a comprehensive knowledge of a rapidly changing complex of institutional processes, we must continue to map the significant structures, practices and spaces of our social systems because the function of art is to register interactions of power and knowledge.

HARAWAY, DONNA: CULTURAL SCIENTIST AND PHILOSOPHER (1944–) Donna Haraway has led the way in formulating a feminist approach to nature and techno-science. Her work forms a cornerstone of the increasingly popular field of techno-theory, which seeks to analyse the impact of technological development on both the **subject** and society.

As a feminist, Haraway is concerned with challenging the traditional postulation of nature as the site of origin and identity: female identity, in particular. Instead, she attempts to portray female subjectivity as contingent upon the influence of class, race and politics, and thus, like nature, a product of society and of history rather than an incontestable 'given'. She also attempts to undermine the **binary** division that makes nature technology's oppositional **other**, with the intention of 'dislocating each term in order to open up new possibilities'.

However, although Haraway 'dislocates' this dualism, she does not do away with it altogether, proceeding instead to envisage it in ironic and disturbing ways. While she may not believe in the 'naturalness' of nature, she nevertheless asserts its importance as a powerful discourse which can be used as a site which forms common ground between diverse peoples and points of view. Because such links are always partial and contradictory, they thus disrupt techno-science's tendency to act as a totalizing force which eradicates difference.

In this context, Haraway's notion of a multiple, refracted subjectivity linked to others by the play of similarities and **difference** seeks to contest techno-science's schematic conception of the human organism, whose systems, like those of a machine, can be mapped, repaired, and replicated through technological intervention. The most popular aspect of Haraway's thought is that which proffers a notion of identity that transcends the polarities of the nature/technology opposition. To exist between such dualisms, suspended between rejection and appropriation, is what Haraway has most famously defined as a '**cyborg**' subject position. Her essay 'A Cyborg Manifesto' was originally published in 1985, but remains her best-known piece of writing. For Haraway, the cyborg, who is neither wholly natural nor artefactual, becomes the embodiment of the **postmodern** condition, where the positioning of the boundaries dividing nature from techno-culture is an increasingly problematic issue.

Haraway's notion of the cyborg operates on both a literal and metaphorical level. In the here-and-now we are all inescapably subject to the operations of a highly technological society, and are therefore all cyborgs. However, the cyborg also functions as a powerful imaginary concept, which, in a 'science-fictional move' can act as the means by which new possibilities and orders of being can be envisaged. As a metaphor, it stands for ironic and partial meaning, the contradictory self, radical fusions between oppositional concepts, and the impossibility of escaping historical processes.

Although increasingly popular, Haraway's ideas have been attacked by some feminists, who see her as operating on the high ground of postmodern theory, and therefore lacking a theory of ideology grounded in a socio-political awareness of feminist struggle. In response, Haraway argues for the 'corporeality' of theory, which 'is not about matters distant from the lived body; quite the opposite. Theory is *anything* but disembodied.'

HARTMAN, GEOFFREY: CRITIC (1929–) Born in Germany, Hartman is Professor of English and Comparative Literature at Yale University, and was together with his colleagues there at the time, **Bloom**, **Miller** and **de Man**, as well as the faculty's Visiting Professor, **Derrida**, a contributor to *Deconstruction and Criticism* (1979). As a collection of essays mostly on Romanticism with its unique historical blend of poetic writing and philosophical criticism, this text is now also referred to as the **Yale School** manifesto, renowned for its particular brand of **American deconstruction**.

Hartman's own work, most often concerned with the relation between literature and criticism, deploys the kinds of deconstructive strategies now familiar from Derrida, which seek to unsettle the rigid demarcations between what is deemed as art and what passes as mere commentary. His confession in *The Fate of Reading* (1975), 'I have a superiority complex *vis-à-vis* other critics, and an inferiority complex *vis-à-vis* art', gives perhaps the best clue as to what propels Hartman to rework, and thus resituate, the secondary status that literary criticism has held in relation to literary creation since after the Romantics. Reacting against the servile critics he associates with a sober Anglo-Saxon formalism, who busily explicate the unique forte and organic unity of a work of art behind which, they naturally assume, lies an even bigger genius in the shape of the masterly figure of the **author**, Hart-

man sets out in *Criticism in the Wilderness* (1980) to induce a new worth in the critic and the reader, to effect a positive revaluation of criticism as literature very much in Bloom's spirit, and of reading as a form of work in **Barthes**' sense.

Literary commentary, therefore, is not just a specialized form of reading which uses writing merely as an incidental aid, a premise that Derrida's stylistically playful writings have, of course, sought to undermine, but this reader-as-a-writer is always 'both an interpreter of **texts** and a self-interpreting producer of further texts'. In this sense, it becomes difficult to separate the work of the commentator from the work that he or she is commenting on; particularly in view of the fact that for Hartman, all texts, literary or critical, are parasitic on other writings, and therefore always already marked by bricolage, citation or theft. The **poststructuralist** tendency to place the activities of reading/writing within the larger framework of **intertextuality**, is also played out in *Saving the Text* (1981), where Hartman's commentary on Derrida's *Glas,* itself a commentary on **Hegel** and Genet and perhaps his most inventive book to date, continually blurs and contaminates the very distinction between critical and creative writing. Here, exposition clearly fulfils Hartman's objective to become 'as demanding as literature', with criticism thus on a par with literature, and the critic, not unlike Bloom's poet-critic, on a par with the artist.

HASSAN, IHAB: CRITIC AND THEORIST (1925–) Ihab Hassan participated in the first Stuttgart Seminar in

Cultural Studies in 1991, which examined the theme of 'The End of **Postmodernism**: New Directions'. Yet throughout his two keynote addresses, Hassan barely mentioned postmodernism at all, apart from a joke he told and a passing (perhaps wistful) reference to 'when we were all postmodernists'. He concentrated, instead, on the virtues of philosophical pragmatism and the vices of political correctness. That Hassan chose to ignore postmodernism in this setting is curious, especially as he himself was one of the prime movers in placing postmodernism on the literary-critical agenda throughout the 1960s and 1970s.

Hassan was born in Egypt in 1925, and graduated from the University of Cairo in 1946. He gained his doctorate in English at the University of Pennsylvania in 1953, and taught at Rensselaer Polytechnic Institute and Wesleyan University before his appointment as Research Professor at the University of Wisconsin at Milwaukee. In this post he has produced works such as *The Right Promethean Fire* (1980) and *The Postmodern Turn* (1987). *The Literature of Silence: Henry Miller and Samuel Beckett* (1968) introduced Hassan's project of a poetics of anti-literature for which silence was a constituent concept. He aligned Miller with the symbolist Stephen Mallarmé, and Beckett with Arthur Rimbaud, thus creating a polar opposition between writers confronting the void by trying to say everything, and writers aspiring to nothingness.

Similar metaphors of alienation, silence and the void are unravelled in Hassan's most effective monograph, *The Dismemberment of Orpheus: Toward a Postmodern Literature* (1971). The decapitated head of Orpheus, still singing as it floats down the River Hebrus, serves as the emblem of anti-literature. As the subtitle indicates, Hassan outlines a family tree of five writers who act as precursors to the postmodern. First is the Marquis de Sade, whose transgressive works embrace destructiveness ('wide-eyed and bodiless, Orpheus glares at the sun, waiting eternally for night'). Second is Ernest Hemingway, whose pared-down style attempts to purify the language of the tribe and show courage in the face of nothingness ('Naked, Orpheus enters the great, empty spaces of violence'). Third is Franz Kafka, the seminal figure for postmodernist writing ('We may even learn to enter, through his words, into an Orphic trance, looking onto the enormous calm of existence'). Fourth is Jean Genet, whose works seek to destroy reason itself ('meanwhile, Orpheus and Narcissus embrace in a black pool'). Fifth is Samuel Beckett, patron saint of the mute and the paralysed ('Such silence – Orpheus of the severed head – speaks not only of vanishing things: it must also sing, on pain of universal stillness, of a new kind of love').

In *Paracriticisms: Seven Speculations of the Times* (1975) Hassan emphasizes the constructedness of the concept of postmodernism by printing it as follows: POSTmodernISM. The capitalization of the prefix and suffix draws our attention to two important points. First, the 'ism' indicates that postmodernism comes after **modernism** itself, rather than simply after the 'modern'. Second, the 'post' suggests not just a historical belatedness, but an agonistic relationship to that earlier movement.

HAWKING, STEPHEN: SCIENTIST: (1942–) There are at least two Stephen Hawkings. The first is an important and respected theoretical physicist whose research has helped to form the way in which other scientists think about **black holes**, the origins of the universe and the relationship between space and time. The other Stephen Hawking is the extraordinary media phenomenon, the figure in an electric wheelchair, the author of the biggest selling scientific book in history, *A Brief History of Time*, who has appeared along with Isaac Newton and Einstein in an episode of *Star Trek* and who has overtaken Einstein in the popular mind as the embodiment of scientific genius. It is this second figure, with its eerie, disembodied, computer-generated voice uttering apparent profundities about knowing the mind of God, that is of particular interest to the student of **postmodernism**.

Stephen Hawking was born in Oxford on 8 January 1942, exactly 300 years after the death of Galileo. After studying physics at Oxford as an undergraduate he moved, in 1962, to Cambridge where, with an occasional sojourn in the USA, he has spent all of his working life. Since 1979 he has held the post of Lucasian Professor of Mathematics, a position once held by Isaac Newton.

Hawking's doctoral research employed Roger **Penrose**'s mathematical work on topology to support the big bang theory of the origin of the universe against the rival 'steady state' theory. Hawking argued that the universe began with '**singularity**', predicted, but not itself penetrated by general relativity, in which the laws of physics held no sway. Time and space came into existence only with the big bang, making it senseless to talk about anything happening before the big bang because the very concept of 'before' did not exist.

Hawking's next major work was on black holes. The existence of black holes had been predicted by J. Robert Oppenheimer in 1939. When a star runs out of fuel one of three things will happen to it, depending on its size. If it is relatively small with a mass less than 1.4 times that of our own sun, it will become a white dwarf; a little larger (between 1.4 and 3 times the sun's mass) and it forms a neutron star. If it began as a very large body (more than 3 times the sun's mass) its collapse creates a body with a gravitational field so strong that nothing, not even light, can escape from it.

As nothing can travel more quickly than light it seemed impossible that anything at all could be emitted from a black hole. Hawking employed **quantum mechanics**, which he combined with general relativity in a startlingly original way, to demonstrate that black holes must emit thermal radiation. Hawking reimagined black holes as physical objects, rather than some form of intensified vacuum – objects which obey the laws of thermodynamics.

We can deduce much about the highly theoretical nature of Hawking's brand of cosmology from the fact that the very existence of 'Hawking radiation' remains a convincing, but unverifiable hypothesis: no one has claimed that the tiny amounts of radiation emitted will ever be measurable. Hawking's hypothesis was based not on any observation, or careful measurement – what we tend to think of as the nuts and bolts of astronomy – but rather was the consequence of a working through of the logic of quantum mechanics and general relativity.

For Hawking the creation of a black hole was much like the creation of the universe in reverse. The former showed a massive body collapsing into a state of singularity, the latter, singularity exploding into the discrete and organized matter of the universe. His later work has returned to those first moments of creation. Hawking's second major contribution to cosmology, the no-boundary principle, posits that there is no definite boundary between space and time, that they exist together as four dimensions. Our universe is a finite sphere of space and time without edges. This theory predicts an origin to the universe in which an initial rapid but organized period of expansion, or 'inflation', preceded the 'hot' big bang. The inflation stage has left its signature on the universe in the form of ripples in space, which, in a convincing verification of Hawking's hypothesis, were detected by the Cosmic Background Explorer Satellite (COBE) project in 1992.

Despite his worthy contributions to theoretical physics and cosmology, however, it is as a cultural icon, as a signifier for the incomprehensible complexities of science, that Hawking attains his true importance. He reminds us that science is a human undertaking, while retaining its mystique.

HEGEL, GEORG WILHELM FRIEDRICH: PHILOSOPHER (1770–1831) Hegel's reputation has waxed and waned over the course of the twentieth century. The founder of modern dialectical philosophy and a critical influence on the work of Karl **Marx,** Hegel's philosophical standing has rarely been very high in the English-speaking world, but in the continental tradition it has been a different matter. From the 1930s onwards in France, for example, he exerted considerable influence, and along with **Husserl** and **Heidegger,** helped to set the agenda for French philosophy up until the advent of **poststructuralism** and **postmodernism.** Within the Marxist tradition in general, Hegel has continued to be a subject of debate.

The Hegelian dialectic operates on the triad of thesis-antithesis-synthesis, where the conflict of the thesis and the antithesis it generates resolves itself into a new state, or synthesis – and then onto a new cycle. Hegel saw this as a method working through history, with successive stages of historical development working towards the ultimate realization of what he called the 'world spirit' (see *The Philosophy of History*, for example). The theory as a whole is highly abstract and, for many, deterministic in nature. Marx found it to be over-idealist, and proceeded to 'turn' the Hegelian dialectic 'on its head' – that is, to relate it to specific developments in the material world, such as the class struggle.

The Marxist tradition has had something of a love–hate relationship with Hegel, although there has been a recognizably Hegelian strain within modern Marxist thought (most notably seen, perhaps, in the work of the Hungarian philosopher and literary critic Georg Lukács). In more recent times there has been a tendency to turn to Hegel in an effort to reconstruct Marxist philosophy, or to register dissatisfaction at the direction Marxism was felt to be taking. Poststructuralist and postmodernist theorists have an even more ambiguous relationship to Hegel. While Jacques **Derrida** can argue that 'We will never be finished with the reading or rereading of Hegel' (he says the same thing of Marx, by the way), others such as Gilles **Deleuze** have been more critical, arguing that Hegelian philosophy's totalizing imperative runs directly counter to what they believe a postmodern philosophy should be. Much of recent French philosophy can be regarded as a reaction against Hegel's previous dominance in French intellectual life. There is no denying that all attempts to provide a 'philosophy of everything' (Marx's no less than Hegel's) are largely out of favour in a postmodern world, which finds such system-building enterprises to be authoritarian – although that has not stopped Hegel from remaining an important presence on the **continental philosophical** landscape.

HEGEMONY The concept of hegemony was most notably used by the Italian **Marxist** theorist Antonio Gramsci, as a way of explaining how the ruling class in a capitalist society managed to impose its ideology on the mass of the population – most of the time without recourse to force. Thus the belief system of bourgeois capitalism could be communicated through the arts and the media, which could present the principles of that ideology as ideals to be aspired to by the general population – or, more simply, as the 'natural' order of things (it is 'natural' for human beings to compete, etc.).

The structural Marxist theorist Louis Althusser later built on Gramsci's ideas to suggest that Western societies consisted of various 'Ideological State Apparatuses' (ISAs), and a 'Repressive State Apparatus' (RSA). It was the role of the ISAs (the educational system, the arts and the media, for example) to disseminate the ideological principles of the ruling class, such that they became part of everyday life for the bulk of the population to the point where the population no longer even recognized that it was being indoctrinated. The RSA (the government, police and army) was there to impose order by violent means if the ISAs failed in their objective.

In **postmodernist** thought, the concept of hegemony has been revised by **Laclau** and **Mouffe**, who in *Hegemony and Socialist Strategy* (1985) emphasized its *contingent* nature, pointing out that it had been devised to explain away (in somewhat *ad hoc* fashion) some apparent failings of Marxist theory. Historical necessity, one of the cornerstones of classical Marxist thought, dictated that the working class eventually *ought* to have risen up against its exploiters; hegemony explained why it generally did not, but in so doing cast doubt on the validity of the classical Marxist conception of historical necessity itself. Neither did Laclau and Mouffe believe in the working class as a homogeneous 'totality' in the manner of classical Marxism, but instead as liable to fragmentation. They concluded that what hegemony demonstrated was the need to develop a **pluralist** Marxism, which would involve the many new social movements that had arisen in the later twentieth century (the **Greens**, for example, as well as various ethnic and sexual minorities).

HEIDEGGER, MARTIN: PHILOSOPHER (1889–1975) Heidegger was born and died in Messkirch. Travelling rarely beyond the Black Forest of southern Germany, Heidegger was rooted to one place like the modern philosopher Immanuel **Kant**. Yet Heidegger also became a pivotal, however controversial, figure for modern philosophy: he marked the beginning of its end. Positively, Heidegger alerted philosophers to the danger of an era that had lost the ability to question deeply and pointed to the possibility of a new beginning. Negatively, Heidegger was caught up in a reflexive circle: in attempting to give up metaphysics, he remained embedded in the categories of Being, truth and language which defined Western metaphysics. **Postmodern** philosophers argue that, although Heidegger developed a number of strategies by which he endeavoured to escape from the era of **modernity**, he could never finally extricate himself from his own age.

Heidegger's project begins with his hermeneutics of *Being and Time* (1927) and culminates in his reversal of time and Being. Some say that Heidegger devoted his life to one philosophical topic: Being, or the being of Being and the Being of beings. However this topic is not so simple, since he systematically exposes the inscrutability of Being as that which eludes our modes of thought. At the very least, Heidegger's relentless attempts to undo the conceptual knots in the history of the philosophy of Being began the destruction of metaphysics which was to be taken up by **deconstruction** and other postmodern strategies.

Initially, Heidegger uses the two concepts, 'Being' and 'time', to establish what metaphysics is. But he finds that the attempt to give them a non-metaphysical meaning is no easy task: How can Being be thought other than as that which never changes? And how can time be thought other than as the perishable, constantly changing realm of existence? Heidegger demonstrates that Being has been thought of in traditional philosophy as a kind of '**presence**'. Roughly stated, the true nature of Being is distorted in the history of Western philosophy because it is always represented as present, rather than being situated in terms of a past out of which it emerges and a future towards which it tends. The traditional emphasis on presence conceals the very question of the meaning of Being.

Heidegger describes the method of his early work as hermeneutical – it interprets one's own understanding and the **texts** of the history of that understanding. The central problem of hermeneutics arises with the recognition that all understanding involves some prejudice. Here one of Heidegger's means to excavate the philosophical tradition is etymology. In seeking the original meaning of a word, he may give the impression of discovering its true sense. Yet this is one of his strategies to escape the tradition of presence: to extricate oneself from the vacuousness of contemporary thought by exposing words which have lost their meaning. So instead of producing a correct account of the meaning of a term, Heidegger unsettles assumptions of meaning.

The word 'Being' itself becomes a problem for Heidegger. Eventually Heidegger develops a strategy of crossing out this word in order to make clear that it does not refer to an object with a unitary character. He gradually abandons 'Being' altogether, replacing it with concepts such as 'appropriation' (*das Ereignis*). In the later Heidegger, Being takes on the sense of appropriation which is supposed to express a being's own way of occurring, i.e. the event of 'the being it itself is' (so not in the sense of 'to be present'). Yet the meaning of such an event virtually coalesces with time, but without simply collapsing into an indifferent sameness. This relation of appropriation and time can be thought of reciprocally: time is the way in which appropriation occurs, while appropriation can be either simply what is or what is given at any moment.

Thus the later Heidegger attempts to leave modern philosophy behind in moving away from his theory of time in *Being and Time*. In his lectures 'Time and Being' (1962) and 'The End of Philosophy and the Task of Thinking' (1963), Heidegger no longer structures time in terms of a present moment such as the Aristotelian 'now'. Neither is time a series of discrete 'nows'. Instead it is a dimension relating the present back into the past and forward into the future. In Heidegger time becomes a relational structure of **difference**, and so heralds postmodern debates about language as a differential system of **signs** which are 'present' only insofar as they relate to another element that is not itself present.

HIRST, DAMIEN: ARTIST (1965–) Fascinated by the realms of advertising, business, medicine, funfairs, art galleries and shopping, Hirst's work comes in two brands: the 'macabre' world of sliced cows and pigs preserved in formaldehyde-filled cases; and the 'whimsical' world of billboards with rotating slats which display cucumbers paired with Vaseline jars, hammers conjoined with peaches, above which we find the logo-like inscription: 'The trouble with relationships'. The common theme running through both forms of his art is the concern with the power of juxtaposition and the authority of framing or classifying objects. Hirst sees the gallery as the home of an ordering system he will 'turn' through his playful transgressions.

Hirst aligns himself with a **postmodernist** aesthetic when he asserts that his exhibitions seek to deny the idea of artistic coherency or continuity. His 1996 *Flash Art* interview contains this statement about *No Sense of Absolute Corruption*: 'I wanted to make a show where every piece somehow undermined every other piece, but not in a negative way. It became a kind of celebration. It looks more like a group show, with the individual artists being aspects of myself, like an exploded view of an artist.' The exhibition, which toured Britain and the USA, confirmed his status as a media star.

Hirst's heroes are Warhol and **Koons**, both of whom he identifies with the power to conflate art and life, the artwork and the self. He, like Warhol and Koons, wants art to shock in the manner of Marcel Duchamp; and his formaldehyde-filled cases of sharks, sheep and pigs repeat the gesture made in 1917 when Duchamp's 'Fountain', an upside-down urinal mounted on a pedestal, was displayed as sculpture at the Salon of the New York Independents group. Like his predecessor, Hirst's art questions the assumption that the art object should be unique or original; like many figures associated with the historical avant-garde he uses a rhetoric that suggests he believes in the capacity of art to be 'radical', although such radicalism seems to be somewhat theatrical: 'I like the idea of rich people buying my burned-out fag-ends', he said of his fag-end pastiche of Claes Oldenburg's giant fag-end and ashtray pop-art sculpture of the early 1960s.

It may well be the case that Hirst's work corresponds to Charles **Jencks**'s characterization of postmodernism as a fluid, flexible and eclectic 'referencing' of the past: in his cows and sheep we find echoes of Rembrandt, Ford Madox Brown, William Holman Hunt and Chaim Soutine; in his spot and dot paintings we find traces of Lichtenstein, Op-Art, Daniel Buren, Niele Toroni and Phillip Taaffe; in the spin paintings we find the ghostly traces of Duchamp's rotoreliefs; in the medicinal cabinets the assimilation of the sweet shop displays by Peter Blake; in the shiny metallic cases the mirrors of **minimalist** serialism.

HOOKS, BELL: CRITIC (1952–) Gloria Watkins, whose pseudonym bell hooks is taken from her maternal great grandmother, is a prolific author and a leading black female cultural critic and commentator. Her first book, *Ain't I a Woman* (1981), made her reputation and she has produced many volumes since, often in the form of collections of essays dealing with fiction, film, feminism and cultural theory. Most prominent among her later works are *Feminist Theory* (1984), *Talking Back* (1989), *Yearning* (1990), *Black Looks* (1992) and *Outlaw Culture* (1994). She has published an autobiography, *Bone Black* (1997), and indeed an autobiographical speculation is often her chosen method of beginning a critical essay. She is one of the few African-American women theorists not only to engage with, but to advocate the use of, **postmodern** theories of subjectivity as an enabling discourse for talking about blackness in non-essentialist ways. *Ain't I a Woman*, a book that grew out of hooks's own working-class experience, introduced one of her most enduring themes: the marginalization of black women in feminism. The title of the work comes from a famous 1850 speech by the ex-slave Sojourner Truth, where she lays claim to an identity, and in many ways *Ain't I a Woman* itself is an act of historical recovery.

hooks is a socialist and her feminism is part of a more general struggle against oppression, not just to end male chauvinism and deliver equal rights for women, but also to eradicate 'the ideology of domination that permeates Western culture'; she is unyielding, therefore, in her criticism of feminists, such as Betty Friedan and Naomi **Wolf**, who leave to one side issues of race and class and take their own (usually affluent, white) experience for that of all women. Both embrace the opportunities capitalism offers successful women. These two, along with Camille **Paglia** and Katie Roiphe, are subjected to a withering critique for their exclusion or patronizing of black women. Indeed, the 'exclusionary use' of the term 'feminism' by white middle-class women leads hooks to shift from using the phrase 'I am a feminist' to saying 'I advocate feminism', for it serves 'as a way women who are concerned about feminism as well as other political movements could express their support while avoiding linguistic structures that give primacy to one particular group'.

In recent years, African-American cultural critics have heatedly debated the value and appropriateness of postmodern theory for black culture. Most prominent in the negative camp has been Barbara Christian in her influential essay 'The Race for Theory' (1987). In *Yearning*, hooks has argued forcibly the other way, but notes white critics' neglect of black contributions to postmodern culture. Though critical of postmodern critics' obsession with '**discourse**' and '**difference**' at the expense of the fight against imperialism, racism and sexism, and their use of '**otherness**' in a very abstract way, hooks argues for a postmodernism which abandons essentialist and restrictive definitions of 'blackness', allows for a multiplicity of black identities and for the construction of selves 'that are oppositional and liberatory'. It is clear that hooks's postmodernism, against the grain of a large amount of theorizing under that name, both is harnessed to and enlivens her emancipatory politics.

HORKHEIMER, MAX: PHILOSOPHER AND CULTURAL COMMENTATOR (1895–1973) Together with Theodor **Adorno** and Herbert **Marcuse**, Horkheimer was the foremost representative of the '**critical theory**' associated with the Institute of Social Research (or **Frankfurt School**). Horkheimer became director of the Institute in 1930, organized its move into exile from Nazi Germany and supervised the return of the Institute to Frankfurt in 1949.

Horkheimer's programmatic essay on 'Traditional and Critical Theory' (1937) enshrined the ambitions of the Institute. It described the necessity of integrating philosophy and social science, and of developing a relationship of integrity between critical theory and political practice. In later years, Horkheimer's vision became increasingly dark and gloomy. His later writings evidence the difficulty – even the impossibility – of fulfilling the original ambition and programme of the Frankfurt School. The result is an increasingly sharp critique of 'enlightened' reason and Western rationality. The *Dialectic of Enlightenment* (1947), written in collaboration with Theodor W. Adorno, was the first and most powerful – if fragmentary – statement of this theme.

After the war, Horkheimer's politics became more liberal but his view of society, more pessimistic (his debt to Schopenhauer became clearer and clearer). Whereas the *Dialectic of Enlightenment* had shown up the problematic, darker side of the **Enlightenment project**, Horkheimer felt more and more constrained to defend the legacy of the Enlightenment against its erosion under late capitalism. The critical impulse which forms a crucial element in the Enlightenment conception of reason had been eroded. Rationality had been reduced to instrumental reason, wholly devoted to the calculation of relating means to (usually unquestioned) ends. Positivism and society's uncritical approval of scientific rationality was one symptom of what Horkheimer and Adorno referred to as 'identity thinking'. The triumph of commercialism and the resulting domination of concrete use values by (abstract) exchange values was another. Both led to the suppression of difference and particularity.

Consistent in Horkheimer's life-work is the attempt to sustain a critique of reason conducted in acknowledgement of suffering, a critique in the name of the entirely '**other**', acknowledging everything dominated and suppressed by the regimes of identity thinking.

HUSSERL, EDMUND: PHILOSOPHER (1859–1938) Husserl's importance to **postmodern** thought lies in his role as founder of the philosophical movement known as phenomenology, a movement that has had a considerable influence on the development of **continental philosophy** in particular.

Husserlian phenomenology is particularly concerned with the structures of consciousness, and also with the need to find an unproblematical starting point, or foundation, for philosophical discourse – one without any metaphysical presuppositions (or assumptions) that could be challenged by other philosophers. Given such a foundation, one could proceed to construct a theory of knowledge.

The desired starting point for a 'presuppositionless analysis' is found by going back to consciousness and phenomenal experience (taken to be things that cannot be doubted), by means of what Husserl called the *epoche*, or 'phenomenological reduction'. This latter is a technique whereby the world and its preoccupations are temporarily suspended, or 'bracketed', thus avoiding all the standard philosophical challenges to one's theories. Critics, however, have tended to treat the *epoche* as the equivalent of a philosophical cheat, arguing that it makes debate all but impossible.

Poststructuralist philosophers have been just as keen as Husserl to find a form of 'presuppositionless analysis', but have queried whether Husserl really provides them with one. Jacques **Derrida**, for example, has criticized Husserlian phenomenology for being in its turn underpinned by metaphysical presuppositions – such as that a theory of knowledge is even possible. To Derrida, the whole idea of a theory of knowledge is based on questionable metaphysical assumptions that go back to the very earliest days of Western philosophy in classical Greece. In general, poststructuralist and postmodernist theorists have been more influenced by the radical phenomenological doctrines of a follower of Husserl, Martin **Heidegger**.

HYPERREALITY Hyperreality is used by Jean **Baudrillard** to indicate the 'loss of the real', where distinctions between surface and depth, the real and the imaginary no longer exist The world of the hyperreal is where image and reality implode. Baudrillard suggests that we no longer need models of analysis such as **Marxism** with its language of surface and depth, for there are no depths. Marxism, which sees the market *behind* everything, must give way to the idea that the market is *in* everything but *behind* nothing. In a famous example, Baudrillard chooses Disneyland as an illustration of a third-order image, a magical space which masks the absence of the real. He argues that, just as prisons exist to mask the fact that society *itself* is one, 'Disneyland is presented as imaginary in order to make us believe that the rest is real, when in fact all of Los Angeles and the America surrounding it are no longer real, but of the order of the hyperreal'. While Baudrillard's concept may be criticized in any number of ways, it seems to capture something of the flavour of the commodified and mediated nature of contemporary life.

HYPERTEXT Hypertext is electronic text that provides links between key elements, allowing the reader to move through information non-sequentially. Now the key technology of the World Wide Web, the idea of hypertext can be traced back to an article published in 1945 by Franklin D. Roosevelt's wartime science adviser, Vannevar Bush. Bush envisaged mechanically linked machines for the storage and retrieval of information, allowing scholars, researchers and others access to large amounts of information without having to deal with the cumbersome storage and classification methods of traditional archives and libraries. Bush proposed a device called the Memex, with translucent screens, levers and motors, which would allow the user to annotate and link information on microfilm.

The term itself was coined by Theodore H. Nelson in 1965: 'By "hypertext", I mean non-sequential writing – text that branches out and allows choices to the reader, best read at an interactive screen.' Nelson envisaged hypertext in utopian fashion as an encyclopaedic gathering together of all printed texts in a global hypertext publishing system called 'Xanadu'.

For some critics and theorists, the non-linearity, linkage and decentredness of hypertext appear to demonstrate empirically the insights regarding reading and textuality advanced by such thinkers as **Derrida**, **Barthes** and **Foucault**. George P. Landow in his book *Hypertext: The Convergence of Contemporary Critical Theory and Technology* (1992), claims that '**critical theory** promises to theorize hypertext and hypertext promises to embody and thereby test aspects of theory, particularly those concerning textuality, narrative and the roles or functions of reader and writer'. At the same time, critics like Landow and J. David Bolter claim that hypertext encourages a more 'natural' and associative way of reading. The inherent utopianism of much hypertext theory has recently come under attack: while the *analogies* between hypertext and the works of Derrida, for example, are clear, it is unclear what the 'realization' or 'fulfilment' of a philosophy like **deconstruction** (not a *project* in any traditional sense) could mean.

I

INCOMMENSURABILITY Many **post-modernists** hold to a version of the 'Sapir–Whorf hypothesis'. In its strongest form it is the claim that linguistic structures condition thought patterns and *determine* our perception of the world. This could be taken to mean that speakers of different languages in a sense inhabit different worlds. Incommensurability is a term taken from mathematical theory where it refers to two qualities or magnitudes which have no common measure. The notion has been loosely transferred to debates about the role of language. Two languages are incommensurable if their structures make exact translation between them difficult or impossible. The term 'incommensurability' has gained currency together with a view (or speculative hypothesis) that all languages are incommensurable one with another.

The most precise formulation of this view is presented by Willard van Orman Quine as part of a more general scepticism about the very idea of meaning. Quine dramatized what he termed 'the indeterminacy of translation'. This is not the same as the platitude that there are shades of meaning which might be lost in the process of translation; instead, it implies that the very notion of shades of meaning which are uncaptured is pointless. Each language posits a different set of objects, maps the world in a different way. Thomas **Kuhn**'s work deals with scientific paradigms. At its most basic, a paradigm is simply an exemplary model. But in the context of scientific theories it is also taken to refer to the interrelationships between a whole system of concepts. There are many postmodern writers on the philosophy of science who suggest that competing scientific paradigms are in principle incommensurable.

The notion of incommensurability reappears in **Lyotard**'s concept of the '**differend**'. The differend is incommensurability politicized. Each party inhabits not simply their own language, and thus their own world; they inhabit a '**phrase**-regime', embodying interests and objectives. One phrase regime exerts dominance over another. Incommensurability captured the idea of opacity between languages. The differend suggests an opacity, and a deformation, created by the action of one language – or phrase-regime – on another.

INSTALLATION ART Associated with Marcel Broodthaers, Hans Haacke, Daniel Buren and Michael Asher, 'installation art' was the term applied to a set of critical practices which emerged in the late 1960s. Concerned with the conditions in which art is displayed, these artists explored the spatial, social and political networks which comprised the art world. Buren's work, which often took the form of structural/architectural elaborations of the spaces where they were displayed, drew attention to the framing systems of the gallery as a cultural space. Haacke's image-and-text work, by contrast, continues to be concerned with mapping the boundaries of art and ideology by revealing the political interests of gallery sponsors, museum trustees and corporate patrons.

INTERNET An electronic space that **cyberpunk** author William **Gibson** has called a 'consensual hallucination', in many ways the Internet, combining a technological reality with immense politically hallucinatory potential, is *the* exemplary **postmodern** object, and arguably even the architecture of postmodern culture. Its technological roots lie in a system developed by the American Advanced Research Projects Agency to link their computers into a network, forming ARPAnet, which went online towards the end of 1969. Since then it has grown geometrically, and has been championed as the source and – although geography is a problem in **cyberspace** – the site of a new, utopian, political order, marking the rise of what Howard Rheingold has famously called 'virtual communities' where information flows without property relations and where anyone can have access to anyone else.

In consequence many of the political conflicts associated with postmodernism, and even the posts one ought to inhabit within postmodern and **post-industrial** societies, are now

being contested on the Net. For example, Jean-François **Lyotard**'s call, as *The Postmodern Condition* (1979) draws to an end, for the public to be given access to all databases stems from his thesis that, in a computerized society, information is power. Lyotard's pronouncement echoes the Internet ideologues' credo 'information wants to be free'; meanwhile, however, corporate concerns have set about the commercialization of the Internet, ensuring that the days of democratized information flow are running out.

This is not, however, a change of direction following the origins of the Internet; rather, the whole purpose of the ARPAnet was to find a means whereby, in the event of a nuclear strike, no single node or post in the network would be responsible for the continuing functioning of the entire net. In other words, the absence of central control on the Net, championed as its chief political virtue by Internet activists, derives from the military necessity that the defence grid remain functional even if some of the nodes in the Net are taken out. To this extent, the democratic impetus of Lyotard's proposals, the anarcho-syndicalism of virtual communities and the ideological sloganizing of the informational libertarians seem, in the long run, doomed to lose their political naivety. The Internet is not beyond war and capital; rather, their territories and markets have been uploaded into cyberspace.

INTERTEXTUALITY Many classic literary **texts**, from Rabelais's *Gargantua* and *Pantagruel,* through Robert Burton's *Anatomy of Melancholy* and on to Sterne's *Tristram Shandy*, are woven from other texts: references, citations and quotations tumbling together in disorienting superabundance. However it was only with Julia **Kristeva**'s *Semiotike* (1969) that it was claimed that *'every* text takes shape as a mosaic of citations, every text is the absorption and transformation of other texts'.

The concept of intertextuality derived from the **poststructuralist** claim that signifiers refer always and only to other signifiers: that language can be transformed, translated, transferred, but never transcended. Words gain their meaning not by referring to some object present to the mind of the language user but from the never-ending play of signification. To use the word 'love' is not to refer to some extra-linguistic biological or psychological object but, consciously or unconsciously, to join in a conversation that takes in the lays of the Troubadours, Shakespearean tragedy, romantic lyrics and the songs of the Beatles.

Postmodernism embraces an extreme notion of intertextuality, in which the play of meaning is infinite, in which anything goes. The limits of interpretation are set only by the boundaries of the imagination.

IRIGARAY, LUCE: PHILOSOPHER AND PSYCHOANALYST (1932–) Luce Irigaray is Director of Research in Philosophy at the Centre National de Recherches Scientifiques, where she has held a research post since 1964. Formerly a member of Jacques **Lacan**'s Ecole Freudienne de Paris, she was expelled as a result of her feminist critique of psychoanalysis

and since then has been one of its most vocal critics, seeking, as she does, to liberate the feminine from masculine philosophical thought. Irigaray's work is challenging and varied, ranging in methodology from the densely psychoanalytic to **deconstructive** to the visionary, lyrical and expressive. *Speculum of the Other Woman* (1974), her first major piece of feminist writing, offers a critique of **Freudian** psychoanalysis and Western philosophy from Plato onwards. Here, Irigaray argues that woman as subject is excluded from Western philosophy, and that this mode of thought allows full **subjectivity** to only one sex: male. Stemming from the primacy accorded the phallus, woman is characterized by absence, lack, negativity. Cast merely as the mirror in which man sees himself reflected, we are only allowed to know woman as man sees her. With this book, Irigaray began a series of publications on language and sexual **difference**, including *This Sex Which is Not One* (1977), *Ethics of Sexual Difference* (1984) and *Sexes and Genealogies* (1987), which continue her quest for the feminine voice, a feminine symbolic order and emphasize the **plurality** of the female sex.

This Sex Which is Not One contains what have become three of Irigaray's most significant essays: 'When our lips speak together', 'Commodities among themselves' and the title essay. The volume, and in particular these essays, demonstrate Irigaray's diverse application of her feminist project. The last two focus particularly upon the economics of patriarchy, in which woman is cast as an object endowed only with use-value for exchanges between men, exchanges which, Irigaray controversially argues, are testimony to the male homosexual nature of patriarchy. In this system of exchange, woman has no agency, and female desire is misrepresented and misconstructed by patriarchal language. However, the title essay of the collection explores Irigaray's own construction and **representation** of female **desire** through the medium of strikingly lyrical prose. In this collection of essays, Irigaray employs what has become her most memorable metaphor, that of the two lips which symbolize the fluidity, plurality and ambiguity of female sexuality: the pun of the sex which is not (even) one in Western philosophical discourse upon the sex which is not (only) one in Irigaray's new method of cultural representation.

While arguing against and critiquing Western philosophy in general, and Freud and Lacan in particular, ultimately Irigaray views the non-subjectivity of women in psychoanalysis and in Western philosophical discourse as an opportunity which women should seize in order to construct their own subjectivity on their own terms. While the feminine is ignored and suppressed in the masculine symbolic order, it is available for women to liberate and reconstruct it in their own symbolic order, argues Irigaray, thereby demonstrating her advocacy of *l'écriture feminine* or female writing.

Luce Irigaray's work has itself been the subject of much critical attention, most notably from Ann Rosalind Jones, Toril Moi, Margaret Whitford and Elizabeth Grosz. She is often grouped together with Julia **Kristeva** and Hélène **Cixous**, although there are considerable theoretical differences between them. The main source of negative criticism is that her writing is too essentialist, too focused upon the physical being of woman, without taking into account the ethnic, economic and political forces which divide the experience of the world's female population. However, her essentialist position is regaining its value as feminists seek to prevent issues of femininity and female sexual difference being obliterated by the **postmodern** insistence upon the **anti-essentialist** subject. As she says in 'Women: Equal or Different' (Jackson *et al.*, eds, *Women's Studies: A Reader* (1993)): 'Trying to suppress sexual difference is to invite a genocide more radical than any destruction that has ever existed in history.'

IRONY We are all familiar with irony as a figure of speech in which the intended meaning is the opposite of that expressed by the words used. In the form of sarcasm or ridicule, irony can express a degree of hostility. It is common in jokes which sometimes separate 'insiders' (who share the joke) from those being laughed at (who do not 'get it' – that is, do not see the irony). Irony is always connected with a requirement not to take things (including ourselves) too seriously, or at least not to take things at face value. Nothing is so characteristic of the current **postmodern** 'mood' as its ironic, detached, self-consciousness. Umberto **Eco** has characterized postmodernism as an attitude in which we cannot give up our cherished hopes and beliefs, but at the same time can no longer embrace them with unqualified or whole-hearted adherence. In *Contingency, Irony, and Solidarity* Richard **Rorty** sketches and recommends the figure of the 'liberal ironist'. 'Ironists' face up to the contingency of their beliefs; 'liberal ironists' are aware that among these lie such things as 'their own hope that suffering will be diminished'.

J

JAMESON, FREDRIC: CULTURAL CRITIC (1934–) Fredric Jameson is the best known and most influential **Marxist** literary and cultural critic writing in English. As such, he has offered one of the most compelling historical analyses of the general climate of **postmodernism** as 'the logic of late capitalism'.

Jameson was a student of Erich Auerbach and an early and enduring influence on his work has been the example of Georg Lukács. During the 1920s, and after his turn to Marxism, Lukács played a crucial role in the reappropriation of **Hegelian** philosophy and the inauguration of a tradition of 'critical' Marxism.

The most influential part of Jameson's own early work concentrated on serious theoretical treatment of figures from this tradition of Hegelian, or 'critical', Marxism. *Sartre; The Origins of a Style* (1961) already focuses on one of Jameson's central themes: the question of narrative. His book *Marxism and Form* (1971) introduced a new generation to the work of Lukács, Bloch, **Benjamin**, **Adorno**, **Marcuse** and Sartre.

Jameson's appropriation of a critical (Hegelian) tradition in Marxism has been complemented by a sustained engagement with French and other **continental** thinking. In *The Prison-house of Language* (1972), Jameson summarized the key concepts and motifs of **structuralist** and **post-structuralist** linguistics and at the same time provided a forceful critique directed against the more pessimistic conclusions that some have derived from such theorizing. In his most ambitious work, *The Political Unconscious* (1981), Jameson developed his own programme for an interpretive framework that was political and historical but which could enrich itself by adopting or adapting the insights of the structural traditions in linguistics.

Jameson's magisterial command of a panorama of theoretical traditions meant that he was well placed to launch a polemic against the depoliticizing, relativist or reactionary tendencies of the age. That polemic was pointedly formulated in the article 'Postmodernism, or the Cultural Logic of Late Capitalism' published in *New Left Review* (1984). This was expanded into a sizeable book with the same title (1991) which is one of the crucial documents in the debate over postmodernism. Jameson interprets postmodernism in historical and political terms. He leans on Ernest Mandel's *Late Capitalism*, which attempted to adapt and update Marx's economic analyses to explain the workings of global capitalism in the post-war, information age. The main aim of Jameson's analysis is the crisis of historicity in the advanced- or late-capitalist countries.

In *The Postmodern Condition* (1979) (whose English-language edition carries a critical foreword by Jameson), **Lyotard** had affirmed the prevailing scepticism towards **meta-narratives**. Jameson was uniquely qualified to instruct the post-modernists about the social relations underlying the symptoms of the 'postmodern condition'. Jameson's own work returns again and again to the question announced in his study of Sartre: 'The question of narrative, or more exactly, . . . the [question of the] relationship between narrative and narrative closure, the possibility of storytelling, and the kinds of experience – social and existential – structurally available in a given social formation.'

'Always historicize!' Jameson calls this 'the one absolute and . . . "trans-historical" imperative of all dialectical thought'. Jameson's thought aims unashamedly at 'totalizing' in a sense elaborated by Sartre (although Jameson's use of commitment in this area connects him also to Lukács and to Adorno).

In the minds of postmodernism's less-critical acolytes, the mere invocation of 'totality' is enough to convict Jameson of an outdated/harmful point of view. But Jameson has consistently rejected the idea of a 'total system'. In fact, in Jameson the attempt to think through the category of 'totality' is part of a defence against totalitarian tendencies in thought. In *Late Marxism: Adorno, or the Persistence of the Dialectic* (1990), Jameson seeks to update Adorno's analysis of the tendencies of late capitalism to function as a negative 'totality'. In the face of drastic changes in the relationship

between the individual and the social system, Jameson proposes the writings of Adorno, especially Adorno's difficult late works *Negative Dialectics* and *Aesthetic Theory*, as the model of the kind of reflexive dialectic needed at the turn of the millennium.

Lukács's early literary work was inspired by the utopian and metaphysical impulses of the early German Romantics. Jameson's work has remained true to this inspiration in a consistent and courageous fidelity to the utopian impulse. He remains one of the most sure-footed guides to the origins of our present predicament.

JARDINE, ALICE: LITERARY THEORIST AND FEMINIST (1951–) Jardine, an academic at Harvard University, is best known as the author of *Gynesis: Configurations of Women and Modernity* (1985), a study examining the relationship between **modernity**, feminism and contemporary French thought. She is also a translator of the French feminist theorist and **semiotician** Julia **Kristeva**.

'Gynesis' is a neologism formed from the Greek root for women ('gyn') and 'sis' for process, and Jardine defines it as meaning the 'putting into discourse of women'. For Jardine, gynesis is a process at work in Western society that has helped to bring about the collapse of its patriarchally based **grand narratives**. Following on from the work of **Foucault**, she has theorized that the crisis of modernity has opened up new opportunities for enquiry in areas that have previously been identified with women, such as madness. The 'putting into discourse of women' (which can also be seen to some extent in the work of male theorists such as **Derrida**), also holds out the possibility of a non-essentialist theory of the **subject** – one of the great concerns of **postmodern** thought.

Jardine has been somewhat critical of Anglo-American feminism for its tendency to promote a 'narrative' of woman, given that the notion of narrative is now under some considerable stress in **poststructural** and postmodern discourse. Critics have responded by pointing to a lack of historical context in her work, and have also questioned her concentration on the idea of woman-as-metaphor.

JENCKS, CHARLES: ARCHITECTURAL HISTORIAN, THEORIST, AND DESIGNER (1939–) A prolific author, Jencks has written and edited over 25 books, including influential studies of twentieth-century architecture. He is best known as the author of a number of books on **postmodern** architecture, most notably for *The Language of Post-Modern Architecture* (1977). The regular updating of this book (now in its seventh edition) and his other writings on postmodernism are part of an ongoing project of definition and redefinition that makes his work both a starting point for many discussions of the forms of postmodernism and an important element of the debate he initially sought to analyse.

The field of architecture has been a useful focus for debates on postmodernism for three main reasons. First because the failure of **modernist** architecture has been so spectacular and so visible: since the early 1960s, urban critics (Jane Jacobs in *The Death and Life of Great American Cities* (1961)) and architects (Robert **Venturi** in *Complexity and Contradiction in Architecture* (1966)) had been critical of the urban destruction resulting from the complacent, brutal aesthetics and social sterility of high-rise modernism. Secondly, and as a consequence of this failure, the difference between modern and postmodern architecture has been so stylistically marked. Finally, leading theorists of postmodernism (including **Jameson** and **Lyotard**) have used architecture as an index of 'the postmodern condition'.

Originally a historian of modernist architectural theory and practice, Jencks's work charts his growing disenchantment with it. Jencks was one of the first architectural critics to introduce **semiotic** analysis into architectural criticism. Using rhetorical, grammatical, and linguistic categories, Jencks 'read' buildings as forms of communication, and he began to see the modernist 'international style' as a very narrow, homogeneous language, 'as if Esperanto had been enforced everywhere'. By the mid-1970s and especially in his most influential work, *The Language of Post-Modern Architecture,* Jencks argued that postmodern architecture was a number of hybrid departures from modernism, using styles from the past as well as the modernist technique in which at that time all architects were trained. If, as Virginia Woolf declared, literary modernism began in December 1910, then Jencks is most famous for precisely dating its architectural and ideological demise; it 'died in St. Louis, Missouri, on July 15th, 1972, at 3.32pm (or thereabouts)', when part of the vandalized and crumbling (and award-winning) Pruitt-Igoe housing project was blown up.

If in 1977, then, 'postmodernism' for Jencks had been 'largely a negative term, its very vagueness appealing', by the second edition of *The Language of Post-Modern Architecture* (1978) he felt able to offer a positive definition, his much-quoted concept of '**double coding**': 'the combination of modern techniques with something else (usually traditional building) in order for architecture to communicate with the public and a concerned minority, usually other architects.' This was not a mere revival of old styles nor a simple anti-modernism, as postmodernism has, for Jencks, 'the essential double meaning; the continuation of modernism and its transcendence'. Among the many examples Jencks uses is the British architect James **Stirling**'s addition to the state gallery in Stuttgart. While obviously a contemporary building, it echoes and plays with past art and architecture, including classical and pop art. Jencks sees this kind of postmodernist building as a way of opening up the minimalist language of modernism to history, context and **difference**; he describes and advocates a **pluralist** approach to cultural communication generally.

During the 1980s, Jencks began to expand his theory of postmodernism as double coding into other areas of culture. 'Double coding' explains the 'postmodern turn' in other arts, for postmodernism has become both 'cultural movement and historical epoch'. His *What is Post-modernism?* (1986) covers fiction and art as well as architecture. This concise little book is a useful guide to Jencks's thought. In art, Jencks sees the return of **representational** painting, self-conscious allegory, eclecticism and hybridity as signs of ubiquitous postmodern double coding. In fiction, Jencks admires writers who neither repudiate nor slavishly imitate the experimental writers of the early years of the century, but who, like John **Barth** and Umberto **Eco** for instance, give us the traditional pleasures of plot and work on a number of other levels too. Jencks's case is less convincing when he strays outside architecture and his obsessive periodizing and categorizing runs against the spirit of postmodern thought as it is generally perceived. He celebrates his humanist version of postmodernism, which has little in common with the **poststructuralist** anti-humanist postmodernism of Lyotard and others.

JOUISSANCE   No adequate translation exists for the French term *jouissance*. *Jouir de* implies the ability to profit from pleasure; *jouissance* connotes the bliss of sexual orgasm. In **postmodern** discourse this psychoanalytic term gains significance from its opposite, the lack accompanying desire. Julia **Kristeva** suggests the existence of a feminine *jouissance* that exceeds the bounds of patriarchal language, remaining within woman's vision but beyond articulation; this pleasurable experience is associated with the child's joyful continuity with the maternal. Luce **Irigaray** defines a 'hysterical' *jouissance* that would not be 'paternal', but would be unrepresentable – remaining for ever a lack within patriarchy.

K

KANT, IMMANUEL: **PHILOSOPHER**
(1724–1804) Kant lived all his life in
Königsberg. After fifteen years as an
unsalaried lecturer (*Privatdozent*)
teaching a wide range of subjects, he
was made professor of logic and
metaphysics in 1770. In 1781 Kant
published the *Critique of Pure Reason*.
Within ten years this immensely
complex and difficult book was being
discussed all over Germany. Over the
next decades responses to what was
called the critical philosophy played
a vital role in the extraordinary
richness of German philosophy as
developed in the writings of Fichte
and the Romantics, Schelling, **Hegel**,
Fries and Schopenhauer.

The *Critique of Pure Reason* argues
that the world as we know it and
experience it, the world as studied by
scientists, is structured by our modes,
or categories, of cognition. Our sense
experience is structured and organized by categorical determinants such
as space and time. Other categories,
such as cause, substance, relation,
totality, are involved in our attempts
to think any 'thing' at all. Thus, for
Kant, in order to be an object, as
opposed to a mere subjective impression, means to be subject to the categories. Objectivity is thus based on
the mental apparatus of the **subject**.
Because he was able to appeal to
categories which he believed to be
universal (part of human nature)

Kant believed that he had definitively
defended the possibility of objective
knowledge. Many attempts to rescue
and secure Kant's achievements by
updating his terms have been made by
a succession of post-Kantians, including **Husserl** and the phenomenolo-
gists as well as many philosophers in
the Anglo-Saxon analytical tradition.

Kant's 'critical philosophy' had
thrust the concept of *critique* into the
foreground of philosophy. During
our own century, the tradition of the
'critique' has become the dominant
motif in philosophy. But a constant
preoccupation with language has
undermined Kant's hopes of providing a 'foundation' for objective
knowledge.

From a **postmodernist** perspective,
what was once presented as 'critical
philosophy' seems compromised by
its ambition to provide a foundation
for knowledge and by its systematic
pretensions. Each of Kant's three
major works was indeed published
under the title of '*Critique*', but in each
Kant attempted by means of analysis
not only to establish the *limits* of, but
also to provide a *foundation* for, a
particular domain of human knowledge.

In the *Critique of Pure Reason* Kant
set out an analysis of the basis of
theoretical or scientific knowledge of
the external world: in the *Critique of
Practical Reason* the basis of our

moral understanding; and in the *Critique of Judgement* the basis of aesthetics. The first two *Critiques* are concerned with the principles pre-supposed in our *objective* judgements as to what *is* the case (pure reason), and what *ought to be* the case (practi-cal reason). The *Critique of Judgement* seeks to uncover the *subjective* princi-ples which underlie (a) the systematic impulse and (b) our apprehension of beauty.

Kant deduced as the fundamental basis of all morality – what he called the 'categorical imperative' – the idea that one should always act in such a way that one's behaviour could become the basis of a universal law. Thus the will to universality – rather than any fixed set of precepts – is seen as the foundation of morality. Kant was attempting to reformulate in philosophical language Jesus of Nazareth's precept: 'Do unto others as you would have them do unto you.'

KIEFER, ANSELM: ARTIST (1945–) Like his teacher and mentor, Joseph **Beuys**, Kiefer's practice is informed by a romantic aesthetic which affirms the mystical unity of art and the world through the mediating agency of the artist. Kiefer follows Beuys in his pre-sentation of art as a form of magical fertility, a fecund force generated by the powers embedded in cultural tradition. In a sense, then, creative power is imagined as a form of bardic incantation: the artist remembers national histories and myths by refiguring the canvas as an organic latticework of drips, inscriptions, erasures and blockages. Hovering between representation and abstrac-tion, the troubled, violent and raw

surfaces of Kiefer's paintings mark the space where paint becomes a nomadic, viscose, bleeding presence. Associating his work with transmu-tation and transcendence, critics have found in Kiefer's compositions a form of alchemy in which painting makes manifest the truths buried within ancient myths and symbols. In the early 1980s this interest in mythological and religious roots of cultural expression could be seen as part of a return to traditional modes of artistic practice; the Italian critic Achillo Bonito Oliva identified Kiefer as one of the most important figures in what he termed the *trans-avant-garde,* although unlike Clemente and Baselitz, Kiefer's work is characterized by its 'expansive' tech-nique: oil, acrylic, emulsion, crayon, shellac, photographs, ferns, straw, lead, steel and glass can be found in 'Niger' (1984), 'Iron Path' (1986) and 'Saturn Time' (1986).

KOOLHAAS, REM: ARCHITECT AND THEORIST (1944–) Very much the current darling of the architectural scene, Koolhaas, founder of the Office of Metropolitan Architecture (OMA), came to architecture late in life having spent numerous years as a scriptwriter in Hollywood, a vocation that has clearly influenced his atti-tude to architecture. A product of the Architectural Association in London during the school's most vibrant years, Koolhaas came to prominence on the back of an illustrated book, *Delirious New York*, which paid hom-age to Coney Island and celebrated 'the culture of congestion' and 'supra rationality' of Manhattanism. The lyrical exuberance of the text, which captured the essential character of the American (as opposed to the European) city, is complemented by a series of eclectic and surreal architectural drawings. Koolhaas is transfixed by the irony that the dream of the most radical of architectural **modernists** – the suprematist city – is actually realized in New York under the auspices of real-estate development rather than the social programming which was at the heart of radical modernism. He also revels in the fact that the immediate architectural manifestation of this tendency – the 'typical' open plan of the office block – is the one that allows the constant shifting and accommodation of multiple architectural programmes that was also the dream of the Russian avant-garde. For Koolhaas, this plan also marks the end of the idea of European architecture and its dominant trait – the plan as the generator.

These ideas have informed his conception of a '**retro**active' architecture – one which reactivates past avantgarde tendencies, but which capitalizes on the unexpected ways in which they have been used. This idea drove OMA's winning competition entry for the Parc de la Villette which is conceived as a horizontal skyscraper, and is structured around a series of strips containing disparate functions which correspond to the floors of a high-rise building. This project led to Koolhaas's inclusion in the infamous exhibition, *Deconstructivist Architecture* at the Museum of Modern Art, New York, where the essentially postmodern aesthetic of extremely stylized or 'stretched' modernism, a style which has since become *de rigueur* among architectural students

worldwide, was made manifest in the OMA drawings.

Since catapulting to fame, Koolhaas has realized many projects including the Kunsthal in Rotterdam, the National Dance Theatre in The Hague and the canonical Villa Dal'ava on the outskirts of Paris. Despite his interest in the real-estate inspired metropolis, Koolhaas has recently become interested in gigantic planning projects, and has realized the master planning of Euro Lille. Koolhaas enjoys the contamination of his projects by other architects (although all seem to work in the stylized modernist idiom) and by commercial processes, and takes his cue from Wallace Harrison, the commercial architect whose contribution supposedly contaminated the purity of Le Corbusier's vision for the UN in New York. His continuing interest in enormous projects is reflected in the publication of *Small, Medium, Large, Extra Large (SMLXL)* a 1,400-page novel about architecture which juxtaposes his writings and projects in the aforementioned categories.

KOONS, JEFF: ARTIST (1955–) Moving to New York from Chicago in 1977 to work at the Museum of Modern Art before becoming a Wall Street broker, Koons came to prominence in the mid-1980s when he exhibited with **Halley**, Steinbach, Taaffe, Bleckner and Levine. During this period it was widely believed that his work was part of a **postmodern** engagement with the role of culture within **post-industrial** society, an economic order where leisure and consumption had become processes of great symbolic and material importance. Like Steinbach's work of this period, Koons positioned domestic and leisure objects within gallery spaces in such a way as to draw attention to their almost totemic significance. His 'New Shelton Wet/ Dry Double Decker' (1981) consists of two vacuum cleaners within Plexiglas boxes. The product, ubiquitous yet elusive, imprisoned yet powerful, seems to be displayed in order to register the **aura**, magic and potency associated with the culture of consumption. A similar process of encapsulating the serene inertia of a frozen micro-world of commodities characterizes his 1985 '2 Ball Total Equilibrium Tank', where the water-filled glass container carrying two basketballs both invites and frustrates a sense of intimacy through its remorseless, cold materialism.

This monumental isolation addresses the interplay between possession and power, consumption and knowledge, desire and control, purity and utility. These hollowed-out icons attracted the interest of writers searching for signs of postmodernism in artistic spaces other than painting, photography and appropriation-based practice. In the important 1987 *Endgame* exhibition at Boston's Institute of Arts, which established a critical overview of postmodernist practice, Koons's 'mediated sculpture' was identified as an example of **simulation** art. In making his art register the power of leisure commodities Koons, it was argued, had revived the language of Duchamp's 'ready-mades', which, seventy years earlier, had seen mass-produced industrial products displayed as art. Koons, like Duchamp, wanted to 'demystify' the art realm. Moreover, in confronting the spectral quality of the commodity Koons had, it was believed, cleverly informed us that it is the ordinary object of consumption rather than the **modern** artwork that seems to possess some mysterious property or principle.

The end of the 1980s saw Koons's work move away from the sublime void of the commodity as he began to assemble a vast army of kitsch objects, all of which demonstrated the disappearance of high art beneath the detritus of mass culture. Where his earlier 'mediated sculpture' bodied forth a vast frozen landscape of endless repetitive inertia, 'Rabbit' (1986), 'Louis XIV' (1986), 'Fisherman Golfer' (1986) and 'Bear and Policeman' (1988) were informed by a welcoming hypervitality, a tacky duplication of luxury. In place of the obsessional clarity and eternal cleanliness of the early work we find a new realm of mass-produced memorabilia. The landscape of leisure utility is supplanted by the frenzied, deranged 'charm' of tourism: now we are confronted with an endless parade of souvenirs in the delirious form of stainless-steel trolls, 'plastic' rococo figurines, camp-Catholic porcelain busts, wooden Yorkshire terriers and other items of 'bingo-prize' ornamental culture. Where the earlier work suggested that as commodities were more interesting than traditional objects the art gallery had become a department store, these later objects appeared to embrace a tourist culture, confirming that the art gallery had become assimilated into the kitsch culture of the souvenir shop.

KRISTEVA, JULIA: FEMINIST PSYCHO-ANALYST, LINGUIST, THEORIST AND CRITIC (1941–) Together with Hélène **Cixous** and Luce **Irigaray**, Julia Kristeva is one of the most famous proponents of French feminist theory (*l'écritique feminin*). Born in Bulgaria, Kristeva moved to Paris in 1966, where her work quickly became associated with the group of **structuralists** and **poststructuralists** attached to the radical journal *Tel Quel*. Kristeva's earliest major work was *Revolution in Poetic Language*, published in 1974, in which she set out her basic theories concerning language and its role in the construction of identity. She differs from **Freud** and **Lacan** in siting the origin of language in the pre-**Oedipal** phase, where the relationship between mother and child is still intact. In what Kristeva terms the '**semiotic**', the child has no sense of itself as possessing an identity separate from its mother, and therefore perceives no need for a means of communication between self and **other**. However, its existence is regulated by physical drives, pulsations and impulses which the child gradually learns to order and control, and it is this which forms the ground for the practice of signification.

The Oedipal crisis signals the intervention of the father in the dyadic relationship between mother and child, and initiates the child's movement into language. Within the symbolic order, the child becomes an independent **subject**, and so depends upon language both to define the content of the world around it and to communicate with other independent subjects. However, the symbolic does not supersede the semiotic: instead, the two 'modalities' combine in order to form a discourse.

For Kristeva, therefore, language is not a fixed system, but an ongoing process, since meaning is generated out of the dynamic interplay between semiotic and symbolic, whereby each modality regulates the other. The energies of the semiotic allow for a flexible and creative use of language to produce new meanings, but without the ordering abilities of the symbolic it becomes incomprehensible 'psychotic' babbling. In contrast, the symbolic attempts to create an exact correspondence between word and object, but without the compensating presence of the symbolic, that deteriorates into a totalitarian urge to control what is 'other' by maintaining an absolute distinction between it and the self.

Different modes of discourse are formed out of the vacillating relationship between symbolic and semiotic. In scientific language, for example, the semiotic is almost entirely repressed, since it allows for very little slippage between the word and the thing described. However, in poetic language, the semiotic's dominance is manifested through rhythm, syntactic irregularities and linguistic distortions such as metaphor, metonymy and musicality.

However, in spite of the fact that the semiotic is identified with the mother, its use is not gender-linked, for Kristeva differs from Cixous and Irigaray in arguing against the kind of linguistic essentialism which claims that men and women have a different relationship to language. By this token, poetic, rhythmic or expressive language is not the especial province of women, any more than scientific discourse is necessarily 'masculine'. Indeed, the writers Kristeva most frequently cites as creative exponents of the semiotic impulse, such as Mallarmé and James Joyce, are male.

Kristeva has kept a consistent distance between herself and the wider feminist movement, claiming that she objects to an agenda that seeks political power within existing bourgeois frameworks. She argues that it runs a danger of becoming another 'master discourse' which, rather than posing a fundamental challenge to the hierarchical distinction between centre and margins, will do no more than reverse the familiar powerful/powerless opposition. As she states in her essay 'Women's Time' (1979): 'The very logic of counter-power and of counter-society necessarily generates, by its very structure, its essence as a **simulacrum** of the combated society or of power.'

In this essay, Kristeva identifies two stages in the history of feminism. Before 1968, the feminist demand was for an equal place *within* history and the order of linear time. After 1968, feminism's second generation emphasized women's essential **difference** from men, and their right to remain *outside* the historical and political realm. Both positions, however, have their disadvantages. While the first generation surrendered the semiotic power of the maternal, the second runs the risk of being completely identified with it, to the extent that any ability to relate to the symbolic may be lost. The challenge for feminism, as Kristeva sees it, is to reconcile maternal time, or motherhood, with the historical and political order of linear time, in order to institute a third option: a fluid discourse which, allowing for multiplicity and difference, abolishes the distinction between centre and margins altogether.

KROKER, ARTHUR: CULTURAL CRITIC (1945–) As a Canadian, Arthur Kroker stands at a marked distance from the domination of the United States. Kroker's response to **postmodernism** contrasts with that of Fredric **Jameson** in being activist and moralizing while ceding nothing to Jameson in its grasp of contemporaneity. In *The Postmodern Scene* Kroker envisages postmodernism as a catastrophe that 'has already taken place'. There is no real, no society, no self, no sexuality (only secretions), no reason (only rationalization), no morality (only seduction and pathos), no life (only death). Kroker's presentation of postmodernism aims to pull together a number of brilliant resources: **Nietzsche**; **Marx** and commodity fetishism; Georges Bataille's vision of waste as the main principle of existence; the view in **Adorno** and **Horkheimer**'s *Dialectic of Enlightenment* that rationality is always bonded to irrationalism; **Baudrillard** and the **simulacrum**.

Prevented by the collapse of reason from using rational argument, immersed in a postmodern world which faces us with a Nietzschean choice between passive and suicidal nihilism, Kroker can only deploy a rhetoric. The effort is to make it seem as bad as it could be but the aim is political: 'Hyper-pessimism today is the only realistic basis for a raging will to political action.' To dramatize this pessimism *The Postmodern Scene* conjures up a vocabulary of horror and despair: '*fin de millennium*'; 'the end of history', 'the resurrection effect', 'panic', 'explosion implosion', 'sign crimes', 'the solar anus', 'excremental culture', 'the death of the social', 'sex without secretions', 'the disembodied eye', '*camera negrida*', 'cynical power'.

Kroker carries forward his rhetorical strategy into a number of texts he has edited, often with others. These include *The Panic Encyclopedia*, dedicated to exciting the 'ecstasy and fear', the 'delirium and anxiety', caused by 'the disappearance of *external* standards of public conduct' and 'the dissolution of the *internal* foundations of identity'. A number of authors write short pieces on 'Panic Art', 'Panic Babies', 'Panic Canada', 'Panic Drugs', etc. 'Panic Seagulls' by Michael Westlake describes how the picturesque Cornish fishing village of St. Ives has been taken over by seagulls, romantic-seeming wanderers of the deep, until the natives counterattack by feeding them bread covered in baking powder which, mixing with acid in the gut, can make a seagull explode in mid-air. In other edited texts, such as *The Hysterical Male* and *Body Invaders*, Kroker exploits postmodernism for its potential to undo any sense that sexuality is based in the real and determined by the body.

KUHN, THOMAS: PHILOSOPHER AND HISTORIAN OF SCIENCE (1922–) Originally trained as a physicist, Kuhn soon moved into the philosophy and history of science, and his work there, particularly on scientific method, has had reverberations well outside his chosen fields. The author of several important books, Kuhn is best known for *The Structure of Scientific Revolutions* (1962), where he outlined his controversial concept of 'paradigm' (basically meaning 'framework of thought'): a concept which has come to be widely adopted in critical debate across a range of intellectual disciplines.

Kuhn adopted a much more radical view of the history of science than most of his peers, for whom it was in general to be seen as a steady process of accumulation of knowledge that led, fairly inexorably, to our current state of technical and theoretical sophistication. For Kuhn, on the other hand, the history of science was a much more exciting and even chaotic affair, where revolutions of thought periodically occurred and new theories swept away older ones. Scientific revolutions were, therefore, the norm, and each successful revolution brought with it a new paradigm which, crucially, was incompatible with the old. Thus the change from Ptolemaic to Copernican astronomy (the earth as the centre of the universe to the sun as the centre), involved two contrasting world views which could not be reconciled: one had to believe either one or the other. Kuhn explored just this topic in *The Copernican Revolution* (1957). A similar **paradigm shift** had accompanied the work of Albert Einstein on relativity (which directly challenged the principles of Newtonian physics), and in recent years such shifts have tended to occur with, as far as the general public is concerned, somewhat bewildering regularity.

Once a paradigm established itself, what Kuhn called 'normal science' took over. Normal science consisted of applying the current set of theories to phenomena in the world around us, and trying to plug as many of the gaps in our knowledge as possible: 'puzzle solving' in Kuhn's terminology. Most scientists' careers consisted, in fact, of just such puzzle solving, conducted according to the principles of the current paradigm. The dominant theory would be persevered with even if it left some problems unanswered, and, if necessary, *ad hoc* adjustments would be made to try and save its authority. Problems that persistently resisted solution (such as the precise path of the planets in Ptolemaic astronomy) would eventually, however, call the dominant scientific theory into question, ushering in a period of instability, featuring various competing theories, that would finally be resolved by the institution of a new paradigm able to explain previous anomalies. Thus Copernican astronomy could predict the positions of the planets with *far* greater accuracy than the Ptolemaic system could, and without the host of *ad hoc* adjustments that Ptolemaic astronomy had latterly required.

The degree of **incommensurability** in world view between an old and new paradigm meant that believers in the old paradigm could not always be converted to the cause of the new, and it was often the case, as Kuhn pointed out, that the new paradigm did not become completely dominant until the older generation of scientists opposing it had died out. For Kuhn, scientific revolution is a necessary and vital part of scientific history, and he sees many parallels with political history in this regard. In both cases the goal is to change institutions which have become set in their ways, and more concerned with maintaining their privileges and aura of authority than admitting the value, indeed the necessity, of new ideas and methods.

Kuhn's importance for **postmodernism** lies in the notion that one paradigm is not necessarily better than another, but simply constitutes another way of looking at things. In postmodern terms of reference, paradigms are effectively 'narratives', some more believable than others no doubt, but none of which can claim to be in possession of the absolute truth. Each constitutes a world view which could be supplanted by other worldviews. Kuhn's ideas have been highly controversial and, particularly in philosophy-of-science circles, the notion of paradigm has been attacked as both vague and too neat an explanation of historical process. Sir Karl Popper was a vociferous critic of Kuhn's views, and the debate conducted between the two men and their supporters dominated philosophy of science for much of the 1960s and 1970s. Outside the philosophy of science, the notion of paradigm has had a considerable vogue, particularly in the context of debates about cultural change.

L

LACAN, JACQUES: PSYCHOANALYST
(1901–81) Along with Claude **Lévi-Strauss**, Michel **Foucault** and Roland **Barthes**, the psychoanalyst and philosopher Jacques Lacan was one of the central figures of French 'high' **structuralism**. Like Foucault and Barthes, his work has proved adaptable and fertile enough to continue to influence **poststructuralist** and **postmodernist** thought. Indeed Lacan is one of the founding fathers of postmodernism – his dense, difficult and convoluted prose, cut with puns, heavy with allusion; his giddying flights of fancy; his often apocalyptic style, have all influenced postmodernist discourse. Lacan became something of a celebrity with the publication of a collection of articles and other pieces, *Ecrits,* in 1966. Transcriptions of his weekly seminars, held for the training of psychoanalysts, continue to appear.

Although Lacan's work could be seen as an extended debate with Sigmund **Freud**, it is a debate illuminated by Lacan's plundering of **Hegel**, surrealism, structuralist linguistics and the anthropology of Lévi-Strauss. Lévi-Strauss had shown how Saussure's structuralist method could be used to understand kinship relationships and primitive myths, and Lacan, from the early 1950s until his death in 1981, attempted to employ the same methods to map the underlying structure of the human psyche.

Like the other great structuralists, Lacan begins with language. In many ways his work is the extension of Saussure's insights into language to the operation of the mind. Perhaps his most famous statement is the claim that the unconscious is structured like a language. This means that the unconscious works with the same tools as language, and that it only comes into existence *because* of language. Saussure had argued that it is the overall structure of a language, the system of **differences**, that gives language the ability to *mean*. For Saussure the link between a word (the signifier) and the idea it conveys (the signified) is purely arbitrary; nevertheless, he argues that there is a certain stability in the relationship. Lacan, like Jacques **Derrida**, challenges that cosy relationship. For Lacan words always refer to other words: signifiers form a chain along which we slip without ever reaching a fixed or definite meaning. A sentence can always be added to, and that addition can completely reverse its meaning. Metaphor and metonymy, both of which involve the substitution of one signifier for another, further disrupt the links between signifier and signified.

Lacan's emphasis on language is part of his reaction against the reductionist, biological reading of Freud prevalent among Freud's American followers. Lacan's 'return to Freud' in reality is a return to the earlier works of the master, such as *The Interpretation of Dreams* and the *Psychopathology of Everyday Life,* in which the biological origins of our thoughts, emotions and behaviour are de-emphasized in favour of social or cultural factors. Lacan extends the reach of these non-biological forces, interpreting, for example, the **Oedipus** complex as a linguistic transaction: the incest taboo is a cultural phenomenon, reliant on the linguistic categories of 'father' and 'mother', quite independent of any biological instinct or need.

Indeed, for Lacan, the biological concept of need is largely displaced by the concept of **desire**. A need can be gratified, but desire is irrepressible. A child has a need for its mother's milk, which can be gratified, but it desires its mother's love and that desire for love can never be satisfied.

Lacan's model of development involves three interlinked 'orders' – the imaginary, the symbolic and the real. The imaginary phase comes with the child's recognition of itself in the mirror, when it sees itself for the first time as a coherent entity, rather than some fragmented, ill-assorted jumble of fleshy odds and ends. But this unity is illusory, an ideal of integration. From the imaginary, the child emerges into the symbolic – the world of culture, of language, and in particular the world of signifiers. It is the realm of culture in which the human subject comes into existence, a world ruled over by the symbolic 'name of the Father', which acts as an enforcer of stability, the word of the law. The real is not in any sense the 'real world' but is that which evades images and symbols, a threatening absence lurking behind the symptoms of neurosis.

Lacan has had a great influence on literary studies and, in particular, feminist theory. Feminists have valued Lacan's emphasis on the cultural/linguistic origins of gender differentiation, which seems to offer an escape from brutalist biological theories of sexual difference. Feminists are, however, sharply critical of the patriarchal assumptions deeply embedded in Lacan's discourse.

LACLAU, ERNESTO: POLITICAL THEORIST (1935–) Laclau is one of the major names in the field of **post-Marxism**, especially in terms of his collaborative work with the political philosopher Chantal **Mouffe** (although he has also published widely under his own name). Born and educated in Argentina, he has since lectured at various universities in England and North America. Laclau and Mouffe's major collaborative work, *Hegemony and Socialist Strategy: Towards a Radical Democratic Politics* (1985) is now regarded as one of the most important contributions to the development of post-Marxism as a distinctive theoretical position in its own right.

As a theoretical movement post-Marxism might best be described as an uneasy coalition between those who have rejected Marxist beliefs altogether, and those who wish to synthesize **Marxism** with more recent cultural and philosophical theories such as **deconstruction**, feminism and **postmodernism**. In the former camp we would place figures such as

Jean-François **Lyotard**, Michel **Foucault**, and Jean **Baudrillard**, all of whom have, in their own way, turned their backs on Marxism in later career; in the latter we would place Laclau and Mouffe, who see their goal as a revitalization of the Marxist tradition to take account of rapidly changing cultural circumstances. Post-Marxism is, therefore, as much as anything a matter of the attitude adopted towards Marxism's heritage. *Hegemony and Socialist Strategy* is a bold plea for Marxism to be revised, such that it sheds some of its authoritarian image and makes itself attractive to a new audience sceptical of the notion of universally applicable theories. Laclau and Mouffe identify a crisis in Marxist thought, arguing that the cultural climate has changed so radically over the course of the twentieth century that most of what were taken to be the 'evident truths' of classical Marxism, such as a belief in homogeneous social classes (the working class, for example), or the historical inevitability of socialism, can no longer stand up to close scrutiny. Put bluntly, Marxism must now reorient itself or go into terminal decline. The authors float the idea of a 'radical democratic politics' that would encompass both Marxism and the various new social movements (such as feminism, the **Greens**, or ethnic and sexual minorities) that have sprung up in recent times, as well as new developments in the field of theory. They describe their approach as broadly deconstructive in that they are trying to point out instabilities and paradoxes in Marxist thought, thus undermining its claims to authority. In effect, they are

arguing that Marxism is in danger of becoming irrelevant and has to be brought up to date, meaning that it must embrace political **pluralism** and dispense with the dogmatism of classical Marxist thought, which saw itself as the theory to end all theories and could only regard any commitment to pluralism as heresy. Laclau and Mouffe therefore call for a 'democratic revolution' where the left consciously establishes as many links as it can with the new social movements, rather than, as was the more usual practice, trying to impose its own ideology on all political struggles in an authoritarian manner. It is precisely that authoritarianism that Laclau and Mouffe wish to see eradicated.

Laclau and Mouffe's ideas have given rise to considerable controversy, with traditionally oriented Marxists dismissing the notion that Marxism is in any need of 'improvement' or has anything of note to learn from theories such as deconstruction. To go beyond Marxism is, for such an audience, to betray its heritage, not to revitalize it. Laclau and Mouffe have replied in robust fashion to their critics (those 'faded epigones' of the Marxist tradition, as they have slightingly referred to them), reiterating their belief in the necessity of reformulating the socialist project such that it is more receptive to new ideas, although for many on the left the new ideas are incompatible with socialism. Their Marxism can seem no more than residual, although there is no doubting the sincerity of their motives.

From a postmodernist standpoint, Laclau and Mouffe are to be seen as representative of the decline of

Marxism as a 'grand narrative' (they are certainly unwilling to defend its claim to be a universal theory in possession of absolute truth), and part of the new wave of pluralism that has taken the place of the grand narrative tradition in general. Where they differ from post-Marxists such as Lyotard, Foucault and Baudrillard is in their desire to retain something of the spirit of Marxism, even if they are no longer prepared to adhere strictly to the letter.

LEGITIMATION To speak of the legitimation of a theory or political system is to speak of what gives it authority. Thus **Marxism** regards itself as based on scientific principles, as opposed to mere ideologies which set out to excuse the domination of one part of society by another: what legitimates Marxism is its status as a 'science of society', rigorous in execution and free of sectional interest. Similarly, Western liberal democracy takes its authority from a particular conception of the individual human being as the possessor of certain inalienable rights (right to equality before the law, to own property, to sell one's labour on the open market, etc.); the political system of Western societies is legitimated by its protection of those rights.

Thinkers like **Lyotard** consider that there is a crisis of legitimation in the **postmodern** world, in that theories such as Marxism (**grand narratives** or **metanarratives** in Lyotard's terminology) have had their authority called into question to the point where there is open incredulity towards them. We can no longer rely on grand narratives to solve all our socio-political prob-lems; rather, we have to realize that they are the *source* of most of these problems, by arousing hopes that they cannot fulfil. Marxism also demands uncritical acceptance of certain key principles (the desirability of the dictatorship of the proletariat, etc.), and for Lyotard this is authoritarian and a suppression of individual creativity. Generally speaking, post-modernist thinkers are suspicious of most means of legitimation in the twentieth century, tending to find authoritarianism lurking behind the scenes in some guise or another.

LÉVI-STRAUSS, CLAUDE: ANTHRO-POLOGIST AND CULTURAL THEORIST (1908–) Lévi-Strauss originally studied law and philosophy, but eventually turned to anthropology to become one of the subject's leading voices in the twentieth century. He has also been one of the most prominent figures in the **structuralist** move-ment, and his various anthropological studies are considered classics of the structuralist approach. Given his classic status in this regard, Lévi-Strauss has been a prime target of the **poststructuralist** movement, which has been highly critical of the methodology lying behind his struc-tural anthropology, in particular its system-building bias.

Lévi-Strauss's overriding concern has been to identify the underlying deep structures of cultural pheno-mena, and his research tends to concentrate on finding patterns and common features within those pheno-mena, which are taken to be struc-tured on the model of language. In one of his most famous pieces of analysis in *The Raw and the Cooked*

(1964), a group of apparently disparate South American tribal myths are argued to be variations on a theme, having a similar underlying structure and narrative elements which undergo subtle modifications (or 'transformations') from tale to tale.

Like all structuralist theorists, Lévi-Strauss makes extensive use of **binary oppositions**, with the nature/culture distinction being one of his main ways of classifying human behaviour. The theory is that all instances of human behaviour must belong to one or other of these mutually exclusive categories, but Lévi-Strauss himself is forced to admit that the incest taboo seems to fall into both. **Derrida** has been particularly critical of Lévi-Strauss on this issue, arguing that his admission casts doubt on structuralist methodology in general and the principle of binary opposition in particular. Lévi-Strauss becomes for Derrida symbolic of the structuralist desire to make everything fit into pre-arranged, ordered systems – a tendency he regards as authoritarian.

LEVINAS, EMMANUEL: PHILOSOPHER (1905–95) Born in Lithuania to a Jewish family, Levinas lived through the Russian Revolution of 1917 in the Ukraine and subsequently departed to France where he began to study philosophy. In 1928 Levinas travelled to Freiburg to study phenomenology with Edmund **Husserl**, and was introduced to the work of Martin **Heidegger**. Later, returning to Strasbourg and gaining French citizenship, it was largely Levinas who introduced German phenomenology to France. Levinas became associated with the French existential branch of pheno-

menology, influencing Jean-Paul Sartre, Simone de Beauvoir, Gabriel Marcel, Jean Wahl, Maurice Merleau-Ponty and Maurice Blanchot. But the first major publication of his own original philosophy appeared in 1961 with *Totalité et infinité*. This work combined a radical critique of Western philosophy with a retrieval of the pre-Platonic tradition of Hebrew thought, bringing Levinas's formative ideas to the attention of the **postmodern** world.

The roots of Levinas's philosophy lie in both his Jewish background and his original work deriving from German phenomenology. But these roots alone do not explain the enormous impact which Levinas's works written after he turned 55 had upon the subsequent generation of philosophers. Jacques **Derrida**'s critical essay of 1964, '*Violence et métaphysique: Essai sur la pensée d'Emmanuel Levinas*', influenced greatly the reception of Levinas internationally by postmodern thinkers. Derrida contributes to Levinas's reputation with respect for and criticism of his efforts to move beyond Western metaphysics. Publication of Levinas's second major work *Autrement qu'être ou Au delà de l'essence* (*Otherwise Than Being or Beyond Essence*) in 1974 represented a new stage in his thinking. Here he endeavours to renew and revise more thoroughly the methods of philosophy after Heidegger. The revisionary core of Levinas has been approached from many perspectives as part of the climate of postmodern thought. But these perspectives converge on Levinas's account of the relation between the other and oneself, elaborating his concern with the external authority that relates the other to the same without, however, uniting them.

Levinas writes movingly of the meeting with the other as an encounter with 'the human in the total nudity of its eyes'. The other is not a potential threat, but a demand that 'Thou shalt not kill'. Levinas's whole oeuvre demonstrates the wisdom of an exhausting love for the other *(philia)* rather than the contemplation of the wisdom that has dominated the history of Western philosophy. The phrase that both encapsulates the wisdom of *philia* and echoes the postmodern claim to the end of Western metaphysics is Levinas's 'ethics as first philosophy'. Here ethics points to something radical and originary. Instead of seeing the theory of the good as the ultimate level of human perfection, Levinas insists that the practice of the good transcends contemplation. Such practice reveals the birthplace of all theoretical relationships as prior to any ontological origin, in one's ethical relation to the other: that is, in 'one's being-for-the-**Other**'. To illustrate this, Levinas uses the face of the other. There is an authority in the face which commands me not to leave this mortal other to dwell alone. This imperative is not a universal command but a particular responsibility of mine for the other.

However, debate continues in feminist circles over Levinas's implicit form of patriarchy. Notwithstanding his highly influential account of otherness, the contention is that Levinas ultimately subordinates the feminine to the masculine. In his 1947 text, *Le temps et l'autre* (*Time and the Other*), the figure of the feminine

serves as the paradigm in Levinas's account of the absolutely other, in his discussion of eros. But even in this early work he exhibits a certain suspicion of femininity. Next in his 1961 text, and later in *Otherwise Than Being* the feminine other is gradually reduced to the role of mother. As Levinas becomes increasingly concerned with the ethical relation between self and other, his early interest in eros and so in the feminine other decreases. Instead he turns to paternity and the face-to-face relation between father and son. The erotic falls short of an ethical relation because it involves a return to self. Levinas defines the other in terms of the paternal God's relation to his son, while leaving the feminine other without her own specific face.

Ultimately for Levinas ethics in its feminine achievement means to be a mother, nothing else, and so the meaning of the other as a passive body and a failure of virility can be learned from the mother. Yet perhaps the feminine can also achieve the disruption of being with goodness beyond maternity in a utopian identity for the other.

LIBIDINAL ECONOMY Libidinal economy is Jean-François **Lyotard**'s term for the various drives within human beings that resist the workings of logic and reason. These are to be seen as analogous to the subconscious drives identified by psychoanalytical theorists such as **Freud**, although Lyotard is perhaps more openly in favour of their free expression than most psychoanalytical theorists, and more prone to celebrate their anarchic, socially disordering effect. One of Lyotard's major objections to **Marxism** is that it fails to allow any place for these drives within its theories, seeing them as irrational and unpredictable, and therefore to be resisted. For Lyotard, however, the denial of libidinal drives in this way is an authoritarian act, and one that ultimately can only be unsuccessful: the drives will always find some means of expression and cannot be suppressed indefinitely. He goes so far as to suggest that the working class in the nineteenth century identified with industrialization as a massive outburst of libidinal energy, and that where Marxists saw simply exploitation the workers instead saw excitement, variety and change. Libidinal economy is therefore to be regarded as a direct attack on Marxism as both a philosophy and a cultural project. In a more general sense it also constitutes a rejection of philosophy's rationalist heritage, to the extent that it has been dubbed a post- and even anti-philosophical notion. The context of the theory is important to note: Lyotard's book *Libidinal Economy* was published in 1974; that is, in the aftermath of the 1968 *événements* when many French left-wing intellectuals had become severely disenchanted by Marxism, largely as a result of the failure of the French Communist Party to support the anti-state cause. *Libidinal Economy* represents one of the most vicious attacks on Marxist thought of the period, and charts a sea change in Lyotard's own career.

LITTLE NARRATIVE In the grand narratives of Jean-François **Lyotard** (all-embracing explanatory theories

such as **Marxism** or **Hegelian** dialectics), individuals are oppressed and find themselves being sacrificed to the objectives of those controlling the **grand narrative**. Thus Marxism in its Soviet model demanded that all individuals follow the Communist Party line, since the Party was assumed to be the repository of all truth. Lyotard points out how this destroys individual initiative, leading to a totalitarian society where dissent is ruthlessly repressed and creativity stifled. The failings of grand narratives have, however, been well recognized by the late twentieth century (thus the collapse of the Soviet Union and its client states), and what we should now be supporting is little narratives. These latter are tactical groupings (or coalitions of interest) which seek to oppose specific social ills. Little narratives, of which the worker–student collaboration in the 1968 *événements* in Paris remains an outstanding example for Lyotard, are not designed to last, but merely to achieve limited, short-term objectives. One might regard the individual as the ultimate little narrative seeking to resist the power of authoritarian grand narratives, such as the state or multinational corporations.

LOGOCENTRICITY Logocentricity is the assumption that words can unproblematically communicate meanings present in individual's minds such that the listener, or reader, receives them in the same way as the speaker/hearer intended. Words and meanings are therefore considered to have an internal stability. This is a standard assumption of discourse in Western culture, but one that has come under attack from the **deconstructionist** movement. Jacques **Derrida** in particular regards this as an unsustainable position to adopt, on the basis that words always carry traces of previous meanings, as well as suggesting other words which sound similar to the one being used.

LYNCH, DAVID: FILM DIRECTOR (1946–) Lynch's work foregrounds the painterly and non-narrative in films of subversive disquiet. His first major film, *Eraserhead*, was completed in 1976, establishing his taste for surrealist juxtaposition and exploration of psyche, through an unsettling use of the absurd and banal. This was followed by *The Elephant Man* of 1980, his most conventional film but equally concerned with the bizarre and monstrous in its account of the deformed John Merrick. *Dune* (1984), a science-fiction thriller, was a much publicized failure, but Lynch recovered to move into mainstream Hollywood cinema with his most popular films *Blue Velvet* (1986) and the Cannes Film Festival Palm d'Or winner *Wild at Heart* (1990). In 1990–91 he embraced the most popular of screen forms, the TV soap serial, becoming a household name with the unprecedented success of *Twin Peaks*, co-written with Mark Frost. This transferred to the big screen as *Twin Peaks: Fire Walk With Me* (1992).

Critics have felt that Lynch's work sits uneasily in commercial Hollywood cinema. It is considered to tread too fine a line between élitist art house and mainstream popular appeal resulting in a series of shocking images lacking substance. Not least,

Lynch's disregard for traditional narrative and plot, transgressing all the conventions of Hollywood film, identify him as an anomaly within mainstream cinema. Lynch's achievement, however, could be said to rest with the very translation of such qualities into commercial success. The mainstay of Lynch's style draws upon the staples of **postmodern** aesthetics. A love of parody and cliché, an eclectic use of film genre, from high art *film noir* and surrealism to horror to pornography, an interrogation of surface image and employment of psychoanalysis to probe that surface and reveal the hidden and abject where least expected.

Lynch's territory is small-town America, his point of crisis, the American dream whose wholesome quality becomes exaggerated to parody and in turn unease. The overstated colour of suburban lawn and picket fence in the opening scene of *Blue Velvet* is façade for a darker, more transgressive, existence. Reinforcing this transgression, our entry into this dangerous but compelling world is in voyeuristic glimpses. In *Blue Velvet* we first see the horror of Dorothy's world through the innocent eyes of Jeffrey secreted in her wardrobe; in *Eraserhead* Henry spies on his seductress through the keyhole of his apartment; and in *Twin Peaks* Audrey witnesses her father's illicit deals through a peephole in his office.

Reflecting postmodern notions of artifice as the reality of contemporary experience, Lynch's world is one of cliché and pastiche with images that exist for themselves rather than for any inherent meaning or interpretation. Trained as a painter, Lynch excels in the purely visual; but criticism of his work as devoid of characterization ignores his iconographic and self-conscious use of motif. The recurring velvet curtain, for example, suggests surface and the intrigue of what surface conceals, providing an anticipation of revelation but not necessarily establishing meaning. Seductive but artificial, it is utilized to aid psychopath Frank's masturbation fantasies in *Blue Velvet* while in *Twin Peaks* it is the fabric of the ambiguous red room containing the unspeakable truth of Laura's death. Lynch's work revolves around the surfacing of what is hidden. In this he remains true to his surrealist beginnings, although his mature style suggests the transformation of these sources through postmodern experience.

LYOTARD, JEAN-FRANÇOIS: PHILO-SOPHER (1928–) Lyotard has been professor of philosophy at the University of Paris VII, Vincennes, and at the University of California at Irvine. A prolific and protean writer, he himself describes his wildly divergent paths through philosophy, politics and art as 'promiscuous'. In the English-speaking world, he is chiefly renowned for *The Postmodern Condition* (1979) a work which has been regarded as unrepresentative of his oeuvre, but in which many of his earlier interests are drawn together, as can be seen from his extended conversations with Jean-Loup Thébaud, concerning that text and his previous works, and published as *Just Gaming* (1979), and from his summative statement of 1988, *Peregrinations*.

In many ways, Lyotard's work has never left the paradigms with which it

began: principally, the synthesis of **Freud** and **Marx** which so troubled French intellectuals, from Althusser to **Deleuze**, in the early 1970s. Although most evident in *Libidinal Economy* (1974), traces of these concerns remain evident in *The Differend* (1984) and in the 1993 re-publication of a collection of essays from 1973 on matters libidinal, political, **postmodern** and aesthetic, *Des dispositifs pulsionnels* (*The Drives and their Apparatuses*).

Like other aspects of his thought, Lyotard's political theory polarizes around events: the Algerian war of independence provided his earliest foray into political terrain, during which time he was teaching in Algeria and monitoring the situation for the radical Trotskyite group, Socialism or Barbarism. During this time, Lyotard professed a faith in the central tenets of Marxism, although this commitment excommunicated him from his comrades in the former group in 1966, when he joined Workers' Power. But his political articles of faith were to disappear altogether with the *événements* of May 1968, where a popular revolt nearly brought down the Gaullist government, despite accusations of 'childishness' directed at the broad coalition of activists by the largely uninvolved official left and fringe left intellectuals. Far from following the French Communist Party in carping about the theoretical and practical inadequacies of the events, Lyotard condemned the Marxists for failing to follow the initiative seized in the streets, and split definitively with them, the bitterest fruit of which can still be sampled in *Libidinal Economy*.

The collapse of this particular **grand narrative** is what provoked Lyotard to adopt the analysis of the 'end of ideology' proferred by the politically right-of-centre theorist of **post-industrial** society, Daniel **Bell**, but also led him to proclaim the dawn of a **postmodernity** in politics, a consistent and extended rewriting of politics, its goals, its methods and its ideals, that has resulted in Lyotard's own philosophical turn to '**Kant** after Marx' and Freud, and in his rejection of the **hegemony** of political – and libidinal – economy in favour of analyses of the potentialities for thought and action offered by the raw materials of the social bond found in exchanges of sentences. This philosophical 'back to basics' campaign, reaching its fullest philosophical statement in *The Differend,* may seem to reduce the scope of Lyotard's focus from politics, aesthetics and philosophy to another, very modern 'linguistic turn' paralleling the later philosophy of Ludwig Wittgenstein, on whose concept of a society linguistically *and therefore* conceptually and practically composed of 'language games' Lyotard drew in *The Postmodern Condition.* However, far from flattening out the field of postmodern **events** and enclosing them within the enfranchisable horizons of linguistic possibilities, linguistic events come to form the 'particles in Brownian motion' that unpredictably coalesce into extremely heterogeneous series of social, political, aesthetic, scientific, and technological phenomena, allowing Lyotard's philosophy to explore everything from the minutiae of the narrative organization of modern philosophies to the fate of thinking after the death of our system's sun.

The question, however, that continues to hang over this body of thought, and to which Lyotard constantly returns, concerns the political bite of his analyses. His famously weak response to the crises of limited information flow in computerized societies, that the public *ought* to be given free access to the data banks, perhaps suggests that nothing has yet replaced the power of **modernity**'s Marxist narrative in terms of its critical and imaginative power, at the same time as, perhaps ironically, the reasons behind Lyotard's often vicious rejection of that programme are more compelling still. This dichotomy lies at the core of Lyotardian postmodernity: our modern programmes are refuted, yet there are no successors. Postmodernity is therefore a period without a programme, working over the accumulated debits against one modernity while experimenting with its roots to invent another. It is in this sense that postmodernity comes not at the end, but at the beginning of modernity.

M

MADONNA: POP-SINGER, PERFORM-ANCE ARTIST AND ACTRESS (1958–)
Although the 1980s was the decade in which Madonna reached the zenith of her stardom in the traditional sense, she has now attained the status of cultural icon. She is, however, an extremely problematic one, as her delight in simultaneously evoking and transgressing cultural stereotypes of femininity makes her exceedingly difficult to categorize. Virgin and whore, material girl and pornographic centrefold, Madonna's endless reproduction of her self in all its varied guises may either, depending on one's point of view, pander to traditional male fantasies which objectify women as sex objects or constitute an **ironic** subversion of such attitudes, in particular through her exploitation of black, lesbian and gay style.

The debate about whether Madonna can be considered an icon for feminism is an ongoing one. One of her most enthusiastic supporters in this regard is Camille **Paglia**, who reads Madonna as the perfect representative of a **postmodern** feminism, which exposes all sexual roles as nothing more than performance. Whereas traditional feminism, claims Paglia, 'says "No more masks"', the multiplicity of personae that constitute Madonna's public face 'says we are nothing but masks'. While there is nothing inherently liberatory about this notion of femininity as masquerade, in the context of the Madonna phenomenon it is assumed that it is an ongoing process of self-fashioning over which she regains full control.

MAGIC REALISM As the term itself suggests, magic realism is a form founded on the juxtaposition of two modes of **representation** which normally exist in opposition: realism and the fantastic. Although the term is now almost exclusively associated with literature, it was originally coined by Franz Roh in 1925 to describe a form of art that portrayed scenes of fantasy and imagination through the use of clear-cut, 'documentary' painting techniques. It is, however, primarily identified with the writing of Latin America, where authors such as Gabriel Garcia Márquez, Carlos Fuentes and Octavio Paz create narratives in which the realistic elements of the text are continually being undercut by the intrusion of impossible or inexplicable events. In this context, magic realism is also a politicized term, since it charts the contradictory responses of a **post-colonial** culture that is engaged in the process of recovering a lost past, while remaining unable completely to escape the lingering influence of its more recent colonial history.

Since the 1970s, however, magic realism has become a fashionable label for any writing that subverts realistic expectations, and has been particularly associated with the work of writers such as Salman **Rushdie**, Angela **Carter** and Jeanette Winterson, all of whom exploit the disruptive potential of fantasy in order to pose a challenge to cultural perceptions of 'normality'.

MANDELBROT, BENOIT: MATHEMATICIAN AND SCIENTIST (1924–) Working both outside the academy, for IBM, and in a variety of academic fields, including pure and applied mathematics, physiology and economics, Mandelbrot found his intellectual feet by inventing what, in 1963, he modestly entitled 'the new scientific discipline' of **fractal** geometry. Fractal geometry studies the form of what traditional, Euclidean geometry expelled from its ideal world of straight lines and perfect curves: the 'pathological' forms of mountains, the exact measure of coastlines, clouds and so on. Mandelbrot's researches, presented in detail in *The Fractal Geometry of Nature* (1977), turn this redundant paradigm's idealist prejudice into a realist error, insofar as they reveal that it is fractals that are the norm in nature, and that perfect curves are, on the contrary, inestimably rare.

It is for this 'revolution' in geometry that **Lyotard** singles out Mandelbrot as an exemplar of **postmodern science**, and, by extension, as providing a model of postmodern practice: if the aim of postmodern science is no longer to seek the known, as Lyotard says, but rather the

unknown, then fractal geometry fits the bill insofar as it both inverts the principles of traditional geometry and creates new regions of ignorance where, it was thought, things had been well and truly settled. So successfully does fractal geometry model the geometries of phenomena such as coastlines, however, that paradoxically, while the scientific community found them initially unacceptably pathological for theoretical reasons, fractals found a niche in the generation of realistic computer images of unknown planets, as in the Genesis planet in *Star Trek II*, or even the damaged death-star in *Return of the Jedi*.

Like René **Thom**, then, Mandelbrot is interested in topology, the mathematics of form. While Thom remains defiantly abstractive, however, abstracting from the local events his **catastrophe theory** is intended to analyse, Mandelbrot insists on natural forms as the core of his earthbound geometry. Fractal dimension, however, is not only analytic, but also generative. Thus, the other objects of fractal geometry are the dynamical systems that exhibit deterministic **chaos**, and ironically, given his commitment to a geometry of natural form, it is in connection with this field that Mandelbrot's work is best known, whether within the academic fields of economics, physiology and mathematics, or, through the ubiquitous images of Mandelbrot sets associated with rave culture, beyond them. Far from disparaging this, Mandelbrot tends to celebrate it as an 'aesthetic' of chaos, tempering the cold formalism of mathematics with the 'pure, plastic beauty' generated by fractals.

MARCUSE, HERBERT: PHILOSOPHER (1898–1979) Marcuse emerged as philosopher and scholar within Weimar Germany. After participating in the attempted social democratic revolution in Berlin in 1917 and becoming familiar with the works of **Marx** he went to study with **Heidegger** at Freiburg University in 1928. Marcuse's hopes for a radical new beginning for philosophy (and a synthesis between existentialism and Marxism) led him back to **Hegel**. In 1932 he published a major study of Hegel and in 1933 he published the first major review of Marx's rediscovered 1844 manuscripts. In 1934 he fled Nazism and emigrated to the USA, where he lived for the rest of his life.

Reason and Revolution (1941) provided a study of the genesis of Hegel's thought and drew Hegel and Marx closer together as social philosophers responding to revolutionary possibilities (and social movements) in the society of their time. Marcuse's thinking was closely related to the Hegelian Marxism – or '**critical theory**' – developed by the members of the **Frankfurt School** (The Institute for Social Research) under the guidance of **Horkheimer** and **Adorno**. *Eros and Civilization* (1955) presented a reading of **Freud** influenced by Marcuse's own existentialist form of Marxism. In it he upheld the view that the liberation of society would need to overcome, or at least transform, that repression which Freud had regarded as constitutive of ego-formation and therefore as a constant in civilization. In 1958 Marcuse published *Soviet Marxism*, a study that was critical of developments in the Eastern bloc. *One-Dimensional Man* (1964) traced similarities between the industrialized and bureaucratized societies under advanced capitalism and under Soviet communism. It argued that technology and bureaucracy have taken on a life of their own, imposing their own forms of institutional domination, buttressed by an unreflective scientific (or scientistic) rationality. Despite the pessimism of his main thesis – that the potential for revolution was being drained from modern, complex, administered societies – Marcuse became the darling of the New Left during the student protests of the 1960s. In an essay oft-quoted on the left, 'Repressive Tolerance', Marcuse **deconstructed** the liberal toleration of dissent which appeared to characterize advanced Western societies (in contradistinction to the tyranny of the Soviet state). In the atmosphere of **postmodernist** relativism and disorientation, Marcuse's demonstration of the repressive function of liberal tolerance retains its polemical edge.

One of Marcuse's most influential essays challenged 'The Affirmative Character of Culture' (1937), by which he meant that tendency to see culture as 'a world essentially different from the factual world of the daily struggle for existence, yet realizable by every individual for himself "from within", without any transformation of the state of fact'. Marcuse promoted the idea of the 'great refusal' and never ceased to challenge the ruses of 'affirmative culture' which aimed to 'contain' the human need for freedom and happiness within the strict limits of a repressive consumer culture and manipulative mass media.

Nevertheless, against the tendencies of our 'one-dimensional' society, Marcuse maintained a lifelong faith in what his last work entitled *The Aesthetic Dimension* (1977). In it he defends art's 'distance from actuality' and invokes Stendhal's definition of beauty as the *'promise* of happiness', rather than its immediate *possession*. 'The basic thesis that art must be a factor in changing the world can easily turn into its opposite if the tension between art and radical praxis is flattened out so that art loses its own dimension for change.'

MARX, KARL HEINRICH: PHILO-SOPHER AND CULTURAL THEORIST (1818–83) What Marx shares with so many **modernists** is his detestation of history. His life was dedicated to the search for political and intellectual means to get a handle on history, to bring history in the form it had always existed – which, according to Marx, has hitherto been a history of ceaseless class struggle – to an end. In the classless (and stateless) society that he struggled to bring about, history would no longer be a demonic force. Instead, social arrangements would make possible the empowerment, the many-sided flowering of each individual.

Throughout his life Marx poured scorn on what he termed 'utopian' socialists who focused their energies on developing elaborate visions of a better society while neglecting both the analysis of actual states of affairs and the political struggle to change them. After a century and a half of 'Marxism' it is clear that despite this taboo on imagining the future, Marx's own thought is utopian through and through.

Marx studied law and philosophy in Bonn and Berlin where he was engaged in the fierce debates over the legacy of **Hegel**. In 1843 he began a lifelong friendship and collaboration with Friedrich Engels. In 1847 Marx and Engels helped found the Communist League, for which they wrote the *Communist Manifesto*. After the failure of the revolutionary upheavals of 1848, Marx went into exile in London.

Living in poverty in London, Marx devoted himself to the task of providing a systematic theory of capitalism. The result was *Das Kapital* (the first volume was published in 1867, subsequent volumes after Marx's death). The International Working Men's Association (1864–72), in which for a while Marx was the moving spirit, promoted communist-inspired opposition to capitalism.

In order to provide the political struggle of the working classes with a sound theoretical framework, Marx had set out to effect a radical transformation of the discipline of political economy. He took over wholesale many aspects of the economic theories of Adam Smith and David Ricardo, but completely recast them so as to reveal the exploitative relation which lay at the heart of the capitalist accumulation of profit.

Marx aimed to provide not only economic analyses but what he regarded as a complete 'science' of society and of history. What he termed the materialist view of history involves both a view of the fundamental role of economic factors in shaping the forms of all social relations and also a periodization of the whole course of human history. It is this that constitutes the basis of the Marxist **grand narrative** repudiated by postmodernists such as **Lyotard**.

One of the most far-reaching implications of Marx's ideas is the development of the critique of ideology. Marx's belief that ideas and ideologies can be traced back to their basis in the material basis of human life has made him – together with **Nietzsche** and **Freud** – a pioneer of what Ricoeur termed the 'hermeneutics of suspicion': the tendency to read all ideas and statements in terms of the interests (economic, political, sexual) they reveal (or conceal).

For over a hundred years after his death Marx's ideas have fed into both trade union organization and the thinking of revolutionary groups in the capitalist countries of Western Europe. During all of this century, almost every serious social theorist – friend or foe – has been influenced by the challenge of Marx. The legacy of Marx's ideas is so immense and complex that we cannot even begin to draw up a balance-sheet. But for many intellectuals, the collapse of Soviet-style communism and the triumph of consumer capitalism as a global system mean that Marx's inspiration is more relevant than ever. Jacques **Derrida**'s *Specters of Marx* (1994) is an impassioned (but philosophically nuanced) plea: in order truly to come to terms with the significance of the events of our time we need to think carefully, responsibly, about Marx's tangled and ambivalent legacy.

MCLUHAN, MARSHALL: CULTURAL THEORIST (1911–80) Marshall McLuhan makes a cameo appearance in Woody Allen's film *Annie Hall* (1977). He pops up in a cinema queue to support an opinion expressed by the central character, who is trying to impress a girlfriend. McLuhan's fame, however, extends far beyond these fifteen seconds. As founder and director of the University of Toronto's Centre for Culture and Technology in the 1960s and 1970s he invented the subject of media and communication studies virtually single-handed.

McLuhan's first book, *The Mechanical Bride* (1951) consists of 59 short pieces which scrutinize adverts, comic strips and the front pages of newspapers for evidence of what he calls the 'replaceable parts' dynamics of Western society. His central thesis is that to industrial man, everything is mechanizable, even – especially – sex (the book's title comes from a hosiery ad in which two detached female legs are displayed on a pedestal). McLuhan has a lynx's eye for the absurd heterogeneous yokings of popular culture, such as the newspaper headline 'Scientists Await Cow's Death to Solve Mathematics Problem'.

The Gutenberg Galaxy (1962) abandons the detached, fixed perspective of the scholarly study and adopts instead a 'mosaic or field approach'. So the book presents 310 short meditations on the consequences of the invention of the printing press and the advent of 'Typographic Man'. Each section is preceded by a provocative gloss: 'The new electronic interdependence recreates the world in the image of a global village' and '**Heidegger** surf-boards along on the electronic wave as triumphantly as Descartes rode the mechanical wave' are two examples. In both statements

– one brilliant, the other banal – we find foreshadowings of **postmodernist** culture. The **Internet** has indeed created a global village, and at least 40 million people worldwide surf its electronic waves on a regular basis.

In *Understanding Media* (1964), McLuhan looks at the threats to the mechanized, print-oriented regime posed by the new electronic media. Separate chapters on telephones, the phonograph and television demonstrate how each development extends the capacities of the human nervous system, and alters our perceptual 'sense-ratio'. Again, many of McLuhan's comments prefigure postmodernist obsessions with machines and distortions of the body, particularly in the work of Jean **Baudrillard** and Paul **Virilio**. After the publication of this book, McLuhan's own life became an exemplification of his ideas. His fame was fed by the very media he flattered. Within a short period of time he was not only the subject of some intense intellectual debate (with contributions by Raymond Williams, Susan Sontag, George Steiner, *et al.*), but he became a kind of guru to the tuned-in and the turned-on. He has some claim to being called the first genuine television talking head.

He has had his critics. Dwight Macdonald moaned about McLuhan's lack of interest in cultural standards, and Christopher Ricks castigated McLuhan's style as a 'viscous fog, through which loom stumbling metaphors'. In many ways, however, it was his catholicness (though not, perhaps, his Catholicness) which led the general public to take him seriously. Like Andy Warhol and the Beatles in

their own respective fields, he championed the breakdown of distinctions between high and low culture which theorists such as Fredric **Jameson** see as symptomatic of the postmodern.

McLuhan's *The Medium is the Message* (1967), *War and Peace in the Global Village* (1968) and *Counterblast* (1969) are visual jamborees, collages of photographs, cartoons, slogans and jokes. Pick any page and you will find an iconic image and an oracular aphorism. One chosen at random from *The Medium is the Message* shows a shadowy profile of Bob Dylan, captioned with lines from one of his lyrics: 'Because something is happening / But you don't know what it is / Do you, Mister Jones?' The same book closes with a 1966 cartoon from the *New Yorker* in which a bemused, besuited gentleman (Mr Jones?) is sitting in his study, while his check-shirted, guitar-toting son explains to him: 'You see, Dad, Professor McLuhan says the environment that man creates becomes his medium for defining his role in it. The invention of type created linear, or sequential, thought, separating thought from action. Now, with TV and folk singing, thought and action are closer and social involvement is greater. We again live in a village. Get it?' By the look on his face, Mr Jones *didn't* get it. Something was happening and he didn't know what it was. McLuhan *did* get it, and he did know what it was: it was nothing other than the 'brand-new world of allatonceness', a.k.a. postmodernism.

METANARRATIVE Jean-François **Lyotard**'s term (used interchangeably with grand narrative) for any theory claiming to provide universal explanations and to be universally valid. **Marxism** is probably the outstanding example of the phenomenon. Lyotard is resolutely opposed to metanarrative, considering it to be authoritarian and restrictive to individual creativity (see also **grand narrative**).

METAPHYSICS OF PRESENCE **Derrida** considers that the history of Western philosophy, and by implication the history of all discourse in the West, is marked by a commitment to what he calls 'presence'. This is the assumption we make that we can grasp meaning in its entirety, and that when we hear a word or phrase it is totally 'present' to us in our minds. Presence is therefore an unacknowledged metaphysical assumption that we make when we engage in communication with others. Behind the metaphysics of presence lies a belief in the stability of words and meanings, which, to a **poststructuralist** thinker like Derrida, invites attack. Derrida's point is that language is much more slippery than believers in presence care to admit, and that, in effect, any given word has a cluster of associations around it that undermine its supposed purity. What language features, to Derrida, is instability and indeterminacy of meaning: never any moment of full presence. Part of the reason for this inability of words to achieve full presence can be found in the nature of time. Derrida makes great play of the fact that time rolls remorselessly on, and that words are constantly being exposed to new states of affairs. There can never be any moment at which full presence, or for that matter full identity, is possible. Full presence and full identity

are two of the main assumptions on which discourse in the West is based, and by his critique of the metaphysics of presence Derrida is calling into question an entire intellectual tradition, which in his opinion is built on an illusion. In the absence of the metaphysics of presence communication appears a much more erratic and anarchic activity than we are normally led to believe, although for the **deconstructionist** it is also a more creative affair.

MILLER, J. HILLIS: CRITIC (1928–) Previously Professor of English at Yale, and then Distinguished Professor of English and Comparative Literature at the University of California, Irvine, Miller has been associated – alongside **Bloom**, **de Man** and **Hartman** – with the **Yale School** of criticism. Described by Hartman as a 'boa-deconstructor' in *Deconstruction and Criticism* (1979), to which he also contributed his perhaps singly most famous essay 'The Critic as Host', Miller is concerned, like Hartman, with the relation between criticism and literature, and in particular the apparently parasitic relation of criticism to literature, that **deconstruction**, especially, is said to entertain. Thus, in the 'The Critic as Host', Miller counters the accusation that a deconstructive reading deliberately feeds off the literary **text**, and thereby kills off its unsuspecting host, by illustrating that both terms, parasite and host, are not opposites, nor adversaries, but are etymologically linked. Insofar as the Greek *parasitos* can be shown to have originally referred to a 'fellow guest' who was invited to share the food of the host, and insofar as the term 'host' itself can be shown to have a common root with 'guest' and 'stranger' in the Latin *hospes*, Miller can conclude that 'a host is a guest, and a guest is a host', a structure reiterated in every encounter between critic and text, criticism and literature.

Miller's method of reading therefore takes the form of painstaking etymological analyses which follow up the multiple roots and unpredictable branches of a word, like 'parasite', not to search for its one true meaning, but to unfold the undecidable structure that cannot be contained in a 'single' word, nor in a single text, but is characteristic, so Miller says, of all language, literary or otherwise. In consequence, not only can no single, critical or deconstructive encounter speak the text in a univocal manner, exhaust its many voices, but rather literature, because it flaunts its own rhetoricity and figurative devices, is so resistant to restatement in a single critical voice that it becomes reciprocally parasitic upon criticism, and deconstructs itself. This is to say, literature subsumes the role of criticism, because for Miller, as for de Man, since a great literary work is likely, as he writes in 'Deconstructing the Deconstructor' (1975), to be ahead of its critics, already having anticipated any deconstruction that the critic might achieve, 'the text performs on itself the act of deconstruction without any help from the critic'.

It remains for the critic then to discover, and identify, the ways in which a text *always already* auto-deconstructs itself. This is also why a work of literature cannot be reduced to a single, definite interpretation, because, marked by ambiguity and indeterminacies, it defies any attempts of interpretive closure by a critic. This, according to Miller, is especially true of great literature. If the traditional critics, including the New Critics, defined a great work of literature according to criteria such as unity and organic form, Miller reverses these criteria to judge a work's greatness not by its unity, but by its heterogeneity and difference within. But rather than seizing on the **writerly texts** associated with **modernism** and **postmodernism**, where one might readily expect plays of difference and multiplicity, Miller turns his close readings instead, on the **readerly texts** of those, such as Hardy, Dickens or George Eliot, who are usually thought of as writers of the realist canon.

MINIMALISM The movement towards minimalism in music began in the early 1960s in America: This movement, which was pioneered by Terry **Riley**, Steve **Reich** and Philip **Glass**, soon spread to Europe where it was further developed by composers such as Michael **Nyman** and Graham **Fitkin**.

Minimalism can be seen as a reaction against the **modernist** aesthetics of the post-war avant-garde which came to be the norm within 'serious' concert music of the 1960s and 1970s. The minimalists rejected modernist music on the following grounds: (a) it was often complex for the sake of complexity and lacked an accessible surface level (thus modernist composers, in alienating their audiences, often harboured élitist attitudes, holding nothing but contempt for the average listener); (b) it maintained the division between 'high' and 'low' art and relegated the role of popular, jazz or folk musics to that of mindless entertainment; (c) the emphasis on dissonance, atonality and loss of regular pulse contradicted the fundamental axioms of music and, again, alienated audiences.

Minimalist music was, for the most part, ignored or vilified by the 'classical' music establishment who often labelled it 'banal', 'retrogressive' or 'not worthy of serious consideration'. Even today, a significant number of European university music departments do not include it in their undergraduate modules, regarding minimalist music as unworthy of serious academic study.

The genre has been diversifying and developing over the past four decades (the term postminimalism often being employed to describe more recent works), but the original features of the music were: *repetition* (often, small musical fragments, maybe only one or two bars long, would be repeated (and developed) over long periods of time); *static harmony* (a sense of stasis was achieved by remaining not just within one key or mode but often on one chord for long periods of time); *rhythmic complexity* (the simplicity of the harmony was often contrasted by complex polyrhythmic and polymetric structures); *process and impersonality* (the composers deliberately avoided self-expression and emotionalism, and maintained a detachment from the music by setting up processes which then generated the flow and structure of the music – this is most evident in the 1960s music of Steve Reich); and

cultural eclecticism (the composers, not content to draw solely on the art tradition, often made studies of jazz, rock and non-Western musics which then informed their own work).

MISE-EN-ABYME Originally a heraldic term denoting an escutcheon bearing in its centre a miniature replica of itself, *mise-en-abyme* was used by André Gide to describe the same technique in literary narratives. In contemporary criticism, it has been used since the 1950s in a more general sense to describe self-reflexivity or self-consciousness in fiction. The term first gained currency in descriptions of the *nouveau roman*, particularly in the criticism of Lucian Dällenbach and Jean Ricardou.

A good example of the technique is provided by John **Barth**'s collection *Lost in the Funhouse*, which includes a story entitled 'Lost in the Funhouse', in which the narrator, Ambrose, describes the difficulty of writing a story called 'Lost in the Funhouse', about a character called Ambrose who is lost in the funhouse. Other examples are the novels described in Nabokov's *The Real Life of Sebastian Knight*, the novels-within-novels of Flann O'Brien's *At Swim-Two-Birds* and Italo **Calvino**'s *If on a Winter's Night a Traveller*. The technique is not only to be found in twentieth-century fiction: Cervantes and Sterne contain early novelistic uses of the *mise-en-abyme*. It has become important for **postmodernism** as a way of denoting the self-reflexive nature of **representation** in general, as this is taken – accurately or otherwise – to be a central tenet of **deconstruction** and postmodern philosophy.

MODERNISM Modernism usually refers to a constellation of intellectual and, especially, artistic movements which emerged around the middle of the nineteenth century. Baudelaire provided early but clear and far-reaching formulations of the doctrines of modernism. **Marx**'s dream of the global abolition of capitalism by means of a proletarian revolution is, in a sense, a modernist vision. Modernist movements included impressionism, symbolism, cubism, futurism, art nouveau, imagism and so on. By the beginning of this century, modernist doctrines came to dominate and define the whole of the literary and artistic landscape. More specifically – if more intangibly – modernism refers to an impulse within artistic and literary circles. For modernism, one's response to the challenge of the 'modern' has become a fundamental issue. Confusions in our terminology result from the fact that modernism is a relatively late development in the history of **modernity**. By the middle of the nineteenth century, modernity had so thoroughly established itself that the sense of scandal and challenge which it once suggested has to some extent been displaced by a belief in progress and evolution. Modernism is a response to these developments which keeps alive an awareness of the conflict, upheaval, and even destruction involved in modernity and modernization. With the emergence of modernism, modernity entered a new, conflict-ridden and self-conscious phase. Modernism and **postmodernism** are intimately interrelated responses to the crises of modernity. In most of its forms, modernism has been characterized by the (often desperate) hope of solving the problems of modernity, by a heightened, more radical (more absolute, more utopian) form of the 'modern'. All too often modernism has been seduced by the vision of a 'final solution' to the problems of history, and of modernity. Postmodernism's even more final solution is to give up the hope of finality. It is thus both a strict and logical continuation of modernist thought and its thoroughgoing revision or reversal.

MODERNITY **Postmodernism** is inevitably confused in its definition by being counterpoised to a whole series of impulses and ambitions which have emerged during the last, say, five hundred years. Postmodernism, **postmodernity**, the postmodern: these are often treated as synonymous. Their 'modern-' counterparts cannot be. Historians commonly refer to the 'early modern' as that broad period in history which encompasses the rise of capitalism, science and technology. Each new expression of these forces represented a challenge to traditional and relatively settled ways of life. In addition they brought with them challenges to the traditional authority of the Christian Church and to the legitimacy of political power. Modernity in this sense is the precondition to the emergence of comparatively liberal regimes as well as to political theories of liberalism.

Equally characteristic of modernity, however, is the emergence of the modern state, and with it the more efficient, and sometimes more ruthless, exercise of political power. During the seventeenth century,

Protestant countries, such as England and The Netherlands, suffered political upheavals and religious wars, but also succeeded in capitalist and imperial expansion and put themselves in the vanguard of modernity. During the **Enlightenment**, modernity became an explicit and central theme of almost all significant thinkers. Modernity, in other words, came to consciousness of itself. It should be remembered that the Enlightenment, the great cultural project of the eighteenth century, was constantly defined in opposition to the continuities of traditional ways of life. It set itself against the arbitrary personal authority of political rulers and the Church's dogmatic (and sometimes violent) defence of superstitious and mysterious rituals. A vision opened up of nature and eventually society (and history) being brought under human control. The Enlightenment proposed one – secular and liberal – route to modernization. Another form of modernization was represented by the absolutism of the French kings, Louis XIV, XV and XVI.

By the nineteenth century, change, transformation and periodic upheaval were increasingly seen as the norm. Doctrines of progress and evolution were and are confronted by revolutionary visionaries and the theorists of crisis and convulsion. Industrial capitalism and, subsequently (and in total opposition) communism, can both be seen to represent the historical movement of modernity. Even until very recently the 'modern' (in the form of new technology, new scientific discoveries, new patterns of behaviour) has generally been the source of enormously inflated hopes.

In recent years – at least from the 1974 oil crisis – we have become much more aware of the costs and the burdens associated with modernity. Postmodernity in this sense could be characterized as the growing awareness that the 'modern' is something to which we are condemned.

MORRIS, MEAGHAN: FEMINIST AND CULTURAL CRITIC (1950–) Meaghan Morris is Australia's best-known feminist cultural critic. The focus of her writing is feminist cultural politics. She has made an enormous contribution to the ongoing international development of the postdisciplinary field of **cultural studies**, publishing work on, for example, intellectuals, **Marxism**, photography, popular cinema, the **postmodern** analysis of Jean **Baudrillard**, David Harvey, Fredric **Jameson** and Jean-François **Lyotard**, power, shopping centres and tourism.

In many ways a reluctant postmodernist, it is Morris's commitment to feminism that has led her into debates on postmodernism. Although she is critical of the reductive sweep of much postmodern analysis, she recognizes that postmodernism is the location where contemporary debates on culture and politics are now taking place. Moreover, she knows that postmodernism has changed the terrain of debate, making previous modes of cultural politics completely ineffective. Therefore, although she does not herself define her work as postmodern, it is certainly defined by others as belonging to the debate that is postmodernism.

Her principal contribution to this debate is her focus on the connection between feminism and postmodernism. She is critical of a paradoxical mode of thought which claims on the one hand that the debate on postmodernism would be unthinkable without the impact of feminist cultural politics, yet on the other that there has been little or no feminist input into this debate. She wonders if the best response is to 'adopt a complacent paranoia, and assume that the male pantheon of postmodernism is merely a twilight of the gods – the last ruse of the patriarchal university trying for power to fix the meaning and contain the damage, of its own decline'. But with less complacency, paranoid or otherwise, she wonders if women still have to ask whether men are reading their work?

MOUFFE, CHANTAL: POLITICAL PHILOSOPHER (1943–) Born in Belgium, Mouffe has since studied and taught at universities in Belgium, France, Britain and Latin America. Although she has published widely under her own name, Mouffe is best known for her collaborative work with her fellow political philosopher Ernesto **Laclau**, and as such is one of the leading voices in the **post-Marxist** movement.

Post-Marxism has become an increasingly important theoretical movement in the later decades of the twentieth century (sparked at least in part by the collapse of communism as a political force in the Western world), and encompasses both theorists who have rejected their **Marxist** past as well as those who, like Laclau and Mouffe, wish to see Marxism reformulated in terms of new cultural and theoretical developments.

On her own Mouffe has written on subjects such as the Italian Marxist theorist Antonio Gramsci, but her reputation rests mainly on *Hegemony and Socialist Strategy: Towards a Radical Democratic Politics* (1985), the book she wrote jointly with Laclau. This call for a more open Marxism in sympathetic dialogue with the various new social movements that had been springing up (especially since the 1960s), is considered to be one of the most significant works of post-Marxist theory, and has been the source of much heated debate on the left. While their detractors have claimed that the book represents a betrayal of the Marxist heritage, Laclau and Mouffe have spiritedly defended their contention that Marxism must change with the times or die.

MULTICULTURALISM Anyone living in a major European or North American city today knows what it means to be part of a multicultural society. Our food, our music, many of the words we utter, much of our literature and television all mark the irruption of non-European traditions and racial groups into the Western cultural landscape.

Multiculturalism is the celebration of this cultural **pluralism** – it welcomes a society made up of diverse racial and cultural groups. Multiculturalism opposes the view that incoming groups must adopt the host society's customs, values and beliefs to avoid conflict. It was once widely believed that society would disintegrate without a common set of values holding together the various groups – and those values would be those of the host country. Integration, it was felt, would be more difficult for those of a different racial origin and this was frequently used as a justification for racist immigration policies.

If conflict is avoided, the danger is that the strands that make up the multicultural society lose their individuality. The challenge for a truly multicultural society is to retain the uniqueness of different traditions and yet simultaneously to create a new entity in which these traditions come together.

N

NEGATIVE DIALECTICS *Negative Dialectics* (1966) was the title given by **Adorno** to his philosophical *magnum opus*. The huge ambitions of the work include both a summation and **deconstruction** of the legacy of what Adorno regards as the tradition of Western philosophy – stretching from Classical Greece up to **Hegel** and **Marx**. In particular, negative dialectics presupposes and incorporates the achievements of Hegel's dialectical philosophy. At the same time, Adorno seeks to hold Hegel's thought at a distance, and indeed, to subject it to a painstaking deconstruction. Hegel's philosophy is historical through and through. It constitutes itself through a historical recapitulation of the ideas and principles which have constituted the whole history of the world as reflected by philosophy. Hegel's thought is dialectical in that it effects a 'reconciliation' of the whole and the part, of unity and **difference**, of individual and society, of particularity and totality. Adorno affirms the need to think in these Hegelian terms because, under late capitalism, the world tends to take on the characteristics of an integrated totality. On the other hand, Adorno asserts the need for dialectics to be thoroughly 'negative' in the sense that it should be alive to the extent of (social) oppression and (individual) repression in the integration of the 'administered world'.

Negative dialectics are needed to allow thought to think the relationships which make up the totality without itself succumbing to the totalitarian tendencies within thought itself. Adorno reverses many of Hegel's dictums. Where Hegel believed only the whole to be true, Adorno (basing himself on the state of the world as he saw it) declared, 'The whole is untrue.' In restoring the critical tension to Hegelian thinking, Adorno believed he was able to represent the perspective of suffering. Hegel's philosophy depends on a logic which proposes 'the identity of identity and non-identity'. Negative dialectics seeks to remain true to the 'non-identical', or to that which is subjugated by thought.

NEO-GEO An art movement (also known as simulationism) active in New York in the 1980s, which was much influenced by the theories of **Baudrillard** and **Foucault** (although it is worth noting that the former disliked their work and the use made of his theories in it). In the work of one of the best-known figures of the movement, Peter **Halley**, neo-geo set out to demonstrate that geometry was an instrument of social control, and to draw attention to the sinister implications of the extensive use of geometric figures in modern art (see also **simulationism**).

323

NEW HISTORICISM The new historicism that emerged during the 1980s insists upon the necessity of studying literature within its historical and social contexts. Centring around the figure of Stephen **Greenblatt** and his journal *Representations*, new historicism's critical heartland is early modern culture. Prominent in new historicist accounts of Renaissance literature are Greenblatt himself, Jonathan Goldberg and Louis Montrose. New historicist strands are also to be found in romantic studies (notably in the work of J. J. McGann, Marjorie Levinson and Alan Liu) and criticism of American literature (most notably Walter Benn Michaels). A transatlantic cousin of American new historicism is the '**cultural materialism**' of British critics Jonathan **Dollimore** and Alan **Sinfield**.

New historicism repudiates new criticism's formalist tendency to address a work of art as a self-sufficient object divorced from its cultural setting. Simultaneously, new historicists argue that the American theoretical orthodoxies of the 1970s, notably **poststructuralism** and **deconstruction**, were as ahistorical in their methodologies as the critical schools – new criticism and myth criticism – which they challenged and replaced. What distinguishes the new historicism from more traditional historical criticism is its problematizing of the division between literary foreground and political background. Following **Foucault**, it foregrounds the concept that 'history' is itself **textually** mediated, and problematizes the mimetic model of previous historicist criticism which viewed a text as simply reflecting the history

around (and thus still outside) it. To use Montrose's phrase, new historicism insists upon the 'the historicity of texts and the textuality of history'.

For Greenblatt, literary works are not 'a stable set of reflections of the historical facts that lie beyond them'; they are 'places of dissension'. From this premise is developed a number of readings of Renaissance literature, many of which address issues of power. For some such writings offer a subversive riposte to the dominant structures of authority, while for others their dissident potential is contained by the power of the state. Renaissance new historicism, though it quarrels with the ahistorical aspects of **postmodernist** theory, borrows heavily from some of its techniques. Greenblatt's founding document, *Renaissance Self-Fashioning* (1980) is heavily dependent upon deconstructionist terminology ('origins', 'rupture', 'inscription' etc.). The new historicism is an attempt to fuse the supposedly dissonant tendencies of postmodern thought with literary historical enquiry. Equally important is the adaptation of critical sources hitherto neglected in historicist writing, notably the work of Foucault, **Lacanian** neo-**Freudianism**, and the anthropological theory of Clifford **Geertz**. For romantic-period new historicism, the French structural **Marxism** of Althusser and Macherey is also an important influence. However, there is no systematic theoretical methodology evident in new-historicist writing: Greenblatt has argued, against two of the major figures in postmodern thought, that the 'historical relation between art and society ... does not lend itself to a single, theoretically satisfactory answer of the kind that **Jameson** and **Lyotard** are trying to provide'. Nonetheless, one can discern certain key preoccupations within this body of writing: structures of authority, the subversion/containment debate, the tendency to use anecdotes to initiate a wider cultural narrative, the inscription of the body within discourse and the social construction of identity. And, throughout all, the devotion to Jameson's injunction: 'Always historicize!'

NIETZSCHE, FRIEDRICH: PHILOSOPHER (1844–1900) Nietzsche is undoubtedly the most important nineteenth-century thinker in relation to **postmodernism**. Among the people he has influenced by his **antifoundationalist** ideas are **Derrida**, **Baudrillard** and **Lyotard**. His aphoristic style of writing has impressed Mann, Kafka and Wittgenstein. 'God is dead', the famous assertion made in *Thus Spake Zarathustra* (1886), has passed into common currency.

The essay 'The Philosopher: Reflections on the Struggle between Art and Knowledge' (1872) outlined clearly the interests which lie behind Nietzsche's critique of the notion of truth. He shows how culture suffers if the demand for truth and certainty is allowed to override the pragmatic implications for knowledge. Lyotard's *The Postmodern Condition* (1979) echoes many of Nietzsche's conclusions. Another essay, 'On Truth and Lies in an Extra-Moral Sense' (1873), distinguishes between two kinds of truths. The first is those truths that fall under the general rubric of illusions, lies and interpretations (i.e. the various world views of metaphysics). The second is those truths that make the world habitable (i.e. scientific insights which yield practical knowledge of the environment). Both are the expression of the general will-to-truth which seeks to appropriate life according to its needs. The difference between them is that the first kind of truth flaunts its reliance upon a particular perspective, while the second seeks to deny its subjective construction. At heart, though, all truth is figurative. As Nietzsche puts it, answering Pilate: 'What, then, is truth? A mobile host of metaphors, metonymies and anthropomorphisms . . . Truths are illusions which we have forgotten are illusions.'

Nietzsche continued to undermine the foundational pretensions of truth throughout the remainder of his philosophical texts, in a manner which was to inspire **Foucault** and others. *The Gay Science* (1882) explores the idea of a science which is aware of its own presuppositions and biases of perspective. The knowledge-drive is to be assessed in terms of its cultural benefits, and not according to its correspondence to an ideal. In *The Genealogy of Morals* (1887), the will-to-truth is traced back to its roots. Behind every system of morality lurks a philosopher seeking to justify his own ethical prejudices. This is why the 'will-to-system is a lack of integrity'.

The Twilight of the Idols (1888) is a series of essays on the theme of the transvaluation of all values, where truth is to be understood as 'true for us' and not 'true to a noumenal world'.

How, though, are we to function in a world of such radical relativism? If all truth is contextual and situational, how can we make sense of the flux of experience? This is one of the most frequently voiced anxieties within postmodern thought. Nietzsche's answer is: through art. He argued that in a healthy culture, aesthetics should replace metaphysics or epistemology as the primary philosophical discipline. As he stated in *The Birth of Tragedy* (1872): 'Only as an aesthetic phenomenon can the world be justified to all eternity.' The supreme artistic discipline for Nietzsche is music, precisely because its content is inseparable from its structure. Music is a process, and is irreducible to any kind of causal account. Its 'truth' is not a product of communicative intent and emotive response, or a correlation with a hidden order of things, but a complex interaction of the personal, social and historical. Such views led Nietzsche to champion Wagner as a modern Aeschylus who could unify the German state through his mythological opera (an allegiance he later regretted).

Another area in which Nietzsche prefigures many concerns of the postmodern is that of identity. Psychology and common sense encourage us to think of the self as something solid and deep. Nietzsche, however, celebrates the surfaces of the self and compares it with a melody or leitmotif. Its end is not its goal, but nevertheless as long as '[it] has not reached its end, it also has not reached its goal', as he states gnomically in *The Wanderer and His Shadow* (1879). It is our very shallowness that is our most profound aspect. *The Genealogy of Morals* goes further

and posits that *'the doer* is merely a fiction added to the deed – the deed is everything'. In other words, we are what we do. This opens the door for a very fluid conception of the self, one which is not based on being and substance, but on the process of 'becoming' and the imposition of style. (When Nietzsche went insane towards the end of his life, he began signing his letters 'Dionysus' and 'The Crucified'. Whether this uncertainty of being was connected in some subterranean way with his earlier speculations is impossible to determine.)

NORRIS, CHRISTOPHER: CRITIC AND PHILOSOPHER (1947–) Christopher Norris's earlier writings include work on the application of **poststructuralist** theory to English literature, on **Derrida** and on music, politics and culture. More recently, his has become a noticeable, some would say strident, voice in the debates about **postmodernity** and **postmodernism**. Norris has launched a series of attacks on what he sees as the principal ideas of postmodernism, and on some of the most prominent postmodern thinkers (notably, **Baudrillard** and **Lyotard**). Three of his books – *What's Wrong With Postmodernism* (1990), *The Truth About Postmodernism* (1993) and *Uncritical Theory: Postmodernism, Intellectuals and the Gulf War* (1992) – have advanced the broad claim that postmodernism is a form of groundless relativism which has not just rejected the *rationalism* of **Enlightenment** thinking, but has in fact abandoned rational and critical thinking entirely, leaving behind in the process the Enlightenment project of emancipation. For Norris, postmodernism is essentially a form of nihilism and political quietism which can provide no basis for an emancipatory politics, and which sees the Enlightenment conception of human liberation as simply part of a broader rationalistic and ultimately totalitarian system of thought. The rejection of rational Enlightenment values takes the form primarily, says Norris, of an aestheticization of politics. It is on these grounds that he launches his attacks on Jean Baudrillard and Jean-François Lyotard.

Norris's reading of Baudrillard – most fully worked out in *What's Wrong With Postmodernism* – takes the latter's position with regard to the real – what Norris calls 'extreme referential agnosticism' – to be one which plays into the hands of the forces of global capitalism and imperialism. While he concedes that Baudrillard is 'a first-rate diagnostician of the postmodern scene', Norris claims that the fundamental mistake Baudrillard makes is to assume that because we live in an age of illusion and misinformation, it therefore no longer makes sense to speak of reference, reality and truth. For Norris, it is precisely because of Baudrillard's first claim that we must resist the second. Accordingly, much of Norris's recent work has aimed at the reclamation of a notion of truth in the face of the perceived abandonment of the concept in postmodernism.

The position Norris adopts with regard to Lyotard is equally dismissive of the latter's claim that it is no longer possible to attach credence to the **grand narratives** of **modernity**, the overarching discourses of truth, enlightenment and progress. When Lyotard proposes a state of affairs in which there are only competing '**phrase** regimens' which are not reducible to the terms of any one political or philosophical discourse (such a reduction is for Lyotard a definition of injustice), he is, according to Norris, rejecting not only the totalizing impulses of modernity, but also disallowing the possibility of radical political action on the basis of critical judgement. Lyotard's thought, then, is for Norris indistinguishable from the quietistic pragmatism of Richard **Rorty** and Stanley Fish. In opposition to the relativism and scepticism of postmodernism, Norris proposes a return to the concept of truth and a notion of rational communication close to that offered by Jürgen **Habermas**.

NYMAN, MICHAEL: CRITIC AND MUSICOLOGIST (1944–) Nyman is most famous for his film music (particularly in collaboration with Peter **Greenaway**) but, as he is always quick to point out, he is also a successful composer of concert music. He undertook a formal music education at the Royal Academy of Music and King's College London, graduating in 1964. For the following twelve years he wrote little or no music but worked as a music critic for, among other publications, *The Listener*, *The New Statesman* and *The Spectator*. As a musicologist, he worked during this period both on a PhD thesis (a study of sixteenth- and seventeenth-century English repetitive and systems music, i.e. rounds, canons and catches) and on his book *Experimental Music – Cage and Beyond* (1974). Many of these techniques studied in his thesis were inspirational to Nyman when he began composing in the late 1970s, whereas *Experimental Music – Cage and Beyond* documents the composers who have, through the influence of John Cage's work, explored alternative compositional aesthetics to the **modernist** mainstream.

It was almost by accident that Nyman took up composition when, in 1976, he was asked to arrange some eighteenth-century Venetian popular songs for a production of Goldoni's *Il Campiello* at the National Theatre. In trying to recreate the sound of a Venetian street orchestra, an ensemble, using a combination of medieval instruments (rebecs, sackbuts and shawms) and more conventional ones, was put together. The production finished but the ensemble wished to stay together and so Nyman took to composing music for them to play. Soon, however, the ensemble redirected itself away from the medieval timbres, employing instead a collection of amplified but conventional strings, wind and pianos. Nyman was then working in a similar fashion to his American counterparts **Reich** and **Glass** in that his music was repetitive and highly diatonic (in contrast to the extreme chromaticism of much twentieth-century music) and he had his own ensemble as a vehicle for his ideas. There are, however, a number of sharp contrasts between Nyman and the American **minimalists**. Unlike Reich and Glass, who drew greatly on non-Western traditions, Nyman found his inspir-

ation in earlier composers from the Western 'classical' tradition.

Music for the Greenaway film *The Draughtsman's Contract* (1982) drew heavily on the music of the English baroque composer Henry Purcell. All the pieces written for this film could be described as chaconnes. This is when the music revolves around a repeated bass line (a ground bass), often with implied harmony, while melodic material is then layered on top in the upper parts. For this project, Nyman took all his ground basses from the works of Purcell. The music for *Drowning by Numbers* (1987), another Peter Greenaway film, draws exclusively on Mozart's Sinfonia Concertante for Violin and Viola (KV364). For the music to the Jane Campion film, *The Piano* (1992), Nyman used, as his source material, nineteenth-century Scottish folk songs and popular piano pieces. The music, while maintaining a melodic lyricism and an emotional intensity, adopts also the repetition and polyrhythmic complexities of minimalist music.

Besides numerous film scores, Nyman has also written many orchestral, chamber and choral pieces for the concert hall. His style, which could be described as a kind of 'English minimalism', is often far more evocative and expressive than that of original minimalism and he has been successful in achieving a sense of tragedy in his music. He has, like Reich and Glass in America, done much to subvert the modernist dialectic of 'high' and 'low' music.

O

OEDIPUS Deleuze and **Guattari**'s term for the body of theories, processes and institutional structures by which modern psychoanalysis sets about repressing **desire** (or **desiring-machines**, as they refer to individual human beings). The Oedipus complex itself (with its source in classical myth) is only one aspect of this repressive mechanism, which attempts to force individuals into socially conformist behaviour such that they are more easily controlled by the political authorities. Psychoanalysis in this reading is an ideologically motivated activity, and Oedipus becomes symbolic of the authoritarianism (and even fascism) felt by the authors to be endemic to modern social existence.

ORIENTALISM Edward **Said**'s path-breaking work, *Orientalism* (1978), leans on **Foucault**'s discussion of knowledge/power as well as Jacques **Derrida**'s insistence that we should '**deconstruct**' certain privileged **binary oppositions**. The words for 'Orient' and 'Occident' derive simply from Latin words for sun rising (*oriens*) and sun setting (*occidens*). Orient and occident are thus by nature entirely relative to the positioning of the observer (for inhabitants of Tokyo the sun rises in the East over Hawaii). However, as Said explains, a huge and ancient historical regime has taken this necessarily mobile and relational positioning and reduced it to a fixity, specifying, for example, the 'Near', 'Middle' and 'Far East' posed in opposition to a supposedly originary point in Europe.

Placed at this imaginary centre, Europe claims to be a **subject** able to know the 'Orient', the entire non-Western world, as an object, so exercising power over it (in his epigraph to the book, Said cites **Marx**: 'They cannot represent themselves; they must be represented'). By bracketing the question of what may or may not be true about 'the Orient', Said opens for interrogation an extraordinary range of writing – 'not only scholarly works but also works of literature, political tracts, journalistic texts, travel books, religious and philological studies'.

This manoeuvre for categorizing and denigrating the Orient secures a particular notion of identity for the West: 'European culture gained in strength and identity by setting itself off against the Orient as a sort of surrogate and even underground self.' If Westerners are, as Said says, 'rational, peaceful, liberal, logical, capable of holding real values, without natural suspicion', then what he terms 'Arab-Orientals' are 'none of these things'; and of course if the Oriental is classified as none of these things this ensures that the Western subject is 'rational, peaceful, liberal', etc.

Thus the West established a good image for itself by disavowing irrational feelings which are then projected on to an Oriental **other**. But the repressed returns: for the West the Orient becomes the place of the unconscious itself – it must, as Said points out, open on to 'terrors, pleasures, desires', an other which is both seductive and terrible.

Said must risk the accusation of functionalism, for in his account orientalism works only too well, perfectly hailing subjects into fixed positions (as Western or Eastern) which they are forced to take up. Homi **Bhabha** asserts that 'there is always, in Said, the suggestion that colonial power and discourse is possessed entirely by the coloniser' and in response he looks for resistance to the power of orientalism. Bhabha draws on psychoanalysis to propose that orientalizing is a struggle always liable to fail since the colonial subject is constructed in 'a repertoire of conflictual positions'; these render him or her 'the site of both fixity and fantasy' in a process which cannot but be uneven, divided, incomplete (Bhabha details mechanisms through which orientalism always threatens to undo itself).

Said's analysis has been extended as a way to understand how any cultural, ethical or racial group may be 'known' and so dominated by a more powerful bloc. For example, his argument that no generalization (about 'races, types, colours, mentalities') remains a neutral description because it always makes an 'an evaluative interpretation' has been foundational for **multiculturalism** in the United States.

OTHER (see **alterity**).

P

PAGANISM Jean-François **Lyotard** terms the state where we make judgements without criteria as paganism. In effect, this describes the **postmodern** condition, since in that condition we no longer have any universal theories to fall back on in order to validate our criteria. Without such universal theories (whether they be theories of truth or politics) we are reduced to making judgements on a case by case basis, which for Lyotard is the only honest way to proceed. Lyotard finds a precedent for this method of making judgements in the work of Aristotle, whom he considers to be a particularly pragmatic thinker. Lyotard wishes to introduce this kind of pragmatism into our public life in a more general way, since it moves us away from an uncritical and slavish reliance on universal theories (**grand narratives**). In his reading of recent history, it has been this uncritical reliance which has been the source of most of our sociopolitical problems, in that it has sanctioned such horrors as Auschwitz, and the many inhuman things done in the name of theories such as **Marxism**, communism and socialism. A 'pagan' society would reject such authorities and examine each demand for political action on its own merits, the assumption being that this would result in a more just society than one based on rigid rules and regulations.

Judgement without preconceived criteria thus becomes one of the defining characteristics of a postmodern society.

PAGLIA, CAMILLE: CULTURAL THEORIST AND COMMENTATOR (1947–) Self-styled 'Amazon of letters', Camille Paglia's notoriety springs more from her headline-grabbing contentiousness than her intellectual achievements. She is a vocal opponent of French theoreticians such as **Lacan**, **Derrida** and **Foucault**, whom she believes to have overrun humanist disciplines with their 'rigid foreign ideology', and is also notable for her hostile relationship with mainstream feminism, whose best-known figures she insults with frequency and enthusiasm. Probably her most famous opponent in this respect is Gloria Steinem, whom she accused in an interview in *Vanity Fair* of becoming 'the Stalin of our time, addicted to the high life and choking off feminist dialogue'. According to Paglia, feminists are 'desensualized, desexualized, neurotic women, who, displacing their personal problems with sex on to society, purvey an appalling diet of cant, drivel and malarkey'. Although not always consistent on this point, she appears to consider herself as a kind of **postfeminist**, who had passed beyond the central tenets of mainstream feminism by the time she began her university education.

Paglia first came to public attention in 1990, when her monumental work *Sexual Personae: Art and Decadence from Nefertiti to Emily Dickinson* was published. Over 700 pages long, it is characteristically audacious in its ambition and eclecticism, and is an early example of Paglia's provocative talent for mingling the canonical with the popular and the sacred with the profane. Edmund Spenser, for example, is approached as an early precursor of the Marquis de Sade, with whom he shares an ability to see 'the daemonism in sex and nature'. Paglia's ultimate intention in this study is to *reclaim* the essentialist notion of the fundamental difference between men and women, arguing for the necessity of abandoning 'the pretense of sexual sameness and admit the terrible duality of gender'. In the universe according to Paglia, the female body, subject to the cycles of menstruation and gestation, is irrevocably tied to the rhythms of nature; while male physiology, symbolized by genitals which point out and away from the body, is identified with culture, which is perpetually attempting to dominate and contain natural processes.

Although, to give her her due, Paglia attempts to portray nature as a powerful, elemental force which persistently evades masculine categorization and control, the dangers of this train of thought are perfectly illustrated by the furore that has sprung up around her apparent defence of 'date rape', a theme that dominates her collection of essays published in 1994, *Sex, Art and American Culture*. Date

rape, pronounces Paglia, is the inevitable consequence of woolly liberal feminist thinking, which teaches young women that the sexes are the same, and are in possession of the same rights. She argues that such a notion is fundamentally flawed, since it ignores the way in which aggression and eroticism are ineradicably entwined in the male psyche. Women should therefore be aware of the risks they run in being alone with a man, and either be prepared to defend themselves against his inevitable advances, or submit. Although that does not absolve the rapist from punishment, it is an event for which the woman should take her fair share of the blame. Although ostensibly still portraying rape as a criminal act, Paglia has at times slipped perilously close to upholding an 'all women want it really' stance; claiming, for example, in an interview reproduced in *Sex, Art and American Culture*, that 'most women want to be seduced and lured'.

The outrageousness of such pronouncements, which often seems to originate more from an addiction to self-publicity than genuine belief or intellectual endeavour, does Paglia few favours. *Sex, Art and American Culture*, for example, is characteristic in not only containing a selection of her essays and interviews, but also an appendix which chronicles her rise to fame. As a consequence, Paglia's repudiation of mainstream feminism and theory can easily be interpreted as pique against more famous or more respected academic competitors. Moreover, her openly displayed ambition and aggressive outspokenness, as well as her public espousal of bisexuality, threatens to act as a repudiation of the very ideas she is promoting, for she certainly does not conform to the notions of 'natural' femaleness she endorses for other women. Nevertheless, beneath the inflammatory rhetoric and endless self-dramatization is work that deserves attention precisely because of its relentless interrogation of academic and ideological orthodoxies.

PARADIGM SHIFT In the work of Thomas **Kuhn**, a paradigm is a framework of thought within which scientific enquiry takes place in any given era. Thus scientists are constrained by institutional and peer pressure to conduct enquiry within the guidelines laid down by currently accepted theories and their prescribed models of practice. This is what Kuhn refers to as 'normal science'. It is in the nature of scientific experiment, however, to generate anomalies that cannot always be explained away by current theories, and when such instances become frequent enough, science finds itself in a state of crisis that can only be resolved by the creation of a new paradigm. The new paradigm is usually **incommensurable** with the old, and we then speak of a paradigm shift, or radical change in perspective. The shift from Ptolemaic to Copernican astronomy (from the earth as the centre of the universe to the sun as the centre) is presented by Kuhn as a classic instance of paradigm shift, where one can believe in one theory or the other, but not both.

Kuhn's theory can be applied outside the sciences, and the notion of cultural paradigm shifts is now widely accepted. One such shift might be from **modernity** to **postmodernity**, although it is also part of the postmodern outlook constantly to challenge the authoritarianism felt to be encoded within almost *any* paradigm. Postmodern thinkers are, as a rule, more concerned with contesting the validity of frameworks of thought in general than upholding their authority.

PENROSE, ROGER: MATHEMATICIAN AND THEORETICAL PHYSICIST (1931–) The grand, synthesizing, speculative sweep of Roger Penrose's recent philosophical works seems profoundly out of phase with sceptical, **postmodern** sensibilities. Concerned, as the title of his recent book has it, with *The Large* (big bangs and **black holes**) *the Small* (subatomic particles) *and the Human Mind* (or consciousness), Penrose's work is animated by a rejection of the idea that **quantum mechanical** paradoxes concerning theory and observation mean that we can never escape the grip of the mathematical formalism of theoretical physics to study reality itself. Rather, since quantum mechanics has also been experimentally successful, it must be taken as a realistic model of naturally occurring phenomena, despite the paradoxes they generate. In other words, there is no unbridgeable gulf between the quantum and classical worlds, they merely model different aspects of one reality; thus the mere fact that observation of quantum states generates the paradoxes it does implicates our consciousness as *part* of a quantum reality, rather than implicating our theories in simply constructing it. Rather than evangelizing quantum mechanics, Penrose is concerned with what modifications it might require to form bridges to the classical world. A modified quantum mechanics similarly underwrites Penrose's attack on **artificial intelligence**, the premature claims of which to simulate intelligence in machinic rather than biological 'hardware' are flawed by the fact that computers remain physically classical systems. It also points to what Penrose proposes as a speculative solution to the problem of consciousness: what if quantum processes were involved in brain activity, and paralleled the 'jump' between quantum and classical reality in observation? Understanding the bridge between the latter might not only provide clues to the physics of consciousness, but also perhaps point artificial intelligence in the direction of 'quantum computing'.

PHILLIPS, TOM: ARTIST (1937–) After visiting France as a small boy, Tom Phillips returned with some old bones. This presaged his interest in death and dissolution, themes permeating his output as a painter, printmaker, composer and film maker. 'Benches', for instance, is a series of 'treated' postcards which feature the ordinary park bench as an emblem of mortality. The images were collected haphazardly – chance is another of his obsessions. In the mid-1960s, he read an interview with William Burroughs about the 'cut-up' technique, whereby words are plucked from a text, shuffled together, and placed in unusual juxtapositions. Enthused, Phillips searched for some randomly chosen source material, and decided that 'the first (coherent) book that I

could find for threepence . . . would serve'. This is how W. H. Mallock's *A Human Document* (1892), a neglected three-decker novel, became his bible. Phillips began painting over the text, isolating certain phrases to extract unusual meanings, and published a completed version of this project as *A Humument* in 1980. The musical opera *Irma* was also composed using this method, and released on Brian **Eno**'s Obscure Records label in 1975. Irma is the robust heroine of Mallock's book, but in the hands of Phillips becomes a shadowy, blurry figure – a **postmodern** equivalent to Wordsworth's Lucy. She is the platonic love-object for Bill Toge, a character who crops up whenever the words 'together' or 'altogether' appear in Mallock's text. *Irma* and *A Humument* deserve to be far better known than the rather ponderous *A TV Dante*, which Phillips co-directed with Peter **Greenaway** in 1990.

PHRASE In Jean-François **Lyotard**, the phrase constitutes the basic element of discourse, and it is to be considered 'open', since it can link to other phrases, thus creating new states of affairs. The term can also be translated as 'sentence', and is a cornerstone of **postmodern** thought in that it is always open to the future and the unexpected. Phrases ensure that discourse remains a process of discovery rather than the mere working out of some predetermined plan, as, for instance, most **grand narratives** would have it. It is the business of philosophers in particular to foster the act of linkage.

PLANT, SADIE: AUTHOR AND FEMINIST
(1964–) An academic who is currently a Research Fellow at the Cybernetic Culture Research Unit at the University of Warwick (UK), Sadie Plant is a proponent of 'cybernetic feminism', which she defines as 'an insurrection on the part of the goods and materials of the patriarchal emergence composed of links between women, women and computers, computers and communications links, connections and connectionist nets'. As this quotation indicates, Plant challenges the notion that technology is antithetical to female concerns. On the contrary, she argues that technological progress and women's liberation have always advanced in tandem, and that in the late twentieth century we have arrived at a situation where an alliance between women and machines is threatening the entire history of patriarchal dominance.

In recent publications such as *Zeroes and Ones: Digital Women and the New Technologies* (1997), Plant traces this association on two levels. One aspect of her concern is sociological, and in a process that is comparable to Elaine Showalter's search for a hidden tradition of female authorship (see **gynocriticism**), she uncovers a forgotten history of female involvement with the advance of information technology. Figures who are central to this project are Ada Lovelace, who assisted Charles Babbage in the development of the world's first programmable machine, the Analytical Engine, in the 1840s, and Captain Grace Murray Hopper, who was the chief programmer of the Analytical Engine's successor,

Mark 1, developed by the United States during the Second World War.

On a more theoretical level, however, Plant sees a more profound connection between women and technology. The Analytical Engine was programmed by a series of punched cards, which was a process taken from the operation of the mechanized Jacquard loom, and Plant makes much of the fact that weaving is a traditionally female art. She persistently returns to, and dramatically reverses, the **Freudian** argument that the activity of weaving stands in a metonymic relationship to the criss-crossing of pubic hair which conceals women's genital 'lack'. In her scenario, which itself weaves together Freudian and feminist theory, history and science-fiction, the computers created to serve patriarchal interests have now far exceeded man's control. Information systems like the **Internet**, which are dispersed and non-hierarchical, cannot be contained by an authority imposed from above. According to Plant, therefore, **cyberspace** is not a disembodied space, but one that is closely identified with the female body and female forms. What Freud saw as a hole, a vacancy that must be decently concealed, Plant reads as a zero, which is the very basis of binary machine code.

PLURALISM It has become all but an article of faith in **postmodernism** to argue against absolute notions of truth or authority, and to encourage plural interpretations of **texts** and situations instead. Thus for Jean-François **Lyotard** there is no overriding **grand narrative** (or universal explanatory theory) in the political domain any more, but rather a plurality of little narratives seeking to achieve limited objectives. Roland **Barthes** argues in *S/Z* that texts are to be seen no longer as having central meanings that critics should be striving to reveal, but instead as sources of plural interpretations. **Poststructuralism** in general has encouraged that view. The idea that there can be any unquestionable central authority (whether in the political or intellectual domain) has been vigorously resisted by poststructuralists and postmodernists alike. Even truth is seen as plural, that is, not reducible to one central meaning that excludes all others, but as relative to the interpreter and situation at hand. **Nietzsche** provides much of the inspiration for this view in his insistence that truth is simply an army of metaphors, available to be wielded on behalf of a specific cause. For poststructuralists and postmodernists there is no one privileged interpretation of any situation, but rather a plurality of possible interpretations.

POLYSEMY Polysemy initially referred to a single word with two or more meanings, e.g. 'pen' which, according to context, can mean either 'a writing instrument' or 'a small enclosure for domestic animals'. More recently, literary theorists have extended the term to include larger units of sense, such as an entire fictional work. The classic demonstration of this is *S/Z* (1975) by the **poststructuralist** Roland **Barthes**. In this study, Barthes dissects the text of Balzac's short story 'Sarrasine' into 512 fragments, or lexias. He then shows how five arbitrary codes (hermeneutic,

proairetic, semic, cultural and symbolic) multiply meaning in each fragment.

POSTCOLONIALISM 'Colonialism' is the conquest and direct control of another people's land, a phase in the history of imperialism, which in turn is the globalization of the capitalist mode of production from the sixteenth century onwards. In the context of cultural production, 'postcolonialism' is 'writing after empire', the analysis of both colonial discourse and the writings of the ex-colonized. In relation to British imperialism, this work would have once been called 'Commonwealth literature', but the field has been transformed by the use of a variety of **postmodern** theories concerning language, gender, subjectivity and race. The proliferation of full-length studies, readers and conferences on the subject testifies to its importance over a range of cultural studies. The two most important dates in postcolonial studies are 1947, which marks the beginning of a massive decolonization of the British Empire, and 1978, when the founding text of postcolonial studies was published: Edward **Said**'s *Orientalism*. Drawing upon the work of **Foucault** and others, Said examines the representation of the Orient in Western discourse and finds there 'Europe's deepest and most recurring image of the **Other** . . . a Western style for dominating, restructuring and having authority over the Orient'. Though much criticized, this book gave an impetus to the study of the culture of post-independent states, from Africa and the Caribbean to South and South-East Asia. It ushered in a period in which the literature of colonial struggle and nationalism, most importantly the writings of Frantz Fanon, was reread from various postmodernist perspectives. More recently, 'post-colonial' has come to mean something other than 'post-independent', and includes writing that resists colonialism in all its forms. This allows postcolonial critics to examine the work of influential anti-colonialists such as Fanon and the huge body of culture affected by the imperial process from the moment of colonization to the present day.

POST-FEMINISM Post-feminism has appeared as a result of contemporary manoeuvres to discredit feminism as passé and bad. The post-feminist contention is that the dangers and damage of feminism 'prove' women are wrong to seek equality with men in a man's world. In particular, the mass media both pronounces the official equality of women and catalogues the ills that this equality brings. Post-feminist doctrine in the media encourages women to blame feminism for their exhaustion and disillusionment with equality. For instance, women's magazines make post-feminist assertions such as the following: feminism spoiled women's right to be sexually attractive, to flirt, to enjoy domestic bliss; it damaged the family, leaving young children to grow up without correct moral standards; it resulted in violence against women and by women. However, acceptance of such messages reveals the public's failure to recognize a political structure that profits, literally, from the inequalities it promotes.

Post-feminism may claim to promote 'the new', e.g. the new femininity or the new monogamy. But the reality is the opposite. It claims that feminism as anti-family stance has destroyed what most people see as the essential foundation of a healthy and just society, while supporting a return to traditional values. Portraying feminism as the disease of 'the terminally single woman', and women's liberation as the source of an endless catalogue of contemporary personal, social and economic evils, post-feminism creates a backlash. It defends men against blame for the oppression of women, and so produces reversals of freedom and justice: the movement for women's liberation is made to appear tyrannical and unrepresentative of the demands of women. If there is any lesson to be learnt from post-feminism, it is that the openness and celebration of **postmodern** relativism can be co-opted into its opposite: an uncritical and absolutist stance.

POSTHUMANISM One of the implications of **postmodern** thought is that we are now deemed to live in a posthumanist age as well. Humanism is identified with the discredited **Enlightenment project**, and in particular with its concentration on the cultural importance of the individual. The individual **subject** was held to be a being with a unique essence, whose goal was self-realization. It was regarded as one of the primary objectives of culture to provide the basis for such self-realization, by guaranteeing the freedom of the individual through the establishment of appropriate institutional structures (governmental, legal, educational, etc.). Various French theorists such as Claude **Lévi-Strauss**, Roland **Barthes** and Michel **Foucault** have argued against this conception of the subject, and can be seen to contribute in their own particular way to the dismantling of the humanist ideal. The **structuralist Marxist** philosopher Louis Althusser gave a particular boost to the development of a posthumanist consciousness by openly declaring himself to be an anti-humanist – that is, to be in opposition to the Enlightenment vision of mankind as the centre of the universe.

More recent **poststructuralist** and postmodernist thinkers such as **Lyotard**, **Deleuze** and **Guattari** have also consciously distanced themselves from the humanist tradition of thought, which they see as an integral component of **modernity**; as do **difference feminists**, for whom humanism is part of the patriarchal ideology they are actively seeking to shake off.

POST-INDUSTRIALISM A post-industrial society relies on service industries, knowledge-production, and information technology to create wealth, rather than, as in most Western societies from the time of the Industrial Revolution onwards, heavy industrial manufacture. Post-industrialism can be identified with the **postmodern**, in much the same way that industrialism, with its commitment to exploitation of the environment in the name of social progress, can with **modernism**. A concern with knowledge-production is in fact now seen as one of the hallmarks of a postmodern society. One of the great proponents of the

notion of post-industrialism is the American sociologist Daniel **Bell**, whose highly influential study *The Coming of Post-Industrial Society* (1973) outlined the likely characteristics involved. Bell envisaged a society where there was a dramatic shift away from manufacturing to services; science-based industries took on a central role; and new élites based on services and science-based industries arose, thus altering the balance of power in that society. Most of the advanced economies in the West can now be described as post-industrial in some sense, in that they have moved significantly towards a position where services, knowledge and information have become the most valuable commodities for trading purposes.

POST-MARXISM The term 'post-Marxist' can be applied in two specific ways: to those who have rejected **Marxist** beliefs, and to those who have attempted to open up Marxism to more recent theoretical developments such as **poststructuralism**, **postmodernism**, feminism and the various new social movements (such as the **Greens**) that have risen to prominence in the latter decades of the twentieth century. In the terminology of Ernesto **Laclau** and Chantal **Mouffe**, arguably the leading theorists of post-Marxism, this would equate to being either *post*-Marxist or post-*Marxist*. In both its main senses, post-Marxism has become an increasingly important theoretical position in the later twentieth century, with such key events as the 1968 *événements* and the collapse of the Soviet bloc in the 1980s serving as catalysts for its development. A whole generation of French intellectuals, including such high-profile figures as Jean-François **Lyotard**, Gilles **Deleuze** and Michel **Foucault**, took a post-Marxist turn in the aftermath of the former event, and proceeded to argue vigorously against what had hitherto been one of the major paradigms of post-war French thought. Lyotard, in *Libidinal Economy* (1974) unleashed a vicious attack on Marxist doctrine, which in many ways sounded the death-knell of the theory as a major factor in French intellectual life. Deleuze and **Guattari**'s *Anti-Oedipus* (1972) also represented a highly symbolic move away from uncritical acceptance of Marxist doctrine in the period. Laclau and Mouffe's *Hegemony and Socialist Strategy* (1985), with its call for a new kind of politics structured around the objectives of the new social movements, as well as rejection of many key Marxist principles as outmoded, created considerable controversy in Marxist circles when it was published. The Marxist establishment has tended to argue that to incorporate ideas from other sources is to compromise the integrity and authority of Marxism itself.

POSTMODERN SCIENCE In Jean-François **Lyotard**'s terms of reference, **postmodern** science is that form of science which seeks to discover the unknown rather the known, and is less interested in solving problems than revealing uncharted territories. Prime examples of this kind of scientific practice would be **catastrophe theory** (which Lyotard relies on heavily in his most famous work *The Postmodern Condition* (1979)), **chaos theory** and **complexity theory**. Such theories feature a host of mysterious entities (strange attractors, dark matter, **black holes**, etc.) that seem to defy any possibility of rational explanation, although of course we cannot prove that they will always do so.

POSTMODERNISM Postmodernism is a wide-ranging cultural movement which adopts a sceptical attitude to many of the principles and assumptions that have underpinned Western thought and social life for the last few centuries. These assumptions, which constitute the core of what we call **modernism**, include a belief in the inevitability of progress in all areas of human endeavour, and in the power of reason, as well as a commitment to originality in both thought and artistic expression. As a cultural ethos, modernism is uncompromisingly forward-looking and, at least implicitly, makes the assumption that present civilization is to be considered superior to past in the extent of its knowledge and the sophistication of its techniques. As an aesthetic, modernism promotes the view that originality is the highest state of artistic endeavour, and that this can best be achieved by experimentation with form. Postmodernism has turned such ideas on their head, by calling into question modernism's commitment to progress, as well as the ideology underpinning it, and encouraging a dialogue between past and present in thought and the arts. Postmodernism has therefore involved a rejection of the modernist commitment to experiment and originality, and a return to the use of older styles and artistic methods – even if this is done in an **ironic** manner. The characteristic postmodernist style is pastiche, with **authors** returning to a realist style of novel-writing, artists moving away from abstraction and back to figurative painting, and architects freely mixing old and new styles in building. Charles **Jencks** has spoken of the latter practice as '**double coding**', and regards it as a way of overcoming the alienating effect of much modern architecture, which was geared towards professionals rather than the public. Jean-François **Lyotard** has encouraged us to see postmodernism as a rejection of all-encompassing cultural theories (such as **Marxism**), and has argued for a much more pragmatic attitude to political life and artistic expression that simply ignores the oppressive rules laid down by **grand narrative**. Postmodernism is therefore as much an attitude of mind as a specific theoretical position in its own right. In general, postmodernism can be regarded as part of a longer-running philosophical tradition of scepticism, which is intrinsically anti-authoritarian in outlook and negative in tone: more concerned with undermining the pretensions of other theories than putting anything positive in their place. Lyotard himself sees postmodernism and modernism as cyclical movements which alternate throughout the course of history.

POSTMODERNITY Postmodernity describes the cultural situation we are now assumed to inhabit, in the wake of **modernity**'s collapse as a cultural ethos. Modernity represented a culmination of several trends in Western culture, including the belief in economic and social improvement and, in a general sense, the inevitability of progress in human affairs (each generation having greater knowledge and technological sophistication than its predecessor). A commitment to progress was built into the politics of modernity, whether this took a capitalist or socialist form, the assumption being that the quality of life could indefinitely be improved, and that science and technology could be utilized to guarantee this. There was in effect an ideology (or **grand narrative**) of progress accepted by most nations, including those in the impoverished Third World. Postmodernity, on the other hand, is the state where scepticism is expressed about notions like the inevitable march of progress, or the necessity to continue exploiting the environment around us irrespective of the long-term effect (from that point of view the **Green Movement** can be seen as a postmodernist phenomenon). It is one of the characteristics of postmodernity that there is a decline in belief in universal theories, and a greater commitment to pragmatism in political affairs. This is accompanied by a generalized suspicion of authority and its grand narratives, and a concern to encourage diversity and cultural **difference**. Against that, it could be argued that grand narratives are still very much with us in the postmodern world in the form of religious fundamentalism. How long postmodernity will last is an open question: as far as theorists like Jean-François **Lyotard** are concerned, the modern and the postmodern alternate over time, in which case our current phase of postmodernity may be no more than a temporary respite before another outbreak of modernity.

POST-PHILOSOPHY Reflection upon the future direction of philosophy has been a fundamental of philosophical discourse since the time of Socrates. But an unusually menacing aura accompanied the repeated announcements of the end of philosophy from **Nietzsche** to **Heidegger** and **Lyotard**, ultimately rendering problematic the very possibility of **postmodern** philosophical discourse. At the least, post-philosophy means after philosophy conceived according to the ideals of autonomous rationality, historical progress and metaphysical truth. Post-philosophy designates the postmodern situation in which these **Enlightenment** ideals have come under criticism. But different responses can be given to this situation. The post-philosopher queries: Has philosophy come to an end or a transformation? The alternative answers offer both strong and weak versions of what comes after philosophy.

Those who seek to transform philosophy admit that an autonomous, fully transparent subject of rationality is no longer beyond critique, that the hoped-for progress of history under the guidance of Enlightenment philosophy has resulted in its own failure, and that a grand truth as the outcome of metaphysical reflection is wisely replaced with the 'local' character of truth. Yet these same metaphysical ideals were already being questioned by Enlightenment philosophers such as **Kant**. For this reason, Kant's critiques offer a useful framework for many in the post-philosophy debates.

Those who make the stronger claim to a decisive end of philosophy find support in a radical critique of the necessity that characterizes Kantian reason. These post-philosophers insist upon the contingency of the rules, criteria, and results of what counts as rational thought and action at any given time and place. They give priority to the empirical and fallible over the a priori and certain, to heterogeneity over unity, to the fragmentary over the total and to the irreducible **plurality** of **incommensurable** language games over the universality of philosophical discourse.

POSTSTRUCTURALISM Poststructuralism is a generic term used to refer to all those theories that came to reject the principles of **structuralism**, which, from the 1950s through to the 1970s constituted the major paradigm of French intellectual enquiry. Among the theories that came to challenge the stranglehold of the structuralist paradigm were **deconstruction**, feminism and **postmodernism**, all of which can be considered as poststructuralist in that they challenged the assumptions on which structuralism was based. Structuralists had held that underlying all phenomena were deep structures that dictated how those phenomena developed (we might think of deep structure as being something in the nature of a genetic programme), and that the world was organized into a series of interlocking systems, each with its own 'grammar' of operation. All systems were amenable to structuralist analysis, given that their grammars were seen to operate in similar ways, and structuralism became an exercise in classification whose goal was the comprehensive mapping of all systems. In principle at least, the world was completely knowable through the analysis of its systems and their grammars.

For poststructuralists this was at once too neat and also oppressive, since it seemed to allow little room for either human agency – individuals being assumed to be mere channels through which deep structure operated – or the workings of chance (an increasingly important factor in scientific enquiry in the later twentieth century). Against this essentially orderly picture of the world, deconstructionists offered a far more anarchic alternative, where **difference** rather than similarity was the defining characteristic, and where there were assumed to be many gaps and paradoxes in the workings of systems, which were not as predictable as structuralists would have had us believe. Jacques **Derrida** spoke of the 'innocence of becoming' rather than the predetermined working out of deep structural patterns, meaning that the future was always to be considered open and unknown. From a deconstructionist perspective structuralism was to be considered authoritarian, since the theory prescribed exactly how systems had to operate. Postmodernists, too, have reacted against the rigidity and apparent authoritarianism of the structuralist model, and have expressed similar sentiments to the deconstructionists – that is, a commitment to the open-endedness of cultural processes, and to the notion of the 'innocence of becoming'. Once again the thrust of the argument is against theories

that claim to offer universal explanations of phenomena, and this dislike of totalizing theory has been a constant feature of the poststructuralist outlook.

PRESENCE Jacques **Derrida** argues that Western thought in general is based on the notion of presence: that is, that the full meaning of words (or concepts) is 'present' to us in our minds when we think them, and that there is no 'slippage' between word and meaning. For Derrida, this is a metaphysical assumption that we are unjustified in making (see also **metaphysics of presence**).

PRINCE, THE ARTIST FORMERLY KNOWN AS: POP MUSICIAN (1958–) Born in Minneapolis, Minnesota, Prince Rogers Nelson has emerged as one of the most prolific and famous musicians of his generation. Coy and private offstage, he has a reputation for being one of the legendary versatile yet controversial performers of all time. The politics of pleasure that surround him can be directly linked to a range of debates surrounding **postmodernism**. Of particular significance is the nature of his address: the binary divides that are central to social constructs of gender, sexuality and identity are fractured through his blurring of essentialist assumptions of social organization. In songs such as 'If I was Your Girlfriend' from *Sign O' The Times* (1987), Prince blatantly privileges the feminine over the masculine by teasing out the complexities of homophobia, misogyny and gynophobia. Ultimately, it is the reinvention of himself across gender, racial and sexual lines that has inflamed the most controversy. Substituting his name for an unpronounceable emblem (depicting the unity of the male and female gender symbols) is the most potent statement regarding his identity. This symbol serves to reconstruct his persona by substituting it for a written word, which thus functions to evaporate the rigid constraints of dominant culture. His music, like his personality, is multilayered, stylistically fragmented and complex; it is the **polysemic** quality of his **texts** and personality that afford him a central role in late-twentieth-century contemporary culture.

PYNCHON, THOMAS: NOVELIST (1937–) Thomas Ruggles Pynchon was born in Glen Cove, New York. He studied Physics and then English at Cornell University, Ithaca, between 1953 and 1955, and then served in the United States Navy in the 1950s as part of the Signals Corps. He also worked as an editorial writer for Boeing Aircraft in Seattle between 1960 and 1962. Little more is known about his private life or public activities. Since his early short stories – collected in *Slow Learner* (1984) – were published in the early 1960s, he has seldom given interviews or attended book-signing sessions. This reclusiveness became his most saleable asset when his later novels *Vineland* (1990) and *Mason and Dixon* (1997) were promoted.

The reputation created by his previous three novels: *V.* (1963), *The Crying of Lot 49* (1966) and *Gravity's Rainbow* (1973) fuelled further media interest. These works are based on complex metaphors which, instead of acting as anchors of sense, scatter meaning across a wide terrain. Exhaustive in scope, they include references to electronics, the history of the US postal system, information theory, ballistics, the second law of thermodynamics and many other weighty topics. Despite this encyclopaedism, Pynchon mocks the urge to construct a **grand narrative** out of these disparate materials.

In *V.,* for instance, Herbert Stencil looks back into moments of European history for evidence of a mercurial woman, possibly his mother, whose nickname, 'V', is the only clue to her identity. But as his search proceeds, the dark lady recedes. These episodes betray Stencil's Rorschach-like projection of meaning into random data and his pulsating paranoia. 'V' becomes a 'remarkably scattered concept', encompassing the jazz club The V-Note, the Via dei Vecchietti, and the sewers where the rat Veronica lives. Then there are the various incarnations of V herself: the Lady V. of Paris, Veronica Mangonese in Malta, Vera Meroving in South-West Africa, and others.

Gravity's Rainbow (1973) is sometimes called the postmodern *Ulysses*, and with good reason. It follows a similar pattern of quest and excess. Tyrone Slothrop, an American lieutenant in Europe after VE Day, is programmed by behaviourist Ned Pointsman to find the advanced V-2 rockets launched by the Germans towards the end of the Second World War. He travels around the Zone (a demilitarized space in Central Europe swarming with bootleggers and conmen and migrants) to seek out a crack group of African rocketeers, called the Schwarzkommando.

However, the rocket is elusive, and allusive too. Throughout the book, it accrues more and more symbolic resonances. It is compared to Zeno's arrow, the arrow of a Zen archer, Time's arrow, and the hour hand of a clock. Some of these resemblances are sharp and pertinent considered in isolation, yet their agglomerative effect is to remove the rocket even further from Slothrop's grasp. Like the letter V, the rocket has to be many things – too many things. Slothrop eventually crumbles under the weight of this information overload. He forgoes his search in favour of the 'mindless pleasures' (the novel's working title) of sex and drugs.

Q

QUANTUM MECHANICS Quantum mechanics grew out of increasing anomalies generated by classical physics and Einstein's modifications of it. Composed of the three spatial dimensions plus one of time, the world of classical physics is the one of large-scale, observable structures and events that we live in. Ironically, Niels Bohr, one of the originators of quantum physics, did not intend to demonstrate the physical limits of classical laws at the scale of sub-atomic particles, but to patch up the fraying fabric of classical reality. Having entered this quantum world, however, Bohr and others have found that it cannot even be comprehended within a classical frame. Thus, a key problem in quantum mechanics, famously described by Heisenberg's uncertainty principle, has it that since all our measurements are macroscopic and classical rather than microscopic and quantum, how can events at the subatomic level be measured by macroscopic means? If we take one classical parameter – position – and measure a subatomic particle accordingly, we not only sacrifice measurement of similarly classical parameters, such as velocity, but actually alter the behaviour of those particles. If we do not measure particles in this way, however, quantum events become undecidable catalogues of classically incompatible possibilities: quantum cats, for example, classically either alive or dead, become superpositions of live cats and dead cats. When an observer physically intervenes, the cat reverts to one or the other classical state, but at the same time, all information about its quantum states is instantaneously dispersed.

QUEER THEORY In the early 1990s, there were a number of articles, conferences and special issues of journals that dealt with lesbian and gay culture by embracing the stigmatized term 'queer'. This was both to remind the reader of homophobic prejudice and to suggest a form of criticism that uses a pejorative signifier of transgressive **desire** and sexual instability as a metaphor to describe a category that goes beyond categories. Heavily marked by **deconstruction**, queer readings use a variety of **postmodern** theories 'to destabilize the entire system of sex regulation, that undoes **binary oppositions** such as gay/straight', as Judith **Butler** has argued. Identity, rather than being the essence of our being, is a '**simulation**', a contingent, provisional performance. Queer theory produces a disturbing, profoundly philosophical kind of criticism that argues not for alternative forms of identity, but for identity's confounding. For Butler and other influential theorists of queer reading such as Eve Kosofsky Sedgwick and D. A. Miller, identity, and in particular sexual identity, is non-essentialist and formed in a material reality that is mediated through discourse. Some critics have argued that this formidable body of criticism plays down sexual **difference** and that its sceptical stance forbids it producing any useful or emancipatory knowledge.

R

RADICAL DEMOCRACY The **post-Marxist** theorists Ernesto **Laclau** and Chantal **Mouffe**'s term for the new left-wing politics they wish to see replace classical **Marxism**. In their highly influential study *Hegemony and Socialist Strategy: Towards a Radical Democratic Politics* (1985), Laclau and Mouffe set out to revise Marxism to take account of the rise of various new social protest movements around the globe (the **Green Movement**, ethnic and sexual minorities, for example). Their ultimate goal is a **pluralist** Marxism informed by recent developments in **postmodernist, poststructuralist** and feminist theory, which will provide a platform for those social protest movements: a new 'articulation' of interests that will bypass the dogmatism associated with classical Marxism as both political theory and practice.

RADICAL PHILOSOPHY Radical philosophy is associated with the journal of the same name, which was founded in the early 1970s with the objective of making **continental philosophy** more accessible to a British philosophical audience. At that time figures like **Hegel**, **Heidegger** and **Marx** were little studied in British philosophical departments, and indeed, often viewed as being of little lasting interest in philosophical terms of reference. *Radical Philosophy* has since pioneered debate about phenomenology, **post-structuralism, postmodernism** and continental feminism in Britain, and has remained a force for continued debate concerning such discourses, which now feature more widely on British academic curricula.

READERLY TEXTS Roland **Barthes** in his later, **poststructuralist**, phase (roughly from the publication of *S/Z* in 1970 onwards) distinguished between readerly and **writerly texts**. The former were taken to impose a meaning on the reader, whereas the latter invited the reader to engage in the production of textual meaning. Barthes argued in *S/Z* that readerly texts encouraged passive consumption, being designed to constrain the exercise of the reader's imagination. In such cases the **author** was exerting power over the reader, and readerly texts therefore played a part in maintaining the cultural status quo. It is difficult to be precise as to what constitutes a readerly text, but nineteenth-century realist novels, with their carefully worked-out plots, omniscient narrators and overt moral purpose, are probably good candidates. In these cases, as Barthes sees it, the reader is forced to respond in a predetermined way and to accept the author's world view as expressed through the narrative. Reading becomes passive consumption, but passive consumption in the service of a particular socio-political structure. To argue in favour

347

of writerly texts (where the reader is assumed to be actively involved in the production of textual meaning) is therefore to take a stance against the prevailing political and intellectual order.

REED, ISHMAEL: NOVELIST, POET, PLAYWRIGHT AND EDITOR (1938–) From the mid-1960s when he began to publish his work, Reed has developed his own style and critical terminology. It was left to others to label it **postmodernism**. His own aesthetic principles, which he calls 'neo-HooDoo', derive from Egyptian myth and Voodoo religious symbolism found in Caribbean and African folklore. These are 'syncretic', taking from other religions what they need, as Reed's fiction does. His novels, from the first, *The Freelance Pallbearers* (1967) to *Japanese By Spring* (1993), are **intertextual** carnivals, hybrid fictions that draw on an enormous range of discourses. As a character in *Yellow Back Radio Broke-Down* (1970) remarks, 'no one says a novel has to be one thing'.

A good example of Reed's approach is *Mumbo Jumbo* (1972). Here we find footnotes, cartoons, photographs, illustrations and a bibliography. Reed, always a disputatious writer, often uses his fiction to settle scores with his critics. He has an implacable hatred of white supremacism, but also both black nationalism for its largely essentialist notions of blackness and its prescriptive aesthetic principles, and feminism for its collusion with white racists in denigrating black men. Very schematically, the black narrative tradition has two major modes: at one pole would be testamentary and confessional writing from slave narratives to tales of self-discovery, while at the

other would be the parodic and 'signifying' tradition represented by the likes of Ralph Ellison, Clarence Major and, most exuberantly but unevenly, by Reed himself.

REICH, STEVE: COMPOSER (1936–) A pioneer of **minimalist** music, Reich's musical language owes a lot to non-Western musics (such as West African drumming and Balinese gamelan), medieval music, jazz and to earlier twentieth-century styles. He came from a musical family, and his early musical training included piano lessons and studying Western percussion and drumming. While studying philosophy at Cornell University (1953–7) he enrolled in a number of music classes and supported himself by playing drums in local dance bands. He then studied composition at the Juilliard School in New York (1958–61) and at Mills College, California (1961–63) with Darius Milhaud and Luciano Berio.

Following his formal education in composition he was quick to reject the **modernist** aesthetics and techniques such as serialism and atonality, which had come to dominate the art tradition of music in the twentieth century. He felt that the so-called avant-garde composers had not only lost touch with the essential ingredients of music (e.g. pulse, rhythm and tonal direction) but had alienated their audiences with music which was mathematical, over-intellectual and preoccupied with structure. His early works (1963–71), being concerned with process, repetition and gradual changes, utilized the technique of 'gradual phase shifting'. This was achieved by playing two identical tape loops on tape recorders, one machine playing fractionally faster than the other, so that they were gradually shifted out of phase with one another. This process was later realized using live musicians.

Reich, who had had a growing interest in traditional African music since the early 1960s, travelled to Ghana in the summer of 1970 to study with a master drummer of the Ewe tribe. He later studied gamelan (in 1973) with a Balinese musician-in-residence at the University of Washington in Seattle. His compositions of the 1970s and 1980s show a marked influence from these two non-Western genres in that the music was complex in its rhythmic aspects but remained, harmonically, relatively simple. Compositions such as *Six Pianos* (1973) and *Music for Eighteen Musicians* (1976), both being written for his own ensemble (formed in 1966), exhibit an intensity and complexity of rhythm coupled with harmony which remains static for long periods. Counterpoint – the technique of layering and intertwining a number of independent melodic lines – was also emerging, in this period, as one of his fundamental techniques. *Different Trains* (1987), *The Cave* (1993) and *City Life* (1995) contain a strong narrative drive and make use of speech samples to generate the fabric of the music. This contrasts sharply with his earlier works which abstained from the dialectics of narratives or self-expression.

Reich's music has, until quite recently, been ignored by academia and, for the most part, been rejected by the modernist music establishment. During the 1960s and 1970s his music, which was almost entirely written for his own ensemble, was often per-formed (away from the established concert halls) in galleries and lofts attracting an audience who might have been more at home in a theatre, art gallery or rock concert than at a 'classical' recital. Reich is, however, one of the most influential composers of the late twentieth century and has not only inspired, but also paved the way for a host of younger composers such as John **Adams**, Michael **Nyman** and Graham **Fitkin**.

REPRESENTATION   **Postmodern** theories of representation take many forms. In painting, for instance, the 1970s and 1980s are said to have witnessed the reintroduction of representation accompanied by **irony**, illusion and disbelief, where content rather than form was deemed to be of central importance. These are ideas primarily associated with American theorists of painting, such as Donald Kuspit and Lawrence Alloway. In continental Europe, however, representation is figured in very different terms by philosophers of the **poststructuralist** school, with **Lyotard** and **Derrida**, for example, pointing to the impossibility of representing reality. In their denial of 'reality' as such, works such as Lyotard's *The Postmodern Condition* (1979) and *The Differend* (1983) emphasize that the 'unpresentable' (or the **sublime**) exists. Attempts to represent the unpresentable are considered to be the defining characteristic of the avant-garde artist.

Following Derrida, **deconstructionists** concentrate on the slippery and ambivalent nature of language, and are similarly negative about the possibility of representing reality. Deconstructionist analyses of representation are **antifoundationalist** in intent, and attack the idea that the Western philosophical tradition provides a transcendental set of beliefs which are 'truthful'. **Foucault**, on the other hand, draws attention to the pervasiveness of power inside representation, particularly as it relates to institutions, and the manner in which certain representations of power are favoured at the expense of others. Consequently, a Foucauldian analysis of representation engages in a more direct fashion with questions of gender, race and class. Postmodern theorists on the left – **Baudrillard** and **Jameson** for example – argue that representation in the arts has been made impossible by the cultural **hegemony** of capitalism.

RETRO As part of its campaign against **modernism** and **modernity**, and their cult of the new and original, **postmodernism** has encouraged dialogue with the past. Perhaps most famously, this change of attitude towards the past can be found in Charles **Jencks'** notion of **double coding**, where a deliberate attempt is made to appeal to both specialists and the general public by mixing together old and new architectural styles in one building. Such reappropriation and recontextualization of older forms and styles, often referred to as retro, has become a hallmark of the postmodern aesthetic and features prominently in areas such as art, music and fashion. Thus in pop music we have the phenomenon of retro-rock, so called, where bands deliberately imitate the style of earlier bands from the 1960s and 1970s (as in the case of Oasis with the Beatles, and the return to favour in

the 1990s of guitar-based groups). In keeping with the postmodern ethos, retro often involves an ironic attitude towards the earlier style, and is not a simple act of homage or mere imitation – more a case of a critical comment on the cult of originality for originality's sake.

RHIZOME In *A Thousand Plateaus* (1980), Gilles **Deleuze** and Félix **Guattari** put forward the notion of the rhizome as a model for how systems should work in a **postmodern** world. Prime examples of rhizomes in the natural world would be tubers or mosses, and it is characteristic of a rhizomatic system that, as Deleuze and Guattari put it, any point on it can be connected up to any other (as in the intertwining of mosses). Rhizomes are contrasted to trees and roots, which, in Deleuze and Guattari's opinion, 'fix an order', and are thus implicitly restrictive and authoritarian. The implication is that since rhizomes do not feature the linear development pattern of trees and roots, they are more democratic and creative, thus forming a better basis for systems in a postmodern world than the tree-like hierarchies most Western societies tend to favour instead.

In common with their **poststructuralist** and postmodernist peers, Deleuze and Guattari are firmly opposed to hierarchy and authority, and concerned to find alternative methods of constructing networks. Something like the rhizome idea can be found in the **Internet**, which similarly allows for connections to be established between any two points of the system, as well as having no clearly identifiable 'centre', or central authority.

RILEY, TERRY: COMPOSER (1935–)
An early pioneer of **minimalist** music,
Riley was one of the first to use techniques which became central to the
minimalist aesthetic, such as repetition, tonality and the building up of a
collage of sound from just a few
musical cells or motifs. While studying
composition at the San Francisco
State College and, later, piano at
the San Francisco Conservatoire, he
supported himself by working as a ragtime pianist. He also studied Indian
classical music with his friend and
mentor, Pandit Pran Nath.

While Riley's early works were
influenced by **modernist** composers
such as Stockhausen, it was in the
1960s that he began to experiment
with repetition, layering and the
superimposition of small rhythmic
cells. He used tape loops and tape
delays to achieve this, producing
works such as *The Five Legged Stool*
(1961) and *Dorian Reeds*. Being an
accomplished pianist he, more than the
other minimalists, gave greater weight
to improvisation and also wrote many
solo piano pieces. The *Keyboard
Studies,* intended for solo performance, were often not written down, or
notated in the briefest possible way.

Perhaps his most famous piece,
often regarded as the first minimalist
piece ever, is *In C* (1964). The piece,
for any number of performers playing
any suitable instruments, consists of 53
short musical figures. While a steady
pulse is established by the continuous
repetition of a high C note, the performers are left to repeat each motif as
many times as they wish before moving
on to the next one. Thus a complex,
overlapping, polyrhythmic web is
created from just a few short motifs.

Riley's music has been hugely
inspirational to both **Reich** and **Glass**
who further developed the minimalist
techniques and aesthetics.

RORTY, RICHARD: PHILOSOPHER
(1931–) Rorty has been among the
foremost American champions of
recent **continental philosophy (Derrida, deconstruction, poststructuralism**, etc.), and also an important voice
in what has come to be known as **post-
philosophy**.

In his early career Rorty is self-
consciously the heir of the American
pragmatist school of philosophy, and
in particular of the work of John
Dewey and C. S. Peirce. Rorty put the
case for pragmatism most famously in
Philosophy and the Mirror of Nature
(1980) and *Consequences of Pragmatism* (1982), both of which
challenged Western philosophy's
commitment to absolute notions of,
for example, truth or goodness. For
Rorty, such notions were chimerical,
and all the apparent problems
surrounding them were in reality non-
problems. He saw pragmatism's role
as the dissolution of such issues as the
nature of truth, arguing that a pragmatist was uninterested in taking sides
or weighing up the pros and cons of the
argument, but instead merely wanted
'to change the subject' to something
more interesting.

Philosophy and the Mirror of Nature
discusses the various theories of mind
and knowledge put forward over the
course of philosophical history, only
in order to demonstrate that the problems they deal with are non-existent –
the product of a particular world view
and set of historical imperatives that
can be changed if we so wish. In this

case, what Rorty wishes to call into question is Western philosophy's long-running obsession with the notion of the mind as a mirror of reality, and he is highly critical of the belief that there can be any such thing as an 'accurate **representation** of reality'.

Consequences of Pragmatism argues that truth is not something we should expect to have philosophically interesting theories about, since such theories tell us very little about our world. Any world they do tell us something about is, in Rorty's view, 'a world well lost'. Rorty feels that theories ought to be judged in terms of their usefulness to us rather than their truthfulness anyway; truth being merely, as another American pragmatist philosopher, William James, had put it, 'what it is better for us to believe'. Seen from this perspective it makes more sense to ask if a theory makes us happy than whether it is true.

Ultimately, Rorty's major concern is to ensure that debate and discussion continue rather than that one theory is allowed to dominate proceedings (politically he describes himself as a liberal). His model for such debate has been academic common-room conversation (and he does tend to regard philosophy as little more than a form of conversation), which he contends is less interested in reaching final conclusions (such as the *real* nature of truth or mind, etc.) than in examining a subject from as many angles as possible. This, rather than the fruitless search for watertight theories, becomes Rorty's ideal. He distinguishes between what he calls 'systematic' and 'edifying' philosophy, with the latter being described as the form of philosophical enquiry that

enables us to break free from outmoded discourses – such as debates on the nature of truth or mind. It is a kind of philosophy that we can find in the work of the American pragmatists, or in Martin **Heidegger** or Ludwig Wittgenstein. Systematic philosophy, the search for watertight theories, is, on the other hand, what Rorty feels we should be trying to avoid at all costs.

In his later work, such as *Contingency, Irony and Solidarity* (1988), Rorty has espoused what can only be called a post-philosophical position, arguing that philosophy is something like a bad habit we should be striving to overcome (there are intimations of this view in the earlier writings too, where he queries whether philosophy even has the right to call itself a professional field of enquiry). For the later Rorty, subjects such as literature or social theory are of much more value to us, as a guide to our behaviour and personal development, than philosophy ever can be, and he often sounds as if he wishes to turn his back on philosophy altogether.

In his disenchantment with the standard narrative of Western philosophy Rorty strikes an authentically **postmodern** note. Certainly, there is no commitment to absolutes or universal theories to be found in his writings, which see no privileged position for philosophy as the supposed arbiter of all other intellectual discourses. Rorty's suggestion that **irony** (or 'liberal ironism' as he dubs it) is the appropriate attitude to adopt towards life, is authentically postmodern too.

RUSHDIE, SALMAN: NOVELIST (1947–) Salman Rushdie was born into a Muslim family living in Bombay a matter of months before two of his most famous characters: Saleem Sinai, the narrator of Rushdie's finest novel *Midnight's Children* (1980), and the State of India. *Midnight's Children* tells the story of modern India through the eyes and other senses of Sinai, an unreliable if entrancing narrator. Rushdie has a political message, but that message never comes between the reader and the joy of the endlessly intricate plot and the moving, comic, tragic characters. As in all of his fiction, Rushdie wears his **postmodernism** a little heavily: 'reality' is a sham, or rather a construct – the true reality is the story, the narrative through which and for which we live. *Midnight's Children* made Rushdie's career. It became a bestseller, and won the Booker Prize in 1981.

Rushdie's third novel, *Shame* (1983), has some of the same elements that made *Midnight's Children* – the extraordinary and the ordinary rubbing shoulders in the East (this time the Pakistan of the 1950s to the 1970s), the same narrative tricks and the same florid prose. The story is a transparent retelling of the Bhutto–Zia feud in which it is difficult to work out who comes out best, the decadent Bhutto or the malevolent Zia. The openly scornful treatment of fundamentalist Islam in *Shame* became a scabrous, scatological attack on the very foundations of the Muslim world in *The Satanic Verses* (1989), a sort of alternative life of the Prophet, in which Mohammed is portrayed as all too human. Like all Rushdie's fiction, the book blurs the boundaries between fact and fantasy, and, in true post-modernist style, the everyday reality of the modern world becomes crazily mixed up with the fantastic and the supernatural.

The publication of *The Satanic Verses* changed Rushdie's life for ever. The *fatwa* issued by the Ayatollah Khomeni means that Rushdie may never again be able to walk openly down a street in his own country. The incident, which has seen massive demonstrations in Iran, India and the United Kingdom, has shown both the gulf in understanding between the West and the Islamic world, and how, for all the postmodernists' irony and detachment, literature can have a deadly impact in the 'real' world.

The Moor's Last Sigh (1995), tells the story of Moraes Zogoiby. Another of Rushdie's bizarre narrators, Zogoiby, who is condemned to age at twice the normal rate, tells the stories of his family, particularly of his artist mother, a Christian, possibly descended from Vasco da Gama, married to a Jew. The model for this cascade of stories is that perennial favourite of postmodernist authors, *The One Thousand and One Nights*.

Not all of Rushdie's critics have been raging clerics. Some secular commentators in India have criticized what they see as Rushdie's patronizing, Western-influenced liberalism. His portraits of Indians have been condemned as Western stereotypes and his own rendering of Anglo-Indian speech idioms has been ridiculed. Many Eastern and Western critics have described his post-*Midnight's Children* work as boring and unreadable.

S

**SAID, EDWARD, W.: CRITIC AND CUL-
TURAL THEORIST** (1935–) Edward
W. Said is Parr Professor at Columbia
University. He was born in Jerusalem
and educated at Victoria College,
Cairo, Mount Hermon school,
Massachusetts, and at Princeton and
Harvard universities. His publica-
tions include *Beginnings: Intention
and Method* (1975), *Orientalism*
(1977), *The World, the Text and
the Critic* (1983) and *Culture and
Imperialism* (1993).

In an afterword to the new edition
of *Orientalism*, Said distinguishes 'two
broad currents: **postcolonialism** and
postmodernism'. He argues that the
prefix 'post' suggests not so much a
'sense of going beyond but rather
continuities and discontinuities'. His
contribution to the current theoretical debate has been in his analyses of
seminal postmodernist thinkers such
as **Barthes**, **Deleuze**, **Derrida** and
Foucault in *Beginnings*. Indeed,
Orientalism, which Said describes as
'an antecedent of postmodernism and
postcolonialism', appears to draw upon
Foucault's notion of the relationship
between knowledge and power. The
first of what can be viewed as a trilogy
of studies examining the relationship
between East and West, Orient and
Occident, *Orientalism* is arguably
Said's most influential work. It resists
notions of a natural and stable human
identity and undermines the belief in
the certain positivity and unchanging
historicity of a culture, a self or a
national identity. The Orient and the
Occident correspond to no stable
'reality' that exists as a natural fact.
The apparatus of orientalism manu-
factures the 'Orient' and thus helps to
regulate colonialist relations. Thus
Said draws on Vico's observation that
human history is made by human
beings, while adhering to the **poststructuralist** idea that there are only
representations in **texts**. This is highlighted in the second and third works
of this 'trilogy': *The Question of
Palestine* (1979) and *Covering Islam*
(1981). Both of these texts are concerned with the representation of the
Arab world by the Western press.

Culture and Imperialism (1993)
focuses, in the early chapters, on
canonical writers such as Jane Austen
and Rudyard Kipling. The focus then
shifts in Chapter 3 to 'national'
writers and colonized intellectuals
with readings of W. B. Yeats and
Ranajit Guha. A later reading of
Yeats (*Field Day Pamphlet 15*) takes
up the question of nationalism and
the dangers inherent in it while pointing to the crucial role of literature in
the re-establishment of a national
cultural heritage, in the re-imagining
and refiguring of local histories,
geographies and communities. The
danger lies in the concept of an
imagined community resulting in a

nativist impasse. Liberation (not nationalism) involves a transformation of social consciousness beyond national consciousness.

The impact of Said's work, in particular his theory propounded in *Orientalism*, has been considerable in the field of postcolonial studies. His attempts to dismantle naturalized assumptions about language and textuality and preoccupation with the importance of ideological construction in socio-textual relations align him with the poststructuralist movement while the accessibility of his works make him a widely read and influential figure in contemporary literary and cultural theory.

SCHIZOANALYSIS A form of anti-psychoanalysis devised by Gilles **Deleuze** and Félix **Guattari** in their controversial study *Anti-Oedipus* (1972), based on the experience of the schizophrenic. The theory is that the schizophrenic provides a better model for resisting authority (as embedded in the procedures of psychoanalysis, for example), than such types as the neurotic – and resisting authority is all but an article of faith for **postmodernists** such as Deleuze and Guattari. Schizophrenics, with their multiple identities, are seen to defeat the efforts of the psychoanalyst to make them conform (that being the point of psychoanalysis, as far as Deleuze and Guattari are concerned), whereas neurotics are more likely to be induced to co-operate, thus helping to perpetuate an authoritarian system.

Psychoanalysis is regarded by the authors as a form of politically inspired social control, and the ability of schizophrenics to frustrate the process turns them into postmodernist role models. Loss of ego amounts to a politically subversive act in this respect. (See also **Oedipus**.)

SEDUCTION A concept in Jean **Baudrillard**, seduction demonstrates how systems can be undermined by more subtle means than the exercise of brute power. Baudrillard argues that systems can in fact be 'beguiled' into submission, thus obviating the need for revolutionary action on the traditional model. There is therefore no need for confrontation or violence when systems are so vulnerable to subterfuge. Not surprisingly, feminist theorists have taken exception to this notion on the grounds of its sexist connotations, and Baudrillard has received some severe criticism from this quarter on the grounds that the theory of seduction reinforces sexual stereotypes.

SEMANALYSIS A synthesis of **semiotics**, **Marxism**, and **Freudianism** put together by Julia **Kristeva** in her first major work of theory, *Semiotike: Recherches pour une semanalyse* (1968). Kristeva's contention was that semiotics was both a critical science in its own right and a critique of science itself. She coined the term semanalysis to describe semiotics in this new critical-political role that she had designed for it, and saw her project as being very close in spirit to the structural Marxism of Louis Althusser and his disciples, with its concern to turn Marxism into a hard-edged 'science of society'. The inspiration behind the development of semanalysis, designed to provide a scientific basis for the study of all **sign** systems, came from such formal sciences as mathematics and logic.

SEMIOTICS Semiotics (or semiology) is for a **structuralist** the science of **signs**, but for a **postmodernist** merely the study of them. Ferdinand de Saussure first broke from the study of language through its history (philology) to investigate language as a structure (linguistics). For Saussure, and all subsequent semioticians, a word is made up of a material component, such as a sound, or a mark on a page, which he terms the *signifier,* and a mental component, the concept or idea represented by the signifier: the *signified.* The signifier and the signified together form a *sign.* Saussurian linguistics became the model for the investigation of all patterned human communication. If a semiotician gives her boyfriend a bunch of roses she knows that it is a sign that can be broken down into the matter of the roses, their petals and leaves – the signifier, and the message they convey: 'I love you' – the signified.

After Saussure, semiologists have concentrated on showing the influence of signs, their power and ubiquity. One classic illustration of the semiotic method is Roland **Barthes'** *Mythologies* (1957). Barthes takes various aspects of French popular culture – car adverts, wrestling, soap-powders – and analyses them to reveal the subtle meanings they convey – often sinister, conservative and repressive.

The emergence of **poststructuralism** towards the end of the 1960s meant a shift in emphasis from the signified to the signifier. In the work of Jacques **Derrida** and Julia **Kristeva**, the links between signifier and signified are broken, replaced by the **intertextual** free interplay of signifiers. Structuralists had sought to find *the* meaning of **texts**; poststructuralists revel in multiple meanings, none of which can be allowed priority.

Postmodernism takes this process one stage further. For Jean **Baudrillard** modern society is so saturated with signs pumped out by the media that it is no longer possible to distinguish between signs and reality.

SHERMAN, CINDY: ARTIST (1954–) Sherman's entry into the American art scene came with her *Untitled Film Stills* (1977–80), a series of black-and-white photographs in which she played out a multiplicity of filmic conventions about women. Initially these images were celebrated for their apparent concern with the 'mythology' of originality. In 1979, Sherman stated: 'Some people have told me they remember the movie that one of my images is derived from, but in fact I had no film in mind at all.' Thus in the early deployments of **postmodernist** criticism – a criticism tending to celebrate those forms of art that registered the simulated nature of modern experience – Sherman's photographic practice was found to be exemplary in its apparent commitment to the view that critical culture should reveal the 'fictive' nature of social experience.

Throughout the *Untitled Film Stills* Sherman positions herself as both 'actress' and 'director', recalling through the use of lighting, depth-of-field, camera-angle, clothing, décor and topography, a range of filmic conventions in which femininity is organized and conventionalized. This sense of inhabiting cultural identities in order to 'foreground' their ideological and institutional nature was seen to be part of a postmodernist package involving Peter **Halley** and Sherrie Levine, both of whom defined art as a technology of power rather than as a neutral aesthetic form. Thus critics like Douglas Crimp and Lisa Phillips applauded work that concentrated on the media construction of reality and the concomitant 'elimination' of the artistic self. It could be affirmed that not only was Sherman revealing the mythic or fictive nature of feminine stereotypes, but through her deliberate use of photography she was demonstrating this medium's complicity in such a process. Therefore her critique was construed as double-fold: it was feminist in that it illuminated the devices by which women were subordinate to the 'industrial' and mass-produced norms of Hollywood; and it was postmodern in that it confirmed the illusory nature of originality, authenticity and individuality

By the early 1980s it was no longer possible to see in Sherman's work a fascination with unravelling the matrix of filmic conventions that articulate female subjectivity. However, *Fashion* (1983–84), *Disasters* and *Fairy Tales* (1985–89), *Civil War* (1991) and *Sex Pictures* (1992) were still identified as exemplars of postmodernist art. In these works she began to use new compositional formats, subjects and truncated plastic mannequins; and these alien commodities, purchased from medical suppliers, were immediately integrated into a new 'somatic' postmodernist discourse that emerged from an engagement with the psychoanalytical writings of Julia **Kristeva**. Laura Mulvey, writing in the *New Left Review* of 1991, claimed that Sherman's 'bulimic' images confront the construction of female identity through a re-evaluation of the relationship between interior and exterior spaces. She saw in Sherman's new bodily landscape of 'disgust' an engagement with the experience of the fear, anxiety and shame of having a body that is always 'unhomely', a body that does not conform to the sanctioned visions of feminine beauty. Anxiety replaces alienation in these deliquescent, decomposing images where the body becomes a viscose web of forms. In this amorphous zone Mulvey discovered the appearance of what Kristeva calls '**abjection**': the confrontation with the primal 'unspeakable abyss' of 'liquidity' and 'decay' that precedes our division between the clean and the unclean, the pure and the impure.

Sherman's career thus far has coincided with the mutation of postmodernist art from that which reveals the fictive qualities of **representation**, to that which affirms that representation is a form of violence or mutilation. In both cases the object of her 'critique' has been the construction of the female body in contemporary culture.

SIGN In Saussurean linguistics, the sign is constituted by the union between a signifier (word) and signified (concept). This union takes place in the individual's mind, and its end product is a recognition of the meaning of the word in question. This meaning is held to be a more or less stable entity, which does not change arbitrarily or at any given individual's whim. It is shared, therefore, by all the members of a given linguistic community at a particular historical moment, although it can change over time. Saussure regarded language as a sign system, which elicited common responses from individuals, and his linguistic theories went on to form the basis for **structuralism**. Structuralist theorists took Saussurean linguistics as the model for the study of all other sign systems, demonstrating how, for example, literary genres were made up of signs (or narrative conventions) that signalled to readers to respond in a particular manner.

Poststructuralist theorists such as Jacques **Derrida** have taken a very different view of the sign, regarding it as a fractured entity which can never capture the 'full' meaning of words. One commentator on Derrida, Gayatri Chakravorty **Spivak**, has spoken of the sign as being 'half not there, and half not that', and as such being open to a wide range of interpretations by individuals. The sign is therefore an *unstable* entity in poststructuralist thought, and meaning shot through with ambiguity.

SIMULACRA, SIMULATION Baudrillard's theories relating to simulation stem from his early work on **sign** systems in the 1970s, where he argued that commodity and sign had combined in order to form a self-referential loop within a closed 'object system'. While the collective imagination may be deceived into thinking that such signs refer to something real and solid outside the system, this is an illusion. What is being generated is a 'simulacrum', which, although the product of the system, also acts as the external referent by which it justifies its function.

In *Symbolic Exchange and Death* (1976), Baudrillard organized the history of the production of simulacra into three parts. In the 'classical' era (from the Renaissance to the Industrial Revolution), simulation takes the form of counterfeiting. This is followed by the 'industrial' era, in which techniques of mass-production allow an order of infinitely reproducible objects. Finally, in our contemporary **postmodern** order, new cybernetics and communications technologies have absorbed human subjectivity itself into a network of busily self-replicating digital systems.

In *Simulations* (1983), Baudrillard sums up the status of the 'real' in the postmodern world. Transformed into the '**hyperreal**', which bears no relation to any reality whatsoever, it has disappeared entirely into the process of simulation, and become 'its own pure simulacrum'.

SIMULATIONISM A development from the mass-media appropriators of the late 1970s, simulationism emerged in New York in the shape of Peter **Halley**, Sherrie Levine, Peter Taaffe, Ross Bleckner, Jeff **Koons** and Ashley Bickerton, most of whom were part of a critical network where the writings of **Foucault** and **Baudrillard** were well known. Two assumptions characterize this art: the idea that the contemporary social order is structured by the **representations, signs** and values embedded in the processes of consumption; and the belief that the scope and power of art must be measured through its capacity to demonstrate that reality has been assimilated into a global image culture.

If Halley, Bleckner, Taaffe and Levine 'copied' the styles of Newman, Stella, Ryman, Mondrian and Malevich, emphasizing the material character of their work, they did so in order to deny the idea that art can establish its own formal purity. Copying is not an act of homage but a parody of the idea that art possesses unique powers, an acknowledgement that it is derived from the mechanical and scientific processes it ostensibly rejects. In abstract art, concerned as it is with fundamental orders and optical regimes, could be seen the technocratic geometries of circuits, networks, and other signs of the architectonic logic of the social order. From these conceptual foundations two forms of practice were developed: first, Bickerton's self-styled 'defiant complicity', where the technocratic object attempts to assimilate all aspects of the infrastructure of art by referring, as Bickerton put it, 'to every station of its operational life, i.e., storage, shipping, gallery access, rack reproduction, and on the wall'; second, Halley's simulated **sublime**, where the painting, composed of grids, nodes, conduits and cells, confirms the priority of abstract codes and languages within a **post-industrial** social system where reality has become the duplication of signs within the simulated spaces of computer circuitry.

SINFIELD, ALAN: CRITIC (1941–) Alan Sinfield is a professor of English in the School of Cultural and Community Studies at the University of Sussex, where he convenes the MA programme 'Sexual Dissidence and Cultural Change'. In such works as *Literature in Protestant England 1560–1660* (1983), *Literature, Politics and Culture in Post-War Britain* (1989) and *Faultlines* (1992) he has been an influential exponent of '**cultural materialism**', a version of ideological critique which has absorbed the insights of Michel **Foucault** on the relationship between sexuality and power. As an extension of that work, his latest books, especially *Cultural Politics – Queer Reading* (1994), are engagements with '**queer theory**' from a cultural materialist perspective. In Sinfield's work we find some of the most familiar themes of **postmodern** criticism – marginality, sexual **difference**, the instability of subjectivity, **cultural relativism**, the politics of identity – but these are anchored by a socialist politics that sets itself against what he calls the 'apocalyptic vision' of postmodern discourse that 'depoliticizes culture by imagining it as flowing, necessarily with the stream of consumer capitalism'. He began his most original work in the early 1980s.

'Against Appropriation' in *Essays in Criticism* (1981) suggests that literary **texts** will serve us better if we allow them to 'challenge rather than confirm ourselves'; the real relevance of texts from the past resides precisely in their distance from our time, their very '**otherness**', a quality critics in the more traditional universalizing humanist tradition seek to suppress in their quest for enduring human values. If, for instance, Shakespeare is our great universal poet, then his world view must in important ways be close to ours. Much of Sinfield's work involves disabusing the complacent reader of this idea. Sinfield suggests that we reverse the principle of relevance; earlier writing illuminates not because it appeals to enduring needs, but because it offers an alternative perspective, a chance to confront our unexamined assumptions. By 1985 and *Political Shakespeare,* Sinfield and his co-editor Jonathan **Dollimore** had worked out a critical approach they called 'cultural materialism'; the politically engaged, materialist analysis of culture.

In *Faultlines,* Sinfield describes what he calls 'dissident reading'. He chooses the term 'dissident' over the more glamorous 'transgressive' or 'subversive' because these terms imply that something has already happened; 'dissident' suggests that the dominant culture tells stories in which there are faultlines, and through which dissident readings can be made. A dominant discourse that speaks of subversion can, in the very act of demonizing it, give it a voice. Sinfield shows in *The Wilde Century* (1994) that nineteenth-century discourses on homosexuality made possible new forms of social control, but also enabled a 'reverse discourse' whereby homosexuality began to speak for itself, often using the very terms in which it was subordinated. A recent example would be the adoption of the pejorative term 'queer' by many gay activists and writers, Sinfield among them. For Sinfield,

the subculture the term names is a source for possible oppositional self-hoods.

SINGULARITY In physics, a singularity is a point (described as being of infinite density) from which a series of effects unfold, but which is not itself 'caused' by anything else. The 'big bang' theory of the universe presupposes one such singularity, claiming that it is pointless to ask what caused the big bang, or existed before it, since the big bang *itself* was the beginning of space and time – thus of causal sequences. Some theorists have speculated that the universe might ultimately collapse back into a singularity again. There are also held to be singularities at the centre of **black holes**.

Singularities have something like the properties traditionally attributed to divinity, in that they transcend physical explanations, such as those of cause and effect (the Christian God similarly creates a universe where there was not one before). The notion of singularity, with its insistence that there are limits to explanation (rather as there are with the **sublime**), appeals to the **postmodern** mind in that it provides one solution to the problem of foundations – although philosophically speaking, it could be said to constitute rather too neat a solution to that problem.

SITE: DESIGN FIRM (1970–) SITE ('Sculpture in the Environment') was founded in New York in 1970 by James Wines and Alison Sky. SITE's buildings have a freshness rarely seen in architecture. They played with the codes and iconographies of ubiquitous contemporary buildings: the supermarket, the highway and the parking lot. Within these recognizably ordinary buildings they made subversive interventions. With gestures located somewhere between the surreal and **spectacle**, such as the corner of a brick supermarket seemingly collapsing (the Indeterminate Facade showroom), or an undulating section of freeway populated by cars, aeroplanes, and boats (Highway 86 at the Vancouver Expo '86), they made these supposedly unarchitectural conditions special. This process of the transformation of the banal or everyday objects was borrowed from a tradition leading back through the conceptual art of the 1970s via pop to Marcel Duchamp. These tactics attempted to open up the restrictive and increasingly irrelevant practice of architecture – proposing a thoroughly contemporary alternative one that embraced the physical and cultural terrains of a highly developed capitalist economy.

SITE's work functions without complex spatial articulation, formal dynamics or esoteric architectural references; rather it engages the building as a means of questioning the nature of architecture – where the building is regarded as a site of communication. Their architecture has thoroughly American flavour, mixing the narrative and iconographic play of Disney with banal suburban conditions. Best Products Company (a suitably low code client) gave SITE numerous opportunities to subvert the generic out-of-town retail unit. This series of buildings demonstrate some of the tactics of what SITE term 'de-architecture' – inversion, inclu-

sion, and indeterminacy, allied with humour and critique.

SITUATIONISM Formed in Italy in 1957, the Situationists were a loose grouping of disputatious political activists, writers and artists who played a significant role in the Paris uprisings of May 1968. The most prominent members of the group were Guy Debord, political theorist and author of *The Society of the Spectacle* (1967), and the artist Asger Jorn. Debord edited the group's journal, which carried articles on Vietnam, urban geography, and cultural and political issues and was full of examples of the Situationists' distinctive and influential approach to graphic design, using political slogans and doctored images from the popular press and advertising. Debord's **Marxist**-influenced *The Society of the Spectacle* suggests that social relations themselves are mediated through images and that we have become spectators in our own lives, while Jorn's technique of *détournement* ('over-painting' found images with political messages) was used extensively by the late 1960s underground press and by punk bands and fanzines in the 1970s. Situationism both prefigures and inaugurates important elements of **postmodern** thinking; **Baudrillard**'s 'hyperreality' has similarities to Debord's spectacle, while the Situationists' concept of the *dérive*, a psycho-geographical 'drift' through an urban landscape, becomes the philosophical 'drifting thought' of **Lyotard**.

SPECTACLE **Situationist** theorists, most famously Guy Debord in his book *The Society of the Spectacle* (1967), promoted the notion of society as a spectacle over which we had no real control as individuals, having become, in effect, mere spectators of our own lives. Debord argued that in a spectacular society we could either accept the role thrust upon us by the state of being mere passive consumers of the spectacle, or, as happened in the Paris *événements* of 1968, revolt against the spectacle in order to wrest back active control over our existence. By taking to the streets, or 'drifting' as the Situationists called it, we were reappropriating the urban environment and striking a blow against the society of the spectacle.

SPIVAK, GAYATRI CHAKRAVORTY: CRITIC, FEMINIST AND CULTURAL THEORIST (1941–) Variously labelled as feminist, **Marxist**, **deconstructivist** and **postcolonialist**, Gayatri Spivak epitomizes **postmodern** subjectivity in her constant reinvention of herself, her refusal to advocate absolutes and her ability to elude absolute definition. Born in Calcutta, West Bengal, from a self-professed 'solidly middle class' background, Spivak was educated as an undergraduate at the University of Calcutta, and as a postgraduate at the University of Cornell in the United States where she was a student of Paul **de Man**. During a distinguished academic career she has lectured both within and outside of the United States and is currently Professor of English and Comparative Literature at Columbia University, New York. Her main works have included *In Other Worlds: Essays in Cultural Politics* (1987), *Can the Subaltern Speak?* (1988), *Poststructuralism, Marginality, Postcoloniality and Value* (1988) and *Outside in the Teaching Machine* (1993).

Spivak's contribution to postmodern thought cannot be overestimated, as she has produced a number of learned disquisitions on a wide range of literary and cultural practices that raise questions about the constitution of identity; challenge the notion of any monolithic, **legitimizing** discourse, and undermine the epistemological status of historical thought within a self/**other binarism** imposed by both patriarchy and imperialism. Spivak's deconstructive practices develop a strategy for reading that inverts the structures of domination by questioning the forms that constitute and disarticulate 'the **subaltern**' (i.e. women) who have been colonized in both a literal and metaphorical sense. Thus she writes at the intersection of postcolonialism and feminism reinstating the marginalized in place of the dominant with what she describes as 'a strategic use of positive essentialism in a scrupulously visible political interest'. She has insisted on the need for the deconstructive and the political to go hand in hand in order to highlight the material reality of racism/sexism in society, stressing the importance of ideology in forming the ideas of the colonial/female subject.

Deconstruction is the theory underlying Spivak's work, whether she is writing as a feminist, Marxist or postcolonialist. An accomplished philosopher who insists that she is described as a 'literary critic', she translated and prefaced Jacques **Derrida**'s *La*

Grammatologie in 1976, which she said was 'a better way of describing what I am trying to do'. Her debt to deconstruction is obvious in her method of questioning the basic assumptions of dominant systems of language and thought in order to unsettle and decentre meaning, yet she is not uncritical of the project, cautioning that the unsettling of meaning *per se* will not promote a feminist future. For Spivak deconstruction should be a companion to the Marxist project. However, she is sceptical of the notion that deconstruction can be practised either as a theoretical discipline or as an ideological/political practice. In relation to feminism she describes Derrida's work as 'solipsistic' and 'marginal' when he writes from a pro-feminist perspective.

Her works on both feminism and postcolonial theory are attached to the notion of marginality which she describes as 'a buzzword in cultural critique now'. She questions the legitimacy of such terms suggesting that the centre (patriarchy/neo-colonialism) fabricates its attitudes by proposing a share of the centre, not by rupture but by displacement, by offering disciplinary support for the conviction of 'authentic' marginality by an aspiring élite. Her argument for postcoloniality as a deconstructive case comes from the illogical, but naturalized, values that are coded within the legacy of imperialism: nationhood, constitutionality, citizenship, democracy and culturalism. Thus, the supposedly 'authentic' cultural narratives from the 'margins' are written elsewhere, in the centre. Spivak articulates the relationship between feminism, **poststructuralism** and the discourse of postcoloniality, examining a number of persistent Western practices crucial to colonization and imperialism associated with what she calls 'othering' (the ideological mechanism that excludes persons or groups from the systems of 'normality' as perceived by oneself). The self is represented by traditional patriarchal authority and British colonization in relation to the subaltern other which is constituted in 'the Self's shadow'. Thus the other is inextricably linked yet fundamentally embedded in the self.

Spivak's contention that 'there is no place from which the subaltern (sexed) subject can speak' exposes the signifying systems of colonialism and patriarchy as oppressive and silencing. She links postcoloniality and feminism by highlighting the fact that both women and colonized peoples have been forced to articulate their experiences in the language of the oppressor. Further, she has remained anomalous to Marxist, feminist and postcolonial schools of thought by her constant critiques of the same through the lens of deconstructivism, and has highlighted the pitfalls or marginality while resolutely refusing to remain in the margin.

STIRLING, JAMES: ARCHITECT (1926–92) Some of Stirling's greatest admirers might well object to his inclusion in a dictionary of **postmodernism** and to some extent they may have a point. Stirling's architecture was very much rooted in the traditions of **modernism**. Particular motifs in his work, such as the emphasis on circulation, the use of ramps, the plays on symmetrical and asymmetrical axes, and the privileging of the plan as the generator, owe a lot to Le Corbusier, of whom Stirling was, in his own idiosyncratic way, a follower. However, it is the very idiosyncratic and highly individual nature of his work which equally marks him out as a postmodernist. For Stirling was never a typical modernist. Nor when his work, like archetypal postmodernist architecture of the 1970s and 1980s, began to display overt historical reference, could he be described as a typical postmodernist. Paradoxically, the postmodernist tactics he employed, such as his predilection for in-built jokes – tended to be much more overt and go much further than more mainstream postmodernists.

Stirling was also a highly controversial figure. For some, he was unquestionably the greatest British architect of the post-war years while for others he was little more than incompetent. Early buildings such as the Engineering Block in Leicester (designed with James Gowan), the Cambridge History Faculty Library, and the Florey Building in Oxford, display a virtuoso control of expressionist neo-constructivist form and a sophisticated grasp of the relationship between form and programme. These buildings constituted an exciting and radical departure from the worthy and sanctimonious brutalism which dominated British architecture at the time. However, for all their formal mastery and the brilliance of their conception, these buildings were to be plagued by technical failures which were to blight Stirling's reputation for years to come.

These problems were a precursor to a barren patch in which Stirling received few commissions but which led to the development of a radical shift in his work. During the 1970s Stirling's work began to display references to historical sources beginning with the unbuilt project for the Derby Civic Centre. This furrow was increasingly ploughed via a number of competition entries for museum buildings in Germany which culminated in Stirling being awarded the commission to design the Staatsgalerie in Stuttgart, arguably his masterpiece. The Staatsgalerie is conceived essentially as an architectural promenade which forms a *public* route through the site. The building itself is anchored around a central open air drum which forms a court within the complex. The public route circulates around the edge of the drum at high level, knitting the museum into the fabric of the city, creating a theatrical expression of integrated and yet separate public and semi-public circulation systems.

The styling of the building is an overblown monumental classicism broken down by the altercation of classical and modernist elements. The building collapses into a series of stratified layers with ramps at the front creating an artificial landscape of levels which contradict and infect the monumentality of the building. Hence the building constitutes a highly sophisticated juxtaposition of object against landscape, of route against axis, of public against semi-public space, of monumental classicism against modernist tropes, and of abstraction against representation. The success of the Staatsgalerie led to the completion of several more high profile projects before Stirling died. These include the Clore Gallery in London and the Fogg Museum in Cambridge, Massachusetts.

Stirling's strength is that he belonged properly to no school. The idiosyncratic nature of his work leaves him much admired but with few followers; however, like Sir Edward Lutyens before him, it would be surprising not to see a resurgence of interest in Stirling in the not too distant future.

STRUCTURALISM When, in the early years of the twentieth century, Ferdinand de Saussure began to study language as a system of interlinked units, each of which had a meaning only in relation to the system as a whole, he inaugurated one of the great movements in Western intellectual history. Saussure sought the underlying rules of language, the deep structures that must exist if language is to perform its function. These deep structures are independent of the human agents who use language, and this displacement of the human subject from the focus of interest is one of the characteristics of structuralism.

For Saussure, language was a system of **signs**. A sign was made up of a 'signified' – a mental component (a concept) and the 'signifier' – a physical component (for example a sound, or a mark on paper). Each took its place in a rigid, and relatively stable, system of **differences**. The sound 'dog' is only capable of carrying a meaning because it is different from the sound 'dig'. Convention then ties the sound 'dog' to the image of man's best friend.

Structural linguistics became a model for researchers in the humanities who were attempting to make sense of the complex products of human cultures. The anthropologist Claude **Lévi-Strauss** was among the first to realize the potential of the structuralist approach. He analysed the intricate rules determining kinship relationships and, later, the myths of 'primitive' peoples in terms of simple **binary oppositions**. In both cases the linguistic/cultural structures produced by these binary oppositions are a reflection of mental structures: the shape of the social world is determined by the structure of the human mind.

After Lévi-Strauss, Roland **Barthes**, Michel **Foucault** and Jacques **Lacan** applied structruralist modes of analysis to, respectively, literary studies, cultural history and psychoanalysis. In each case, the aim was to find the underlying system of relationships, the structure, within which any individual **event** could come to have a meaning.

By the late 1960s, however, a radical reaction to structuralism's ambitious claims to have explained the world had set in. Jacques **Derrida**, and other **poststructuralists** launched a series of devastating critiques of structuralist poetics, anthropology, and historiography, focusing on the inability of structuralists to understand the radicalism inherent in their own view of language. Derrida emphasized the fragility of the conventional link between signifier and signified, thus rendering 'meaning' a more elusive and slippery beast than the structuralists had supposed.

SUBALTERN THEORY *Webster's Dictionary* defines subaltern thus: 'A commissioned officer below the rank of captain / a person holding a subordinate position / particular with reference to a related universal.' This links subalternity with the notions of *marginality* and **Derrida**'s notion of *presence* as the subaltern subject is, owing to either race, class or gender, marginalized and placed in a subordinate position in relation to the determining authority of 'the centre'. In other words, the centre is designated an invariable 'presence'; it is a point of reference or authority from which norms are established. That which is outside the centre or in the margins is designated '**other**'.

Postcolonial theorists such as Gayatri Chakravorty **Spivak** and the Subaltern Studies Group led by Ranajit Guha examine this process of 'othering' by examining the way in which the signifying system of the centre, i.e. colonialist discourse, renders the experience of the subaltern, or colonial subject, as irrelevant as it is outside the system of normality and convention. Thus the colonial subject is 'muted' owing to its being constructed within a disabling master discourse. The alternative to this silencing is espoused by Homi K. **Bhabha** in his notions of 'mimicry' and 'parody' in which the subaltern's voice is characterized by inappropriate imitations of the master discourse of the centre .

Subaltern studies can be viewed as a form of postcolonial historiography which interrogates the centre from the margin using **deconstructive** and **poststructuralist** practices. It focuses attention on the function of the centre as a site of the operation of power and thus confers insight on the marginalized or subaltern by exposing the oppressive nature of this discourse.

SUBJECT **Postmodernism** has rejected the concept of the individual, or 'subject', that has prevailed in Western thought for the last few centuries. For that latter tradition, the subject has been a privileged being right at the very heart of cultural process. Humanism has taught us to regard the individual subject as a unified self, with a central 'core' of identity unique to each individual, motivated primarily by the power of reason. **Modernity** encouraged the notion of the entrepreneurial subject exploiting the world of nature and bringing it under his (the pronoun being appropriate in this case, given the patriarchal bias of modernity as a cultural movement) domination. Rights and privileges could be ascribed to that subject, whose development and self-realization came to be regarded as a central objective (if not *the* central objective) of Western culture.

This model of the subject as a rational, unified, powerful and controlling being has come under increasing attack from the days of **structuralism** onwards and, particularly in France, there has been a concerted move on the part of theorists to destabilize this model. Claude **Lévi-Strauss** spoke of the **death of man**, arguing that deep structures worked *through* mankind, using it as a channel; Roland **Barthes** spoke of the **death of the author** as a controller of **textual** meaning (the reader becoming the key element instead); Michel **Foucault** spoke of the modern conception of the subject as something that could be erased quite easily, rather as marks made in the sand could be. For **poststructuralists** and postmodernists, the subject is a fragmented being who has no essential core of identity, and is to be regarded as a process in a continual state of dissolution rather than a fixed identity or self that endures unchanged over time. The old model of the subject is held by such thinkers to inhibit creativity and cultural change; as **Deleuze** and **Guattari** put it, 'there is no fixed subject unless there is repression'.

SUBLIME As an aesthetic concept the sublime can be traced back to classical times and the work of Longinus, but in its modern manifestation it dates from the eighteenth century and the work of Edmund Burke and Immanuel **Kant**. It has since come into prominence again in **postmodern** theory, particularly in the work of Jean-François **Lyotard**, for whom it has become an increasingly important concept in his later philosophy (much of which is a conscious dialogue with Kant). In Burke and Kant the sublime represents a force larger than the human, which holds human beings in a state of awe. Essentially, the sublime cannot be comprehended by individuals, who can at best come to recognize the incomprehensibility of its magnitude and power (as in the case of the power of nature), and their inferiority before it. For Lyotard the sublime is the 'unpresentable', the element which always militates against the

possibility of any complete understanding of the world. **Grand narratives** (or universal theories) always try, ultimately unsuccessfully, to deny the existence of the sublime. Great art, on the other hand, makes us aware of the unpresentable, and Lyotard proceeds to judge works of art in terms of their attitude to the unpresentable.

SUKENICK, RONALD: NOVELIST (1932–) American writer Ronald Sukenick's distinctive brand of **postmodernist** fiction substitutes improvisation for plot, split selves for characters, and explores the fluid **subjectivity** of experience. *Up* (1968) presents what seems to be thinly veiled fictionalizations of his early struggles to make a living as a writer in Brooklyn. But the Ronald Sukenick who authors the novel-within-the-novel is not necessarily co-extensive with the Ronald Sukenick on the jacket cover. In *Out* (1973), too, the author adopts a variety of disguises: (a) Ronald, who describes himself as a shapeless bag of protoplasm; (b) Sukenick, who shoots one of his own characters; and (c) Roland Sycamore, who dissolves into the enigmatic 'R'. The chapter numbers reverse from 9 to 1, a countdown determining the number of lines in each section's short blocks of prose. The last pages are blank except for an insouciant 'O'. *98.6* (1975) is also written in fragments, or the 'law of mosaics' as Sukenick puts it. The mosaic patterns are retained in *Long Talking Bad Conditions Blues* (1979), in which conventional forms of punctuation disappear altogether. Sukenick's most extreme gesture towards doing away with the artificial filters of plot, characterization and setting is 'Roast Beef: A Slice of Life' from *The Death of the Novel and Other Stories* (1969). This is a transcription of a taped conversation between Sukenick and his wife as they prepare a meal in the kitchen. It attempts to make us 'hemidemisemiquaveringly interested' in the complex nuances of reality-in-the-raw, an admirable project for the postmodernist writer.

SUPERSTRING THEORY Haunted by the incompatibility of general relativity and **quantum mechanics**, twentieth-century physics' most recent 'theory of everything' is superstrings. To combine these theories, superstring theorists explain, we need to explore the subatomic world at a much smaller scale, one-thousandth of one-billionth the size of a nucleus. As we descend the scale of subatomic particles, the theory goes, we find that the smallest – quarks – are composed of oscillating strings. Each string vibrates at a particular frequency and assumes a particular tension, like a violin string, producing quarks that will form neutrons, protons, electrons and so on, depending on the string's particular frequency. As we ascend the scale, everything dances to 'the music of the strings'. Apart from its successes in explaining 'high-energy' subatomic physics, advocates of superstring theory hold that its mathematics also make sense of the 'low-energy' planetary gravity to which Einsteinian relativity applies. However, in order to explain subatomic particles in terms that make equal sense of cosmic gravity, superstring theory suggests that at sub-quark scales, strings 'unfold' into at least six extra dimensions. Since the energies required to observe real strings in the four dimensions we inhabit would be at least ten million billion times as high as current particle accelerators are capable of they remain elegant mathematical fictions that must yet explain how ten 'stringy' dimensions fold up into our apparently four-dimensional world.

SUPPLEMENT In its **poststructuralist** sense, the term originates from **Derrida**'s *Of Grammatology* (1967) and his reading of Rousseau, who is accused of devaluing writing in favour of speech. Rousseau's contention is that writing is a supplement to speech, is inessential and therefore inferior. By this reckoning, writing adds nothing affirmative to speech and is in itself unnatural, creating, according to Rousseau, a distance between those in communication, and distorting intention and meaning. Rousseau's **logocentrist** discourse is then **deconstructed** by Derrida, for whom speech and writing exist as **binary oppositions** in a 'violent' hierarchy, in which positive value is always accorded to the first term.

The French verb *suppléer* (root of *supplément*) has two meanings: in the first instance it means 'to make up' (as in adding to); it can also mean 'to take the place of' or 'to substitute'. The distinction in what seem to be oppositions is, however, difficult to maintain upon close analysis. The supplement appears as a replacement and/or addition for the terms that the deconstructionist herself has 'violently' reversed. In the endless process of deconstructive reading, the instability of the **sign** ensures that as the newly inverted hierarchy begins to take shape it too is subverted by the supplement. Other examples include active/passive and good/evil; the first term is deemed 'natural', but is subverted by the second, which is in turn supplemented by another.

SVELTENESS Jean-François **Lyotard** has svelteness as a concept which attempts to capture the flexibility and lack of dogmatic belief found in the postmodern individual, when freed from the constraints of **grand narrative** (or universal theory). To be svelte is to be open to events as they unfold around one, and to be able to respond to them without the prejudices that for Lyotard inevitably accompany belief in grand narratives. An example of svelteness, drawn by Lyotard from the work of Stendhal, would be the ability to go to a ball in the evening and then to go to battle in the morning.

T

TERRITORIALITY In **Deleuze** and **Guattari**'s *A Thousand Plateaus* (1980), a territoriality is any entity or institution that restricts the free flow of individual **desire**. The family and the state count as prime examples of territorialities, and they conspire to produce the modern **subject** – the controlled and, as Deleuze and Guattari see it, inhibited subject of liberal humanism and the **Enlightenment project**; 'there is no fixed subject unless there is repression', they insist. They argue that desire needs to be 'deterritorialized', and treat nomadic existence as some kind of ideal of deterritorialization.

TEXT In **postmodern** thought, 'text' refers not only to written materials but also to painting, architecture, information systems and to all attempts at **representation**, whatever form this may take. **Derrida**'s famous dictum that 'there is nothing outside the text', for instance, has been badly misrepresented as a call for a kind of super-formalism. This reading of Derrida's key works has been advanced by members of the so-called **Yale School**, such as Geoffrey **Hartman**, whose work on the use of the pun in literature has been highly influential in the American academy. There is, however, more to postmodern usage of the word 'text' than an endless game of word-play. For postmodernists, it would be more accurate to state that the world is constituted by text.

THOM, RENÉ: MATHEMATICIAN AND SCIENTIST (1923–) Thom, who developed **catastrophe theory** in a work entitled *Structural Stability and Morphogenesis* (1972), is not an easy character to get to grips with, whether his work is approached from the point of view of his native discipline of mathematics; from that of sciences resistant to theoretical modelling in general, and to mathematical treatment in particular (such as biology); or from what looks at first sight like perhaps the most unpromising and certainly uninvitingly tortuous perspective of the social, cultural and philosophical theories of **postmodernism**. Yet Thom's work has had enormous impact on each of these fields, despite infrequent recognition, especially in the latter case.

In mathematics, catastrophe theory (CT) shares the language, now familiar from **chaos theory**, of 'non-linear dynamics', of 'attractors' and 'bifurcations', so that many theorists are currently seeking, under the provisional rubric of 'bifurcation theory', to synthesize its insights with chaos; if CT is concerned to model catastrophic changes in form, which Thom calls 'morphogenesis', at the formal and abstract level, chaotic systems are found very much embodied at the material level. If CT remains avowedly deterministic, emphasizing predictability, the emergence of chaotic behaviour introduces novelties and casts physical laws, especially the second law of thermodynamics, into question as regards their universal applicability.

In biology, while Thom has waged war on what he claims to be an inappropriate metaphorics of information, his work has also had some constructive impact. Drawing the term 'morphogenesis' from that discipline, where it refers to the development of organs, Thom has developed it into an abstract mathematical theoretical framework and re-exported it, thus modified, whence it came; and as biologist C. H. Waddington's enthusiastic introduction to Thom's first major work demonstrates, the graft has taken. But morphogenesis does not stop there. Perhaps ironically, from the point of view of the history of postmodern thought, Thom extends it – in *Structural Stability*, in the essays collected in the French bestseller, *Mathematical Models of Morphogenesis* (1983) and most recently in *Semiophysics* (1990) – to the human sciences (linguistics, **semiotics**, sociology and anthropology) whose scientific status Michel **Foucault** had so rigorously challenged in *The Order of Things*. While the human sciences finally become susceptible of mathematization through CT, the term and the theory of morphogenesis subjects this newfound scientificity to a peculiarly postmodern twist: science itself can no longer be taken to be 'the investigation of the ultimate nature of reality', so that the

'objectivity' associated with that ethos, along with the universalist pretensions of modern science, fall simultaneously. With the demise of the 'era of grand, cosmic synthesis', science becomes postmodernistically local: the analytical tools and the mathematical models remain intact but, as **Lyotard** has it of the postmodern in general, they give rise only to islands of 'local determinism' and 'institutions in patches'.

The proximity between Lyotard's and Thom's formulations is not accidental; Thom is one of the principal references in the characterization of **postmodern science** from which Lyotard would like to draw political lessons. Indeed, if it seems absurdly reductionist to attempt to model politics on science, this is one of the many questions that Thom's work insistently raises: at what degree of abstraction do phenomena of whatever nature, whether scientific or cultural, become susceptible of a single method of modelling? In other words, Thomian speculations with CT invite us to consider to what extent the general applicability of a concept (such as morphogenesis or postmodernism) guarantees a correspondingly global theory; or whether, on the contrary, the generality of a concept is an index, as perhaps **Baudrillard** might say, of its loss of content, the concept thus becoming, in Thom's words, 'a pure play of forms'. Thom's answer, one to which Lyotard lends support, is that only science, with its relentless quantification of phenomena into abstract form, can provide a theory suitably abstract and plastic to chart the profound cultural morphogenetic catastrophe called postmodernism.

TRACE As a translation of the French for a track or footprint, 'trace' indicates something that is no longer present, yet has left its mark. Understood as a structure of difference, trace marks a relation to what is not present. Following **Levinas** and **Derrida**, the structure of every linguistic **sign** is determined by the trace of that other which is forever absent. Breaking with the classical sense of an empirical mark standing for an original non-trace, its origin is equally a trace. A lack of nostgalia for what has been lost gives the term its **postmodern** distinctiveness: its differential relation to a non-origin.

TRANS-AVANT-GARDE The term *trans-avant-garde* was coined by the Italian critic Achille Bonito Oliva to distinguish the works of Anselm **Kiefer**, Francesco Clemente, Sandro Chia, Georg Baselitz and Markus Lupertz from their **modernist** predecessors. According to Oliva, who became an important commentator in the 1980s, this group of European painters, eschewing the utopian rhetoric of modernism, had escaped the burden of art history by using it as a resource-base for their elaborations of myth, will and self-expression. In place of the universalism of modernism, the *trans-avant-garde* was to reveal the magical roots of art in the conflation of ego and cultural tradition, thus producing a new generation of 'nomadic' artists. The visual eclecticism of such painters was taken to offer the possibility of re-investigating traditional styles, techniques and iconographies.

TSCHUMI, BERNARD: ARCHITECT (1944–) 'To experience architecture', Tschumi proclaims in *Advertisements for Architecture,* 'one might have to commit murder'. His confrontational and provocative work set the tone for much architectural theory in the 1980s. Influenced by the **Situationists**, and initially concerned with **representation**, he argued that the traditional forms of architectural drawing excluded ideas of occupation and event. *The Manhattan Transcripts* presented an alternative and inclusive form of spatial representation and notation. Taking the form of film stills and storyboarding, the project outlined a series of events, movements and incidents intertwined with both the drawing style and the space depicted.

Tschumi was soon given the opportunity to speculate by building, winning one of the highest-profile commissions of the 1980s, Le Parc de la Villette, in north-eastern Paris. The required programme of the park was exploded across the site and placed on an abstract grid. The ground plan of the park was layered with three organizational systems, based upon different types of spatial occupation – route, encounter and event, which set out an organization of territory which is subsequently programmatically defined. Since then he has built little, but continues to exert influence through publications and competitions.

Tschumi's belief that programme is as much the medium of architecture as iconography has led to a series of propositions that attempt to engage with the experience of the contemporary urban situation. His current work manages to retain the radical ideas of his theory while proposing new architectural scenarios – coining new terminologies such as crossprogramming and disprogramming, opening up fresh possibilities for architectural practice.

VATTIMO, GIANNI: PHILOSOPHER (1936–) Gianni Vattimo studied philosophy at the University of Turin, completing his doctorate under Luigi Pareyson, and later working with Hans-Georg Gadamer and Karl Löwith at the University of Heidelberg. His first book was *Essere, storia e linguaggio in Heidegger* (*Being, History and Language in Heidegger*), published in 1963, and he has published studies of **Heidegger**, Schleiermacher and **Nietzsche**. Since 1982 he has been Professor of Theoretical Philosophy at the University of Turin. In the late 1960s and early 1970s, he played an active role in the politics of the Radical Party. Vattimo is known best for his writings on *il pensiero debole* ('weak thought'); in 1983, he co-edited, with Pier Aldo Rovatti, a collection of essays entitled *Il pensiero debole*. Vattimo conceives of weak thought as a refusal of the **Enlightenment** identification of the intellectual as avant-garde legislator: *il pensiero debole* refuses the strength of will which is assumed by **modernity**.

Vattimo defines the modern as that era in which being modern itself becomes a value. The new becomes a value, for Vattimo, at the end of the fifteenth century with the beginnings of a conception of the artist as creative genius whose work is characterized by *originality*. This is linked, says Vattimo, with the more general perspective from which human history is seen in terms of an emancipation conceived as advancement, progression and refashioning. Such a conception of history is by definition a linear one. This modernity ends, says Vattimo, when it no longer seems possible to regard history as unilinear. Vattimo sees the philosophical challenge to the unilinear model as coming from a project in the nineteenth and twentieth centuries that exposes this view of history as an ideological one. Walter **Benjamin**'s 'Theses on the Philosophy of History', for example, 'maintained that unilinear history is a **representation** of the past constructed by dominant groups and social classes'. It is in relation to the writings of Nietzsche and Heidegger, however, that Vattimo's ideas are most fully developed.

In *The End of Modernity* (1985), Vattimo argues that what he calls 'the scattered and often incoherent theories of **post-modernity**' only begin to make sense when placed in direct contact with Nietzsche's concept of the eternal return and Heidegger's notion of the overcoming of metaphysics. If the works of Nietzsche and Heidegger can be placed in productive relation to those of **post-modernism**, that project involves first of all, for Vattimo, a careful attention to the prefix 'post' in postmodernism.

'Post' signifies for Vattimo the same relation with the past of European thought – with the modern – that is advanced by the two thinkers in question. Both Nietzsche and Heidegger, he claims, recognize the necessity of calling into question the tradition of European metaphysics and of breaking with it in some fundamental sense. At the same time, though, they acknowledge the paradox of claiming to have severed all ties with a tradition which considers itself as a process of constant development or overcoming in the first place: simply to claim to have broken with the modern, then, would be to repeat the logic of the modern. Both Nietzsche and Heidegger recognize in the modern not merely an impulse toward progress or novelty, but also the basis of this drive in a notion of 'origin' or 'foundation', and it is towards this concept that their respective critiques of metaphysics are oriented. According to Vattimo, what is postmodern in Nietzsche and Heidegger is not an abrupt break with metaphysics, but an attempt to *rethink* this origin. Postmodernism is, then, to be seen as a weakening of the relation to an origin, a weakening which takes place philosophically in Nietzsche's 'accomplished nihilism' and the Heideggerian concept of *Andenken* (rethinking). For both thinkers, Vattimo points out, the aesthetic is the site of this weakening, which institutes an altered conception of truth, 'not as an object which can be appropriated and transmitted, but as a horizon and a background upon which we may move with care'.

In later works such as *The Transparent Society* (1992) and *Beyond Interpretation*, Vattimo has extended these arguments while, in the latter volume, warning against any hasty reduction of the thought of modernity to a purely aesthetic phenomenon. Truth, argues Vattimo in a rejection of what he sees as the groundless relativism of much postmodern thought, requires an act of interpretation, but this does not excuse us from attending to *historicity*.

VENTURI, ROBERT: ARCHITECT AND ARCHITECTURAL THEORIST (1925–)
Possibly the first architect whose work attracted the label **postmodern**, Venturi revolutionized architectural thinking in the 1960s and 1970s via the design of a number of controversial buildings which reintroduced ornament and historical motif as generators of architectural meaning. This approach amounted to an unprecedented attack on the hitherto unquestioned doctrine of architectural **modernism**. However, while the offending buildings did little more than dent the ubiquitous monolith of modernist practice, two books, *Complexity and Contradiction in Architecture* (1966) and *Learning from Las Vegas* (with Denise Scott Brown and Stephen Izenour, 1972) met with huge popular acclaim and blew a gigantic hole in the dominance of modernism.

Venturi persists in being a controversial and paradoxical figure. While continuing to oppose the mythical 'heroic and original' ambitions of modernism, the phrase 'complexity and contradiction' became itself a heroic slogan for those opposing the sanctimonious and esoteric purity exhibited by the aesthetics of modern architecture. *Complexity and Contradiction* calls for evolutionary rather than revolutionary change and promotes an attitude of 'both/and' rather than 'either/or', in opposition to the singularity and univalence of modernist functionalism. Perhaps the most blasphemous of the book's proposals is the promotion of ornament and historical reference as a means of architectural communication. When placed in the context of slogans such as 'ornament is crime', Venturi's position, in terms of the modernist doctrine of progress, appears conservative but, in respect of the overriding élitism and authoritarianism of modernist humanism, it seems extremely liberating. Venturi takes delight in the parody of modernist slogans. Mies van der Rohe's 'less is more' becomes in Venturi's words, 'less is bore'.

If the first book, with its emphasis on legitimate historical architecture, was just about acceptable to the modernists, *Learning from Las Vegas*, which extended the analysis of ornament to a study of the symbolism of the commercial strip, sent the architectural establishment into apoplexy. The apparent political ambivalence implied by the acceptance of commercial codes has, however, been read by other practitioners, such as the artist Dan Graham, as a complex form of political commentary.

In engaging with commercial signification, Venturi refuses to submit to the modernist myths of rationality and transparency which, in the buildings of modernist masters such as Mies van der Rohe, served as alibi for capitalist bureaucracy and economic imperialism. Recognizing his own contribution to twentieth-century

architecture, Venturi is at pains to stress his role as an architect rather than as writer. However, it is likely that posterity will disappoint him in this matter. This not because he has not produced buildings of quality and note. The Vanna Venturi House and North Penn Nurses Association Building are highly sophisticated dialogues between the codes of conventional architecture and those of a prevailing modernism. The Benjamin Franklin Museum in Philadelphia manages to incorporate references to popular significations of shelter, pop art and minimalism, and the Sainsbury wing to London's National Gallery, designed in response to a fierce debate between the modernist architectural establishment and the Prince of Wales, managed, in its witty and knowingly paper-thin appropriation of the host building's mediocre classicism, to undermine both the sanctimoniousness of the former and the pomposity of the latter. This, his only excursion into the British architectural scene, serves as a prime example of the complexity and contradiction with which this architect's career and reputation are riddled.

VIRILIO, PAUL: CULTURAL COMMENTATOR (1932–)   Paul Virilio trained as an artist in stained glass, working with Braque and Matisse, and studied philosophy at the Sorbonne. At eighteen, inspired by the Abbé Pierre and the movement of worker-priests, he became a Christian and a militant. In 1975 he became director of the Ecole Spéciale d'Architecture in Paris. With Georges Perec, he created the *Espace critique* series at the publishers Galilée. He has worked on journals such as *Esprit* and *Cause Commune*.

Virilio's thought begins from the idea that **modernity** is characterized less by the control of spatial territory than by the 'government of time'. In *Speed and Politics* (1977) he argues that the city is founded first of all on a temporal phenomenon: the advantage of speed afforded by a vantage point. To see one's enemy from an elevated lookout position is to gain a temporal advantage, a period of time in which crucial tactical decisions can be made. Virilio extends this observation to his examination of the modern city, where, he claims, the technological infrastructure is geared toward the control of time: 'The new capital is no longer a spatial capital like New York, Paris or Moscow, a city located in a specific place, at the intersection of roads, but a city at the intersection of the practicabilities of time, in other words, of speed.' The crucial political relations in modernity have to do, he says, with speed, which Virilio calls 'the hope of the West'. He takes this to mean that the political must now be thought of in terms of a 'chronopolitics', rather than in the geopolitical or spatial terms we are used to.

Much of Virilio's work is concerned with what he calls the 'logistics of perception'. In a line of argument that is partly indebted to Michel **Foucault**'s theorization of the relations between power and vision, Virilio claims that there is an intimate link between modern technologies of vision and the speed of which he wrote in his earlier work. In *War and Cinema* (1984) he outlines the complicated connections between the development of military technology and the optical technology that is now – in cinema, television and video – a part of everyday life. According to Virilio, the logic of this technology – and of the form of the state of which it is part – results from the insight that *that which can be seen can also be destroyed*. This leads Virilio to posit an 'aesthetics of disappearance', in which the dominant relation in modernity turns out not to be (as modern philosophy had conceived it) the relation between appearance and reality, but that obtaining between appearance and disappearance.

While he is sometimes seen as occupying a 'nihilistic' position close to that of Jean **Baudrillard**, Virilio's work exists outside of the terms of recent intellectual movements and debates in **postmodern** thought. He does not expressly couch any of his insights in terms of the postmodern; indeed, it would be impossible to extract from his work any periodizing formulation of a modern/postmodern distinction. Rather, Virilio thinks of the phenomena he describes as various 'flows' or drifts, a notion reflected in his difficult and deceptively seductive writing. Virilio's method takes the form of the piling-up of examples in a kind of flow that both resists any hasty assimilation into rigid 'positions' and appears not to be bound by the limits of any one of his works. It is easy to get the impression when reading Virilio that his work is one long **text** rather than discrete books, an impression which Virilio has himself justified in interviews.

Virilio's later work has seen an inevitable critical engagement with the new technologies of the **Internet**.

As with his earlier work on visual technology, he sees here a continuation of the impulse towards speed: it is a question here, though, of an apparently achievable *simultaneity* which will destroy, in what Virilio calls a 'generalized planetary accident', our relations to our bodies, time and space. In the instantaneity of the transfer of information, Virilio sees the end of the possibility of critical distance: his call to resist the 'government of time' which he identifies in this technology, is revealed in works such as *The Vision Machine* (1992), *The Art of the Motor* (1996) and *Open Sky* (1997) as an attempt to rescue a notion of a localized *present* in the face of the generalized instantaneity of technology. The argument has a clear precedent in **Benjamin**'s mystical invocation of *Jetztzeit* or 'now-time', a parallel that perhaps suggests Virilio's continuing proximity to the theological impulse evident at the beginning of his career.

VIRTUAL REALITY The oxymoron 'virtual reality' was coined by Jaron Lanier in 1986 to describe technology that attempts to create computer-generated interactive environments, in which users can immerse themselves by means of 3D goggles and gloves which act as computer-input devices. Initially developed in the late 1960s, virtual reality is now an increasingly common phenomenon in the world of entertainment, art, and scientific and medical research. However, in the popular imagination it still has more than a hint of the science-fictional about it, and it is therefore not surprising that the concept is capable of arousing feverish speculation and paranoia far beyond what its current capabilities would allow.

Virtual reality is certainly a common theme in contemporary science-fiction, where it becomes the focus of both horror and celebration. David Cronenberg's film *Videodrome* (1982), for example, led the way in portraying it as an invasive technology which hijacks the human brain, making it incapable of distinguishing between the virtual and the real. *Videodrome* anticipates by two years what is probably the most famous fictional evocation of virtual reality: William **Gibson**'s *Neuromancer*. Gibson's vision of the world within the computer is more equivocal than Cronenberg's, however, for he invests the concept of computer-generated worlds with a sense of vertiginous freedom, in which, free of the body's 'meat', the disembodied mind can traverse the limitless realm of **cyberspace**.

The concept of virtual reality, therefore, is inherently double-edged, offering us a window into a world of imagination and exciting possibility, while also threatening us with its implicit challenge to our assumptions concerning 'authentic' reality. With good enough technology, perhaps no one will be able to tell where the computer simulation ends and reality begins. Indeed, who would want to accept the limitations of the 'real', anyway, when one can be and do anything one wants in the world behind the screen – even if it means sacrificing a society of human interaction? It is such speculations that continue to energize the work of science-fiction writers and film-makers, and make virtual reality a potent motif through which the increasingly tenuous status of reality within **postmodern** culture can be foregrounded and problematized.

VONNEGUT, KURT: NOVELIST (1922–) Kurt Vonnegut was born in Indianapolis, and his Mid-west birthplace may well explain his fiction's uneasy balance between high-art and pulp, gravity and levity. After abandoning his science degree at Cornell University because of ill-health, Vonnegut was drafted into the US Army in 1943. His capture during the Battle of the Bulge led to internment in an abattoir in Dresden during the intense Allied fire-bombing in February 1945. This experience inspired his most popular novel, *Slaughterhouse-Five* (1969). Disillusioned with technology after the war, he enrolled as an anthropology student at the University of Chicago; worked for the General Electric Company for a while; then became a freelance writer in the 1950s. His apprentice works – *Player Piano* (1952) and *The Sirens of Titan* (1959) – both explored standard science-fiction themes. The former is a Wellsian view of a mechanistic society and the latter a comic space opera.

It was with his next book, however, that Vonnegut found his **postmodernist** voice. *Mother Night* (1961) is written in a multitude of short chapters with oddball titles. His other novels of the 1960s – including *Cat's Cradle* (1963) and *God Bless You, Mr. Rosewater* (1965) – adopted this fragmented style. So too did several novels of the 1970s and 1980s, including *Breakfast of Champions*

(1973), *Slapstick* (1976) and *Deadeye Dick* (1982). Vonnegut explained his organizational preference in this way: 'My books are essentially mosaics made up of a whole bunch of tiny little chips; and each chip is a joke.'

Vonnegut compensates for his extremely fragmented structures through repetition. Every book has its running typographical joke. *Slapstick*, for instance, refers to metric measurements throughout, instead of feet and inches (Vonnegut brags that it was probably the first American book to do so). *Jailbird* (1979) spells out each year instead of using numerals and has a helpful index at the back. In *Galapagos* (1985), an asterisk is placed before the names of those characters who will shortly die.

Several of his books contain recurrent catch-phrases. The refrain of 'So it goes' follows every death (human, animal or otherwise) in *Slaughterhouse-Five*. 'And so on' crops up persistently in *Breakfast of Champions*, which ends with a giant hand-drawn 'ETC'. The equally nonchalant 'Hi ho' peppers *Slapstick*. These phrases migrate from book to book. The same is true of many of Vonnegut's characters. Kilgore Trout appears in at least five works, and Eliot Rosewater plays major roles in several novels. Sometimes characters who make cameo appearances in earlier works are later given star billing: Rabo Karabekian, the Armenian abstract expressionist, appears briefly in *Breakfast of Champions* and is the subject of a full biography in *Bluebeard* (1987). Vonnegut's locations are repeated, too. The cities of Ilium and Midland City, and the alien planet of Tralfamadore, are particular favourites.

These repetitions of typography, diction, character and place are postmodern because the descriptions of them are often mutually incompatible across different books. A Vonnegut text is a 'chrono-synclastic infundibulum', a Tralfamadorian term for a place where all spaces and times merge.

WOLF, NAOMI: FEMINIST THEORIST
(1962–) Wolf's first book, *The Beauty Myth* (1990) begins with a paradox: since the late 1960s, affluent women in the West have had an increasing amount of political and social autonomy; they have entered the workforce in boardrooms, offices, in the main political institutions and on the shop floor. They have gained reproductive rights over their own bodies, and they have more money and power than at any other time in human history. Concurrently, however, there has been an exponential rise in women with eating disorders and cosmetic surgery has become the fastest-growing medical speciality. So, while women have gained both respect and self-respect, in relation to their own bodies women are 'worse off than [their] grandmothers'. Wolf explains this paradox by means of 'the beauty myth', a violent backlash against women that uses images of female beauty as a weapon against female betterment. It is one of the last remaining ways of controlling women. The myth says that the quality called 'beauty', which women need because men want to possess it, is natural and universal. Wolf says that none of this is true; ideals of beauty are culturally relative. The oppressive concept of 'beauty' is not about women at all, but about male institutional power. The book has been criticized (most force-fully by bell **hooks**) for its assumption, in keeping with the beauty myth itself, that black women do not exist. *The Beauty Myth* was an international bestseller though many feminists criticized it for lack of originality.

Wolf's second book, *Fire with Fire* (1993) is a good example of what she calls 'power feminism'. She argues that feminists need to be critical of their own movement; she attacks radical feminism's 'reflexive anti-capitalism' and 'rigid ideology' and argues for a 'flexible feminism to reclaim the majority'. She quickly dismisses the work of Adrienne Rich, Andrea Dworkin, Catherine McKinnon and Audre Lorde as varieties of 'victim feminism': their attitude of blaming men holds back the women's movement. Only women themselves stand in the way of their empowerment. They need to adopt a 'bad girl' persona and leave behind the 'good girl' image internalized from the age of three. Women need to take responsibility for the fact that they can be equally aggressive and violent as men. From this follows the argument that women therefore need to use the same tactics as men to gain political and economic power: 'Whether used to scar or illuminate, whether used by men or women, fire is fire.' While feminists have argued this position before, Wolf's 'fire' is quite capable of burning other women, despite her rhetoric of sisterhood. From a socalist-feminist perspective, a notion of sisterhood that calls for women to enter the workforce as both workers and bosses is politically confused. Emblematic of this approach is her only example of a power feminist who is black: Madame J. C. Walker. This ex-slave became the richest woman, black or white, in nineteenth-century America by selling hair-straightening products which were, as bell hooks notes, the very sign of white supremacy and black women's oppression until at least the late 1960s. The book therefore reproduces earlier, predominantly middle-class feminists' marginalization of black women. *Promiscuities* (1997) uses her own and her friends' early sexual experiences to generalize about women's sexuality. Critics argue that this is what Wolf has done in her other work too; taken her own relatively privileged experience as an example of women's in general.

WRITERLY TEXTS Roland **Barthes** divides narrative fiction into two main types in his **poststructuralist** study *S/Z* (1970): writerly and **readerly**. The latter comprises narratives that promote passive consumption on the part of the reader, whereas the former invite the reader to participate in the production of **textual** meaning. **Modernist** texts are good examples of the writerly category in that the reader frequently has to fill in gaps in the narrative, thus, in Barthes' terms of reference, becoming part of the production of textual meaning. Such texts are to be regarded as 'open' to the exercise of the reader's invention and imagination. Readerly texts, on the other hand, are designed to prevent such invention and imaginative play. A candidate for this category would be the nineteenth-century realist novel, which, with its meticulously structured plot, omniscient narrator, and overt moral agenda, severely constrained the nature of the reader's response. Readerly texts are therefore in the service of the cultural status quo, whereas writerly ones help to undermine it by calling into question the extent of the **author**'s control over interpretation. Many critics have taken the line, however, that writerly texts are just as manipulative in their way as the readerly texts that Barthes accuses of being ideologically suspect.

Y

YALE SCHOOL The Yale School comprised a group of literary critics at Yale University who, in the 1970s, came under the sway of the **decon-structionist** Jacques **Derrida**, a visiting professor at Yale and several other American universities during the period. Its members included Harold **Bloom**, Paul **de Man**, Geoffrey **Hartman**, and J. Hillis **Miller**. They can be considered a 'school' only in the loosest sense, and there were marked differences in the way each critic responded to deconstruction, and utilized its techniques. Their best-known collaborative effort (with Derrida) is the book of essays *Deconstruction and Criticism* (ed. Harold Bloom (1979)).

YOUNG, IRIS MARION: PHILOSOPHER AND FEMINIST THEORIST (1949–) Young is a political activist, contemporary philosopher and feminist academic who has written on democratic theory, feminist social theory, female bodily experience and the politics of **difference**. In particular, Young objects to the liberal theory of distributive justice which answers questions such as 'What would be a fair distribution of property?' and 'What rights should individuals have?' with appeals to abstract ideals of formal equality and individual freedom. Young's studies of embodiment led her to formulate an alternative theory which recognizes concrete issues of difference among persons and incorporates substantive content into an account of justice. This means challenging the presumption that justice is a question of distribution. Young's philosophy differs from not only the liberal tradition of J. S. Mill, but from the post-**Enlightenment** tradition of German philosophy in raising fundamental questions about oppression and domination. In response to such questions, political theories of liberal democracy need to address the problem of an inclusive participatory framework. Young contends that democratic theorists generally assume a conception of the public which excludes people not culturally identified with white European male norms of reason and respectability.

Although deriving her method from German **critical theory**, Young resists any modern commitment to a homogeneous public. Instead Young proposes that normative theory and public policy can undermine group-based oppression by affirming rather than suppressing social group difference. Her vision of the good society is the differentiated, culturally plural network of contemporary urban life. Her goal is a principle of group representation in democratic publics, along with group differentiated policies. She resists feminist theories of embodiment which retain an ideal of a shared subjectivity and unified **desires** over the basic opacity and asymmetry of subjects and their desires. She fears the suppression of difference and of concrete **otherness**.

Her distinctive passion for the **postmodern** finds the desire for community among the members of radical organizations dangerous. Community produces homogeneity; it directs energy away from political goals, creating a clique atmosphere which excludes difference. Instead Young proposes an ideal of urban life, nurturing diversity and co-operation in providing services conceived, distributed and administered justly. Critics worry that Young is against friendship, but arguably she has realistic doubts concerning the transparency and affection of face-to-face relationships. Ironically, the problem attributed to Young constitutes her distinctiveness: rejection of identity and community for difference and diversity is criticized as often as it is celebrated. Modern feminists are sympathetic with, but ultimately critical of, Young's postmodern account of difference over identity, multiplicity over unity, heterogeneity over homogeneity. Possibly overstating her case, Young objects that the identity of the modern self as a unified centre of desire is a mere fiction. Yet Young recognizes that the child must separate from its joyful continuity with the maternal in order to enter language and become a self – the consequence of which is the identity and the difference of individual persons. Simply stated, it is difficult to realize both a social ethic of care (preserving identity and unity) and a politics of difference.

Z

ZAPPING The technique of rapidly cutting between television channels using a remote control device, or 'zapping' as it is colloquially known, can lay claim to being one of the most characteristically **postmodern** acts. The channels themselves are treated like some kind of continuous narrative which can be connected together in any order at all, according to the whims of the individual viewer. There are clear similarities in this respect with the way that **hypertext** or the **Internet** work. The effect of zapping is to break up the flow of linear narrative and, arguably, to empower the viewer to a certain extent by giving her control over the sequencing, if not the content, of her viewing. If nothing else, the **grand narratives** of the programme makers, which demand passive viewers who consume what is given to them in a relatively uncritical manner, is challenged by the process of zapping.

ZERO DEGREE The term originates in a book written by Roland **Barthes** in 1953, entitled *Writing Degree Zero*, where he posits a **paradigm shift** in the literary history of France. The dates that Barthes considers to be particularly significant are 1650 and 1848. According to Barthes, pre-1650 the French language was insufficiently established to maintain a literary mode of expression. Between 1650 and 1848, a period he refers to as the 'classical age', thought and language are unified – in fact, the two are synonymous and are created simultaneously. Post-1848, however, French literature witnesses a move away from such unities, and Barthes substitutes instead a **Marxist** model predicated upon antagonistic social classes.

Although the argument of the book is firmly Marxist in its methodology, it points forward suggestively to the debates about language which figure so prominently in **structuralist** and **poststructuralist** thought.

INDEX